AF789334

The International Law Commission's Draft Conclusions on Peremptory Norms

The International Law Commission's Draft Conclusions on Peremptory Norms

DIRE TLADI

OXFORD
UNIVERSITY PRESS

OXFORD
UNIVERSITY PRESS

Great Clarendon Street, Oxford, OX2 6DP,
United Kingdom

Oxford University Press is a department of the University of Oxford.
It furthers the University's objective of excellence in research, scholarship,
and education by publishing worldwide. Oxford is a registered trade mark of
Oxford University Press in the UK and in certain other countries

© Dire Tladi 2024

The moral rights of the author have been asserted

All rights reserved. No part of this publication may be reproduced, stored in
a retrieval system, or transmitted, in any form or by any means, without the
prior permission in writing of Oxford University Press, or as expressly permitted
by law, by licence or under terms agreed with the appropriate reprographics
rights organization. Enquiries concerning reproduction outside the scope of the
above should be sent to the Rights Department, Oxford University Press, at the
address above

You must not circulate this work in any other form
and you must impose this same condition on any acquirer

Public sector information reproduced under Open Government Licence v3.0
(http://www.nationalarchives.gov.uk/doc/open-government-licence/open-government-licence.htm)

Published in the United States of America by Oxford University Press
198 Madison Avenue, New York, NY 10016, United States of America

British Library Cataloguing in Publication Data
Data available

Library of Congress Control Number: 2023946011

ISBN 978–0–19–284609–9

DOI: 10.1093/law/9780192846099.001.0001

Printed and bound by
CPI Group (UK) Ltd, Croydon, CR0 4YY

Links to third party websites are provided by Oxford in good faith and
for information only. Oxford disclaims any responsibility for the materials
contained in any third party website referenced in this work.

MIX
Paper | Supporting
responsible forestry
FSC
www.fsc.org
FSC® C013604

For Mama Eva
Nearly three decades later, your absence is acutely felt

Acknowledgements

This book, a commentary on the work of the International Law Commission on Peremptory Norms of General International Law (*jus cogens*), would not have been possible without the support of many people and I wish to thank them all. In particular I wish to acknowledge the contribution and support of the following:

First, as the holder of the DST/NRF SARChI Chair in International Constitutional Law, I wish to express my gratitude to the NRF South African Research Chairs Initiative. The support from the programme, particularly at the tail end of the ILC project and the beginning of the book project, made the completion of the book much easier.

Second, since the book would not have been possible without the ILC project, I wish to thank the ILC, and its members between 2014 and 2022. I thank the Commission and its members, for the courage to accept the proposal to place the topic of *jus cogens* on its programme of work, for the trust it showed in me by appointing me Special Rapporteur, and for the support throughout the duration of the project. It is perhaps a little-known fact that it was not the first time that an attempt had been made to place the topic of *jus cogens* on the agenda of the ILC. Because of the sensitivity of the topic, the ILC initially declined to place the topic on the agenda, citing at the time lack of practice. The reason for the initial reticence was probably because, as Georg Nolte, then a member of the Commission and now judge of the International Court of Justice, would recall when I proposed the topic, *jus cogens* is one of those topics that sits above the glass ceiling. Nolte also described *jus cogens* as the 'topic of topics'. Another former member, Alain Pellet, famously observed that *jus cogens* had the same initials, JC, as Jesus Christ. Yet in 2015, courageously, the ILC decided to reach beyond that glass ceiling, to address the 'topic of topics', and to demystify the divinity of *jus cogens*—an act of courage for which I am grateful.

Because this book would not exist without the work of the Commission, a special word of thanks to the Commission for the work done is called for. Within the Commission there are many individuals that I would like to thank individually, but experience has taught me that that is a slippery slope that I best not step on, so I express my gratitude to all the members of the Commission. There is a cliché within the Commission—that the work of the Commission is collegiate, which simply means that the work of the Commission is the result of a collective effort. That cliché was certainly true in relation to the work of the Commission on *jus cogens*. The text of the draft conclusions is what it is because of the interactions and exchanges between members of the Commission and the Drafting Committee. I am thus grateful to the entirety of the Commission for making the conclusion of the project, and thus the commencement of this book, possible. A particular debt of gratitude is owed to those members of the Commission that served on the Drafting Committee. I would however be remiss if I did not mention all the Chairs of the Drafting Committee—in 2016 (Šturma), 2017 (Rajput), 2018 (Jalloh), 2019 (Grossman), and 2022 (Park)—who exercised such diligence in guiding the work on this topic in what is, without question, the most important phase of the Commission's working process. I am grateful also to the Secretariat which always did what was necessary to oil the machine enough to make sure that we were able to complete our work in time.

Unlike many other Special Rapporteurs, save for the final year of work on this topic, I did not have a grant or pot of money or a group of paid assistants to help me with the sourcing and analysis of materials. I relied on volunteer-researchers who, without any remuneration whatsoever, searched for and provided me with relevant materials for the preparation of reports. Of course, given the voluntary nature of their assistance, their contribution was always going to vary, both in terms of quantity and quality. Given the selflessness of their contribution, it is appropriate to mention each and every one of them: in 2016, Emily Buist-Catherwood, Manar Mohsen, Mawuse Vormawor, Tjasa Tanko, Evelyn Mogere, Aniel de Beer, Romain Pinchon, Marija Đorđeska, Christina Hioureas, Amy Belsher, Aldana Rohr (also 2017 and 2018), Varin Singh (also 2017), and Annelize Nienaber; in 2017, Juan Pablo Pérez-León-Acevedo; in 2018 Paula Kates and Sean Yau; and in 2019, Francisco Lobo, Tanishta Vaid, and Cheree Olivier. I am also grateful to many other assistants that have served as interns with me during the various sessions of the International Law Commission.

The ILC adopted the final version of the Draft Conclusions and Commentaries in August 2022, but I began working on this book while also trying to imagine what the final text and commentaries of the ILC's work would look like—in January 2022. I should say a special word of thanks to Ms Rachel Foreman, not only for her general role as the ILC librarian, but also for allowing me the freedom of the 'UNOG library' during that early period of work on this book. It will sound like hyperbole but trust me when I say I have never met such a combination of kindness and efficiency in my life.

Having spent January 2022 in wintry Geneva writing the opening salvos of the book, I wrote the final few chapters in the warm embrace of Singapore, where I spent time as a Distinguished Visiting Fellow at the Centre for International Law of the University of Singapore. I want to express my deepest gratitude to my good friend, member of the ILC, Nilufer Oral, Director of the Centre for International Law for making this happen. Not only did that visit afford me the opportunity to 'sit and write' but also allowed me an opportunity to interact with the Office of the Attorney-General in Singapore—these interactions were not only pleasant, but they also allowed me to see things from a perspective I had not seen before. So in that respect, I am grateful not only to Nilufer, but also to the Office of the Attorney-General of Singapore for making a very valuable contribution to this book.

I would also like to thank a small group of young assistants who helped me with the finalisation of the book, crossing the t's and dotting the I's: Shubhangi Agarwalla, Karem Luisa Cárdenas Ynfanzón, Yasmine Luhandjula, Lisa Ndyulo, and Anjana Sathy. Thank you to all of you. I am looking forward to seeing your contributions to the world of international law.

Finally, to all my friends, family, loved ones, thank you for the unending support.

Contents

Table of Cases and Other Materials

INTERNATIONAL COURT OF JUSTICE CASES

OTHER INTERNATIONAL CASE LAW

DOMESTIC CASE LAW

DOCUMENTS OF THE INTERNATIONAL LAW COMMISSION

TREATIES

1

The International Law Commission's Draft Conclusions

Setting the Scene

1. Introduction

In August 2022, during its seventy-third session, the International Law Commission (the 'ILC' or the 'Commission') adopted a set of twenty-three draft conclusions on peremptory norms of general international law (*jus cogens*) (the 'Draft Conclusions').[1] The work of the Commission on this topic, which began in 2015, seeks to clarify the contours of *jus cogens* by providing a framework for the identification of norms of *jus cogens* and describing the main general consequences of *jus cogens*.[2]

The concept of *jus cogens* is an important one in international law and yet, at the same time, a mysterious one. It has been described in a variety of ways that attest to its special nature. Pellet, for example, recalled that it shared the same initials as Jesus Christ—a figure said to have turned water to wine, walked on water, and raised people from the dead, among many other miracles.[3] Other images that have been invoked to capture the special character of *jus cogens* include magic[4] and the supernatural.[5] The special character of *jus cogens* potentially challenges the very structure and horizontal nature of international law.

Given its special character and status, providing clarity on how norms of *jus cogens* are to be identified and what the general consequences of those

1 ILC Draft Conclusions on Peremptory Norms of General International Law (*Jus Cogens*), *Report of the International Law Commission at its Seventy-Third Session* (A/77/10).

2 Id. Draft Conclusion 1 ('The Present Draft Conclusions concern the identification and legal consequences of peremptory norms of general international law (*jus cogens*)').

3 Alain Pellet 'Conclusions' in Christian Tomuschat and Jean Thouvenin (eds) *The Fundamental Rules of the International Legal Order: Jus Cogens and Obligations Erga Omnes* (Martinus Nijhoff, 2005), 217.

4 Andrea Bianchi 'Human Rights and the Magic of *Jus Cogens*' (2008) 19 *European Journal of International Law* 491.

5 Anthony D'Amato 'It's a Bird, It's a Plane, It's *Jus Cogens*' (1990) 6 *Connecticut Journal of International Law* 1.

norms are in international law is no easy task. The controversy and debates surrounding *jus cogens* have stirred fierce contestations and disagreements producing mountains of literature.[6] The ILC's decision to embark on this topic was thus brave and some might say unwise, ill-advised, imprudent, injudicious, and maybe even irresponsible. Yet, precisely because of the controversy it generates coupled with the far-reaching implication of the concept, its consideration by international law's leading codification and progressive development body was important and necessary. This is particularly the case since more courts and tribunals and other forums, both domestic and international, including those without expertise in public international law, are being called upon to address questions pertaining to *jus cogens*.

The present book is about the ILC's Draft Conclusions.[7] While it serves, in part, as a commentary on the ILC's work, it seeks to provide a broader understanding of the text, from the perspective of an insider. Certainly, the book provides a commentary on the ILC's Draft Conclusions, including the

[6] See e.g. the many essays in Dire Tladi (ed) *Peremptory Norms of General International Law: Disquisitions and Disputations* (Brill, 2021). See, amongst many others, essays in a special volume of (2015) 46 *Netherlands Yearbook of International Law*; Robert Kolb *Peremptory International Law Jus Cogens: A General Inventory* (Hart, 2015); Levan A. Alexidze 'Legal Nature of *jus cogens* in Contemporary International Law' (1981) 172 *Collected Courses of the Hague Academy of International Law* 219; Antonio Augusto Cançado Trindade '*Jus Cogens:* The Determination and the Gradual of its Material Content in Contemporary International Case Law' (2008) XXXV *Curso de derecho internacional organizado por el Comite Juridico Interamericano* 1; Lauri Hannikainen *Peremptory Norms (Jus Cogens) in International Law: Historical Development, Criteria, Present Status* (Helsinki Finnish Lawyers, 1988); Andreas Jacovides *Treaties Conflicting with Peremptory Norms of International Law and the Zurich/London Agreements* (Nicosia, 1966); Sevrine Knuchel *Jus Cogens: Identification and Enforcement of Peremptory Norms* (Schulthess, 2015); Ulf Linderfalk *Understanding Jus Cogens in International Law and International Legal Discourse* (Edward Elgar, 2019); Aldan Rohr *La responsabilidad internacional del Estado por violación al jus cogens* (SGN Editora, 2015); Hélène Ruiz Fabri 'Enhancing the Rhetoric of *Jus Cogens*' (2012) 23(4) *European Journal of International Law* 1049; Eric Suy 'The Concept of *Jus Cogens* in Public International Law' in *Papers and Proceedings: Report of a Conference in Lagonisi, Greece, April, 1966* (Geneva, 1976); Grigori Tunkin '*Jus cogens* in Contemporary International Law' (1971) 3 *University of Toledo Law Review* 107; Thomas Weatherall *Jus Cogens: International Law and Social Contract* (Cambridge, 2015); Alfred Verdross 'Jus Dispositivum and Jus Cogens in International Law' (1966) 60 *American Journal of International Law* 55; Karl Zemanek 'The Metamorphosis of *Jus Cogens:* From an Institution of Treaty Law to the Bedrock of the International Legal Order?' in Enzo Cannizzaro (ed.) *The Law of Treaties beyond the Vienna Convention* (Oxford, 2010).

[7] In addition to my reports as Special Rapporteur, this book also draws liberally on my previous works on the topic of *jus cogens*. These include: 'Grotian Moments and Peremptory Norms of General International Law: Friendly Facilitation or Fatal Foes' (2021) 42 *Grotiana* 334; 'The ILC's Draft Conclusions on Peremptory Norms of General International Law: Personal Reflections of the Special Rapporteur' (2019) 24 *Austrian Review of International and European Law* 121; 'The International Law Commission's Draft Conclusions on Peremptory Norms of General International Law (*Jus Cogens*): Making Wine from Water or More Water than Wine?' (2020) 89 *Nordic Journal of International Law* 244; 'Codification, Progressive Development, New Law, Doctrine, and the Work of the International Law Commission on Peremptory Norms of General International Law (*Jus Cogens*): Personal Reflections of the Special Rapporteur' (2019) 13 *Florida International University Law Review* 1189; *Peremptory Norms of General International Law (Jus Cogens): Disquisitions and Disputations* (Brill, 2021) (edited volume).

Commentaries accompanying the Draft Conclusions. But more than merely commenting on the Draft Conclusions and the associated Commentaries, the book provides a deep analysis and evaluation of the issues raised by the Draft Conclusions. Thus, while the Draft Conclusions serve as the main source and anchor of the book, they are by no means the only source for the book. In particular, issues that are not addressed in the Draft Conclusions, or that are not adequately addressed, but that are related to the main elements of the Draft Conclusions, i.e. identification of *jus cogens* norms and their consequences, are addressed in the book.

A small note on terminology. The Draft Conclusions use the phrase 'peremptory norms of general international law (*jus cogens*)'. In this book, the terms '*jus cogens*', 'peremptory norms', and 'peremptory norms of general international law' are used interchangeably. Save where it is explicitly mentioned, there is no particular significance to the choice of one or the other.

The next section of this chapter will briefly describe the main contestations and controversies surrounding *jus cogens*. It is these controversies and contestations that gave rise to the Commission's decision to undertake this work. This will be followed by an overview of the Commission's work on the topic, including the processes leading up to the inclusion of the topic on the agenda of the Commission and the substantive issues that arose during those processes. As will become clear as the book unfolds, these substantive issues would remain for the duration of the Commission's consideration of the topic and would greatly influence the Commission's work. The chapter will then provide a broad overview of the Draft Conclusions adopted by the Commission on second reading.

2. Peremptory Norms: The Great Debate

There is, today, little doubt about the place of *jus cogens* in international law. This is in large part because of Article 53 of the 1969 Vienna Convention on the Law of Treaties (the 'Vienna Convention' or the 'VCLT'). Article 53 provides as follows:

> A treaty is void if, at the time of its conclusion, it conflicts with a peremptory norm of general international law. For the purposes of the present Convention, a peremptory norm of general international law is a norm accepted and recognized by the international community of States as a whole as a norm from which no derogation is permitted and which can be

modified only by a subsequent norm of general international law having the same character.

While the place of *jus cogens* in modern international law is today undisputed, debates about its nature, content, and effects remain. The Commission's 2022 Draft Conclusions tackle these issues through an assessment of how *jus cogens* norms are to be identified and what legal consequences flow from *jus cogens* and the breach of *jus cogens* norms. Each of these is the subject of its own debate, but in many ways these two debates are a microcosm for a broader debate. For the question of identification, the debate concerns whether norms of *jus cogens* emerge from State consent or whether they have a more natural law basis.[8] As for consequences, on one side of the debate are those that take the view that the consequences of *jus cogens* are limitless, while on the other side of the debate, the consequences of *jus cogens* are limited to the invalidity of conflicting rules of international law in the mould of Articles 53 and 64 of the 1969 Vienna Convention, and possibly, though in some cases grudgingly, the consequences of serious breaches spelt out in the Articles on the Responsibility of States for Internationally Wrongful Acts.[9] Needless to say, between these two extreme positions is a continuum of positions.

In fact, the two debates (on identification and on consequences) described above, while presented here as two different debates, could also be seen as manifestations of the same debate. On the one side of this debate are those that seek to maximise *jus cogens* and its potential (let's call these the maximisers) and on the other side of the debate those that would call for more caution (let's call them cautioners).[10] There may even be anti-*jus cogeners*—those that deny the existence of the concept to begin with. But the latter are outliers and will not be accounted for here. From the perspective of the maximisers, the objective is to make the most of *jus cogens*. That means, for the debate on content and identification, freeing *jus cogens* from the strictures of positivism and the requirements of consent. For these maximisers, the establishment,

[8] See, for discussion, Dinah Shelton *Jus Cogens: Elements of International Law* (Oxford University Press, 2020), 3 *et seq*. See also Mark W. Janis 'The Nature of *Jus Cogens*' (1988) 3 *Connecticut Journal of International Law* 359.

[9] See *First Report of the Special Rapporteur on Jus Cogens* (A/CN.4/SR.3414) 'for some, including some in the Commission, *jus cogens* was super brilliant and could perform magic beyond the dreamer's wildest dreams, while for others, its consequences were no different from those of other rules of international law'.

[10] See e.g. Thibault Moulin 'Un nouveau "cheval de Troie"? Regard sur la codification des normes impératives du droit international général (*jus cogens*)' [2020] *Canadian Yearbook of International Law* 225. See, for a detailed description of this debate, Linderfalk (above note 6), which he refers to as a debate between legal positivism and legal idealism.

or, better yet, the emergence and formation, of *jus cogens* should not be dependent on the consent and practice of States. For them, the identification of *jus cogens* is a more fluid process heavily dependent on values. In the context of consequences, making the most of *jus cogens* means allowing *jus cogens* to affect international law and practice in more significant ways. Its consequences cannot simply be invalidation—a consequence that is most unlikely to come to pass since it is not expected that States would adopt rules that, on their face, violate peremptory norms of international law.[11] Rather the consequences must flow further,[12] affecting such issues as the scope and application of immunity,[13] compensation,[14] and, perhaps, even the rules on jurisdiction,[15] and the rules on the use of the veto in the Security Council.[16] Mbengue and Zouapet provide an interesting consideration of the potential consequences of *jus cogens*, not often considered, in international economic law.[17] For the cautioners, on the other hand, there must be strict requirements for the identification of peremptory norms of general international law—quantitatively and qualitatively stricter than for normal customary international law—since these rules can have such a massive impact on other rules. Moreover, for these cautioners, and in keeping with the rules of traditional international law, the consequences of *jus cogens* must be limited to those agreed to by States in accordance with the ordinary rules for law-making.[18] This means the only clear consequences flowing from *jus cogens* are those contained in the Vienna Convention on the Law of Treaties or those clearly established in customary

[11] See Catherine Maia '*Jus Cogens* and (In)Application of the 1969 Vienna Convention on the Law of Treaties in the Jurisprudence of the International Court of Justice' in Tladi (above note 6).

[12] Ulf Linderfalk *Understanding Jus Cogens in International Law and International Legal Discourse* (Edward Elgar, 2020), 1 ('The concept of *jus cogens* has attracted remarkable attention among international scholars, who have used it, in particular in the context of human rights and international criminal law, to argue such things as the invalidity of UN Security Council resolutions, the non-applicability of amnesties, immunity rules, and extradition agreements').

[13] This view has been put forward by Alexander Orakhelashvili 'Audience and Authority—the Merit of the Doctrine of *Jus Cogens*' (2015) 46 *Netherlands Yearbook of International Law* 115, 138 *et seq*. See also Alexander Orakelashvili *Peremptory Norms in International Law* (Oxford, 2008), 320 *et seq*. See also Thomas Weatherall '*Jus Cogens* and Sovereign Immunity: Reconciling Divergence in Contemporary Jurisprudence' (2015) 46 *Georgetown Journal of International Law* 1151.

[14] See generally Rosalind (with John Dugard) '*Jus Cogens* and Compensation' in Tladi (above note 6), 413.

[15] Orakhelashvili *Peremptory Norms in International Law* (above note 13), 489 *et seq*.

[16] See e.g. Rana Essawy 'The Responsibility Not to Veto Revisited under the Theory of "Consequential *Jus Cogens*"' (2020) 12 *Global Responsibility to Protect* 299. See also Jennifer Trahan *Existing Legal Limits to the Security Council Veto Power in the Face of Atrocity Crimes* (Cambridge University Press, 2020).

[17] Makane Moïse Mbengue and Apollin Koagne Zouapet 'Ending the Splendid Isolation: *Jus Cogens* and International Economic Law' in Tladi (above note 6), 509.

[18] See Daniel Costelloe *Legal Consequences of Peremptory Norms in International Law* (Cambridge, 2017), 17 ('The legal consequences of peremptory norms are grounded in practice but are closely associated with the values that certain legal norms represent and seek to protect').

international law, i.e. there should be clear evidence of practice as accepted as law of a particular consequence.[19]

The ILC's Draft Conclusions navigate the issues, i.e. identification of *jus cogens* and its consequences, without necessarily attempting to find a solution to these debates. This might be somewhat frustrating for those that see the Commission's function as being to resolve these theoretical debates. Yet the Commission's intention not to attempt to resolve theoretical debates was made clear at the very beginning of the work. The First Report of the Special Rapporteur stated that it was 'not the objective of either the present report or the consideration of the topic, to resolve the theoretical debates concerning *jus cogens*'.[20] At the same time, those theoretical debates could not be completely ignored. Thus, the First Report suggested that attempts to address the identification and consequences questions 'must be based on the appreciation of the theoretical debate surrounding its foundations'.[21] In other words, the Commission's work, while not addressing or attempting to address the theoretical debates (and certainly not solving them), was to be undertaken with an appreciation of the debates.

3. The Work of the Commission on the Peremptory Norms

3.1 Previous Work of the Commission

The notion of peremptory norms has been firmly established as part of the corpus of international law since the adoption of the Vienna Convention in the 1960s. Yet, the concept has featured prominently mainly in academic circles and scholarship. In the practice of States, *jus cogens* was not as commonly utilised, leading to the now famous retort that *jus cogens* had become like a car stuck in the garage.[22] It seems that if any institution could help bring the car out of the garage, it was the International Law Commission. After all, it was the Commission that had taken the topic of *jus cogens* from the periphery

[19] Id., 18, stating that '[e]ach legal consequence of a peremptory norm requires a legal basis in international practice and cannot be freely inferred'.

[20] Dire Tladi *First Report of the Special Rapporteur on Jus Cogens*, 2016 (A/CN.4/693), para 23.

[21] Id. The Report proceeded to state that these theoretical debates could thus not be avoided and that 'even if not providing "the solution" to the theoretical debate, the work of the Commission must be based on a sound and practical understanding of the nature of *jus cogens*, which necessitates a study of some of the theoretical bases that have been advanced'.

[22] See Georges Abi-Saab 'The Third World and the Future of the International Legal Order' (1973) 29 *Revue egyptienne de droit international* 27, 53; Ian Brownlie 'Comment' in Antonio Cassese and Joseph Weiler (eds) *Change and Stability in International Law-Making* (Walter de Gruyter, 1988), 110.

of international law, where it was asserted in scholarly writings, to the mainstream of international law by introducing it in the Articles on the Law of Treaties, which eventually became the Vienna Convention on the Law of Treaties.[23]

The central idea behind *jus cogens*, i.e. the notion that some rules of international law are superior to other rules and can invalidate them, was introduced into the work of the Commission on the law of treaties by Sir Hersch Lauterpacht.[24] In his First Report as Special Rapporteur, which was the fourth overall report on the topic of *jus cogens* at the time, Lauterpacht proposed Draft Article 15, according to which '[a] treaty, or any of its provisions, is void if its performance involves an act which is illegal under international law'.[25] Lauterpacht postulated that 'international law' in Draft Article 15 referred to 'such overriding principles of international law which may be regarded as constituting principles of international public policy (*ordre international public*)'.[26] Lauterpacht himself did not use the term '*jus cogens*' or 'peremptory norms'. The term '*jus cogens*' was introduced into the lexicon of the Commission's work much later by Sir Gerald Fitzmaurice in his Third Report, and what was the eighth overall report.[27] Draft Article 16(2) proposed by Fitzmaurice describes the 'international law' that has the power to invalidate treaties as 'those principles and rules of international law which are in the nature of *jus cogens*'.[28] In proposed Draft Article 17, Fitzmaurice makes a distinction between *jus cogens* and *jus dispositivum*, providing that 'it is only if the treaty involves a departure from or conflict with absolute and imperative rules ... of international law in the nature of *jus cogens* that a cause of invalidity can arise'. Finally, Sir Humphrey Waldock, in his Second Report—the twelfth overall report on the topic—then proposed that '[a] treaty is contrary to international law and void if' it 'involves the infringement of a general rule or principle of international law having the character of *jus cogens*'.[29]

[23] See Dire Tladi 'The ILC's Draft Conclusions on Peremptory Norms of General International Law: Personal Reflections of the Special Rapporteur' (2019) 24 *Austrian Review of International and European Law* 121, 122.

[24] Hersch Lauterpacht *Report by the Special Rapporteur on the Law of Treaties*, (A/CN.4/63), *Yearbook of the International Law Commission*, 1953, Vol. XX, Part XX.

[25] Id., Draft Article 15.

[26] Id., Paragraph 4 of the Commentary.

[27] See Gerald Fitzmaurice *Third Report of the Special Rapporteur on the Law of Treaties* (A/CN.4/115 and Corr.1), *Yearbook of the International Law Commission*, 1958, Vol. II.

[28] Id., 27. The text of Article 16(2) reads as follows: 'It is essential to the validity of a treaty that it should be in conformity with or not contravene, or that its execution should not involve an infraction of those principles and rules of international law which are in the nature of *jus cogens*.'

[29] Article 13(1) in Humphrey Waldock *Second Report of the Special Rapporteur on the Law of Treaties*, 1963 (A/CN.4/156 and Add.1–3).

While these proposals were, in the context of international law as it stood at the time, nothing short of spectacular, they were generally accepted by other members of the Commission and eventually by States.[30] Indeed the only State that opposed the notion of *jus cogens* on a *substantive basis* was Luxembourg, which saw the provision as an attempt to 'introduce as a cause of nullity criteria of morality and "public policy" such as are used in internal law', and consequently questioned 'whether such concepts are suitable for transfer to international relations which are characterized by the lack of any authority, political or judicial, capable of imposing on all States standards of international justice and morality'.[31] Of course France is the State that is most known for having opposed *jus cogens*. But elsewhere, I have described this notion of France as the poster child for anti-*jus cogens* sentiments as a 'false narrative', suggesting that, at least, at the time, France's concern did not relate to the substance of *jus cogens*, but merely to the lack of adequate mechanisms to prevent abuse.[32]

Thus, the Commission took a concept that had little pedigree in the practice of States—a concept whose life was confined to the pages of academic writings—and thrust it into the mainstream of international law. It was again, moreover, the Commission that kept the ventilator on, thus keeping *jus cogens* alive (although barely) through its subsequent work. The Commission's decision to include particular aspects of peremptory norms in its Articles on States Responsibility,[33] as well as other topics such as fragmentation of international law,[34] provided a lease of life for the ailing *jus cogens*. The Commission

[30] The reception of these proposals is considered by me elsewhere. See Tladi 'Grotian Moments' (above note 7), 340 *et seq.* See, for more comprehensive discussion, First Report (above note 20), paras 29–39. See e.g. Mr Yasseen (A/CN.4/SR.828) ('the concept of *jus cogens* in international law was unchallengeable', supporting this statement by noting that '[n]o specialist in international law could contest the proposition that no two States could come to an agreement to institute slavery or to permit piracy, or that any formal agreement for either purpose was other than void').

[31] See Humphrey Waldock *Fifth Report of the Special Rapporteur on the Law of Treaties* (A/CN.4/183), *Yearbook of the International Law Commission* 1966, Vol. II, 21.

[32] Tladi 'Grotian Moment' (above note 7), 343 ('This false narrative no doubt arose (and became entrenched) because of France's vote against both Article 53 and the Vienna Convention as a whole. Yet, the records indicate France, both in response to the ILC's work on the topic and during the Vienna Conference, expressly supported the concept but was concerned about the lack of adequate of safeguards against abuse and the potential for destabilisation of treaty relations. France declared for example, that "the substance of *jus cogens* was what represented the undeniable expression of the universal conscience, the common denominator of what men of all nationalities regarded as sacrosanct, namely, respect for and protection of the rights of the human person" and that it "could hardly formulate an objection to such" a concept'). See also First Report (above note 20), para 36.

[33] Articles on the Responsibility of States for Internationally Wrongful Acts, *Yearbook of the International Law Commission*, 2001, Vol. II, Part II. See especially Articles 26, 40, and 41.

[34] Conclusions of the work of the Study Group on the Fragmentation of International Law: Difficulties arising from the Diversification and Expansion of International Law, *Yearbook of the International Law Commission*, 2006, Vol. II, Part II. See also *Report of the Study Group on the Fragmentation of International Law: Difficulties Arising from the Diversification and Expansion of International Law (finalised by Martti Koskenniemi)* (A/CN.4/L.682). Other topics of the

has thus played a very important role not only in bringing *jus cogens* from the periphery to the mainstream of international law, but also in developing it further when it seemed destined to remain stuck in the garage.

It is thus appropriate that, if any institution should further clarify the most fundamental aspects of *jus cogens*, the Commission would be the institution to take on that responsibility. It is against this background that, in 2013, a proposal was submitted for the Commission to consider more comprehensively than before the topic of *jus cogens*.[35]

3.2 Placing the Topic on the Agenda: Premonitions of Potential Pitfalls

The 2013 proposal to place the topic on the agenda of the Commission was not the first attempt to have the Commission study the topic. In 1993, Mr Andreas Jacovides presented a paper to the ILC's Working Group on the Long-Term Programme of Work to study *jus cogens*.[36] In the paper, Mr Jacovides noted that, notwithstanding its 'regular invocation, there existed no definitive statement of what peremptory norms are or where they may be found',[37] and suggested that the time had come for the International Law Commission to study the subject 'with a view to establishing which rules of international law are indeed peremptory'.[38] At the time, the Commission decided not to take up the topic on account of the scarcity of practice relating to *jus cogens*.[39] As noted in the 2013 proposal, this reason was very similar to that put forward by the Commission in not identifying norms of *jus cogens* in the Draft Articles on the Law of Treaties.[40]

Commission that invoked *jus cogens* are: Guide to Practice on Reservations to Treaties, *Yearbook of the International Law Commission*, 2011, Vol. II, Part III, and Guiding Principles Applicable to Unilateral Declarations of States Capable of Creating Legal Obligations, *Yearbook of the International Law Commission*, 2006, Vol. II, Part II.

[35] Annex.

[36] The paper is contained in *Yearbook of the International Law Commission*, 1993, Vol. II, Part I, 213.

[37] Id.

[38] Id.

[39] See Dire Tladi 'Jus Cogens' Syllabus, *Report of the International Law Commission, Sixty-Sixth Session* (A/69/10), Annex, para 4.

[40] Id. See para 3 of the Commentary to Draft Article 50 of the Draft Articles on the Law of Treaties, *Yearbook of the International Law Commission*, 1966, Vol. II ('The emergence of rules having the character of *jus cogens* is comparatively recent, while international law is in process of rapid development. The Commission considered the right course to be to provide in general terms that a treaty is void if it conflicts with a rule of *jus cogens* and to leave the full content of this rule to be worked out in State practice and in the jurisprudence of international tribunals').

The proposal of 2013 suggested that since the proposal by Mr Jacovides, practice had developed at a rapid pace and that the time had now truly come to undertake a study of *jus cogens*.[41] The proposal submitted to the Working Group on the Long-Term Programme of Work identified four areas to be considered by the study:

(a) the nature of *jus cogens*;
(b) the requirements for the identification of a norm as *jus cogens*;
(c) an illustrative list of norms which have achieved the status of *jus cogens*;
(d) consequences or effects of *jus cogens*.

While most members of the Working Group in that year supported the topic, there were several members that did not. In addition, there were some other members that raised a number of questions.[42] The criticisms and objections raised against the proposal can be placed into three groups, some of which are interrelated. As will become clear, each of these has impacted in some way on the work of the Commission on this topic. As will become evident in the following chapters, some of the issues raised were reflected in criticisms that would later be directed at the project.

First, there was concern that there was simply insufficient practice on which the Commission could base its work. Some members of the Working Group worried that while the proposal suggested that there had been practice, in fact the State practice that was there was insufficient. Since the work of the Commission was meant to be based on State practice, the dearth of practice available for the Commission to study would create difficulties for the Commission in its mandate for the codification and progressive development of international law. This is interesting because, in so far as this view places an emphasis on State practice, it already indicates that, at least from the perspective of the proponents of this view, the posture of the Commission is generally inclined towards cautioners.[43]

The second concern, which is related to the first, was that there was very little value that the Commission could add to this topic. The view here was that, in

[41] Tladi Syllabus (above note 39).

[42] Since the discussions of the Working Group are held in closed sessions, the views expressed therein will not be attributed, save for the views expressed by Mr Georg Nolte, now judge on the International Court of Justice and Mr Mathias Forteau, both of whom have acceded to my request to have them identified.

[43] See e.g. Alexander Orakhelashvili 'Audience and Authority: The Merit of the Doctrine of Jus Cogens' (2015) 46 *Netherlands Yearbook of International Law* 115, 135, describing the approach of the ILC as 'narrow'.

the light of the scarcity of State practice, all that the Commission could do was to restate texts already adopted, i.e. the Vienna Convention and the Articles on State Responsibility. Mr Forteau,[44] a proponent of this view, gave as an example the illustrative list of norms of *jus cogens* and famously said that elements could be done in either five minutes, by relying on the list in the Articles on State Responsibility, or it would take fifty years, if the Commission were to attempt a *de novo* elaboration of a list.

The third concern was raised by Mr Nolte.[45] He suggested that there should be a glass ceiling above which not even the Commission should dare to go and that *jus cogens* was a topic that fell above the glass ceiling. This concern is, in a sense, based on reverence for *jus cogens*. Those that shared this concern also suggested that, given the dearth of practice, the Commission could cause damage to the evolution of *jus cogens* by freezing its development in an authoritative text. This is a concern that I, as the author of the proposal, also shared. In particular, I wondered whether a conservatively constituted Commission might result in regression rather than progress.

After several rounds of discussions, with some slight (mainly editorial and technical) amendments, the Working Group approved the topic and recommended that the Commission place it on its long-term programme of work.[46]

With the topic on the long-term programme of work of the Commission, the next step was to place it on the agenda. While not bound by the views of States on the inclusion or not of a topic on the agenda, in its recent practice the Commission does take into account the views of States in deciding whether or not to place a topic on its agenda. With respect to *jus cogens*, the views of States were understandably mixed, yet most States supported the inclusion of the topic.[47] In 2014, after the inclusion of the topic on the long-term programme of work, statements by States commented on the inclusion.[48] Of these, thirteen statements, representing forty-eight States, spoke in favour of the inclusion of the topic.[49] Only three States explicitly opposed

[44] While the discussions in the Working Group are confidential, Mr Forteau has given approval for his view on this particular matter to be revealed.

[45] While the discussions in the Working Group are confidential, Mr Nolte has given approval for his view on this matter to be reflected. Nonetheless, in so doing Mr Nolte asked that it be made clear that his was not an objection against the Commission taking up the topic, but only a cautionary remark about the dangers of taking on the topic.

[46] See *Report of the International Law Commission, Sixty-Sixth Session* (A/69/10), para 268.

[47] See, for discussion, First Report (above note 20), para 7 *et seq*. Most States, however, supported the inclusion of the topic on agenda of the Commission. See Ecuador (on behalf of CELAC) (A/C.6/70/SR.17), para 32; Peru (A/C.6/70/SR.17), para 51; Romania (A/C.6/70/SR.17), para 96; the United Kingdom (A/C.6/70/SR.18), para 9; Japan (A/C.6/70/SR.18), para 23; and El Salvador (A/C.6/70/SR.18), para 50.

[48] First Report (above note 20), para 6.

[49] Id.

the inclusion of the topic, namely France, the Netherlands, and the United States.[50] Common to the objections of these States was the refrain that there was currently insufficient State practice to justify the Commission taking on the topic. In addition to these explicit objections, there were some States that, while not objecting, expressed sufficient discomfort with the project to suggest they would have been content with a decision of the Commission not to proceed.[51]

4. An Overview of the Methodology and the Draft Conclusions

4.1 Method and Methodology

In the lead-up to the inclusion of the topic on the agenda of the Commission, some members of the Commission and some States emphasised the importance of relying on State practice. This methodological question has accompanied the work of the Commission from the beginning until the completion of the work. The First Report of the Special Rapporteur addressed the question of the methodology and the role of State practice. That Report stated that there was no need to depart from what it termed 'the Commission's normal method of work'.[52] According to this normal method of work, the Commission would proceed by 'considering a variety of materials and sources, in an integrated fashion'.[53] The Report explained that this involves

> conducting a thorough analysis of State practice in all its forms, judicial practice, literature and any other relevant material. As is the case with the other topics, the Commission will need to assess the particular weight to be given to the various materials.[54]

[50] France (A/C.6/70/SR.20), para 25; the Netherlands (A/C.6/70/SR.17), para 78; the United States (A/C.6/70/SR.19), para 17.

[51] See e.g. Israel (A/C.6/70/SR.18), para 5 ('Ultimately, her Government questioned whether the codification of rules relating to *jus cogens* was appropriate at the current juncture, reiterating its request for the Commission to proceed with caution on that topic'); China (A/C.6/70/SR.18), para 19 ('Given that there had not been any fundamental change in that situation, the Commission should collect information on State practice before undertaking an in-depth study on the topic. It should also adopt a cautious approach when referencing the limited practice of international bodies and institutions').

[52] First Report (above note 20), para 14.

[53] Id.

[54] Id.

These would include the types of materials that might ordinarily be referred to for the purpose of establishing State practice or *opinio juris* for the purposes of customary international law,[55] and decisions of international courts and tribunals.

While most States supported the approach of the Commission,[56] there has been a constant refrain from several States that the work of the Commission on this topic has not been based on State practice. The States making this claim most strongly have been the United States, Israel, Turkey, and the United Kingdom. Israel, for example, notes as a general point that 'the Special Rapporteur has relied greatly on theory and doctrine rather than on a thorough survey of State practice'.[57] An equally strong statement is that of the United States, noting that in general '[t]here is little State practice related to peremptory norms of general international law', that the Commentary 'cites no examples', and that it is 'not aware of any examples of' any new rules of international law conflicting with existing *jus cogens* norms.[58] Other States, while generally supportive of the approach of the Commission, also referred to the dearth of State practice.[59] Similarly, there were other States, notably the United Kingdom and the Nordic countries that noted, not as a criticism but as a fact, that there was little practice available.[60] For these countries, this scarcity of practice required that the Commission adopt a cautious approach to the Draft Conclusions.

The veracity of the criticism can only be assessed by looking at each Draft Conclusion separately and the subsequent chapters will, to some extent, undertake this type of assessment. For the purposes of the current discussion,

[55] See e.g. Draft Conclusion 6 of the Draft Conclusions on the Identification of Customary International Law, *Report of the International Law Commission, Seventieth Session* (A/73/10). The materials listed there are: diplomatic acts and correspondence; conduct in connection with resolutions adopted by an international organisation or at an intergovernmental conference; conduct in connection with treaties; executive conduct, including operational conduct 'on the ground'; legislative and administrative acts; and decisions of national courts.

[56] See e.g. Spain, Peremptory Norms of General International Law (*Jus Cogens*): Comments and Observations received from Governments (A/CN.4/478) (Spain), stating that it 'commends the Commission and the Special Rapporteur for their efforts to base the draft conclusions and the commentaries thereto on practice, jurisprudence and doctrine on the topic'; South Africa, Comments and Observations received from Governments (A/CN.4/478), expressing the view that the 'Commission has managed to deliver a well-balanced text of draft conclusions, supported by practice and judicial decisions of international courts and tribunals'; Cyprus, Comments and Observations received from Governments (A/CN.4/478); Japan, Comments and Observations received from Governments (A/CN.4/478); Bulgaria (A/C.6/74/SR.26), para 105 welcoming 'the constructive approach', which struck a 'balance between State practice and theory'; Romania (A/C.6/74/SR.23), para 75. See also Thailand (A/C.6/74/SR.24), para 107.

[57] Israel, Comments and Observations received from Governments (A/CN.4/748).

[58] The United States, Comments and Observations received from Governments (A/CN.4/478).

[59] These included the Netherlands (A/CN.4/478); Malaysia (A/C.6/74/SR.26), para 102.

[60] The United Kingdom (A/CN.4/478) and Sweden on behalf of the Nordic countries (A/CN.4/478).

it suffices to point out that some States had taken a rather narrow view of practice. For example, some of the reliance on judicial decisions—presumably also domestic judicial decisions—has been criticised as not being in keeping with the methodology of the Commission.[61] Other States seemed to include, under the rubric of State practice, only examples of breaches of *jus cogens* norms.[62] Yet the approach adopted by the Commission appears more akin to that favoured by the African group of States, which had stated that 'the process of progressive development and codification of international law must be all-embracing by including the consideration of texts of laws, State practice, precedents and doctrine'.[63]

The criticism surrounding the lack of State practice also seems to call into question the importance of the jurisprudence of international courts and tribunals. The Fifth Report of the Special Rapporteur, produced to account for the comments of States on the Draft Conclusions adopted on first reading, put forward a particularly strong response to this:

> While the Special Rapporteur believes that work on this topic is, in fact, supported by State practice, he would also like to stress that he finds it curious that reliance on the jurisprudence of international courts, including the International Court of Justice, the principal judicial organ of the United Nations, is regarded by a few vociferous States with such disdain. He would point out that one of the most, if not the most, successful topics addressed by the Commission since the adoption of the 1966 articles on the law of treaties, i.e., the 2001 articles on responsibility of States for internationally wrongful acts, relied significantly on the jurisprudence of international courts. Indeed, the foundational principle in that set of articles, namely Article 1, relies wholly on international jurisprudence and scholarly writings. Ditto for Article 2. This is also true of the topics adopted by the Commission over the course of the quinquennium. For example, the basic rule in the Conclusions on Identification of Customary International Law, conclusion 2, putting forward the two constituent elements, includes, in the commentaries thereto, only decisions of international courts. Similarly, the commentaries on Conclusion 5 do not reference any State practice. The same is true of the Commission's

[61] See, e.g. the Netherlands (A/CN.4/478).

[62] See the United States, Comments and Observations (above note 58) ('The commentary cites no examples, and the United States is not aware of any examples, of new treaties, customary international law, or acts of international organizations that contradicted existing *jus cogens*, and incidences of existing treaties violating later-emerging *jus cogens* are exceedingly rare').

[63] Sierra Leone on behalf of the fifty-three States that make up the African Group (see A/C.6/74/SR.23, para 36).

> Conclusions on Subsequent Agreements and Subsequent Practice in relation to treaty interpretation. For the Special Rapporteur, this is not a criticism of those works of the Commission. Quite to the contrary, it is a recognition of the fact that judgments of international courts, in particular the International Court of Justice, are seen as authoritative.

This debate on the reliance on practice and the appropriate methodology for the Commission is captured well in an exchange between the Special Rapporteur and the then President of the International Court of Justice, Judge Joan Donoghue.[64] In her remarks, Judge Donoghue had said that the Commission ought to be more meticulous in supporting its work with State practice.[65] The Special Rapporteur pushed back against the sentiment, suggesting that the standard of rigour relied upon by Judge Donoghue, namely the two-element approach in the Commission's Draft Conclusions on Customary International Law, was itself based on the jurisprudence of the Court and that, by her logic, even that rigorous standard ought to be approached with a level of scepticism.[66] Judge Donoghue seemed to acknowledge, albeit cautiously, that the standards may, in reality, be impractical:

> Whenever that approach to the two-element test was taken, the conclusion almost always drawn was that there was no customary international law rule, since evidence of State practice and opinio juris was so difficult to find. While there was no perfect solution, it was important to provide clear reasoning when determining the existence and content of a rule of customary international law.[67]

Yet, the response of the Special Rapporteur in the Fifth Report, punctuated by the exchange with Judge Donoghue, while pointing to apparent double standards does not tell us what we should make of judicial decisions.[68]

64 The exchange is reflected in A/CN.4/SR.3548. However, due to the editing process, the summary records do not quite capture the essence and intensity of the exchange. To see it in full, see ILC Video Record, Meeting 3548 available at https://media.un.org/en/asset/k11/k11dzifl33 (accessed 20 January 2022).

65 Judge Donoghue (A/CN.4/SR.3548), 7. See ILC Video Recording (above note 64), from minute 23:30.

66 Tladi (A/CN.4/SR.3548), 9; See ILC Video Recording (above note 64), at minute 46:40.

67 Id. In the video version, ILC Video Recording (above note 64), at minute 53:01, not captured in the summary records, she continues to say: 'but I don't know a better way [and] I know it's frustrating. It's a fair to point to say but where does that come from. I just don't have a better answer'.

68 On the role of judicial decisions in international law, see Shabtai Rosene 'International Court of Justice' *Max Planck Encyclopedia of Public International Law* (online 2006) and Leo Park 'The International Court and Rule-Making: Finding Effectiveness' (2018) 39 *University of Pennsylvania Journal of International Law* 1965.

How should the ILC account for decisions of international courts, particularly those of the International Court of Justice? It is beyond dispute that they are relevant but what does this mean?[69] What weight is to be accorded to them? The starting point in assessing the role of decisions of international courts and tribunals is to acknowledge that these decisions are not binding. Yet the function of the Court to resolve international disputes (as well as its function to provide advisory opinions) necessarily requires that the Court provide an assessment of the state of the law. For it to have any effect, even as 'between the parties and in respect of that particular case' the Court's statement of the law has to be authoritative. In other words, the judicial function of settling disputes cannot be easily separated from its function of authoritatively stating the law.[70] The authority of decisions of the Court, beyond the parties to the dispute and in respect of that particular dispute, however, is relative. As the Commission observed in the Commentaries to the Draft Conclusion on Customary International Law:

> The value of such decisions varies greatly, however, depending both on the quality of the reasoning (including primarily the extent to which it results from a thorough examination of evidence of an alleged general practice accepted as law) and on the reception of the decision, in particular by States.[71]

This quoted extract serves to emphasise that, ultimately, international law is made (and developed) by States. Thus, the extent to which decisions of the Court are to be taken as law, as opposed to being merely persuasive, falls to be determined by the extent to which they are based on State practice—that is the import of the description of the phrase 'quality of the reasoning'—and/or the extent to which such decisions are accepted subsequently by States—that is the import of the phrase 'the reception of the decision'. Thus, decisions of the International Court of Justice, and international courts in general, that have not been widely rejected by States acquire an enhanced level of authority *because*

[69] See Dire Tladi 'The Role of the International Court of Justice in the Development of International Court' in Kate Parlett and Carlos Esposito (eds) *The Cambridge Companion to the International Court of Justice* (Cambridge, 2023).

[70] See also Pierre-Marie Dupuy 'The Danger of Fragmentation or Unification of the International Legal System and the International Court of Justice' (1999) 31 *New York University Journal of International Law and Policy* 791, 802 ('In other words, to settle a particular dispute, the judge must "state the law" to be applied ... this jurisdiction amounts, in some respect, to the exercise of a residual legislative function').

[71] Paragraph 3 of the Commentary to Draft Conclusion 13 of the Draft Conclusions on Customary International Law, *Report of the International Law Commission, Seventieth Session* (A/73/10).

of the implied acceptance of those decisions by States. Thus, in assessing the Commission's reliance on judicial decisions for particular Draft Conclusions, the extent to which those decisions have been 'received' by States is important. That is to say, if States have not widely criticised a decision (or rejected the proposition contained therein), then it ought to be readily accepted as an authoritative statement of the law.

4.2 An Overview of the Draft Conclusions

The ILC began its work on the Draft Conclusions in 2015. Between 2016 and 2019, the Special Rapporteur produced four reports, on the strength of which a full set of Draft Conclusions was adopted on first reading in 2019.[72] Contrary to the normal practice of the Commission, the Commission did not adopt any Draft Conclusion before a full set was adopted on first reading, opting instead to keep the full text in the Drafting Committee.[73] The ILC's text of the Draft Conclusions consists of twenty-three Draft Conclusions, divided into four different parts.

Part One of the Draft Conclusions, titled 'Introduction', consists of three Draft Conclusions on 'Scope' (Draft Conclusion 1), 'Nature of Peremptory Norms of General International Law (*Jus Cogens*)' (Draft Conclusion 2), and 'Definition of Peremptory Norms of General International Law (*Jus Cogens*)' (Draft Conclusion 3). Draft Conclusion 1 describes the scope of the set of Draft Conclusions as being the identification and legal consequences of peremptory norms. Based on Article 53 of the Vienna Convention on the Law of Treaties, Draft Conclusion 3 defines *jus cogens* as a norm that is 'accepted and recognised by the international community of States as a whole as a norm from which no derogation is permitted and which can be modified only by a subsequent norm of general international law (*jus cogens*) having the same character'. While these two Draft Conclusions were understandably uncontroversial, Draft Conclusion 2 did elicit some controversy. It provides that norms of *jus cogens* 'reflect and protect fundamental values of the international

[72] Adoption on first reading occurs when the Commission adopts a full instrument (set of Draft Articles, Draft Principles, Draft Conclusions, or Draft Guidelines) and submits it to States for comment, before final adoption (on second reading).

[73] On the controversy caused by this departure from the traditional procedure see *Fourth Report of the Special Rapporteur on Peremptory Norms of General International Law (Jus Cogens)* (A/CN.4/727), paras 6, 13, and 15. See also *Fifth Report of the Special Rapporteur on Peremptory Norms of General International Law (Jus Cogens)* (A/CN.4/747), para 30.

community, are hierarchically superior to other rules of international law and are universally applicable'.

Part Two concerns the identification of peremptory norms and consists of six Draft Conclusions covering various aspects of the identification of *jus cogens*. The first of these, Draft Conclusion 4, draws on the definition of *jus cogens* to put forward the criteria to be satisfied when identifying the peremptory norms of general international law. Based on the definition, the Draft Conclusion provides that the criteria for the peremptory character of norms are, first, that the norm in question must be a norm of general international law and, second, that it must be accepted and recognised as a norm from which no derogation can be made and which can only be modified by a norm having the same character. The rest of the provisions in that part are dedicated to fleshing out the criteria. Thus, Draft Conclusion 5 describes what is meant by a norm of general international law. It identifies customary international law as the most common basis of *jus cogens* norms, while not excluding the possibility that treaty rules and general principles of law (within the meaning of Article 31(1)(c)) may also serve as sources for *jus cogens* norms. Draft Conclusion 6 describes further what is meant by acceptance and recognition, this being the core element that separates *jus cogens* norms from other norms of international law. The phrase 'the international community of States as a whole' is the subject of Draft Conclusion 7. Draft Conclusion 8 describes the materials that can be relied upon to show that the international community of States as a whole accepts and recognises the peremptory character of a norm. From the language of the text, it can be concluded that any material in which the views of the State are reflected would be included. Draft Conclusion 9 addresses the subsidiary means for identifying norms of *jus cogens*. This category includes decisions of international courts and tribunals, in particular the International Court of Justice, as well as the work of expert bodies, most notably the International Law Commission.

Part Three consists of ten Draft Conclusions and addresses the legal consequences of peremptory norms. Draft Conclusions 10 to 13 address consequences of *jus cogens* for treaty law. The basic rule of invalidity is contained in Draft Conclusion 10, while Draft Conclusion 11 addresses the possibility of severability of treaty provisions. Draft Conclusion 12 describes the legal effects of invalidity of treaties on account of conflict with *jus cogens*. These Draft Conclusions are generally based on relevant provisions in the Vienna Convention on the Law of Treaties. Draft Conclusion 13, although also addressing consequences of *jus cogens* for treaty rules, is not based on the Vienna Convention but rather on the ILC's previous work on reservations to treaties. It describes the consequences of *jus cogens* for reservations to treaties as being two-fold. First, a reservation to a treaty provision that reflects a *jus cogens* norm does not affect that *jus cogens* norm, i.e. whatever the effect on the treaty norm, the *jus cogens* norm continues to apply as such. Second, a reservation cannot affect a treaty provision in such a way as to violate a peremptory norm.

Draft Conclusions 14 to 16 apply the rules concerning the consequences of *jus cogens* norms for treaties to other sources of obligations, namely customary international law (Draft Conclusion 14), unilateral acts, and decisions of international organisations.

Draft Conclusions 17 to 19 concern the consequences of *jus cogens* for the secondary rules of responsibility under international law and are based on the ILC's Articles on State Responsibility. Draft Conclusion 17 provides that *jus cogens* norms establish *erga omnes* obligations and describes the relationship between *erga omnes* obligations and *jus cogens* norms in general terms. Draft Conclusion 18 describes the general idea that circumstances precluding wrongfulness may not be invoked in relation to *jus cogens* norms. Draft Conclusion 19 sets out particular consequences for serious breaches of *jus cogens* norms, including the duty to co-operate to bring to an end such breaches and the duties not to assist in maintaining or recognising situations created by such serious breaches.

Part Four of the Draft Conclusions, titled 'General Provision', consists of three unrelated Draft Conclusions. Draft Conclusion 20 is an interpretative provision based on the principle of systemic integration. It provides that, as far as possible, rules of international law ought to be interpreted in such a way as to render them consistent with *jus cogens* norms. Draft Conclusion 21 sets forth a recommended procedure for dealing with disputes concerning *jus cogens* norms, in particular disputes concerning the invalidity of rules on account of conflict with *jus cogens*. Draft Conclusion 22 is a without prejudice clause that explains that the set of Draft Conclusions are limited to the consequences of a *jus cogens* of a general nature and do not address particular consequences related to specific norms. While the provision appears bland and non-controversial, it is intended to cover perhaps the most controversial issue surrounding *jus cogens*, namely the impact of *jus cogens* on the rules of international law of immunity. Finally, Draft Conclusion 23, together with its Annex, provides a list of norms previously recognised by the International Law Commission as *jus cogens*.

5. Structural Issues

5.1 Outline of the Book

This book is about the ILC's Draft Conclusions on Peremptory Norms of General International Law (*jus cogens*). It provides a commentary on the set of Draft Conclusions and provides insight and context into how the Draft Conclusions were arrived at and elaborated upon. In putting together the analysis, the book relies not only on the historical materials that are readily available—reports of the Special Rapporteur, Summary Records of the Commission, Statements of the Chair of the Drafting Committee, reports of the Commission, and Summary Records of the Sixth Committee—but also on personal notes taken during the plenary deliberations as well as informal papers produced during the Drafting Committee which are not readily available.

While this book provides comment on the set of Draft Conclusions it is not a conventional commentary. It seeks to provide more than explanations and comments on the individual Draft Conclusions and seeks to engage in an analysis and evaluation of the issues underlying, and themes running through, the set of Draft Conclusions. Thus, very often the book will discuss, in addition to what is contained in the Draft Conclusions and their Commentaries, issues that are not addressed there. In respect of those, the book will offer not only reasons why the issues were not addressed but also how those issues might be understood in the light of the Draft Conclusions.

As with the Draft Conclusions, the book does not attempt to resolve many of the theoretical and philosophical debates underlying questions of *jus cogens*. Yet, since, as explained earlier, these theoretical debates do inform many of the discussions, the book will attempt a more explicit appraisal of the underlying theoretical tensions than would have been possible in a set of Draft Conclusions with Commentaries negotiated by a group of thirty-four international lawyers with vastly differing approaches to international law.

The book is divided into different parts. Part I consists of two chapters. Chapter 2 will discuss the scope of the set of Draft Conclusions (Draft Conclusion 1). In Draft Conclusion 1, the Commission excludes from the scope of its work many substantive issues, including the question of regional *jus cogens*. Some of the choices made by the Commission in respect of the scope of the Draft Conclusion had an impact on how the Commission would address (or not) other issues, such as the question of immunity, the illustrative list, and aspects of consequences such as grounds precluding wrongfulness. Chapter 3 will discuss definitional issues and in particular Draft

Conclusion 2 (general nature) and Draft Conclusion 3 (definition). With respect to the definition, the chapter will assess the Commission's decision to treat Article 53 of the Vienna Convention as *the* definition of *jus cogens*. While this was generally not a controversial question, there certainly were some calls to consider it more carefully. At any rate, the decision to stick with the Article 53 definition also implicates the theoretical debates underlying *jus cogens* simmering below the surface of the ILC's work. Central to the relationship between the definition and the theoretical debates, is the general nature of *jus cogens*, described in Draft Conclusion 2. The general nature, at times referred to as 'characteristics', of *jus cogens*, as described in Draft Conclusion 2, has been the source of much controversy. Where do these characteristics come from? Is the ILC justified in putting forward these characteristics? What is the relationship between these characteristics and the definition of *jus cogens*?

Part II of the book will focus on the identification of peremptory norms and will consist of Chapters 4, 5, 6, and 7. The criteria for *jus cogens* are derived from the definition of *jus cogens* in Article 53 of the Vienna Convention. While there is some convergence that the definition of peremptory norms contained in Article 53 of the Vienna Convention provides the point of departure for the criteria of peremptory norms, there has nonetheless been a wide divergence of views about what the criteria are. In Draft Conclusion 4, which is the subject of Chapter 4, the Commission determines that there are two criteria for *jus cogens*. First, the norm in question must be a norm of general international law. Second, the norm of must be accepted and recognised by the international community as a whole as one from which no derogation is permitted. Chapter 5 will address the first criterion, norm of general international law. Since there is general acceptance that customary international law is a common basis for *jus cogens*, the focus of the chapter will be on the relevance of treaty provisions and general principles as possible bases for *jus cogens*. Chapter 6 is concerned with the second criterion, the elements of which are contained in Draft Conclusions 6 (acceptance and recognition) and 7 (community of States as a whole). One of the more controversial issues in the Draft Conclusions, the threshold for acceptance and recognition, is addressed in Chapter 6 in the context of the meaning of the concept 'the international community of States as a whole'. Finally, in Part II, Chapter 7 is concerned with the evidence for acceptance and recognition of a norm as one from which no derogation is permitted. Materials that can be used as evidence for acceptance and recognition are provided for in Draft Conclusions 8 (evidence for acceptance and recognition) and 9 (subsidiary means).

Part III of the book consists of four chapters. Chapter 8 addresses treaty-related consequences of *jus cogens*. The chapter will thus cover the issues raised in Draft Conclusions 10 to 13. *Jus cogens* has been most closely associated with invalidation of treaties. Issues relevant to the invalidity of treaties, such as the separability of treaties conflicting with *jus cogens*, are also addressed in Chapter 8. Many of these issues are addressed in the Vienna Convention on the Law of Treaties. Yet, the Draft Conclusions also address issues to which answers cannot be found in the Vienna Convention, in particular the effects of *jus cogens* on reservations to treaties.

Chapter 9 addresses consequences of *jus cogens* for other sources of international law, namely customary international law (Draft Conclusion 14), unilateral acts of States (Draft Conclusion 15), and decisions of international organisations (Draft Conclusion 16). An issue not covered in any Draft Conclusion is the effect of *jus cogens* on general principles. It is briefly addressed in the chapter. In the context of customary international law, the chapter also addresses the question of modification of *jus cogens*—an issue not addressed at any great length in the ILC's set of Draft Conclusions. It also considers the question of the persistent objector doctrine and its application to *jus cogens*.

In Chapter 10, the consequences of peremptory norms for the secondary rules of State responsibility are considered. Issues that are covered in this chapter include the relationship between peremptory norms and *erga omnes* obligations (Draft Conclusion 17) and circumstances precluding wrongfulness (Draft Conclusion 18). Finally in Part III, Chapter 11 addresses particular consequences of breaches of *jus cogens*. The subject of Chapter 11 is addressed in two Draft Conclusions, namely Draft Conclusion 19 on particular consequences of serious breaches of *jus cogens* and Draft Conclusion 22, which is a without prejudice clause concerning those consequences of *jus cogens* that are not addressed in the Draft Conclusions.

Part IV of the book consists of four chapters covering Part Four of the Draft Conclusions. Chapter 12 addresses the impact of *jus cogens* on the interpretation of rules of international law, the subject of Draft Conclusion 20. A related issue is dispute settlement. It is well-known that Article 53 of the Vienna Convention became possible because of an agreement to include a dispute settlement provision in order to avoid the possibility of auto-interpretation in relation to *jus cogens*. What does this mean for the Draft Conclusions since these Draft Conclusions do not constitute a treaty? The Vienna Convention dispute settlement procedures are obviously not applicable as treaty law to the Draft Conclusions, but are they applicable as customary international law? Could reliance on the Draft Conclusions be made subject to a dispute settlement procedure? The ILC, in its Draft Conclusions, included a provision recommending a procedure for dispute settlement (Draft Conclusion 21) which is addressed in Chapter 13.

The final substantive chapter is Chapter 14, which addresses Draft Conclusion 23 and the Commission's non-exhaustive list of norms of *jus cogens*.

By way of conclusion, Chapter 15 will offer some thoughts on the prospects of the Draft Conclusions. This discussion on the prospects will include a discussion of the reception of the Draft Conclusion by States, more particularly in the Sixth Committee.

At the end of the book, a collection of relevant resource materials that are not easily obtainable is provided. These include: Drafting Committee Working Papers, both formal and informal, including handwritten notes of the Special Rapporteur made on the working papers containing reflections of some members on the proposals by the Special Rapporteur.

5.2 Structure of Each Chapter

The book departs from the traditional structure of commentaries in two ways. First, each Draft Conclusion is not necessarily allocated its own chapter. Thus, in cases where there is a particularly strong connection between specific Draft Conclusions, these are addressed together. This is the case with Draft Conclusions 2 and 3 (Chapter 2); Draft Conclusions 6 and 7 (Chapter 6); Draft Conclusions 10, 11, 12, and 13 (Chapter 8); Draft Conclusions 14, 15, and 16 (Chapter 9), Draft Conclusions 17 and 18 (Chapter 10), and Draft Conclusions 19 and 22 (Chapter 11).

The second way in which the book departs from the traditional structure of commentaries concerns the symmetry of the chapters. Commentaries tend to have a particular symmetry in terms of structure. While there is a degree of symmetry pursued in the book, where the content dictates, there is a departure from the symmetrical structure. Most of the chapters begin with an introduction, followed by a discussion and then a comment on the text adopted by the Draft Conclusion(s). The chapters then close with concluding observations. In the discussion, the main issues and areas of contestation are addressed. This then allows the text to be commented upon with the issues of contestation in mind. This basic structure is not followed for this chapter for obvious reasons, nor is it followed in Chapters 2 and 3. For Chapter 2, dealing with scope, the reason is fairly straightforward. The Draft Conclusion is not addressing any substantive issue such that the discussion/text dichotomy would not make sense. For Chapter 3, addressing Draft Conclusion 2 (general nature) and Draft Conclusion 3 (definition), the reasons are less self-evident. While those Draft Conclusions are substantive in nature, making the discussion/text dichotomy possible, because the conclusions reached therein permeate the whole set of Draft Conclusions, it was better to address them in a more fluid way such that the descriptions of the texts were intertwined with the discussions on the issues raised.

Quite apart from the structure, the book is also not always symmetrical in terms of methodology or approach. Depending on various factors, including the content of the particular Draft Conclusion, the controversy surrounding the debate, the source of the content of the provision, and the extent to which issues remain unresolved, some chapters are more descriptive while others are more analytical. Other chapters may focus more on controversies, while in others the accent may fall on the text and its evolution. Examples of chapters that are more descriptive or focused on the text include Chapter 8 on consequences of *jus cogens* for treaties and Chapter 12 on interpretation of other rules of international law. Chapter 11 on particular consequences and Chapter 9 on other sources of obligations are of a more analytical nature. Chapter 3 which concerns the definition and nature of *jus cogens* and Chapter 6 on acceptance and recognition of peremptory status have a bias in favour of the internal discussions. Of course all of the chapters are a mixture of analysis, internal deliberations, and description, but there is definitely a difference of emphasis of which the reader should be aware.

6. Concluding Observations

I write this book having served as Special Rapporteur for the topic under consideration. This creates a real risk of bias (in favour of the outcomes). That is not my intention and I hope I have been successful in striking an objective tone, and not being too defensive of the Draft Conclusions. The Draft Conclusions are, after all, the work of the Commission as a whole and not of the Special Rapporteur. I do think there are particular issues that the Commission could have approached somewhat differently and this I hope is evident from the book. I myself, in hindsight (yes, even this early), could have approached some things somewhat differently. At any rate, I hope the book succeeds in its attempt to be an honest assessment of the International Law Commission's Draft Conclusions on *Jus Cogens*, with the benefit of an insider's perspective.

PART I
INTRODUCTION

2

The Scope of the Draft Conclusions

1. Introduction

The subject of peremptory norms of general international law can be very broad. The scope of the Draft Conclusions is provided for in Draft Conclusion 1, which is the subject of this chapter.

The scope provision in any text of an instrument is important because it explains why certain aspects that a reader might expect to be covered are not covered. In the case of the International Law Commission's topic on *jus cogens*, examples of subjects that might be expected to have been covered but which are not covered include the impact of *jus cogens* on the rules of international law on immunity and the relationship between the exceptions to the prohibition on the use of force, such as self-defence, and *jus cogens* in the context of the rule that circumstances precluding wrongfulness do not apply in the case of *jus cogens*.

In keeping with the general approach of this book to provide context even beyond the Draft Conclusions, the relevant chapters of the book will provide some insights into how those issues might be viewed in the light of the Draft Conclusions. Moreover, the Commentaries to the Draft Conclusions are more comprehensive in setting out aspects that lie beyond the scope of the Draft Conclusions. This is the case, for example, with respect to regional *jus cogens*, which is not addressed in the Draft Conclusions. Similarly, the Commentary to Draft Conclusion 1 also explains which actors are to be addressed and how.

Section 2 provides a discussion of the text of the Draft Conclusion. From this text, the section identifies three issues which are discussed in turn. These issues are: the methodological nature of the Draft Conclusions, and its implications for the full set of Draft Conclusions (Section 2.1); the question of regional *jus cogens* (Section 2.2); and the actors that are covered in the Draft Conclusions (Section 2.3). Concluding Observations are offered in Section 3.

2. Scope of the Draft Conclusions

Conclusion 1
Scope
The present draft conclusions concern the identification and legal consequences of peremptory norms of general international law (*jus cogens*).

2.1 The Methodological Character of the Draft Conclusions

The text of Draft Conclusion 1 on the scope describes the Draft Conclusions as being concerned with 'the identification and legal consequences of' *jus cogens*. The Commentary to Draft Conclusion 1 explains that the implication of this scope is that the set of Draft Conclusions is limited to what it refers to as 'methodological' issues.[1]

In part, the 'methodological' nature of the topic appears to be justified by the underlying reasons for the elaboration of these Draft Conclusions. In the Commentary to Draft Conclusion 1, the Commission observes that peremptory norms have 'increasingly' been invoked 'by national courts, States and other actors' and that the purpose of the Draft Conclusions is to provide 'guidance to all those who may be called upon' to apply *jus cogens*.[2] Similar wording was previously used by the Commission in its Draft Conclusions on the Identification of Customary International Law.[3] What is not said, but may well be implied, is that, as in the case of the identification of customary international law, the Commission is concerned with the uncontrolled proliferation of statements about *jus cogens* and its consequences made without the application of an appropriate methodology. Under these circumstances, any court can determine the existence of *jus cogens* based on little more than policy preferences. The list of norms that have been identified as *jus cogens* in recent times include a diverse number of norms such as the prohibition on the use of force, prohibition of genocide, prohibition of crimes against humanity, basic rules of international humanitarian law, prohibition of racial discrimination and apartheid, prohibition of slavery, prohibition of torture, right to life, prohibition of discrimination against women, prohibition

[1] See paras 2–6 of the Commentary to Draft Conclusion 1 of the Draft Conclusions.
[2] Id., para 2.
[3] Paragraph 2 of the Commentary to Draft Conclusion 1 of the Draft Conclusions on the Identification of Customary International Law, *Report of the International Law Commission, Seventieth Session* (A/73/10).

of discrimination on the basis of sexual identity, right to a fair trial, right to a name, and many others.

In addition to concern about the proliferation of norms identified as *jus cogens* without the application of an appropriate methodology, presumably the Commission is also concerned about the invention of novel consequences of peremptory norms. As explained in Chapter 1, consequences of *jus cogens* have been said to include, in addition to the invalidation of conflicting treaty rules, evisceration of immunity and the establishment jurisdiction of international courts without the consent of the States involved.

From one perspective, the Commission's work in this area may be seen as efforts to ensure the systematic development of a very important area of international law.[4] While the need for systematic development of international law may be particularly important for *jus cogens* because of the 'importance and potentially far-reaching implications' of the rules concerned, it is equally important for other rules of international law. This may explain the recent focus by the Commission on topics concerning sources. In the last twelve years, the Commission has completed five source-related topics,[5] and it is currently engaged in two others (general principles of law and subsidiary means). Yet, from another perspective, the Commission's work may be seen as an attempt to retard the development of *jus cogens* by placing impossible criteria for the identification of *jus cogens* norms, thus ensuring that there will be few norms of *jus cogens* (fewer even that the ones on the list customarily accepted). The right to self-determination, for example, long accepted without objection, is one norm which has, since the adoption of the Draft Conclusions on first reading, come under severe pressure from a few States (see Chapter 14). It is certainly the case that, without a strict set of criteria, developed by a body with *some authority*,[6] it becomes easier for anyone to claim that his or her preferred norm has peremptory status. These sentiments were certainly present in the minds of some members of the Commission, at the onset of the project.

[4] According to para 2 of the Commentary to Draft Conclusion 1, the reason why the systematic development of the peremptory norms was important was because of the 'importance and [the] potentially far-reaching implications of' those norms.

[5] The Commission adopted the Guide to Practice on Reservations to Treaties (2011), Draft Conclusions on the Identification of Customary International Law (2018), Draft Conclusions on Subsequent Agreements and Subsequent Practice in Relation to Treaty Interpretation (2018), Guide to Provisional Application of Treaties (2021), and Peremptory Norms of General International Law (*Jus Cogens*) (2022).

[6] On this see Zuzana Trávníčková 'The International Law Commission and the International Law Codification Market' and Monica Pinto 'The Authority and the Membership of the Commission in the Future', both in United Nations *Seventy Years of the International Law Commission: Drawing a Balance for the Future* (Brill/Nijhoff, 2021).

In the Commentary to Draft Conclusion 1, the Commission identifies a number of implications of its distinctly methodological approach to the topic. The first one is more a cautionary note than anything else, but it is worth mentioning because, as will be seen, particularly in the context of the consequences of *jus cogens* for treaties and the secondary rules of responsibility, the Commission was often constrained in the examples of State practice that it could put forward. In the Commentary, the Commission states that because the approach adopted is methodological, the Commission is not concerned with the content of individual peremptory norms and for that reason the 'materials referred to as examples of practice' only 'serve to illustrate the methodology for the identification and consequences of' *jus cogens* but 'do not imply the agreement with, or endorsement of, the views expressed therein by the Commission'.[7] In the adoption of the report, the reference to many examples was very contentious precisely because some members did not agree with those examples, with the result that, in some cases, those examples were not retained, and in others the Commentaries were redrafted to under-emphasise the examples.[8] On second reading, for example, the Draft Commentaries referred to examples concerning the Russian intervention in Ukraine, resulting in protracted debates and informal consultations on the appropriateness of such references. On first reading, various examples pertaining to the decisions on the war in Iraq and the Israeli occupation of the State of Palestine were similarly contested.[9]

The idea that the Commission is not, in relation to this topic, concerned with individual peremptory norms had a second implication for the project as a whole, namely the Commission's approach to an illustrative or non-exhaustive list. It is noteworthy that the issue of whether to have a list was raised in each of the first four debates leading to the adoption of the first reading texts. Indeed the reports of the Special Rapporteur indicate that he himself oscillated between different views throughout the life of the project. This aspect is discussed further in Chapter 14.

Third, the Commission also used the methodological nature of the topic as a reason for not addressing particular consequences of specific peremptory

[7] Paragraph 3 of the Commentary to Draft Conclusion 1.

[8] See Murphy (A/CN.4/SR.3499), 7, who, having expressed support for the insertion of these words, emphasised that this language 'would not obviate the need to discuss certain examples used in the [draft] commentary in due course'.

[9] See *ILC Draft Report of the International Law Commission on the Work of Seventy-First Session*, Chapter V (A/CN.4/L.929/Add.2). See *ILC Draft Report of the International Law Commission on the Work of Seventy-Third Session*, Chapter IV (annotated with comments) (A/CN.4/L.960/Add.1) available as an Annex in this book.

norms. Incidentally, the effect of this choice was to exclude from the scope of the topic perhaps the most debated consequence of *jus cogens*, and the aspect that many were certainly hoping the Commission would address: the impact of *jus cogens* on the rules of international law concerning immunities.[10] Chapter 11 addresses this aspect of the Commission's choice.

2.2 Regional *Jus Cogens*

The topic proposed in the Syllabus and initially placed on the agenda of the Commission was *jus cogens*.[11] However, in the second year of the Commission's consideration of the topic, the Commission decided to change the name to peremptory norms of general international law (*jus cogens*). While, as is clear from the Commentary and the Second Report on *jus cogens*, the reason for this shift was simply to ensure consistency with the terminology in the Vienna Convention and the Commission's previous work,[12] the Commission ascribed this change to another consequence of the scope of the topic, certainly not foreseen when the new name was adopted:

> The phrase 'peremptory norms of general international law (*jus cogens*)' also serves to indicate that the topic is concerned only with norms of general international law. *Jus cogens* norms in domestic legal systems, for example, do not form part of the topic. Similarly, norms of a purely bilateral or regional character are also excluded from the scope of the topic.[13]

Before changing the name of the topic, the First Report of the Special Rapporteur had already suggested, although as a preliminary point, not only that the Commission would not deal with regional (and/or bilateral) *jus cogens*, but that international law did not recognise such concepts.[14] Moreover, in that first debate, it was not suggested by any other member that regional *jus cogens*, though it exists in international law, ought to be excluded from the scope of the topic. The relationship between the exclusion of regional *jus*

[10] *Report of the International Law Commission, Seventieth Session* (A/73/10), paras 141–8.
[11] 'Jus Cogens' Syllabus, *Report of the International Law Commission, Sixty-Sixth Session* (A/69/10), Annex.
[12] *Second Report of the Special Rapporteur on Jus Cogens* (A/CN.4/706), paras 5 and 90.
[13] Paragraph 8 of the Commentary to Draft Conclusion 1.
[14] *First Report of Special Rapporteur on Jus Cogens* (A/CN.4/693), para 68.

cogens and the phrase 'of general international law' is thus, at best, coincidental and first appeared during the adoption of the Commentary. While the First Report offered, in preliminary and tentative terms, the view that regional (and by definition bilateral) *jus cogens* was incompatible with the very idea of *jus cogens*, the Fourth Report presented a more comprehensive assessment of the potential for regional *jus cogens* in international law.[15] The conclusion in that report was that international law does not recognise the notion of regional *jus cogens*.[16]

The Fourth Report identified several conceptual difficulties with the idea of regional *jus cogens*. First, the rationale for the exceptional power of *jus cogens*, such as being capable of binding States without their consent and invalidating conflicting rules, can be found in the fact that these are norms so fundamental to the international community that derogation from them cannot be permitted. It would be difficult to explain the extraordinary force of a regional peremptory norm on an individual State which has not consented to that norm (or its peremptory character) if that norm did not reflect the fundamental values of the international community as a whole.

The second conceptual difficulty relates to the question of the definition of 'region'. Regional *jus cogens*, as a matter of law, is indeterminate. For example, to which States would a regional *jus cogens* in Southern Africa apply? Would such a regional *jus cogens* apply to Burundi or the Democratic Republic of the Congo? What about Europe? Does it include Eastern Europe? What do we mean by Eastern Europe? This question can be asked about any other region. In the light of this uncertainty, the concept of regional *jus cogens* would create the conceptual and practical difficulty of identifying the States to which a regional *jus cogens* applies.

Both the first and second conceptual difficulties could potentially be addressed by reference to treaties. In other words, the binding and peremptory character of a regional *jus cogens* norm could be explained based on a treaty acceptance.[17] Similarly, the 'region' to which a regional *jus cogens* applies might be determined by a treaty or treaty regime. It is these treaty-based arguments that underpin the proposition that certain rights constitute *jus cogens* in Europe

[15] *Fourth Report of the Special Rapporteur on Peremptory Norms of General International Law (Jus Cogens)* (A/CN.4/727), paras 21–47.

[16] Id., para 47.

[17] See Robert Kolb 'Peremptory Norms as a Legal Technique Rather than Substantive Super Norms' in Dire Tladi (ed.) *Peremptory Norms of General International Law (Jus Cogens): Disquisitions and Disputations* (Brill, 2021), 35 who makes the following observation: 'This means that peremptory position does not need to be embedded in a universal norm ... It can be cast into a regional treaty, when the latter does not allow its parties to depart from its rules by more special acts.'

or under the inter-American system for the protection of human rights.[18] In putting forward the possibility of regional *jus cogens*, for example, Kolb refers to the 'European public order, which goes further than the universal one on issues of democracy, pre-eminence of law and separation of powers'.[19] He also refers, at the same time, to the practice of the Inter-American Commission particularly in its decision in *Roach and Pinkerton* concerning the imposition of the death penalty on minors.[20] Yet, as treaty systems based on the agreement of the parties to those regional systems, it is difficult to characterise the norms emanating therefrom as *jus cogens*, regional or otherwise. Moreover, to take Kolb's assertion that *jus cogens* 'can be cast into a regional treaty, when the latter does not allow its parties to depart from its rules by more special acts',[21] if a new treaty rule is established contrary to such a regional treaty, such new treaty rule would not be invalid as would be the case if it were a *jus cogens*. Indeed, it is the inapplicability of the consequences of *jus cogens* that provide the most difficult conceptual hurdle for regional *jus cogens*.

The main conceptual difficulty identified in the Fourth Report concerns the consequences of *jus cogens*. How might the consequences that are generally accepted to flow from *jus cogens* apply to a norm of regional *jus cogens*? Is a treaty concluded between a State from that region and another State invalid? If the answer is that the treaty is valid because the third State is not part of the region, then that norm can hardly be said to be non-derogable. Indeed, even as between members of the region, if two States from the region conclude a treaty contrary to the regional *jus cogens* norm, it is not at all clear why the provisions of the treaty would not trump the regional *jus cogens* norm on the strength of the rule contained in Article 30 of the Vienna Convention on the Law of Treaties—assuming the regional *jus cogens* norm is based on a treaty rule. Of course, the conclusion of the subsequent treaty conflicting with regional norms may well constitute a breach of international obligations and entail the responsibility of the relevant States, but it is not at all clear that the subsequent treaty would be invalid. It would also be difficult to imagine how the duty not to recognise situations arising from a breach of a regional *jus cogens* would apply.

[18] See, for discussion, Pavel Šturma 'Is There Any Regional *Jus Cogens* in Europe? The Case of the European Court of Human Rights' in Tladi (above note 17); Juan José Ruda Santolaria 'The Treatment of Peremptory Norms of General International Law (*Jus Cogens*) in the Inter-American Human Rights System' in Tladi (above note 17). See also Ulf Linderfalk *Understanding Jus Cogens in International Legal Discourse* (Edward Elgar, 2020), 137.

[19] Robert Kolb *Peremptory International Law: Jus Cogens—A General Inventory* (Hart, 2015), 97.

[20] Id. See also Erika de Wet 'The Emergence of International and Regional Value Systems as a Manifestation of the Emerging International Constitutional Order' (2006) 19 *Leiden Journal of International Law* 611, 617.

[21] See Kolb (above note 17), 35.

Thus, while several authors have expressed the view that regional *jus cogens* was possible,[22] the conceptual difficulties outlined above make the proposition untenable. Of course, it is possible to respond to each of these conceptual difficulties. The Fourth Report responds as follows:

> It is true that some responses to these theoretical problems can be advanced. These responses, however, require intellectual gymnastics which, in the end, take non-derogability out of regional *jus cogens*. However, even if these responses to the theoretical problems were acceptable, there is a more serious (and insurmountable) problem with the notion of regional *jus cogens*, namely the lack of State practice supporting such a notion.[23]

The notion of a regional *jus cogens* may well be consistent with a purely positivist and technical approach to *jus cogens*, for example the one adopted by Kolb.[24] Yet, as will be discussed momentarily, the Commission opted for the more substantive and more traditional approach to *jus cogens*, which is based on fundamental values of the international community and is of universal application. This approach to *jus cogens* is not compatible with the idea of regional *jus cogens*.[25]

The non-recognition of regional *jus cogens* does not, of course, mean that regions (or other groups of States) cannot establish, whether through treaty or particular custom, rules of elevated importance applicable in their relations and attach particular consequences to those norms. This, however, is not the same as *jus cogens*. Nor does the approach mean that regions (or other groups of States) cannot determine that some rules enjoy a heightened status in relations with each other. But neither does this equate to *jus cogens*.

States have, in response to the work of the Commission, distanced themselves from the possibility of regional *jus cogens*.[26] The debate within the Commission

[22] For literature supporting the proposition of regional *jus cogens*, see also Kolb (above note 17). See further de Wet (above note 20), 37; Alain Pellet 'Comments in Response to Christine Chinkin and in Defense of *Jus Cogens* as the Best Bastion against the Excesses of Fragmentation' (2006) 17 *Finnish Yearbook of International Law* 83, 83; Giorgio Gaja '*Jus Cogens* Beyond the Vienna Convention' (1981-III) 172 *Collected Courses of the Hague Academy of International Law* 271, 284 ('No convincing reason has ever been given for ruling out the possibility of the existence of non-universal, or "regional" peremptory norms. Values prevailing in regional groups do not necessarily conflict with values operating in a larger framework. There may be norms which acquire a peremptory character only in a regional context').

[23] Fourth Report (above note 15), para 37.

[24] See generally Kolb (above note 17).

[25] See Patrícia Galvão Teles 'Peremptory Norms of General International Law and the Fundamental Values of the International Community' in Tladi (above note 17).

[26] For a summary of the views of States, see Fourth Report (above note 15), para 22.

on this point was revealing. Most members of the Commission explicitly expressed the view that the notion of regional *jus cogens* was not recognised under international law as it stood.[27] Only a few members of the Commission spoke in favour of regional *jus cogens* as a doctrinal proposition.[28] Other members, while accepting that international law as it stood did not recognise regional *jus cogens*, were of the view that the Commission should not foreclose the possibility that norms of regional *jus cogens* may, in the future, emerge.[29]

[27] See e.g. Murase (A/CN.4/SR.3459), 12 ('he fully supported the Special Rapporteur's position on the exclusion of any mention of regional *jus cogens* in the draft conclusions, because the concept of regional *jus cogens* contradicted the very notion of peremptory norms of general international law and was not supported in practice'); Lehto (A/CN.4/SR.3459), 19 ('With regard to regional *jus cogens*, she agreed with the main reason given by the Special Rapporteur for omitting references to the concept in the draft conclusions, namely, that regional *jus cogens* could not easily be reconciled with the Commission's approach to the present topic. According to that approach, *jus cogens* was based on a hierarchy of norms and seen as reflecting and protecting the core values of the international legal order, which were necessarily universal'); Galvão Teles (A/CN.4/SR.3460) ('Even though it could be argued that different regions or groups of States might have a common set of unifying and binding norms that had a higher status than other rules, at least among those regions or groups—as in the case, for instance, of the prohibition of the death penalty in the countries of the European Union—that did not mean that such norms had the status of regional *jus cogens*. She therefore agreed with the Special Rapporteur's proposal, in paragraph 47 of his report, that no draft conclusion should be adopted on regional *jus cogens* and that an appropriate explanation should be included in the commentary'); Oral (A/CN.4/SR.3460), 5; Hmoud (A/CN.4/SR.3460), 13; Hassouna (A/CN.4/SR.3460), 15 ('Nonetheless, he shared the views of the Special Rapporteur, whose report included a detailed discussion of the lack of practice to substantiate the existence of regional *jus cogens* and the practical and conceptual difficulties deriving from the inherently universal character of *jus cogens*'); Nguyen (A/CN.4/SR.3460), 17 ('Acceptance of the existence of different regional *jus cogens* norms might thus contradict the universality of human rights values'); Jalloh (A/CN.4/SR3461), 8; Rajput (A/CN.4/SR.3461), 13 ('If the commentary were ultimately to make mention of regional *jus cogens*, it should be to reject the concept, for the convincing arguments laid out by the Special Rapporteur in his report'); Aurescu (A/CN.4/SR.3462), 3; Saboia (A/CN.4/SR.3462), 5 ('The notion of regional *jus cogens* thus seemed difficult to accept. As indicated in previous reports of the Special Rapporteur, norms could not be considered peremptory unless they belonged to general international law and were accepted and recognized by the international community of States as a whole as being non-derogable'); Petrič (A/CN.4/SR.3462), 8 *et seq.* ('He fully endorsed the Special Rapporteur's approach and agreed that the existence of a "common set of unifying and binding norms in different regions" did not translate into a recognition of regional *jus cogens* and that the notion of regional *jus cogens* did not find support in the practice of States'); Argüello Gómez (A/CN.4/SR.3462), 11 ('he had doubts as to the existence of regional *jus cogens*, which seemed to be a contradiction in terms. So-called regional *jus cogens* norms did not derive from general international law, were not non-derogable and could not be invoked against peremptory norms of general international law. By their very definition, they were not peremptory norms of general international law'); Escobar Hernández (A/CN.4/SR.3462), 14 ('she had expressed serious reservations about the existence of regional *jus cogens*'); Ruda Santaloria (A/CN.4/SR.3462), 17 ('On the question of regional *jus cogens*, he fully agreed with the Special Rapporteur that the concept was difficult to reconcile with the concept of *jus cogens* proper, which, by its very nature, was universal'); Laraba (A/CN.4/SR.3463), 3 ('the notion of regional *jus cogens* did not find support in the practice of States and it was not necessary to propose a draft conclusion on the question'); Šturma (A/CN.4/SR.3463), 16;

[28] Nolte (A/CN4/SR.3461), 3–4; Ouazzani Chahdi (A/CN.4/SR.3463), 12; Valencia Ospina (A/CN.4/SR.3463), 13 ('Regional international law and, by extension, regional *jus cogens* were particularly germane from a Latin American perspective, and thus he could not agree totally with the finding that regional *jus cogens* did not exist; he supported the strong objective arguments put forward by Mr. Nolte in that regard); Cisse (A/CN.4/SR.3462), 7.

[29] Wood (A/CN.4/SR.33459), 6 ('As demonstrated by the Special Rapporteur, "the notion of regional *jus cogens* does not find support in the practice of States". But rather than taking the position

Thus, the wording of the Commentary, while on its face non-committal as to the possibility of regional *jus cogens*, was adopted against the background of very strong opposition and very little support for the idea of regional *jus cogens*.

2.3 The Actors to Which the Draft Conclusions Apply

The Draft Conclusions apply in general to States. Although there is much literature proclaiming the increased role of non-State actors in international law,[30] States remain the main subjects of international law. The text of the ILC's Draft Conclusions adopt this traditionalist approach and cover mainly States, perhaps a reflection of the fact that the ILC remains faithful to the traditional conception of international law. The definition of *jus cogens*, for example, is centred around the acceptance and recognition by States.[31] Similarly, with only one exception in which international organisations are referred to (Draft Conclusion 16 on decisions of international organisations), the Draft Conclusions refer only to consequences attaching to States.

Yet there were certainly members of the Commission that called for a more inclusive approach that accounts for the greater role that non-State actors can play and have played in international law. During the very first debate on the topic, for example, Mr Park suggested that it would be appropriate 'to broaden the scope of the topic to include non-State actors, whose role had undeniably grown'.[32] He noted in particular that the Commission would have to consider extending the scope of its work to include non-State actors since they were capable of committing the types of atrocities that would undoubtedly be covered

that "international law does not recognize the notion of regional *jus cogens*", he believed that the Commission should acknowledge that the matter was more nuanced, either by saying nothing or by saying, somewhere in the commentaries, that the draft conclusions did not deal with any question concerning the possibility of regional rules having a *jus cogens* character'); Park (A/CN.4/SR.3459), 16; Reinisch (A/CN.4/SR.3461), 6; Grossman Guiloff (A/CN.4/SR.3463), 5.

[30] See e.g. Andrea Bianchi 'The Fight for Inclusion: Non-State Actors and International Law' in Ulric Fastenrath *et al.* (eds) *From Bilateralism to Community Interest: Essays in Honour of Judge Bruno Simma* (Oxford University Press, 2011).

[31] Draft Conclusion 2, Draft Conclusion 4, Draft Conclusion 7, and Draft Conclusion 8. The traditionalist view that only States were relevant in the formation and identification of *jus cogens* was held by a number of members: Nguyen (A/CN.4/SR.3369), 12 ('A non-State actor had no right to modify a *jus cogens* norm'); Murphy (A/CN.4/SR.3369), 15 ('the Special Rapporteur was correct to focus on the acceptance and recognition by States, rather than other actors'); Hmoud (A/CN.4/SR.3370), 6 ('While material from actors other than States might be useful in assessing acceptance and recognition by States, acceptance and recognition by non-State actors was not at stake'); Kolodkin (A/CM4/SR.3372), 3.

[32] Park (A/CN.4/SR.3316), 15. See also Vásquez Bermúdez (A/CN.4/SR.3322), 5–6.

by *jus cogens*.[33] In concrete terms, Vásquez Bermúdez stated that norms of *jus cogens* were 'applicable to all subjects of international law, including States and international organisations'.[34]

The Draft Commentary to Draft Conclusion 1, proposed during second reading, attempted to take these views into account by making the following clarification:

> In general, the present draft conclusions apply to States, as the primary subject of international law. For this reason, the text of the draft conclusions refers in the main to 'States'. Nonetheless, there are instances in which the draft conclusions apply to entities other than States, in particular, international organisations. However, even in these cases, the draft conclusions often refer simply to States. Where a particular draft conclusion applies to entities other than States, in particular international organisations, the commentaries will make this clear.[35]

Curiously, while it was Mr Park, on first reading, who had suggested broadening the scope, it was largely at the insistence of Mr Park that this proposed formulation was narrowed to finally refer only to international organisations.[36] In consequence, the relevant part of the Commentary now states:

> In general, the present draft conclusions apply only to States, as the primary subjects of international law. For this reason, the text of the draft conclusions refers in the main to 'States'. Nonetheless, there are instances in which the draft conclusions also apply to international organisations. Where a particular draft conclusion applies also to international organisations, the commentaries will make this clear.

[33] Park (A/CN.4/SR.3316), 15. In the same statement, Park said that the work of the Commission should cover 'questions pertaining to international organisations and to the criminal responsibility of legal persons'. See also Nguyen (A/CN.4/SR.3425), 7; Lehto (A/CN.4/SR.3317), 18.

[34] Vásquez Bermúdez (A/CN.4/SR.3322), 6. See also Vásquez Bermúdez (A/CN.4/SR.3418), 12; Hassouna (A/CN.4/SR.3419), 6.

[35] Paragraph 10 of the Commentary to Draft Conclusion 1, in UN A/CN.4/L.960 + Add.1.

[36] Park (A/CN.4/SR.3595) ('said that the reference in the third and fifth sentences to "entities other than States, in particular international organizations" was puzzling. He wished to know what precisely was meant by "entities other than States". Was it intended to encompass non-governmental organizations, private individuals and non-State armed groups? The term "non-State actors" appeared three times in the text of the commentary, but in each case, it was made clear that it referred solely to international organizations. He therefore proposed that the third sentence should be changed to read "Nonetheless, there are instances in which the draft conclusions apply also to international organizations", and the fifth sentence should read "When a particular draft conclusion applies to international organizations, the commentaries will make this clear"'). See also Murphy (A/CN.4/SR.3595).

In other words, even where the Draft Conclusions speak only of States, they may also still apply to international organisations. It is therefore important, when assessing the scope of any of the Draft Conclusions and their applicability to international organisations, to look carefully at the accompanying Commentaries.

What this Commentary leaves open is the impact of the Draft Conclusions on other non-State actors. Does the fact that entities other than States and international organisations are not mentioned in the Draft Conclusions mean that there is no duty on these other entities to co-operate to bring to an end serious breaches of *jus cogens*, or that these other entities are permitted to assist in the maintenance of situations created by serious breaches of *jus cogens*? This seems unlikely. While the Draft Conclusions are themselves limited to States and international organisations, there may well be particular consequences of peremptory norms attaching to non-State actors although these are not addressed in the Draft Conclusions.

3. Concluding Observations

The underlying objective of the Draft Conclusions is to provide guidance to those that are called upon to identify *jus cogens* and to apply its consequences. Yet, both in respect of identification and legal consequences, the Draft Conclusions are not comprehensive. This is particularly the case with respect to consequences. The Commission does not cover, for example, consequences flowing from specific norms of *jus cogens*, including the prohibition of acts constituting international crimes. With respect to identification, the Commission does not cover, for example, how norms of *jus cogens* are modified. The explanation for this limited scope is provided in Draft Conclusion 1 on Scope.

In assessing the content of the Draft Conclusions, the limitations on scope must be taken into account. This is particularly true of the consequences of *jus cogens*. In other words, the fact that the Commission did not address a particular consequence in the Draft Conclusion should not necessarily be taken as an indication of the Commission's position one way or another.

3

Definitional Issues

1. Introduction

This chapter is concerned with definitional issues. The definition of *jus cogens* is addressed in Draft Conclusion 3. Draft Conclusion 2 concerns the general nature of *jus cogens*. These two Draft Conclusions are addressed in this chapter.

It is appropriate to address these two Draft Conclusions together because the general nature of *jus cogens* will tell us much about how to define it. In other words, the general nature of *jus cogens* contributes to an understanding of *jus cogens*. Indeed, as will become clear in the discussion below, the debate within the Commission on Draft Conclusion 2 centred very much on its relationship with the definition of *jus cogens*. In the end, the Commission decided that the characteristics of *jus cogens*, contained in Draft Conclusion 2, are not part of the definition and do not, in general, contribute to the criteria for *jus cogens* derived from the definition in Draft Conclusion 3. And yet, as will be seen below, there are elements of ambivalence in the Commentary. Given this close relationship, or in the view of some, possible confusion between the general nature and the definition, it is appropriate that the two Draft Conclusions are addressed in one chapter.

Draft Conclusion 3 on definition was not contentious at all, while Draft Conclusion 2 was one of the most contentious Draft Conclusions in the whole set. Moreover, much of the discussions on Draft Conclusion 2 invoked Draft Conclusion 3. For that reason, this chapter proceeds by discussing first Draft Conclusion 3 in Section 2 and then reverts to Draft Conclusion 2 in Section 3. Indeed, in the original order of the Draft Conclusions adopted on first reading, the definition came before the general nature. The order was reversed on second reading only to create an optical separation between the general nature (Draft Conclusion 2) and the criterion in Draft Conclusion 4 (addressed in Chapter 4). Section 4 provides some concluding observations.

2. The Definition of *Jus Cogens*

Draft Conclusion 3
Definition of a peremptory norm of general international law (*jus cogens*)
A peremptory norm of general international law (*jus cogens*) is a norm accepted and recognized by the international community of States as a whole as a norm from which no derogation is permitted and which can be modified only by a subsequent norm of general international law (*jus cogens*) having the same character.

2.1 The Source of the Definition: The Vienna Convention

In Draft Conclusion 3, the Commission chose to base its definition of *jus cogens* on the second sentence of Article 53 of the Vienna Convention. The definition that was initially proposed in the First Report of the Special Rapporteur, while also relying on the Article 53 definition, left out some elements and introduced others:

> Peremptory Norms of international law (*Jus Cogens*) are those norms of general international law accepted and recognised by the international community of States as a whole as those from which no modification, derogation or abrogation is permitted.[1]

This definition was subject to strong criticism from members of the Commission.[2] Members questioned the use of the words 'modification' and 'abrogation'.[3] The strong sense in the Commission was that the Commission should retain the language in Article 53.[4] This view was perhaps best captured

[1] See Proposed Draft Conclusion 3, para 74 of the *First Report of the Special Rapporteur on Jus Cogens* (A/CN.4/693).

[2] See, for support of the proposals, Caflisch (A/CN.4/SR.3314), 10 ('He supported that proposal, as well as the three draft conclusions proposed in paragraph 74, which could be referred to the Drafting Committee, although perhaps the order of draft conclusions 2 and 3 should be inverted').

[3] See e.g. Wood (A/CN.4/SR.3314); Hassouna (A/CN.4/SR.3315), 4, suggesting that these concepts went beyond the scope of the project; Kittichaisaree (A/CN.4/SR.3315), 6; McRae (A/CN.4/SR.3315), 8; Nolte (A/CN.4/SR.3315); Murphy (A/CN.4/SR.3316), 12; Candiotti (A/CN.4/SR.3317), 2; Forteau (A/CN.4/SR.3317), 14; Vásquez Bermúdez (A/CN.4/SR.3322), 7; Niehaus (A/CN.4/SR.3323), 5.

[4] Statement of the Chair of the Drafting Committee, 9 August 2016 ('As regards the first paragraph, the Drafting Committee, on the basis of suggestions made in the plenary, decided to reformulate the provision in order to track the language of the second sentence of Article 53 of the Vienna Convention').

by the comments of Commissário Afonso who 'endorsed Draft Conclusion 3' which he said 'was of crucial importance'.[5] At the same time, however, he said the Commission 'should be cautious in its approach and not depart from Article 53 of the Vienna Convention' and that the definition in the Draft Conclusions 'should reproduce the text of Article 53, with minor adaptations'.[6]

The reliance by the Commission on Article 53 is of course a safe option.[7] Yet, at least one member of the Commission consistently expressed the view that the definition of peremptory norms in Article 53 applies only to the law of treaties and that a definition has to be identified to cover other areas of international law, in particular the law of State responsibility.[8] The view adopted by the Commission, however, is that the definition of *jus cogens* in Article 53 of the Vienna Convention applies also to other areas in international law, including the law on State responsibility.

It is true, as has been pointed out, that Article 53 states that the definition contained there is '[f]or the purposes of the Convention'. Yet, whatever the position may have been at the time of the adoption of the Vienna Convention, it is 'now hardly tenable' to view the definition contained in Article 53 as being applicable only for the purposes of the Vienna Convention.[9] As the Commentary points out, the definition is 'the most widely accepted definition in the practice of States and in the decisions of international courts and tribunals' for peremptory norms.[10] The Commentary refers to decisions of national courts[11]

[5] Commissário Afonso (A/CN.4/SR.3323), 6.

[6] Id.

[7] Cf. Dire Tladi 'The International Law Commission's Draft Conclusions on Peremptory Norms of General International Law (jus cogens): Making Wine from Water or More Water than Wine' (2020) 89 *Nordic Journal of International Law* 244 ('An unsympathetic view of the Draft Conclusions might suggest that the Draft Conclusions are nothing more than a "cut and paste" of existing instruments. From this perspective, the Draft Conclusions might be seen, to borrow from Valencia-Ospina, as more water than wine').

[8] See e.g. generally Murase (A/CN.4/SR.3314), 7 ('He was not convinced, however, that the legal nature, content and function of *jus cogens* were the same in the law of treaties as in the law of State responsibility. If that were the case, a broad definition of *jus cogens* would have to be elaborated, applicable to both of branches of law').

[9] Ulf Linderfalk *Understanding Jus Cogens in International Legal Discourse* (Edward Elgar, 2020), 8.

[10] Para 2 of the Commentary to Draft Conclusion 2.

[11] See e.g. *Al Shimari et al. v CACI Premier Technology, Inc., No. 1:08-cv-827 (LMB/JFA)*, Opinion of 22 March 2019, 2019 WL 1320052 (E.D. Va. 2019), p. 26; *Committee of United States Citizens Living in Nicaragua v Reagan*, Case No. 87-5053, Opinion of 14 October 1988, 859 F 2d 929 (DC Cir 1988), p. 940; *Youssef Nada v State Secretariat for Economic Affairs and Federal Department of Economic Affairs, Case No. 1A 45/2007*, Administrative appeal judgment of 14 November 2007, Federal Supreme Court of Switzerland, BGE 133 II 450, para 7.1; *National Commissioner of The South African Police Service v Southern African Human Rights Litigation Centre and Another*, Case No. CC 02/14, Judgment of 30 October 2014, Constitutional Court of South Africa, [2014] ZACC 30, para 35; *Priebke, Erich s/ solicitud de extradición*, Case No. 16.063/94, Judgment of 2 November 1995, Supreme Court of Argentina, para 70; *Bouzari v Islamic Republic of Iran, Docket C38295*, Decision of 30 June 2004, Court of Appeal for Ontario, 71 OR (3d) 675 (Ont CA), ILDC [*International Law in Domestic Courts*] 175 (CA 2004), para

and international courts and tribunals.[12] States have also in their statements endorsed Article 53 as containing the definition of *jus cogens* in general.[13] The literature on *jus cogens* also supports Article 53 of the Vienna Convention as the definition of *jus cogens* in general terms and not only for the purposes of the Vienna Convention.[14] The Commission itself, whenever it has considered the notion of peremptory norms in the context of its previous works, has relied on the definition in Article 53 of the Vienna Convention.[15] Perhaps the strongest indication that the definition of *jus cogens* in Article 53 applies generally is the fact that few States objected to the content of Draft Conclusion 3 (at the time Draft Conclusion 2).[16] Indeed, most States chose not to address the

86; and *Gabriel Orlando Vera Navarrete, EXP. No. 2798-04-HC/TC*, Decision of 9 December 2004, Constitutional Tribunal of Peru, para 8.

[12] The list of cases referred to in the *Legality of the Threat or Use of Nuclear Weapons*, Advisory Opinion, *ICJ Reports* 1996, p. 226, p. 258, para 83; *Prosecutor v Furundžija*, Case No. IT-95-17/1-T, Judgment of 10 December 1998, Trial Chamber, International Criminal Tribunal for the Former Yugoslavia, *Judicial Reports* 1998, p. 571, para 155; and *Prosecutor v Jelisić*, Case No. IT-95-10-T, Judgment of 14 December 1999, Trial Chamber, International Criminal Tribunal for the Former Yugoslavia, *Judicial Reports 1999*, pp. 431–3, para 60. See also *Jaime Córdoba Triviño*, Case No. C-578/95, Sentence of 4 December 1995, Constitutional Tribunal of Colombia. See, especially, the Separate Opinion of Judge ad hoc Dugard in *Armed Activities on the Territory of the Congo (New Application: 2002) (Democratic Republic of the Congo v Rwanda), Jurisdiction and Admissibility*, Judgment, *ICJ Reports* 2006, p. 6, p. 88, para 8.

[13] The Commentary refers to the statement by the Czech Republic (A/C.6/71/SR.24), para 72. See also the statements by Canada (A/C.6/71/SR.27), para 9; Chile (A/C.6/71/SR.25), para 101; China (A/C.6/71/SR.24), para 89; the Islamic Republic of Iran (A/C.6/71/SR.26), para 118 ('The aim of the Commission's work on the topic was not to contest the two criteria established under article 53 ... On the contrary, the goal was to elucidate the meaning and scope of the two criteria'); and Poland (A/C.6/71/SR.26), para 56. See, further, the statement by Ireland (A/C.6/71/SR.27), para 19 ('Her delegation agreed with the view that articles 53 and 64 of the 1969 Vienna Convention on the Law of Treaties should be central to work on the topic').

[14] Examples referred to in the Commentary are: Makane Moïse Mbengue and Apollin Koagne Zouapet 'Ending the Splendid Isolation: *Jus Cogens* and International Economic Law' in Dire Tladi (ed.), *Peremptory Norms of General International Law (Jus Cogens): Disquisitions and Disputations* (Brill, 2021) at 510; Sévrine Knuchel *Jus Cogens: Identification and Enforcement of Peremptory Norms* (Zurich, Schulthess, 2015), 19 ('Given that Article 53 provides the only written legal definition of the effects of *jus cogens* ... as well as of the process by which such norms come into being ... it is the necessary starting point for analyzing this concept'); Stefan Kadelbach 'Genesis, Function and Identification of *Jus Cogens* Norms' (2016) 46 *Netherlands Yearbook of International Law* 147, 166, noting that 'treatises on *jus cogens* usually start' with Article 53 of the 1969 Vienna Convention and, at 162, assessing enhanced responsibility and the *erga omnes* effects of *jus cogens* on the basis of Article 53 of the 1969 Vienna Convention; and Ulf Linderfalk 'Understanding the *Jus Cogens* Debate: the Pervasive Influence of Legal Positivism and Legal Idealism' (2015) 46 *Netherlands Yearbook of International Law* 51, 52. See also, generally, Daniel Costelloe *Legal Consequences of Peremptory Norms in International Law* (Cambridge, 2017), 15 *et seq.*, who, though never stating that Article 53 of the 1969 Vienna Convention is the definition, certainly proceeds on that basis. Similarly, see Lauri Hannikainen *Peremptory Norms (Jus Cogens) in International Law: Historical Development, Criteria, Present Status* (Helsinki, Finnish Lawyers' Publishing Company, 1988), especially at 5–12; and Levan Alexidze 'Legal Nature of *Jus Cogens* in Contemporary International Law' (1981) 172 *Collected Courses of the Hague Academy of International Law* 219, 246.

[15] See, for examples, para 38, fn 88 of the *Second Report of the Special Rapporteur on Peremptory Norms of General International Law (Jus Cogens)* (A/CN.4/706).

[16] See generally Dire Tladi *Fifth Report of the Special Rapporteur on Peremptory Norms of General International Law* (A/CN.4/747), paras 40 and 41.

Draft Conclusion at all, with only the Czech Republic, Cyprus, and the United Kingdom expressing support for its content.[17] It would thus be difficult to depart from the definition in Article 53, even if an alternative definition were readily available.

2.2 The Content of Draft Conclusion 3

One issue that was not addressed in the Commentary was whether the definition in Article 53 of the Vienna Convention was a definition at all. It has been asserted that what is contained in Article 53 is not a definition and that, if it is a definition, it is a circular definition since it defines *jus cogens* by reference to consequence.[18] Part of the reason for this is undoubtedly the fact that the Article 53 definition reflects an intersection between a consensualist and non-consensualist approach to *jus cogens*.[19] As noted in Chapter 1, the tension between the consensualist and non-consensualist approaches to *jus cogens* represents a broader tension which the Commission sought to steer clear of, but which remains reflected throughout the Draft Conclusions.

Emblematic of the consensualist/non-consensualist tension is the question of whether the definition should refer to the acceptance and recognition of the international community of States, or whether it was sufficient to refer to the international community without qualifying it by 'of States'. While this issue did not receive much attention in the plenary debate on the First Report, it was the subject of much deliberation within the Drafting Committee. Although there was no formal written proposal made in this direction, the first proposal that the Special Rapporteur presented to the Drafting Committee, based on the Article 53 definition,[20] had the words 'of States' bracketed in pen in

[17] Peremptory Norms of General International Law (*Jus Cogens*): the Cyprus Republic, Comments and Observations received from Governments (A/CN.4/648), 6; the United Kingdom, Comments and Observations received from Governments (A/CN.4/648), 19. See also the United States, Comments and Observations received from Governments (A/CN.4/648), 20, stating that Draft Conclusion 2 'reflects provisions in the Vienna Convention in the Law of Treaties'.

[18] See, for discussion, Knuchel (above note 14), 2; Linderfalk (above note 14), 56.

[19] See para 59 of the First Report (above note 1). See also Martti Koskenniemi *From Apology to Utopia: The Structure of Legal Argument* (Reissue with new Epilogue) (Cambridge, 2006), 307 *et seq.*, especially at 'Initially, *jus cogens* seems to be descending, non-consensualist. It seems to bind States irrespective of their consent. But a law which would make no reference to what States have consented would seem to collapse into a natural morality [but] the reference to recognition by "international community" [makes it] ascending, consensualist.'

[20] International Law Commission Drafting Committee Working Paper, ILC/LXVIII)/DC/JC/WP.1, 20 July 2016: 'A Peremptory norm of general international law (*jus cogens*) is a norm accepted and recognised by the international community of States as a whole as a norm from which no derogation is permitted'.

response to comments on the text by members of the Drafting Committee.[21] When presenting the interim report of the Drafting Committee, the Chair of the Drafting Committee, Pavel Šturma, referred to this discussion as the 'main issue':

> The main issue discussed was whether the Drafting Committee might modify the language of the Vienna Convention, in particular by deleting the reference to 'of States' in the formula 'international community of States as a whole', which was a suggestion supported by some members. Their view was that including the reference to 'of States' did not accord with the approach recently taken by the Commission in other topics, which also took into account the practice of international organizations and other actors. The concern also expressed was that the reference to 'of States' was based on a notion of the international community at the time of the Vienna Conference, which no longer reflected the present reality.[22]

It is no surprise that this discussion dominated the first Drafting Committee because it represented an important marker for the approach that the Commission would take in its work on the topic. The proposal to remove 'of States' from the definition would bring *jus cogens* closer to a non-consensualist vision of international law, one which was more idealist and in which the role of the State is diminished, including in law-making. In such an approach the role of values would be enhanced. The decision of the Commission to retain 'of States' in the definition thus suggests that the Commission has taken a position in the debate between positivists and idealists.[23] It suggests a more consensualist approach to peremptory norms.

[21] Id.

[22] Statement of Drafting Committee Chair of 9 August 2016.

[23] See e.g. Valencia Ospina (A/CN.4/SR.3322), 19 ('The approach taken by the Special Rapporteur in chapter V (C) of the report, on the core elements of *jus cogens*, was also problematic. By taking the requirement of "a norm accepted and recognized by the international community of States as a whole" from article 53 of the Vienna Convention, the Special Rapporteur included among the core elements of *jus cogens* a criterion for identification centred on consent. However, some of the limitations of a consent-based approach were highlighted in the report itself, in relation to the issue of States inability to withdraw their consent at a later stage. As indicated in para 53 of the report, "even if there were a way to address the question of emergence of peremptory rules through consent—or consensus—it is not clear why those States that have joined in the consensus could not later withdraw their consent, thus damaging the consensus". Ultimately, basing *jus cogens* on State consent failed to provide a plausible explanation of what made a peremptory norm peremptory').

Yet, for some members, acceptance and recognition by the *international community of* States *as a whole*, rather than simply 'States', meant something different than mere acceptance and recognition of States.[24] This would certainly be in accordance with Simma's (tentative) definition of community interests as 'a consensus according to which the respect for fundamental values is not left to the free disposition of States individually' but rather 'is recognised and sanctioned by international law as a matter of concern to all States'.[25] In other words, the qualification 'of States' by the notion of the 'community as a whole' has the effect of emphasising a 'much more socially conscious legal order' in a way that reflects 'community interests' moving beyond the interests of individual States.[26] Therefore, in this choice of language, the Commission navigates the tension between the idealist and consensualist approaches, with the former reflected in the requirement of acceptance and recognition of States, while the latter is reflected through the qualification of States by 'community as a whole'. What precisely is meant by the international community of States is not addressed in the Commentary to Draft Conclusion 3. A full draft conclusion, Draft Conclusion 7, is dedicated to it and will be considered in Chapter 6.

Intimately connected with the question of the role of values, consensualism, and the meaning of the international community of States as a whole is Draft Conclusion 2, which is said to contain the nature of peremptory norms. It is discussed in the next section.

3. The General Nature of *Jus Cogens*

Conclusion 2

Nature of peremptory norms of general international law (*jus cogens*)

Peremptory norms of general international law (*jus cogens*) reflect and protect fundamental values of the international community. They are universally applicable and are hierarchically superior to other rules of international law.

---

[24] See e.g. Caflisch (A/CN.4/SR.3314), 10; Petrič (A/CN.4/SR.3318), 3; Nolte (A/CN.4/SR.3370), 7 ('In terms of substance, any rule of general international law that was elevated to the status of *jus cogens* should have to reflect the existing fundamental values of the international community of States. He agreed with the Special Rapporteur that the Commission should not revert to theories of natural law for the identification of such fundamental values. It must point to a more generally accepted way in which existing fundamental values could be identified').

[25] Bruno Simma 'From Bilateralism to Community Interests in International Law' (1994) 217 *Recueil des Cours de l'Académie de Droit International de la Haye* 217, 233.

[26] Id., 234.

3.1 To Include or Not to Include the Nature of *Jus Cogens*

The arrival at a definition of *jus cogens* in the Draft Conclusions was not a contentious affair. This is evident from the fact that the Commentary to Draft Conclusion 3 only has three short paragraphs, while very few States submitted comments on it. The path towards the adoption of Draft Conclusion 2, which sets forth the characteristics of peremptory norms, could not have been rockier.[27] While the Draft Conclusion, in more or less its original form, was finally adopted, this was achieved at the cost of much friction and contestation.

In the original proposal contained in the First Report, the characteristics referred to in what is now Draft Conclusion 2 were in the same Draft Conclusion as the proposed definition. Paragraph 2 of that proposed text provided as follows:

> Norms of *jus cogens* protect the fundamental values of the international community, are hierarchically superior to other norms of international law and are universally applicable.

In 2016 when the text was proposed, it was opposed vociferously by a few members—Mr Forteau, Mr Huang, Mr Murase, Mr Kamto, Mr Murphy, Mr Singh, and Mr Wood.[28] The other members that took part in that first

[27] In an article written just before the adoption of the Draft Conclusions on first reading, I stated that the 'real fight [in the first year that the topic was considered] was the proposal in the first report that norms of *jus cogens* were hierarchically superior to other norms, universally applicable and reflected and protected the fundamental values of the international community of States'. See Dire Tladi 'Codification, Progressive Development, New Law, Doctrine, and the Work of the International Law Commission on Peremptory Norms of General International Law (*Jus Cogens*): Personal Reflections of the Special Rapporteur' (2019) 13 *FIU Law Review* 1137, 1144.

[28] Wood (A/CN.4/SR.3314), 13 ('In his view those elements were not helpful, and by adding them the Special Rapporteur seemed to depart from his initial commitment to ensure that his reports reflected contemporary practice'); Murphy (A/CN.4/SR.3316), 12 ('These concepts seemed to be unsubstantiated extrapolations of Article 53 of the Vienna Convention'); Huang (A/CN.4/SR.3373), 14 ('Those elements differed sharply from the provisions of Article 53 of the Vienna Convention and introduced new elements that were problematic'); Murase (A/CN.4/SR.3314), 9; Singh (A/CN.4/SR.3322), 17; Kamto (A/CN.4/SR.3323), 9; Forteau (A/CN.4/SR.3317), 14 ('He was not in favour of adopting draft conclusion 3(2), which did not appear to be grounded in practice or jurisprudence and contained legally ambiguous terms. The concepts of "fundamental values" and "hierarchy", in particular, did not appear in the Vienna Convention and including them in the draft conclusions would amount to [an unnecessary] legal innovation'). Forteau's rejection of these elements was somehow surprising given that, in the same statement, he had said '*Jus cogens* and natural law were of the same nature, in that they were legal vehicles that conveyed the fundamental values of a society in a given moment in time' (at 12). Although Hmoud (A/CN.4/SR.3322), 14, was initially opposed to the characteristics, he did subsequently endorse them. See Hmoud (A/CN.4/SR.3370), 4. Similarly, while Nolte (A/CN.4/SR.3315), 11, might be read as being opposed to the characteristics, in 2017, Nolte (A/CN.4/3370), 5, expressed support for the fundamental values characteristic, even going beyond the proposal to suggest that that characteristic was a criterion ('*jus cogens* should have to reflect the existing fundamental values of the international community of States').

debate supported, in general terms, the content of the second paragraph of Draft Conclusion 3.[29] Notwithstanding the strong support, the objections of the small minority were strong enough, mainly due to their influence within the Commission, to prevent the adoption of that paragraph in the Drafting Committee in that first year. Writing about this episode, the Special Rapporteur said that, unlike many other provisions, he could not fathom the possibility of a text without these basic characteristics.[30]

Of course, in 2017, the second year of the consideration of the topic, the Commission was very differently configured. The elections of 2016 brought new members that strongly supported the provision. Thus, while the size of the majority did not grow significantly, new members like Mr Jalloh,[31] Ms Galvão Teles, and Ms Oral changed the dynamics in the Commission and made the adoption of the text an almost foregone conclusion.[32] Indeed, of the twelve new members taking their seats in the Commission in 2017, only one member opposed the inclusion of the characteristics.[33]

[29] Caflisch (A/CN.4/SR.3314), 10; Hassouna (A/CN.4/SR.3315), 5; Kittichaisaree (A/CN.4/SR.3315), 6 ('the core elements chosen by the Special Rapporteur seemed appropriate'); Saboia (A/CN.4/SR.3316), 16 ('Paragraph 2 should be retained as it incorporated into the definition of Vienna Convention on the Law of Treaties the important elements of the fundamental values of the international community, the hierarchical superiority of *jus cogens*, and their universal acceptance (*sic*)'); Candioti (A/CN.4/SR.3317), 11, suggesting that the first Draft Conclusion should contain a definition of *jus cogens* consisting of the elements contained in Draft Conclusion 3; Petrič (A/CN.4/SR.3322), 5; Vásquez-Bermúdez (A/CN.4/SR.3322), 8; (A/CN.4/SR.3322), 8 ('Rather than merely reproducing the language of Article 53 of the Vienna Convention, draft conclusion 3 should clarify the legal nature of *jus cogens*. In that respect, paragraph 2 contained two important elements—norms of *jus cogens* protected the fundamental values of the international community as a whole and were hierarchically superior to other norms'); Jacobsson (A.CN.4/SR.3322), 16 ('While she supported the inclusion of draft conclusion 3(2), its wording should be refined'); Niehause (A/CN.4/SR.3323), 5; Comissário Afonso (A/CN.4/SR.3323), 6 ('He supported the main thrust of paragraph 2, which was well founded'). See, however, for somewhat ambiguous views, McRae (A/CN.3315), 9; Park (A/CN.4/SR.3315), 15. Šturma's comments (A/CN.4/SR.3322), 11, were particularly interesting, suggesting that he himself supported the elements but that they ought to be discussed elsewhere because of the criticism ('Judging from the comments made thus far, he believed that draft conclusion 3(2) was the most problematic. Although he approved of the three elements contained in that paragraph, which were in his opinion particularly important, he believed that they could be moved to another draft conclusion supported by a more detailed analysis').

[30] See Tladi (above note 27), 1144, where I state that I was 'willing to "fall on my sword"' for this provision and that had the Commission not seen its way to adopting this provision, I would have resigned as Special Rapporteur.

[31] Charles Jalloh, before becoming a member of the Commission, upon hearing that these characteristics were not being accepted by some members of the Commission remarked 'But I thought this was international law 101!'

[32] The brevity of the Statement of the Chair of the Drafting Committee on this issue provides some evidence of the ease with which the then Draft Conclusion 3 was adopted in the Drafting Committee, with few substantive issues being seriously debated. See Statement of the Chair of the Drafting Committee, 26 July 2017.

[33] The newly elected member that opposed Draft Conclusion 3 was Rajput (A/CN.4/SR.3369), 6 ('The Special Rapporteur appeared to want draft conclusion 3 to reflect the general nature of jus cogens norms, and draft conclusions 4 to 8 to reflect the criteria for identifying such norms. Although the theoretical distinction between the two concepts was comprehensible, its practical use was unclear.

Even after the adoption of the text in 2017, resistance to it continued. The Commentary to the first reading text revealed this disagreement in a stark manner. In the first paragraph of the accompanying Commentary, the Commission stated that a 'view was expressed, however, that such "characteristics" have an insufficient basis in international law, it unnecessarily conflates the identification and effects of these norms, and risks being viewed as additional criteria for determining whether a specific peremptory norm of general international law (*jus cogens*) exists'.[34] Another minority view reflected in the Commentary was that 'the difference between "criteria" and "characteristics" is obscure, as is the proposition that such "characteristics" provide supplementary evidence' for the existence or not of peremptory norms.[35] The inclusion of minority views in the Commentary during the adoption of the first reading text is intended to emphasise to States when they comment on the text, that this was an issue of disagreement within the Commission, so that States might focus on those issues of disagreement.

The response of States to Draft Conclusion 3 of the first reading text was thus of particular interest.[36] According to the Fifth Report of the Special Rapporteur 'most States in their comments expressed enthusiastic support for draft conclusion 3'.[37] States that expressed explicit support for

A provision on the general nature of jus cogens might simply serve to create confusion.'). Newly elected members that supported Draft Conclusion were Lehto (A/CN.4/SR.3372), 6 ('She therefore agreed with the Special Rapporteur's statement, in paragraph 76 of his second report, that the content of peremptory norms and the values that such norms served to protect were the underlying reasons for the norms' "peremptoriness"'); Jalloh (A/CN.4/SR.3372), 12 ('He himself supported the Special Rapporteur's ultimate finding, rooted in both practice and doctrine, that the three features identified in draft conclusion 3 were indeed the generally accepted characteristics of *jus cogens* norms and, like him, he had found the controversy around those characteristics somewhat surprising'); Ruda Santolaria (A/CN.4/SR.3372), 13 ('Reference could be made to the fundamental values and interests of the international community when the overwhelming majority of States accepted and recognized that there could be no derogation from the norms that reflected those values and interests'); Cisse (A/CN.4/SR.3373), 3–4, although he spoke protection of fundamental human rights; Galvão Teles (A/CN.4/SR.3373), 8 ('In her view, the protection of fundamental values was the key distinguishing feature of *jus cogens* norms; it explained why they were limited in number and were non-derogable. The unique character of *jus cogens* norms resulted not from their sources but from their content and their purpose of protecting values that the international community as a whole recognized as fundamental and thus non-derogable'); Oral (A/CN.4/SR.3373), 9 ('At the core of those norms that had attained the status of *jus cogens* lay a shared set of fundamental values of the international community'); Reinisch (A/CN.4/SR.3372), 15, did not express a view on the issues. Similarly, Ouazzani-Chahdi (A/CN.4/SR.3373), 13, had been somewhat ambiguous.

[34] Paragraph 1 of Commentary to Draft Conclusion 3 of the Draft Conclusions on Peremptory Norms of General International Law (*Jus Cogens*) adopted on first reading, *Report of the International Law Commission, Seventy-First Session* (A/74/10).

[35] Id., para 16.

[36] See generally Fifth Report (above note 16).

[37] Id., para 43.

Draft Conclusion 3 included the Cyprus,[38] Czech Republic,[39] Ecuador,[40] El Salvador,[41] Greece,[42] Ireland,[43] Micronesia,[44] Peru,[45] Portugal,[46] Sierra Leone,[47] Slovenia,[48] South Africa,[49] Spain,[50] Switzerland,[51] and Togo.[52] Presumably States that commented on the Draft Conclusions but did not mention Draft Conclusion 3 supported it, or at worst did not have concerns with it. In contrast, 'out of the nearly 60 States that expressed their views on the topic, it was only [these] 5 States [that] expressed negative sentiments against draft conclusion 3'.[53] States that, in the written comments,

[38] Id., Cyprus, 19–20 ('The Republic of Cyprus shares the Commission's comments on the definition, general nature and criteria for the identification of peremptory norms of general international law (Draft Conclusions 2, 3 and 4)').

[39] The Czech Republic, Comments and Observations (above note 17), 6 ('We also concur with the characterisation of peremptory norms of general international law as reflecting and protecting fundamental values of the international community, which are hierarchically superior to other rules of international law and universally applicable').

[40] Ecuador (A/C.6/74/SR.27), para 35 ('They also served to confirm that such norms reflected and protected the fundamental values of the international community, were hierarchically superior to other rules of international law and were universally applicable').

[41] El Salvador, Comments and Observations (above note 17), 7 ('The concept *of jus cogens* is based on the acceptance of fundamental and superior values within the international system').

[42] Greece (A/C.6/74.SR.24), para 36 ('Her delegation particularly welcomed draft conclusion 3 which, inter alia, provided that *jus cogens* norms reflected and protected fundamental values of the international community').

[43] Ireland (A/C.6/74/SR.24), para 40 ('It welcomed the confirmation in the commentary to draft conclusion 3 that peremptory norms were universally applicable').

[44] Micronesia (A/C.6/74/SR.24), para 99, applying Draft Conclusion 3 to the protection of the environment.

[45] Peru (A/C.6/74/SR.27), para 63 ('She said that, with regard to draft conclusion 3, her delegation agreed that peremptory norms of general international law reflected and protected fundamental values of the international community, were hierarchically superior to other rules of international law and were universally applicable').

[46] Portugal, Comments and Observations (above note 17), 20 ('Portugal is of the opinion that the references in Draft Conclusion 3 ... do not raise confusion nor generate new criteria for identifying a norm as a *jus cogens*. Consequently Portugal supports those references as a clarification of the general nature of *jus cogens*').

[47] Sierra Leone (A/C.6/74/SR.27), para 9 ('With regard to the draft conclusions adopted on first reading, his delegation fully endorsed draft conclusion 3').

[48] Id., Slovenia, 23 ('With regards to Draft Conclusion 3 the Republic of Slovenia supports the notion that the peremptory norms reflect and protect fundamental values of the international community and are hierarchically superior ... [and] must also be universally applicable').

[49] South Africa, Comments and Observations (above note 17), 23 ('We believe that this a very important draft conclusion which should be retained').

[50] Id., Spain, 15, noting that notwithstanding 'the doubts of a few States', it was clear that peremptory norms 'reflect and protect the fundamental values of the international community, are hierarchically superior to other rules of international law and are universally applicable'.

[51] Id., Switzerland, 24 ('The essential characteristics associated characteristics with *jus cogens* norms, as set out in draft conclusion 3, reflect the understanding of the general nature of such norms').

[52] Togo (A/C.6/74/SR.26), para 27 ('Togo supported draft conclusion 3, because it believed that peremptory norms of general international law reflected and protected fundamental values of the international community, were hierarchically superior to other rules of international law and should be universally applicable').

[53] Fifth Report (above note 16), para 51. The Report includes the Netherlands in the five, although it asserts that is unclear that the Netherlands opposed Draft Conclusion 3 ('To stay on the side of caution, I also include the Netherlands, even though it only criticised one element of draft conclusion 3, namely hierarchical superiority. In fact, to put the observations of the Netherlands in context, it is necessary to refer to the

were opposed to Draft Conclusion 3 were France,[54] Germany,[55] Russia,[56] the United States,[57] and the United Kingdom.[58]

The minority views, both within the Commission and of States, can be summarised in two basic points. First, it is argued that the characteristics in Draft Conclusion 3 are not well founded in law and State practice. Second, that the inclusion of Draft Conclusion 3 could lead to the conflation of the characteristics with the criteria of *jus cogens*. Each of these will be taken in turn, but for convenience, I begin with the second point.

3.1.1 The Conflation of the Criteria and Characteristics

A different way of presenting the concern about the conflation is that the characteristics might be interpreted as being additional criteria for the determination of *jus cogens*. Given the source of these concerns—both in terms of

Commissie van Advies Inzake Volkenrechtelijke Vraagstukken *Advisory Report on the Draft Conclusions of the International Law Commission on Peremptory Norms of General International Law*, Advisory Report No. 37, July 2021, which the government of the Netherlands invited us to take note of in considering its observations. The *Advisory Report* states that Commission "believes that these essential characteristics do indeed reflect the general nature of peremptory norms". However, it continues to state they do require some additional comments. Thus, it appears that Commission, and therefore, the Netherlands, in fact support draft conclusion 3, but believe there are issues that can be better or more articulated in the commentaries').

[54] France, Original Comments and Observations (on file with the author), ('*Cependant, la France recommande la suppression de la référence aux termes de "valeurs fondamentales". Outre que cette notion ne figure pas dans la CVDT, elle peut être sujette à diverses interprétations et controverses. Sur le plan méthodologique, la caractérisation d'une norme de jus cogens procède de deux critères énoncés par la Commission : leur généralité et leur inderogeabilité. Cette référence à la notion de "valeur fondamentale" pourrait être comprise comme introduisant un troisième critère de fond, allant très au-delà de ce que prévoit la CVDT*') ('Nonetheless, France recommends deleting the reference to the term "fundamental values". Apart from the fact that this notion does not appear in the Vienna Convention, it may be subject to various interpretations and controversies. From a methodological perspective, the characterization of a norm of *jus cogens* proceeds from two criteria set out by the Commission: their generality and their non-derogation. This reference to the notion of "fundamental value" might be understood as introducing a new substantive criterion, moving far beyond the Vienna Convention').

[55] Germany, Comments and Observations (above note 17), 22 ('With regard to the current wording of draft conclusion 3, Germany sees the risk that the wording "reflect and protect fundamental values of the international community" could be interpreted as an additional criterion for determining whether a specific peremptory norm of *jus cogens* exists or not. To avoid a conflict with the definition of *jus cogens* in Article 53 of the Vienna Convention, which contains no such reference to "fundamental values of the international community", it is suggested to remove the reference in the draft conclusion and to elaborate on this feature in the commentary only').

[56] Id., Russian Federation, 23 ('These characteristics are not of a legal nature and should not be accorded the status of additional criteria, of sorts, for the identification of peremptory norms of general international law (*jus cogens*), which they appear to have been accorded in the draft conclusions').

[57] Id., the United States, 25 ('The United States agrees with the view expressed by some ILC Members that the "characteristics" described in draft conclusion 3 "have an insufficient basis in international law, unnecessarily conflate the identification and effects of these norms, and risk being viewed as additional criteria for determining whether a specific peremptory norm of general international law (*jus cogens*) exists" ').

[58] Id., the United Kingdom, 24 ('the UK considers that it is neither necessary nor helpful to include draft Conclusion 3 on "the general nature" of peremptory norms of general international law (*jus cogens*). The UK finds the Commission's commentary to this draft conclusion unconvincing').

the States and the members of the Commission that put them forward, all of which would, at best, be described as supporting 'a cautionary' approach to *jus cogens*[59]—it would not be a reach to suggest that the underlying concern is the fear that these characteristics might lead to a lack of rigour and the proliferation of *jus cogens* norms based on 'fundamental values'. To this concern, the Commentary to the Draft Conclusion only offers a brief response:

> The characteristics contained in Draft Conclusion 2 are themselves not criteria for the identification of peremptory norms of general international law (*jus cogens*). Thus, Draft Conclusion 2 is not to be read as imposing additional criteria for the identification of peremptory norms of general international law (*jus cogens*). The criteria for the identification of peremptory norms of general international law (*jus cogens*) are contained in Part Two of the draft conclusions.[60]

Yet, this is really not a response to this criticism, because it does not answer the question: if they are not criteria then what purpose do they serve? All the more so since it should be recalled that when the Special Rapporteur had first proposed this provision, it had been a second paragraph in a draft conclusion containing the definition—suggesting a strong connection between the definition (from which we get the criteria) and the characteristics. Moreover, several of the statements supporting the content of the Draft Conclusion assumed, contrary to the assertions in the Second Report, that the characteristics will be used also to identify the peremptory character of a given norm. As far as these members of the Commission are concerned, for example, these elements had been 'incorporated into the definition of the Vienna Convention'.[61] In this context, Candiotti, suggesting that the first provision should be the definition, stated that such definition should consist of the elements in Draft Conclusion 2 and 'thus indicate that such norms served to protect the fundamental values of the international community; were universally applicable; were hierarchically superior to other norms of international law'.[62] The sentiment was also strongly echoed by Lehto:

> In paragraph 18 of his report, the Special Rapporteur referred to three 'descriptive and characteristic elements, as opposed to constituent elements

[59] In Chapter 1 I suggested that it was possible to characterise the fault line in many *jus cogens*-related debates as being between the maximisers and the cautioners. See Chapter 1, Section 2. This characterisation of the fault lines is similar to Linderfalk's positivist/idealist characterisation of the debate.
[60] Paragraph 18 of the Commentary to Draft Conclusion 2.
[61] Saboia (A/CN.4/SR.3316), 16.
[62] Candioti (A/CN.4/SR.3317), 11.

> (or criteria) of norms of *jus cogens*'. It might be asked, however, whether there were any peremptory norms that were not characterized by fundamental values, hierarchical superiority and universal applicability. She echoed the view expressed by Mr. Nolte, Mr. Hmoud and Mr. Šturma that the three elements, in particular the notion that *jus cogens* norms reflected and protected fundamental values of the international community, were essential in complementing the criteria drawn from article 53. Mr. Nolte had pointed out that peremptory status must be linked to the substantive content of *jus cogens* norms and to the values they reflected.[63]

This sentiment had also been expressed by several States. The Czech Republic, for example, stated that the characteristics and the criteria were closely interconnected and should be read together.[64] Greece was particularly direct in this respect:

> Her delegation particularly welcomed draft conclusion 3 which, inter alia, provided that *jus cogens* norms reflected and protected fundamental values of the international community. However, that cardinal characteristic of *jus cogens* norms provided also a criterion for their identification, given that, for a norm to qualify as peremptory, it should be accepted and recognized by the international community of States as reflecting and protecting such values.[65]

There is thus some ambiguity. On the one hand, the characteristics are presented as merely descriptive. Yet, on the other hand, at least some endow with them some normative quality. The Commission attempts to address this apparent contradiction in the following way:

> Though themselves not criteria, the existence of the characteristics contained in draft conclusion 2 may provide context in the assessment of evidence for the identification of peremptory norms of general international law (*jus cogens*). For example, evidence that a norm reflects and protects fundamental

[63] Lehto (A/CN.4/SR.3372), 6.

[64] The Czech Republic, Comments and Observations (above note 17), 6.

[65] Greece (A/C.6/74/SR.24), 36. The statement by the Federated States of Micronesia (A/C.6/SR.24), para 99, in which the protection of the environment is put forward as a *jus cogens* norm because the protection of the environment is a fundamental value of the international community, also suggests that it views the characteristics as part of the criteria for determining *jus cogens* normativity.

> values of the international community, is hierarchically superior to other norms of international law and is universally applicable, may serve to support or confirm the peremptory status of a norm. This supplementary evidence cannot, however, in and of itself, constitute the basis for identifying peremptory norms of general international law (*jus cogens*). Evidence supporting the criteria, as described in Part Two of the present draft conclusions, must always be present.[66]

The essence of this explanation is that these characteristics can contribute to the assessment of whether the criteria identified have been met. This proposition was considered in the Drafting Committee in 2017. There, on the basis of the plenary debate on the Second Report, the Special Rapporteur produced a revised Draft Conclusion on the meaning of acceptance and recognition for the purposes of identification of peremptory norms (see Chapter 7), which would provide that evidence that a norm 'protects and reflects fundamental values ... is hierarchically superior ... and is universally applicable can contribute' to the identification of peremptory norms.[67]

This is of course rather imprecise, but should be seen in the context that the assessment of the criteria is not a mathematical but, rather, a qualitative exercise.[68] In respect of norms where there is some, but perhaps not extensive, evidence of the criterion of acceptance and recognition by the international community of States as a whole of non-derogation, then evidence of the characteristics might be used to supplement the criteria. While this proposal was not, in the end, adopted, it does serve to indicate that, at least in the minds of some members of the Commission, there is a strong relationship between the criteria and the characteristics of *jus cogens*.

The relationship between the criteria and the characteristics has another (related) dimension, apart from the evidentiary one, described above. It seems clear that the inclusion of the characteristics, alongside the more formal criteria derived from Draft Conclusion 3, serves also to mediate between the tension between the idealist and the consensualist approaches to *jus cogens*. Thus, again, without attempting to resolve this tension, the Commission has sought to nimbly navigate it by supplementing the formal criteria with value-laden characteristics.

66 Paragraph 19 of Draft Conclusion 2.

67 Revised Proposal by the Special Rapporteur for Draft Conclusions 6, 7, and 9, ILC(LXIX)/DC/JC/WP.4.

68 See para 6 of Commentary to Draft Conclusion. See, for further discussion, Chapter 7.

3.1.2 Little Authority to Support the Characteristics

The criticism that Draft Conclusion 3 is not grounded on a solid base of authority has also been directed at other parts of the Draft Conclusions and was, as a result, also addressed in Chapter 1 of the book. The approach of the Commission to the evidence was described in the very first Special Rapporteur's report in the following terms:

> The Commission should proceed on the established practice of considering a variety of materials and sources, in an integrated fashion. As is customary, the Commission approaches its topics by conducting a thorough analysis of State practice in all its forms, judicial practice, literature and any other relevant material.[69]

This approach received general agreement from members of the Commission.[70] It should therefore be against this general approach that Draft Conclusion 2 should be assessed. All three elements of the characteristics appear well-supported by the relevant authority.

In support of the first element, on fundamental values, the Commentary to Draft Conclusion 2 refers to decisions of international courts, in particular the International Court of Justice and State practice in the form of domestic judicial decisions.[71] The decisions of the International Court of Justice include the Court's Advisory Opinion on *Reservations to the Convention on the Prevention and Punishment of the Crime of Genocide*,[72] and the *Application of the Convention on the Prevention and Punishment of the Crime of Genocide* cases.[73] In the Advisory Opinion, the Court linked the prohibition of genocide—which is undoubtedly a norm of *jus cogens*—to fundamental values.[74] According to the Court, the Convention was inspired by the commitment 'to condemn and punish genocide as "a crime under international law" involving a denial of the right of existence of entire human groups, a denial which shocks the

[69] First Report (n 1), para 14.

[70] *Report of the International Law Commission, Sixty-Eighth Session* (A/71/10), para 113 ('Members expressed support for the Special Rapporteur's recommendations on the methodology to be pursued. Agreement was expressed with his view that, in principle, the study should be based on both State and judicial practice, and supplemented by scholarly writings').

[71] See para 5 of Commentary to Draft Conclusion 2.

[72] *Reservations to the Convention on the Prevention and Punishment of the Crime of Genocide*, Advisory Opinion, *ICJ Reports* 1951, p. 15.

[73] The Commentary referred to *Application of the Convention on the Prevention and Punishment of the Crime of Genocide (Bosnia and Herzegovina v Serbia and Montenegro)*, Judgment, *ICJ Reports* 2007, p. 43, pp. 110–11, para 161; and *Application of the Convention on the Prevention and Punishment of the Crime of Genocide (Croatia v Serbia)*, Judgment, *ICJ Reports* 2015, p. 3, p. 46, para 87).

[74] *Reservations to the Genocide Convention*, Advisory Opinion (above note 72), 23.

conscience of mankind and results in great losses to humanity, and which is contrary to moral law and to the spirit and aims of the United Nations'.[75] As the Commentary notes, the reference to 'conscience of mankind' and 'morality' has obvious connections to fundamental values. The reference to values was more direct in the later ICJ decisions.[76] The Commentary also refers to decisions of other tribunals in which the *jus cogens* norms were linked to fundamental values.[77]

A similar approach is adopted in the paragraphs of the Commentary in respect of the elements of hierarchical superiority and universal applicability.[78]

Moreover, as the Commentary notes, all three characteristics are ubiquitous in scholarly writing on *jus cogens*.[79] Even Kolb, although not a supporter of the doctrine of international law that puts forward the elements in Draft Conclusion 2 as characteristic of *jus cogens*, describes it as the 'predominant' approach.[80] The pedigree of these elements can thus hardly be questioned.

3.2 The Content of Draft Conclusion 2

Draft Conclusion 2 describes what it terms the 'nature' of peremptory norms. This 'nature' is in turn described in terms of three elements that are said to be 'essential characteristics' of *jus cogens*.[81] This means that a norm of *jus cogens* will invariably exhibit these characteristics.

What is now Draft Conclusion 2 was initially the second paragraph of a draft conclusion on the definition. Once a definition based on Article 53 of the Vienna Convention was adopted, the Drafting Committee had to decide what to do with the second paragraph of the proposed Draft Conclusion containing the characteristics. Some of the options considered by the Drafting Committee were to relocate the characteristics as part of Draft Conclusion 7 on the meaning of the international community of States as a whole, to combine it with a new reworked Draft Conclusion on acceptance and recognition,

[75] Id.

[76] For example, in the 2007 case *Bosnia and Herzegovina v Serbia and Montenegro* (above note 73), para 147 ('That is so even if the alleged breaches are of obligations under peremptory norms, or of obligations which protect essential humanitarian values, and which may be owed *erga omnes*').

[77] See para 4 of Commentary to Draft Conclusion 2.

[78] Paragraphs 10–17 of Commentary to Draft Conclusion 2.

[79] See id., paras 6, 13, and 16.

[80] See, generally, Robert Kolb 'Peremptory Norms as a Legal Technical Rather than Substantive Super Norms' in Dire Tladi (eds) *Peremptory Norms of General International Law (Jus Cogens): Disquisitions and Disputations* (Brill, 2021), especially 21–26.

[81] Paragraph 1 of the Commentary to Draft Conclusion 2.

to merge it with the proposed Draft Conclusion 9 (evidence of acceptance and recognition), or to include it as part of the preamble.[82]

Combining the characteristics with elements of acceptance and recognition by the international community of States would, of course, have the effect of turning them into another manifestation of the consensualist approach to *jus cogens* in the sense that it would imply that those characteristics were relevant only to the extent that they had been accepted and recognised by States. Those options were thus summarily discarded within the Drafting Committee. The proposal to instead have these characteristics in the preamble was also rejected out of hand for fear that it would undermine the normative pull if the characteristics were not included in the operative provisions—this is even before considering that the Draft Conclusions did not, then or now, include a preamble.

While some members sought to have the characteristics incorporated as a second paragraph to what is now Draft Conclusion 3, other members felt that placing the provision within Draft Conclusion 3 would create the impression that these elements were part of the criteria, since the criteria were synthesised from the definition. As a result, the characteristics are contained in a separate draft conclusion, initially as Draft Conclusion 3, but relocated to Draft Conclusion 2 on second reading.

The text of Draft Conclusion 2 largely follows the proposal made in the First Report of the Special Rapporteur.[83] The first difference between, on the one hand, the text originally proposed and the text adopted on first reading, and, on the other hand, the final version of the Draft Conclusion, is that the text is now divided into two sentences. This was done on the basis of a proposal by Mr Wood.[84]

The main difference relates to the first characteristic, namely the fundamental values. While the proposal in the First Report provided that the norms of *jus cogens* 'protect the fundamental values', the final text adopted by the Commission states that norms of *jus cogens* 'reflect and protect the fundamental values of the international community'.

The insertion of 'reflect', as an additional qualifier to 'fundamental values', emerged because the Second Report used both terms.[85] While the Second

[82] See Statement of the Chairman of the Drafting Committee 26, July 2017.

[83] Proposed Draft Conclusion 3(2) in the First Report of the Special Rapporteur provides as follows: norms of *jus cogens* protect the fundamental values of the international community, are hierarchically superior to other norms of international law, and are universally applicable.

[84] See Proposal by Mr Wood of 27 April 2022 (unnumbered).

[85] *Second Report of the Special Rapporteur on Peremptory Norms of General International Law (Jus Cogens)* (A/CN.4/706), para 22.

Report suggested that 'reflect' and 'protect' could be used interchangeably,[86] at least one member of the Commission identified this as a problem.[87] From his perspective, authorities 'supporting one concept thus could not be marshalled in support of the other'.[88] The Drafting Committee, and eventually the Commission, did not accept the argument that because some authorities used the qualifier 'protect' while others used 'reflect', the whole notion of fundamental values ought to be discarded. As a result, the Drafting Committee considered several options. One option was to use 'protect', which was contained in the original proposal in the first reading, while another was to use 'reflect', which some members of the Drafting Committee felt best described the role of 'fundamental values' in relation to *jus cogens*. A further option, in order to recognise that both may play a role, was to state that *jus cogens* norms 'reflect or protect' fundamental values. In the end, the Drafting Committee decided that a norm could, at the same time, 'protect' and 'reflect' a fundamental value. The choice of using both qualifiers was motivated by two reasons. First, both 'reflect' and 'protect' are found in the relevant authorities.[89] Second, using both words would serve to signify that a norm in

[86] Id. ('Of course, different authorities use different terms to describe the central notion, but the notion itself is generally accepted in international law. For example, some authorities state that *jus cogens* norms "protect" the fundamental values, while others state these norms "reflect" the fundamental values').

[87] Murphy (A/CN.4/SR.3369), 15 ('Another difficulty with Draft Conclusion 3(2) was that the arguments contained in paragraphs 20 to 22 of the second report conflated the idea that *jus cogens* "protected" fundamental values with the idea that it "reflected" those values, yet those were two very different things'). See, however, Jalloh (A/CN.4/SR.3372), 12 ('He did not share the views of some Commission members that *jus cogens* norms protected, but did not necessarily reflect, such fundamental values').

[88] Murphy (A/CN.4/SR.3369), 15.

[89] Authorities that used the word 'protect' include 2007 *Bosnia and Herzegovina v Serbia and Montenegro* (above note 73), para 147 ('That is so even if the alleged breaches are of obligations under peremptory norms, or of obligations which protect essential humanitarian values, and which may be owed erga omnes'); *Prosecutor v Furundžija*, Judgment of the ICTY Trial Chamber, Case No. IT-95-17/1-T, para 153; *Arancibia Clavel, Enrique Lauturo s/Homicidio Calificado y Asociación Ilícita y Otros*, Causa No. 259, Judgment of 24 November 2004; Germany (A/C.6/55/SR.14), para 56 ('His government reiterated its conviction regarding the need to define more clearly peremptory norms of international law that protected fundamental humanitarian values'); Italy (A/C.6/65/SR.13), para 15 ('The Vienna Convention on the Law of Treaties contained a tautological definition of peremptory law, which doctrine and jurisprudence had endeavoured to interpret as being a framework of rules prohibiting conduct judged intolerable because of the threat it posed to the survival of States and peoples and to basic human values'); Mexico (A/C.6/56/SR.14), para 13 ('The very concept of peremptory norms had been developed to safeguard the most precious legal values of the community of States'). Authorities that used the word 'reflect' (or related terms) include *Kaunda and Others v President of the Republic of South Africa* 2005 (4) SA 235 (CC), 169 ('norms of *jus cogens* reflect the most fundamental values of the international community'); *Siderman de Blake v the Republic of Argentina*, United States Court of Appeals for the Ninth Circuit, 965 F 2d 699, 715, which stated that norms of *jus cogens* were 'derived from' fundamental values of the international community; see also *25% del número legal de Congresistas contra el Decreto Legislativo N° 1097, EXP. No. 0024-2010-PI/TC*, Judgment of the Jurisdictional Plenary of 21 March 2011, Constitutional Tribunal of Peru, para 53 (*de la extraordinaria importancia de los valores que subyacen a tal* [jus cogens] *obligación* ('of the extraordinary importance of the values that underlie [the *jus cogens*] obligation')).

question can exist for the purposes of protecting the value ('protect') while also serving as an underlying rationale for the value ('reflect'). The statement of the Chair of the Drafting Committee that the decision to refer to the phrase 'reflect and protect' is meant to 'indicate the process of identification of peremptory norms, as well as their consequences', in part, but not fully, captures this rationale.

The choices concerning 'reflect' and 'protect' were not the only terminological issue that arose in the context of the first element of Draft Conclusion 2. The Commission also had to choose between 'fundamental values' and 'fundamental interests'. While Draft Conclusion 2 refers to 'fundamental values', the term 'fundamental interests' has also been used in this context.[90]

Another terminological debate concerned the term 'international community as a whole' and whether it should be qualified by 'of States'. In its written comments, the United States had suggested that if Draft Conclusion 2 (then Draft Conclusion 3) were retained, the phrase 'international community of States as a whole' as opposed to just 'international community' should qualify 'fundamental values' in order to be consistent with the definition and the criteria contained in Draft Conclusion 4.[91] This suggestion was meant, it appears, to entrench the consensualist approach to the identification of *jus cogens*, by ensuring that any element that might be relevant in the determination of peremptoriness was, somehow, tied to acceptance of States. The Commission, by not taking up the suggestion, appears to have decided that the concept of 'values of the international community' in Draft Conclusion 2 means 'something different, although related', from the notion of 'international community of States as a whole'.[92] The values that *jus cogens* norms reflect and are supposed to protect are broader and more inclusive than those of States, but include the values espoused by other actors in the international arena. Nonetheless, in identifying *jus cogens* norms (and thus attaching particular consequences), it is the attitude of States as a whole (acceptance and recognition), that must be looked to.

[90] Second Report (above note 85), 22.

[91] The United States, Comments and Observations (above note 17), 26, and the Russian Federation, Comments and Observations (above note 17), 23. A related but slightly different suggestion was made by Mr Argüello Gomez (A/CN.4/SR.3568), who suggested that the Draft Conclusion 'should state that peremptory norms "reflect and protect fundamental values of the international community, which find their principal expression in the Charter of the United Nations"'. This proposal is intimately connected with the non-exhaustive list and will therefore be considered in Chapter 7.

[92] See position in the Fifth Report (above note 16), para 54.

The second element of Draft Conclusion 2, hierarchical superiority, is intended to signify that *jus cogens* is normatively higher than other norms of international law. This normative superiority can be described using different terms:[93] 'higher rules of international law',[94] 'hierarchically higher than any other rules of international law',[95] 'superior legal order norms',[96] 'primacy in the hierarchy of rules',[97] 'prevail over' other rules of international.[98]

One of the key issues of debate concerning hierarchical superiority was whether it was a characteristic or more a consequence or an effect.[99] The approach adopted in the Draft Conclusions is that hierarchical superiority is a characteristic of a norm of *jus cogens* that produces particular effects as outlined in Part III of the Draft Conclusions (See Chapters 8, 9, 10, and 11).

The third and final element contained in Draft Conclusion 3 is that *jus cogens* norms are universally applicable. As with hierarchical superiority, it is possible to view universal applicability as an effect of peremptoriness rather than a characteristic. At the same time, there is no reason why universal applicability cannot be both a characteristic and a consequence. Moreover, universal applicability itself might produce particular effects. One such possible effect, discussed already in Chapter 1, is the exclusion of the concept of regional *jus cogens* in international law. Another possible consequence, to be considered in Chapter 9, is the non-applicability of the persistent objector doctrine to *jus cogens* norms.

[93] See more comprehensively paras 12 and 13 of the Commentary to Draft Conclusion 3.

[94] *Yassin Abdullah Kadi v Council of the European Union and Commission of the European Communities*, Case No. T-315-01, Judgment of 21 September 2005, Second Chamber, Court of First Instance of the European Communities [2005] ECR II-3649, para 226.

[95] *Al-Adsani v United Kingdom*, Application No. 35763/97, Judgment of 21 November 2001, Grand Chamber, European Court of Human Rights, para 60.

[96] *Michael Domingues v United States, Case 12.285*, Inter-American Commission on Human Rights, Report No. 62/02 of 22 October 2002, para 92.

[97] *Mann v Republic of Equatorial Guinea*, Case No. 507/07, Judgment of 23 January 2008, High Court of Zimbabwe, p. 12 ('the principle against torture has evolved into a peremptory norm or *jus cogens*, viz. a principle endowed with primacy in the hierarchy of rules that constitute the international normative order').

[98] *Mani Kumari Sabbithi et al. v Major Waleed KH N.S. Al Saleh et al.*, 605 F Supp 2d 122 (United States District Court for the District of Columbia 2009), p. 129.

[99] See e.g. Kittichaisaree (A/CN.4/SR.3315), 6 ('Rather than being a requirement for identification, hierarchical superiority was a consequence of *jus cogens*. Therefore, although the idea of superiority should be mentioned, he was concerned that addressing it in Draft Conclusion 3(2) might blur the difference between identification of *jus cogens* and its consequences and thereby risk making the its definition circular'); Nolte (A/CN.4/SR.3315), 11 ('The meaning of "hierarchical superiority" was wrapped up with the issue of legal consequences of *jus cogens* rules'); Murphy (A/CN.4/SR.3369), 15 ('Further, the notion that *jus cogens* norms were hierarchically "hierarchically superior to other norms" primarily concerned the consequences of *jus cogens*').

4. Concluding Observations

Draft Conclusions 2 and 3 describe what we are to understand by *jus cogens* through a statement of the characteristics and definition. These two provisions appear to be an attempt at mediating between two approaches to peremptory norms, namely the consensualist and idealist approaches to international law. The role of 'acceptance and recognition' by states versus the role of values, the distinction between the international community on the one hand, and the international community of States on the other, serve as elements for mediating the tension between the two approaches to peremptory norms of general international law (*jus cogens*).

The criteria for the identification of *jus cogens* developed and applied in the set of Draft Conclusions are based on the definition of *jus cogens* in Draft Conclusion 3. The criteria, including whether, and the extent to which, they interact or leave room, is the subject of Part Two of the book.

In addition to revealing the tension between the consensualist and idealist approaches to *jus cogens*, Draft Conclusions 2 and 3 also illustrate the balance that the Commission had to strike between faithfulness to existing instruments, such as the Vienna Convention, and openness to innovation (albeit based on existing practice). This balance is reflected throughout the Draft Conclusions. Draft Conclusions 2 and 3, and their relationship to each other, are thus something of a microcosm of the full set of Draft Conclusions.

The relationship between the two Draft Conclusions cannot be overstated. It is no coincidence that many States that had strongly opposed Draft Conclusion 2 had, during the Sixth Committee's deliberations on the final outcome of the Draft Conclusions, adopted a less hostile approach to Draft Conclusion 2 precisely because the Commission had moved Draft Conclusion 2 to come before the Draft Conclusion 3.[100] This, in the view of these States, served to decouple the two Draft Conclusions and, more specifically, excludes the possibility of Draft Conclusion 2 playing a role in the identification of *jus cogens*.[101] At the same time, there were States according to which the relationship between the elements in Draft Conclusion 2 should have been explicitly connected to

[100] See e.g. the United States, Sixth Committee of the General Assembly, Seventy-Seventh Session, 25 October 2022 ('We recognise that the Commission has addressed some of those concerns, including with respect to the adjusted placement of what is now Draft Conclusion 2'); Norway, Sixth Committee of the General Assembly, Seventy-Seventh Session, 25 October 2022 ('While many of the Nordic countries' comments and observations ... have not resulted in changes, we are pleased to observe that [former] Draft Conclusion 3 has been moved in order to avoid the perception that it forms part of the criteria for the identification of a peremptory norms of general international law').

[101] Id.

the criteria for *jus cogens*.[102] That the ambiguity was not resolved by the change made on the second reading is captured by the statement of Germany.[103]

As described above, the Commentary to Draft Conclusion 2 adopts an ambiguous posture to the relationship between Draft Conclusion 2, on the one hand, and Draft Conclusion 3 and the criteria, on the other hand. How those charged with identifying *jus cogens* will mediate between the different views on the role of Draft Conclusion remains to be seen.

[102] See Greece, Sixth Committee of the General Assembly, Seventy-Seventh Session, 25 October 2022 ('We also note with appreciation that Draft Conclusion 2 provides, inter alia, that *jus cogens* norms reflect and protect the fundamental values of the international community. We are however of the view that this cardinal characteristic of *jus cogens* provides also a criterion for their identification given that, for a norm to qualify as peremptory, it should be accepted and recognised by the international community of States as reflecting and protecting such values ... For this reason, we are of the view that affirmative language in this respect should have been inserted'). In its statement, South Africa suggested that the substance of Draft Conclusion 2 was relied upon by its Constitutional Court in identifying particular norms as *jus cogens*. See South Africa, Sixth Committee of the General Assembly, Seventy-Seventh Session, 26 October 2022. See also the Czech Republic, Sixth Committee of the General Assembly, Seventy-Seventh Session, 25 October 2022, which seemed to conflate the characteristics with the definition ('We agree with the adopted definition and characterisation of [*jus cogens* norms] as universally applicable and hierarchically superior rules of international law'). See also further Pakistan, Sixth Committee of the General Assembly, Seventy-Seventh Session, 25 October 2022.

[103] See Germany, Sixth Committee of the General Assembly, Seventy-Seventh Session, 25 October 2022, stating that 'the ambiguity in the commentary the risk of misinterpretation still remains and has not been mitigated'.

PART II
IDENTIFICATION

4

Identifying Peremptory Norms

The Criteria

1. Introduction

This chapter addresses the International Law Commission's Draft Conclusions on the criteria and methodology for the identification of peremptory norms of general international law. The methodology for the identification of norms of *jus cogens* is provided for in Draft Conclusions 4, 5, 6, 7, 8, and 9. This chapter, however, will address only Draft Conclusion 4, which describes the criteria for the identification of *jus cogens* in general. Chapter 5 will discuss in more detail the first criterion, i.e. what is to be understood by the term 'a norm of general international law' (Draft Conclusion 5). The second, cumulative criterion, acceptance and recognition by the international community of States as a whole of the non-derogability of the norm, will be the subject of Chapter 6 (Draft Conclusions 6 and 7). Chapter 7 will address the evidence that may be relied upon to illustrate the acceptance and recognition of the international community of States as a whole that a norm is non-derogable (Draft Conclusions 8 and 9).

The chapter will begin, in the next section, by a discussion of the issues raised in connection with the criteria. Chief amongst these is what the source of the criteria is and whether Article 53, given its drafting by reference to consequences, can provide the criteria. This discussion itself has several elements. First, whether the criteria ought to be more value-based in the tradition of the idealist approaches to *jus cogens*. Second, if the Vienna Convention were to be used as the basis for the criteria, whether other elements could be drawn from elsewhere. Section 3 of the chapter will then provide an analysis of the text adopted by the Commission. Some concluding observations are offered in Section 4.

2. Discussion

Draft Conclusion 4 puts forward two requirements as criteria for the identification of *jus cogens*. The first criterion is that the norm in question must be shown to be a 'norm of general international law', while the second criterion is that such a general norm of international law must be 'accepted and recognized by the international community of States as a whole as a norm from which no derogation is permitted and which can be modified only by a subsequent norm of general international law having the same character'. The second criterion is described in the Commentaries as 'a single composite criterion'.[1] By this it is meant that while the second criterion has several elements, these elements together make up a single criterion. The individual elements of the second criterion are:

(a) acceptance and recognition;
(b) by the international community of States as a whole;
(c) non-derogation;
(d) which can be modified only by a subsequent norm;
(e) having the same character.

Some of the elements will be considered in greater depth in subsequent chapters. What is important for the purpose of the present chapter is that, together, these elements constitute the second criterion. This, together with the first criterion, i.e. a norm of general international law, is necessary for the identification of a norm as *jus cogens*.

According to the Commentary to Draft Conclusion 4, these criteria are derived from the definition of *jus cogens* in Article 53 of the Vienna Convention and affirmed in Draft Conclusion 3 (see Chapter 3).[2] From the beginning of the Commission's consideration of the topic, many States took the view that whatever criteria the Commission put forward should be based on Article 53.[3] The

[1] See para 3 of the Commentary to Draft Conclusion 4.

[2] See para 1 of the Commentary to Draft Conclusion 4 ('The criteria are drawn from the definition of peremptory norms contained in article 53 of the 1969 Vienna Convention'). See also para 3 ('On the basis of the definition contained in draft conclusion 3, draft conclusion 4 sets forth two criteria').

[3] See e.g. Peremptory Norm of General International Law (*Jus Cogens*): The Czech Republic, Comments and Observations received from Governments (A/C.6/71/SR.24), 72; see also Canada, , Comments and Observations received from Governments (A/C.6/71/SR.27), 9; Chile, , Comments and Observations received from Governments (A/C.6/71/SR), 101; China, , Comments and Observations received from Governments (A/C.6/71/SR.24), 89; The Islamic Republic of Iran, Comments and Observations received from Governments (A/C.6/71/SR.26), 118: ('The aim of the Commission's work on the topic was not to contest the two criteria established under Article 53 . . . On the contrary the goal was to elucidate the meaning and scope of the criteria'); Poland, Comments and Observations received from Governments (A/C.6/71/SR.26), 56. See further Ireland, Comments and Observations received

Second Report of the Special Rapporteur, however, stated that this view should not be interpreted 'to mean that the Commission may not move beyond Article 53 even if practice so determined'.[4] On this basis, the Second Report adopted the following approach:

> The present report therefore takes, as its point of departure, the elements of Article 53 of the Vienna Convention as the basis for the criteria for the identification of *jus cogens* norms. However, State practice and the decisions of international courts and tribunals are relied upon to give content and meaning to Article 53.[5]

While the Commentary states that these criteria are based on Article 53 of the Vienna Convention, it is not always clear that the definition of *jus cogens* in the Vienna Convention sets forth any criteria for its identification. Nor is it unquestioned that Article 53 provides a definition at all. It has, for example, been suggested that what stands in Article 53 cannot be a definition and therefore does not provide criteria.[6] Indeed, in formulating what eventually became Article 53 of the Vienna Convention, the International Law Commission in 1966 pointed out that 'there [was] no simple criterion by which' to identify norms of *jus cogens*, suggesting that the Commission did not, at that point, consider that it was providing the criteria for peremptory norms.[7]

It has been pointed out that the problem with Article 53 of the Vienna Convention is that it appears to define *jus cogens* by reference to its consequences, namely non-derogation.[8] To this end, Linderfalk says that the

> remarkable thing about the definition laid down in Article 53 of the Vienna Convention is that it does not say anything about the particular properties of

from Governments (A/C.6/71/SR.27), 19: ('Her delegation agreed with the view that Articles 53 and 64 of the 1969 Vienna Convention on the Law of Treaties should be central to work on the topic').

[4] Dire Tladi *Second Report of the Special Rapporteur on Peremptory Norms of General International Law (Jus Cogens)* (A/CN.4/706), para 32.

[5] Id.

[6] See statements in footnote 3.

[7] See para 2 of the Commentary to Draft Article 50 of the Draft Articles on the Law of Treaties, *Yearbook of the International Law Commission*, 1966, Vol. II ('The formulation of the article is not free from difficulty, since there is no simple criterion by which to identify a general rule of international law as having the character of *jus cogens*'); see also Shoji Matsumoto *Jus Cogens and the Right to Self-Determination: The Falsiability of Tests* (Policy Centre for the New South, 2020), 12, noting that the Vienna Convention does not specify any tests for *jus cogens*.

[8] Sévrine Knuchel *Jus Cogens: Identification and Enforcement of Peremptory Norms* (Schultess, 2015), 41; Ulf Linderfalk *The Creation of Jus Cogens—Making Sense of Article 53 of the Vienna Convention* (*Zeitschrift für ausländisches öffentliches Recht und Völkerrecht*, 2011), 373.

> *jus cogens* norms. Instead, as the definition provides, a norm of *jus cogens* is to be identified based on its acceptance among States and their recognition of the existence of some very particular legal obligations tied to it.[9]

There are several conclusions that one can draw from this.[10] First, it might be argued that this means that the criteria are to be identified on the basis of 'acceptance and recognition'. Second, it may be claimed that there are no criteria at all. From this perspective, the identification of *jus cogens* becomes like art, whose beauty, or existence, lies in the eye of the beholder. Third, it may be asserted that there are criteria, but that these criteria are not to be found in Article 53, but rather that they are to be found elsewhere. The most common example of this approach is the argument that *jus cogens* norms are to be identified through what has been referred to as the 'normativist approach' to the identification of *jus cogens* norms.[11]

The ILC Draft Conclusions adopt the approach that there are criteria for the identification of *jus cogens* and that these criteria are to be found in the definition contained in Article 53 of the Vienna Convention. This view was endorsed almost universally by both States and members of the Commission when the topic was considered on second reading. Indeed, for the most part, members of the Commission simply did not comment on Draft Conclusion 4.[12] There were, of course, some exceptions. Mr Murase, for example, suggested that Draft Conclusion 4 was not acceptable to 'some states'—without mentioning which States these were—'in part' because 'there were two different types of *jus cogens*', one applicable under the law on State responsibility and the other applicable under the law of treaties.[13]

Although in the end the Commission took the view that from the definition contained in Article 53, the criteria for *jus cogens* could be identified, that was not the end of the matter since, from the definition in Article 53, it was possible

[9] Ulf Linderfalk *Understanding Jus Cogens in International Law and Legal Discourse* (Edward Elgar, 2020), 10.

[10] See generally id., 10–11.

[11] See generally Mary H. Hansel '"Magic" or Smoke and Mirrors? The Gendered Illusion of *Jus Cogens*' in Dire Tladi *Peremptory Norms of General International Law (Jus Cogens): Disquisitions and Disputations* (Brill, 2020). See especially Alexander Orakhelashvili *Peremptory Norms in International Law* (Oxford University Press, 2006), 49, specifying that morality can 'explain a norm's peremptory character'.

[12] Members that did explicitly express support for Draft Conclusion 4 were Cisse (A/CN.4/SR.3567), 11 and Vásquez-Bermúdez (A/CN.4/SR.3568), 7: in both cases, the support for Draft Conclusion 4 was explicitly stated in order to draw a distinction between the criteria for identification and the nature of *jus cogens*.

[13] Murase (A/CN.4/SR.3565), 3.

to conceive of the criteria in different ways.[14] The Second Report notes, for example, that it is possible to interpret the phrase 'accepted and recognised' as qualifying only 'general international law' and not 'non-derogation'.[15] If that were the case, Article 53 would have three criteria. The first criterion would be a norm of general international law which is accepted and recognised (as a norm of general international law) by the international community of States as a whole. The second criterion would, under this construction, be a norm from which no derogation is permitted, and the third criterion, a norm that can only be modified by another *jus cogens* norm. Another approach, similar to but not the same as that adopted by the Commission, is that put forward by Knuchel.[16]

The Commission thus, in adopting Draft Conclusion 4, made several choices. First, that there were in fact particular criteria for the identification of peremptory norms, i.e. whether a rule is or is not *jus cogens* is not simply in the eye of the beholder. Second, that those criteria were to be found in Article 53. And finally, that the notion of 'acceptance and recognition' by the international community of States as a whole was central to the process of identification. Taken together, these choices *may* suggest that, contrary to its stated intention, the Commission has adopted a particular, voluntarist, approach to the topic. Yet, a different way to view the approach taken by the Commission, particularly in light of the inclusion of Draft Conclusion 2 and its appeal to values, is an interaction of the consensualist and non-consensualist philosophies. The First Report on *Jus Cogens* suggested that 'the binding and peremptory force of *jus cogens* is best understood as an interaction between natural law and positivism'.[17] The Report cites Koskenniemi's proposition that *jus cogens*, in the first place, reflects descending non-consensualism, with reference to the recognition of the international community of States adding a consensualist flavour.[18]

[14] See generally Dire Tladi 'The International Law Commission's Draft Conclusions on Peremptory Norms of General International Law *(Jus Cogens)*: Making Wine from Water or More Water than Wine?' (2020) 89 *Nordic Journal of International Law* 244, 263.

[15] Second Report (above note 4), para 38.

[16] Knuchel (above note 8), 7. See, for a further alternative formulation, Ulf Linderfalk 'Understanding the *Jus Cogens* Debate: The Pervasive Influence of Legal Positivism and Legal Idealism' (2015) 46 *Netherlands Yearbook of International Law* 51, 65, according to whom positivism draws from Article 53 two criteria: (a) a general practice, namely that States generally do no derogate from the rule and generally do not modify through the rule through ordinary sources of law; (b) an *opinio juris generalis* of the peremptory character of the rule in question.

[17] Dire Tladi *First Report of the Special Rapporteur on Peremptory Norms of General International Law (Jus Cogens)* (A/CN.4/693), para 59.

[18] Martti Koskenniemi *From Apology to Utopia: The Structure of Legal Argument (Reissue with New Epilogue)* (Cambridge University Press, 2006), 308.

3. The Content of Draft Conclusion 4

Conclusion 4

Criteria for the identification of a peremptory norm of general international law (*jus cogens*).

To identify a peremptory norm of general international law (*jus cogens*), it is necessary to establish that the norm in question meets the following criteria:

(a) it is a norm of general international law; and

(b) it is accepted and recognized by the international community of States as a whole as a norm from which no derogation is permitted and which can be modified only by a subsequent norm of general international law having the same character.

The initial text of Draft Conclusion 4 proposed in the Second Report of the Special Rapporteur provided as follows:

> To identify a norm as one of *jus cogens*, it is necessary to show that the norm in question meets two criteria:
> (a) It must be a norm of general international law; and
> (b) It must be accepted and recognized by the international community of States as a whole as a norm from which no derogation is permitted.[19]

In substance, the final text of Draft Conclusion 4 remains the same with one exception. The original proposal of the Special Rapporteur did not include the 'modification element'. The approach taken in the Second Report was that the element of modification in Article 53 of the Vienna Convention—a norm that can only be modified by a subsequent norm of *jus cogens*—was not so much a criterion of peremptoriness but rather a description of how a peremptory norm could be modified.[20] While this view received some support, there were some members of the Commission who did not agree with this proposition and were rather of the view that the 'modification element' was an integral part of the criteria.[21] It must be said that the reason advanced seemed to be more related

[19] Second Report (above note 4), para 91.

[20] Id., para 37.

[21] *Report of the International Law Commission, Sixty-Ninth Session, Yearbook of the International Law Commission*, 2017, Vol. II, Part II, para 165 ('While most members agreed with the Special Rapporteur that the modification element referred to in article 53 of the 1969 Vienna Convention could not be a criterion, some expressed disagreement in that regard').

to fidelity to the text of the Vienna Convention than anything else.[22] As a result, in substance, the text adopted that year followed the proposal of the Special Rapporteur, with the addition of the phrase 'and which can be modified only by a subsequent norm of general international law having the same character'.

Within the Drafting Committee, there were suggestions that the formulation of the second criterion—the one referred to earlier as a 'composite criterion'—was overly complex and messy. In response, the Special Rapporteur presented a revised proposal, which would separate the elements of the criteria. The revised proposal read as follows:

> To identify a norm as one of *jus cogens*, it is necessary to show that the norm in question meets two criteria:
> (a) It must be a norm of general international law; and
> (b) It must be accepted and recognised by the international community of States as a whole as:
> (i) a norm from which no derogation is permitted;
> (ii) a norm that can be modified only by a subsequent norm of general international law having the same character.[23]

This formulation, while easier to read, had the potential to create confusion and uncertainty as to the meaning of the Draft Conclusion. The revised formulation had the potential to be read as implying that the two elements of the second criterion were separate and independent, requiring that evidence for both be presented. Yet such an understanding would be inconsistent with the general idea behind the proposal as contained in the Second Report. The Commission thus decided to revert to the original formulation in the Second Report, with only minor modifications. First, the word 'show' was replaced by 'establish' while the phrase 'two criteria' was replaced by 'following criteria'. In addition, the 'modification' element was inserted in the second criterion, thus completing the composite criteria.

With respect to the chapeau, the Commentary emphasises the words 'it is necessary to establish', which indicate that the criteria have to be shown to exist in law and cannot just be assumed.[24] There were some members of the Commission, in the course of the discussions in the Drafting Committee

[22] Id. ('The view was also expressed that the first sentence of article 53 ought to be inserted as a criterion').
[23] See Drafting Committee, Peremptory Norms of General International Law, Revised Proposal of the Special Rapporteur for Draft Conclusion 4 ILC(LXIX)/DC/JC/WP.1, 13 July 2017.
[24] See para 2 of the Commentary to Draft Conclusion 4.

during the second reading, who seemed to suggest that the phrase 'it is necessary to establish' was evidence that the characteristics in Draft Conclusion 2 did not play *any role* in the identification of peremptory norms. Yet, this reading would not be consistent with the Commentary to Draft Conclusion 2 which does suggest that the characteristics might play some role in the identification, especially in the assessment of the evidence.[25]

The first criterion, that the norm in question be a norm of general international law, is discussed in the next chapter. The second criterion, which consists of several elements, will be addressed in subsequent chapters.

4. Concluding Observations

Draft Conclusion 4 is one of the Draft Conclusions that was least controversial in the whole set of Draft Conclusions. At the same time, Draft Conclusion 4 is at the heart of the Draft Conclusions and sets out the basic requirements necessary for the identification of *jus cogens*. These criteria, derived from Article 53 of the Vienna Convention, suggest a consensualist approach. At the same, as discussed in Chapter 3, the elements contained in Draft Conclusion 2 may have some role to play in the assessment of the criteria, thus introducing a non-consensualist or idealist flavour.

Each of the individual criteria that make up the Draft Conclusion will be addressed in the following chapters.

[25] See para 19 of the Commentary to Draft Conclusion 2 ('Though themselves not criteria, the existence of the characteristics contained in draft conclusion 2 may provide context in the assessment of evidence for the identification of peremptory norms of general international law (*jus cogens*). For example, evidence that a norm reflects and protects fundamental values of the international community of States as a whole, is hierarchically superior to other norms of international law and is universally applicable, may serve to support or confirm the peremptory status of a norm').

5

The First Criterion

A Norm of General International Law

1. Introduction

The criteria for *jus cogens* are set forth in Draft Conclusion 4, which is considered in Chapter 4. It identifies two criteria, namely, first, that the norm in question must be a norm of general international law, and second, that the norm must be accepted and recognised as a norm from which no derogation is permitted and which may only be modified by a subsequent norm having the same character.

This chapter focuses on the first criterion, i.e. the norm of general international law, which is provided for in Draft Conclusion 5, while subsequent chapters will address the second composite criterion. What is uncontested is that customary international law is the main basis for peremptory norms. This view can be seen in both doctrine and practice. The main issue of contestation in relation to Draft Conclusion 5 was whether the other sources of international law, in particular treaties and general principles, can also form the basis of *jus cogens*.

The next section will provide an overview of the issues surrounding the first criterion. The section will focus in particular on the role of treaties and general principles of law as bases of *jus cogens*. Section 3 will provide an overview of the text adopted by the Commission. Section 4 will provide final observations.

2. Discussion

Draft Conclusion 5 concerns the first criterion for peremptory norms of general international law, namely that the norm in question must be a norm of general international law. The basic import of this criterion is that, even before assessing whether the norm in question is recognised and accepted as being peremptory, it has to be shown to be a rule of international law, and in particular, a rule of general international law.[1]

The Second Report declared that the notion of 'general international law' in the context of the first criterion referred to the scope of application.[2] It could of course, in other contexts, have a different meaning. The Commission's Study Group on Fragmentation, for example, made the distinction between *lex specialis* and general international law.[3] Yet, that distinction is not what is meant in the context of *jus cogens* since this would exclude *lex specialis* rules from the ambit of *jus cogens*.[4] In the context of *jus cogens*, rather, the phrase 'general international law' is meant to refer to norms which 'by their very nature must have equal force for all members of the international community'.[5]

It was on this understanding of 'general international law' that the Second Report proposed a three-tiered approach for Draft Conclusion 5.[6] The first tier was customary international law, which was described as the most common basis for *jus cogens*. There was much authority in support of this proposition, in the form of State practice,[7] decisions of international courts and

[1] See Ulf Linderfalk 'The Creation of *Jus Cogens*: Making Sense of Article 53 of the Vienna Convention' (2011) 71 *Zeitschrift für ausländisches öffentliches Recht und Völkerrecht* 359, 371 ('by "the creation of a rule of *jus cogens*" I mean, not the creation of a rule of law, but rather the elevation of a rule of law to a *jus cogens* status').

[2] Dire Tladi *Second Report of the Special Rapporteur on Peremptory Norms of General International Law (Jus Cogens)* (A/CN.4/706), para 42.

[3] Id., para 41; *Report of the Study Group of the International Law Commission, finalised by Mr. Martti Koskenniemi* (2006) (A/CN.4/L.682 and Add.1).

[4] Second Report (above note 2), para 42.

[5] *North Sea Continental Shelf Cases (Germany/Denman; Germany/the Netherlands)*, Judgment, *ICJ Reports* 1969, p. 3, para 63.

[6] Second Report (above note 2), para 46.

[7] The Second Report cited, *inter alia*, the following statements by States in the General Assembly: Statement by Pakistan at the Thirty-Fourth Session of the General Assembly (A/C.6/34/SR.22), para 8 ('The principle of the non-use of force, and its corollary, were *jus cogens* not only by virtue of Article 103 of the Charter but also because they had become norms of customary international law recognized by the international community'). See also the statements by the United Kingdom (A/C.6/34/SR.61), para 46 and Jamaica, (A/C.6/42/SR.29), para 3 ('The right of peoples to self-determination and independence was a right under customary international law, and perhaps even a peremptory norm of general international law'). The Report also cited the following decisions of national courts as a form of State practice: *Siderman de Blake v Republic of Argentina*, United States Court of Appeals for the Ninth Circuit, 965 F.2d 699 (9th Cir. 1992), 715, where *jus cogens* norms were described as 'an elite subset of the norms recognized as customary international law'; *Kazemi Estate v Islamic Republic of Iran* [2014] Supreme Court of Canada 62, 3 SCR 176, para 151; *Steen v Islamic Republic of Iran*, 2013 ONCA 30, 114 OR (3d) 206, para 30 ('Peremptory norms of international law, or *jus cogens*, are high forms of customary international law from which no derogation is permitted'); *Arancibia Clavel, Enrique Lautaro s/ Homicidio Calificado y Asociación Ilícita y Otros*, Causa No. 259, judgment of 24 August 2004, para 28; EXP. No. 0024-2010-PI/TC, Sentencia del Pleno Jurisdiccional del Tribunal Constitucional del Perú, 21 March 2011, para 53 ('Las normas de *jus cogens* parecen pues encontrarse referidas a normas internacionales consuetudinarias que bajo el auspicio de una opinio juris seu necessitatis'); *Bayan Muna as represented by Representative Satur Ocampo et al. v Alberto Romulo*, Supreme Court of the Republic of the Philippines, GR 15968 (2011); *Kenya Section of the International Commission of Jurists v Attorney-General and Others*, Judgment of the High Court of Kenya of 28 November 2011, [2011] eKLR, para 14; *Germany v Milde (Max Josef)*, Appeal Judgment of 13 January 2009, 1st Criminal Section, Case No.

tribunals,[8] and doctrinal writings.[9] Unsurprisingly, this proposition was universally accepted, both within the Commission and by States commenting on the Draft Conclusions.[10]

In the second tier of sources identified in the Second Report were general principles of law within the meaning of Article 38(1)(c) of the Statute of the International Court of Justice—a source of law which, incidentally, would be included in the programme of the Commission two years after the debate on the Second Report.[11] The Second Report begins by noting that 'like customary

1072/2009, ILDC 1224 (IT 2009), para 6 ('customary rules aiming to protect inviolable human rights did not permit derogation because they belonged to peremptory international law or *jus cogens*').

[8] For decisions of international courts and tribunals, the Second Report cited, *inter alia*, the following: *Questions relating to the Obligation to Prosecute or Extradite (Belgium v Senegal)*, Judgment, *ICJ Reports* 2012, p. 422, para 99, where the Court recognised the prohibition of torture as 'part of customary international law' that 'has become a peremptory norm (*jus cogens*)'; *Legality of the Threat or Use of Nuclear Weapons*, Advisory Opinion, *ICJ Reports* 1996, p. 226, para 79, describing 'many rules of international humanitarian law' as constituting 'intransgressible principles of international customary law'; *Prosecutor v Delalić et al.*, Judgment, Case No. IT-96-21-T, T.Ch., 16 November 1998, para 454; *Prosecutor v Jelisić*, Judgment, Case No. IT-95-10-T, T.Ch., 14 December 1999, para 60; *Prosecutor v Furundžija*, Judgment, Case No. IT-95-17/1-T, T.Ch., 10 December 1998, para 153.

[9] For literature supporting the proposition, the Second Report referred to the following authorities: Gérard Cahin *La Coutume internationale et les organisations internationales: l'incidence de la dimension institutionnelle sur le processus coutumier* (Pedone, 2001), 615 ('voie normale et fréquente sinon exclusive'); Raphaële Rivier *Droit international public* (2nd edn, Paris, Presses Universitaires de France, 2013), 566 ('Le mode coutumier est donc au premier rang pour donner naissance aux règles destinées à alimenter le droit impératif'); Antonio Cassese *International Law* (2nd edn, Oxford, Oxford University Press, 2005), 199 ('a special class of general rules made by custom has been endowed with a special legal force: they are peremptory in nature and make up the so called *jus cogens*'); João Ernesto Christófolo *Solving Antinomies between Peremptory Norms in Public International Law* (Zurich, Schulthess, 2016), 115 ('As the most likely source of general international law, customary norms would constitute *ipso facto* and *ipso iure* a privileged source of *ius cogens* norms').

[10] See e.g., for views of members of the Commission, Forteau (A/CN.6/SR.3564), who, while expressing concern with Draft Conclusion 5 said: 'It was generally accepted that a norm of *jus cogens* was necessarily customary and, to date, no convincing example had been provided to suggest otherwise'; Jalloh (A/CN.4/SR.3565) explained, with approval, that the import of Draft Conclusion 5 was that customary international law was the 'most common basis for a *jus cogens* norm [and that] custom was the most obvious manifestation of general international law' and 'that factor explained the higher status that it enjoyed in Draft Conclusion 5'; Hassouna (A/CN.4/SR.3566); Hmoud (A/CN,4/SR.3566) ('As to the content of the draft conclusion, practice supported the argument that customary international law was the basis for *jus cogens*'). For the views of States on the first reading text of the Draft Conclusions, see Peremptory Norms of General International Law (*Jus Cogens*): Australia, Comments and Observations received from Governments (A/CN.4/748), March 2022, 27; Czech Republic, Comments and Observations received from Governments (A/CN.4/748), 28 ('In our view, customary international law norms are the primary means of formation of *jus cogens* norms, since its "general binding character" makes it the most appropriate vehicle for peremptory norms'); Germany, Comments and Observations received from Governments (A/CN.4/748), 29 ('concurs that customary international law—as opposed to treaty law or other sources—is the most common basis for peremptory norms of general international law (*jus cogens*)'; the Russian Federation, Comments and Observations received from Governments (A/CN.4/748), 31; Slovenia, Comments and Observations received from Governments (A/CN.4/748), 32; the United States, Comments and Observations received from Governments (A/CN.4/748), 32 ('it is well established that *jus cogens* is a species of customary international law').

[11] *Report of the International Law Commission on the Work of Its Sixty-Ninth Session*, 2017 (A/71/10), Annex.

international law' general principles of law 'are generally applicable'.[12] Yet, almost immediately, the Report makes the following declaration which casts doubt on the role of general principles as a basis for peremptory norms:

> However, while there is ample authority in practice for the proposition that customary international law rules form the basis of *jus cogens* norms, there is significantly less authority for the proposition that general principles of law also constitute a basis for *jus cogens* norms.[13]

The choice of language is noteworthy. For customary international law, the extract refers to 'authority *in practice*', while for general principles, the Report not only qualifies the authority as 'significantly less' but also does not refer to it as practice. In fact, the 'significantly less' authority relied upon in the Second Report is limited to doctrinal literature[14] and the negotiating history of Article 53 of the Vienna Convention.[15] Unlike the position of customary international law, the idea of general principles of law as a basis for peremptory norms did not receive overwhelming support. While the proposition received some support within the Commission and from some States,[16] there was also some criticism of the proposition.[17] Between these

[12] Second Report (above note 2), para 48.

[13] Id.

[14] For this proposition, the Second Report cites the following: Sévrine Knuchel *Jus Cogens: Identification and Enforcement of Peremptory Norms* (Schultess, 2015), 51 ('general principles [of law] may be elevated to *jus cogens* if the international community of States recognise and accept them as such'); Dinah Shelton 'Sherlock Holmes and the Mystery of *Jus Cogens*' (2015) 46 *Netherlands Yearbook of International Law: Jus Cogens—Quo Vadis?* 23, 30; Thomas Weatherall *Jus Cogens: International Law and Social Contract* (Cambridge University Press, 2015), 6–7 ('Although the Vienna Convention concerns the law of treaties and binds only signatories... Article 53 reflected a concept with legal effect beyond the treaty context.... The contemporary practice of international and domestic judicial organs, to refer to Article 53 for any consideration of *jus cogens*, is consistent with this view of a concept existing outside the treaty context').

[15] Second Report (above note 2), paras 49–50.

[16] Vázquez-Bermúdez (A/CN.4/SR.3568) ('It was also worth noting that the sources of international law referred to in Article 38 of the Statute of the International Court of Justice did not operate in silos but interacted with one another. Thus, to exclude treaties and general principles of law from serving as bases for peremptory norms of general international law would risk creating an artificial division among the sources of international law'); El Salvador, Comments and Observations (above note 10), 28.

[17] For statements by members of the Commission opposing the idea of general principles of law as a basis for peremptory norms see: Forteau (A/CN.4/SR.3564); Argüello Gómez (A/CN.4/SR.3568) ('He agreed with the comments of Italy, Spain and the United States of America on draft conclusion 5, a provision he considered unnecessary. All peremptory norms were rules of customary law that had acquired a kind of added value. The rules contained in treaties and in general principles of law necessarily became customary rules before being viewed as peremptory norms'); Park (A/CN.4/3369) ('He generally agreed with the wording of draft conclusion 5. However, paragraph 3 thereof required further discussion, primarily because it was difficult to find a case where a general principle of law had served as the basis for *jus cogens*; actual State practice could not be ignored for theoretical purposes. It was indeed questionable whether there was any State practice which supported the status of

two positions, there were also members that adopted somewhat ambiguous stances.[18]

The third tier in the categorisation of the Second Report is treaty law. According to the Second Report, treaties do not constitute general international law, and therefore treaty provisions as such cannot form the basis of peremptory norms of general international law.[19] Yet the Report acknowledges that there are certain treaty rules that are widely accepted as constituting *jus cogens*—a typical example of this being the prohibition on the use of force as contained in the Charter of the United Nations. In this context, the Report notes that the treaty rule reflects an autonomous rule of customary international law as observed by the International Court of Justice in the *Military and Paramilitary Activities* case[20] and that it is that underlying customary international law rule that forms the basis of the peremptory norm.[21] Like the proposition concerning general principles, that proposition received varying responses from States and members of the Commission. Several members of the Commission believed that, contrary to the claim in the Second Report, treaties could in fact form the basis for peremptory norms,[22] with some members even suggesting that treaties were the most obvious basis for peremptory norms.[23] Yet other members agreed with the proposition of the

general principles of law as the basis of *jus cogens*'). See statements by The Netherlands, Comments and Observations (above note 10), 31; Czech Republic, Comments and Observations (above note 10), 28; Israel, Comments and Observations (above note 10), 29; Italy, Comments and Observations (above note 10); Russia, Comments and Observations (above note 10), 31; the United States, Comments and Observations (above note 10), 33.

[18] Park (A/CN.4/SR.3565), stating that the Commentary should make clear that the proposition was progressive development; Hassouna (A/CN.4/SR.3565) ('Although there were currently no treaty rules or general principles that served as a basis for *jus cogens*, that did not mean that the situation might not change one day'); Hmoud (A/CN.4/SR.3566); see statements by Australia, Comments and Observations (above note 10), 27; Slovenia, Comments and Observations (above note 10); United Kingdom, Comments and Observations (above note 10), 33.

[19] Second Report (above note 2), para 55.

[20] *Case Concerning Military and Paramilitary Activities in and Against Nicaragua (Nicaragua v United State)*, Judgment, Merits, *ICJ Reports* 1986, p. 14, para 94 ('But in addition, even if a treaty norm and a customary norm relevant to the present dispute were to have exactly the same content, this would not be a reason for the Court to take the view that the operation of the treaty process must necessarily deprive the customary norm of its separate applicability').

[21] Second Report (above note 2), para 55.

[22] See, for members that believed that treaties could form the basis of *jus cogens*, Vázquez-Bermúdez (A/CN.4/SR.3568); Park (A/CN.4/SR.3565); Rajput (A/CN.4/SR.3369).

[23] See e.g. Rajput (A/CN.4/SR.3369) ('The role of treaty rules in initiating the process of the creation of a *jus cogens* norm could not be relegated to a secondary or tertiary status, as was done in draft conclusion 5, because those rules represented the clearest statement of the views of States and conveyed direct consent, unlike customary international law and general principles of law, which conveyed tacit consent'); Kolodkin (A/CN.4/SR.3372).

Second Report.[24] A similar pattern can be discerned from the comments of States.[25]

In the light of these positions and, in particular, the lack of agreement with respect to general principles and treaty law, the Commission adopted a somewhat ambiguous provision which treats general principles of law and treaty provisions on an equal footing with respect to their potential to serve as bases of *jus cogens*.

3. The Content of Draft Conclusion 5

Conclusion 5

Bases for peremptory norms of general international law (*jus cogens*)

1. Customary international law is the most common basis for peremptory norms of general international law (*jus cogens*).
2. Treaty provisions and general principles of law may also serve as bases for peremptory norms of general international law (*jus cogens*).

Draft Conclusion 5 consists of two paragraphs. The first paragraph concerns customary international law and the second one concerns the other sources of international law, namely treaties and general principles. The text initially proposed in the Second Report of the Special Rapporteur contained four paragraphs. The first paragraph provided a general description of 'general international law'. The second, third, and fourth paragraphs concerned customary international law, general principles of law, and treaty provisions, respectively. Draft Conclusion 5, as proposed by the Special Rapporteur, thus read as follows:

1. A norm of general international law is one which has a general scope of application.

[24] Park (A/CN.4/SR.3369); Nguyen (A/CN.4/SR.3369); Hmoud (A/CN.4/SR.3370); Šturma (A/CN.4/3370); Vasquez-Bermúdez (A/CN.4/SR.3372).

[25] States that believed that treaties could 'reflect' norms of *jus cogens*, but not form the basis of *jus cogens* included: Australia, Comments and Observations (above note 10), 27; Israel, Comments and Observations (above note 10), 29; Italy, Comments and Observations (above note 10), 30; The Netherlands, Comments and Observations (above note 10), 31; South Africa, Comments and Observations (above note 10), 32; States that believed that treaties could not only 'reflect' *jus cogens* norms but could also form the basis of *jus cogens* norms included: Belgium, Comments and Observations (above note 10), 28; Czech Republic, Comments and Observations (above note 10), 28; Germany, Comments and Observations (above note 10), 29; Russian Federation, Comments and Observations (above note 10), 31; Switzerland, Comments and Observations (above note 10), 33.

2. Customary international law is the most common basis for the formation of *jus cogens* norms of international law.
3. General principles of law within the meaning of Article 38(1)(c) of the Statute of the International Court of Justice can also serve as the basis for jus *cogens* norms of international law.
4. A treaty rule may reflect a norm of general international law capable of rising to the level of a *jus cogens* norm of general international law.

In the Drafting Committee, over and above the substantive issues discussed in Section 2 above, a number of drafting issues had been raised. First, it was felt that the first paragraph was not necessary and that its content could go into the Commentary. Second, the view was expressed that 'basis' was an obscure term and that it would be better to refer to 'source'. Finally, it was suggested that 'treaty rule' was overly broad and that what the text should really be concerned with was multilateral treaties or treaty provisions. On the basis of these observations, the Special Rapporteur reformulated the text to delete the first paragraph and replace the word 'basis' with 'source'.[26] More substantively, paragraph 4 was reformulated to provide not only that treaty rules 'may reflect' norms of general international law capable of rising to the level of *jus cogens*, but that they may also '*give rise to*' *jus cogens*—language that suggests that treaty rules as such may also be the basis of *jus cogens*.[27]

In the end, the Drafting Committee, and subsequently the Commission, adopted a different text. First, with respect to the use of the word 'sources', the Drafting Committee decided that 'sources' was not the appropriate term and that the better term was that which was initially proposed in the Second Report, namely 'basis'. The problem with 'source', according to the Drafting Committee, was that it risked creating confusion with the sources as understood in the context of Article 38(1) of the ICJ Statute.[28] Commenting on the

[26] Drafting Committee, Peremptory Norms of General International Law, Revised Proposal of the Special Rapporteur for Draft Conclusion 5 ILC(LXIX)/DC/JC/WP.2, 17 July 2017; Drafting Committee, Peremptory Norms of General International Law, Revised Proposal of the Special Rapporteur for Draft Conclusion 5 ILC(LXIX)/DC/JC/WP.3.

[27] Draft Conclusion 5 ILC(LXIX)/DC/JC/WP.2, para 4 (read: 'Provisions in multilateral treaties may reflect and give rise to peremptory norms of general international law (*jus cogens*)').

[28] Peremptory Norms of General International Law (*Jus Cogens*), Statement of the Chair of the Drafting Committee, Charles Chernor Jalloh, 26 July 2018 ('the Drafting Committee adopted the word "basis", out of the concern that the word "source" was a term used in Article 38(1)(c) of the Statute of the International Court of Justice, where no reference was made to peremptory norms of general international law. The accompanying commentary will indicate that the word "basis" is to be understood flexibly, so as to capture a range of ways in which the traditional sources of law might feed into the formation of *jus cogens* norms').

first reading text, many States had also expressed support for the use of the word 'sources' instead of 'bases'.[29] Responding to these comments, the Fifth Report observed 'that sources of international law are not sources of *jus cogens* norms' and the replacement of the word 'bases' by 'sources' 'would imply that a source of law (customary international law, for example) is a source of a rule of law (for example, the prohibition of the use of force)'.[30] The 'better construction' according to the Fifth Report, would be to 'view the source of law (customary international law) as the underlying basis of the *jus cogens* rule'.[31] Nonetheless, the Fifth Report proposed making the amendment as a way to be responsive to the views of States. However, many members of the Commission opposed this change, citing the very reasons provided in the Fifth Report.[32]

The second change was more substantive. Since there were differences of opinion as to the potential for treaty provisions and general principles to form the bases of peremptory norms, both sources of law were treated in a single paragraph, which provided that both treaty provisions and general principles may also serve as bases for peremptory norms.

Thus, as finally adopted by the Commission, Draft Conclusion 5 consists of two paragraphs. The first paragraph provides simply that customary international law is the most common basis for *jus cogens*. The second paragraph provides that treaty provisions and general principles of law 'may also serve as bases for' *jus cogens*. As explained in Section 2 above, the first paragraph was generally well accepted. The Second Report and the Commentary also

[29] Austria, Comments and Observations (above note 10), 27 ('it would be preferable to refer to "sources" … instead of "bases" for such [*jus cogens*] norms, in conformity with the terminology normally used in connection with Article 38 of the Statute of the International Court of Justice'); El Salvador, Comments and Observations (above note 10), 29 ('International law, in essence, is an interrelated system of legal norms by which States and other subjects of international law, such as international organizations, are bound. This interrelationship must also be highlighted in terms of the sources of such norms, which give rise to distinct effects. Accordingly, and bearing in mind the nature of *jus cogens* norms, it is important to retain a reference to other sources'); France, Comments and Observations (above note 10), 29 ('the idea developed here refers to the sources that confer on certain norms the character of *jus cogens*. Hence, it may be legally more appropriate to use the term "sources"'); Italy, Comments and Observations (above note 10), 30 ('legally speaking, one may wonder to what extent "the range of ways" that "various sources of international law may give rise to the emergence of a peremptory norm" describes anything different from the concept of "source of a peremptory norm"'); Slovenia, Comments and Observations (above note 10), 32 ('suggests that the word "bases" be replaced with the word "sources" in both paragraphs of draft conclusion 5. That would align the wording of the paragraphs with the terminology usually associated with Article 38 of the Statute of the International Court of Justice'); Spain, Comments and Observation (above note 10), 32 ('It would have been preferable in this case to refer to "sources" of international law').

[30] *Fifth Report of the Special Rapporteur on Peremptory Norms of General International Law (Jus Cogens)* (A/CN.4/747), para 69.

[31] Id.

[32] Forteau (A/CN.4/SR.3564); Park (A/CN.4/SR.3565); Jalloh (A/CN.4/SR.3565); Hmoud (A/CN.4/SR.3566); Oral (A/CN.4/SR.3567); Šturma (A/CN.4/SR.3567); Vázquez-Bermúdez (A/CN.4/SR.3568); Wood (A/CN.4/SR.3568).

provided much support in the form of practice, judicial decisions, and scholarly writings for the view that customary international served as the main basis for peremptory norms.[33]

With respect to the second paragraph, because the role of treaties and general principles of law as bases for *jus cogens* was more contentious, the Commission opted to use the phrase 'may also'. According to the Commentary, this was meant to indicate that while there was little in practice to support the emergence of *jus cogens* from these sources of international law 'the possibility of these other sources ... forming the basis of' *jus cogens* 'cannot be *a priori* excluded'.[34] Indeed, for some members, the second paragraph was best seen as a without prejudice clause, preserving, without being definitive about, the possibility of norms of *jus cogens* arising from treaty provisions and general principles of law.[35]

Specifically in the case of general principles, while it was accepted that there is no practice to support the proposition that general principles of law could form the basis of *jus cogens*,[36] the inclusion of general principles is based on the fact that general principles could be described as 'general international law' as they had a general scope of application in the sense that they applied to all States.[37]

With respect to treaty provisions, while the text leaves open the possibility that treaty provisions may serve as a basis for peremptory norms, the Commentary retains remnants of the Special Rapporteur's scepticism. The Commentary makes references to the Commentary to Draft Article 50 of the Articles on the Law of Treaties, which referred to the 'law of the Charter [of the United Nations] concerning the prohibition of the use of force' as a

[33] Second Report (above note 2), paras 42–7. See paras 4–6 of the Commentary to Draft Conclusion 5.

[34] See para 5 of the Commentary to Draft Conclusion 5.

[35] Hmoud (A/CN.4/SR.3566). See also Tladi (A/CN.4/SR.3569) (when summing up the debate: 'Part of the difficulty lay in the fact that Commission members and States held differing opinions on whether treaties and general principles really did serve as a basis of *jus cogens*. Any attempt by the Commission to resolve that issue would be mere conjecture. It therefore had two options: the first would be to leave the compromise text intact; and the second would be to ask the Drafting Committee to consider redrafting the second paragraph as a "without prejudice" clause—although that, in essence, was what the current version actually was').

[36] Of course, the Commentary to Draft Conclusion 5, para 8, does provide some references to jurisprudence which may be read to support the proposition that general principles of law can form the basis for *jus cogens*: *Prosecutor v Jelisić*, Case No. IT-95-10-T, Judgment of 14 December 1999, Trial Chamber, International Tribunal for the Former Yugoslavia, *Judicial Reports 1999*, p. 399, para 60 and *Juridical Condition and Rights of Undocumented Migrants*, Advisory Opinion OC-18/03 of 17 September 2003, *requested by the United Mexican States*, Inter-American Court of Human Rights, *Series A*, No. 18, p. 113, para 101.

[37] See para 8 of the Commentary to Draft Conclusion 5 ('General principles of law are part of general international law since they have a general scope of application with equal force for all members of the international community'), relying on the *North Sea Continental Shelf* cases (above note 5), para 63.

'conspicuous example of a rule of international law having the character of *jus cogens*'.[38] The Commentary then proceeds to make the following statement:

> The role of treaties as a basis for peremptory norms of general international law (*jus cogens*) may be understood as a consequence of the relationship between treaty rules and customary international law as described by the International Court of Justice in *North Sea Continental Shelf* cases. In that case, the Court observed that a treaty rule can codify (or be declaratory of) an existing general rule of international law, or the conclusion of a treaty rule can help crystallise an emerging general rule of international law, or that a treaty rule can, after adoption, come to reflect a general rule [of international law] on the basis of subsequent practice.[39]

This extract seems to suggest that treaty rules cannot, in and of themselves, form the basis of *jus cogens*, except through one of the processes described in the *North Sea Continental Shelf* cases. Put differently, a treaty rule will only be the basis of a norm of *jus cogens* if such a treaty rule is a codification of a rule of customary international law, or if the treaty rule contributes to the emergence of a rule of customary international law or through some other means reflects a rule of customary international law. The net result of this is that it is the customary international law rule, albeit reflected in a treaty provision, which forms the basis of the *jus cogens* norm.

This point is also reinforced in the Commentary to an unrelated provision, Draft Conclusion 13, on the effects of *jus cogens* on the reservation to treaties. There the Commission states that, 'even when reflected in a treaty provision, a peremptory norm of general international law (*jus cogens*) continues to *exist independently of the treaty provision*'.[40]

4. Concluding Observations

While the role of customary international law in *jus cogens* is virtually undisputed, with some even referring to *jus cogens* as 'super customary international law', it is the role of other sources of international law in the identification of *jus cogens* that is less settled. As illustrated in this chapter, the Commission

[38] See para 1 of the Commentary to Article 50 of the Articles on the Law of Treaties, 1966.
[39] See para 8 of the Commentary to Draft Conclusion 5.
[40] Id., para 2.

addresses the uncertainty by adopting a tentative and ambivalent provision which can be read in different ways. It is tentative and ambivalent because there is little authority in practice for general principles of law and treaty provisions to serve as bases for peremptory norms of general international law. The provision is capable of being understood as recognising that the two sources can serve as a basis of *jus cogens*, that the two sources can reflect customary international law and in that indirect way can serve as bases of *jus cogens*, or that the possibility of the two sources serving as bases of *jus cogens* is not precluded.

The ambivalence is particularly pronounced in respect of treaty provisions, where, at various places the Commentaries point out that treaty provisions can form the basis of *jus cogens* because treaty provisions can reflect customary international law.

While some States remain adamant that the Commission ought to have addressed this ambivalence,[41] it seems that the ambivalence and tentativeness are a reflection of the reality that there is some uncertainty in international law about the role of treaties and general principles of law as a bases for *jus cogens*.

[41] See South Africa, Sixth Committee of the General Assembly, Seventy-Seventh Session, 25 October 2022; Australia, Sixth Committee of the General Assembly, Seventy-Seventh Session, 25 October 2022. See especially Jordan, Sixth Committee of the General Assembly, Seventy-Seventh Session, 25 October 2022, in which it is stated without equivocation that 'only customary international law forms a basis of *jus cogens* norms'.

6

The Second Criterion

Acceptance and Recognition by the International Community as a Norm from which no Derogation is Permitted

1. Introduction

The second criterion for the identification of peremptory norms is the main one. The first criterion involves 'merely' showing that the norm in question is a norm of general international law or, put differently, that it is a norm of customary international law. But it is the second criterion that sets the norm in question apart from other 'less special' rules of international law—the one that endows the norm in question with the magic and the miracle-creating quality that comes with having the elevated status of *jus cogens*.

The Draft Conclusions relevant to the second criterion are Draft Conclusion 6 ('acceptance and recognition'), Draft Conclusion 7 ('international community of States as a whole'), Draft Conclusion 8 ('evidence of acceptance'), and Draft Conclusion 9 ('subsidiary means for the determination of the peremptory character'). This criterion, which was described by the Commission as a composite criterion, has three separate elements. The first element, acceptance and recognition, is the essential element. The second element describes who should do the accepting and recognising. The third element describes what it is that should be accepted and recognised, namely that no derogation is permitted. These elements are described in Draft Conclusions 6 and 7, while Draft Conclusions 8 and 9 concern the evidence necessary for showing acceptance and recognition.

This chapter will provide a commentary on Draft Conclusion 6 and Draft Conclusion 7. The chapter will thus cover all three elements of the second criterion. The evidence for showing acceptance and recognition, contained in Draft Conclusion 8 and Draft Conclusion 9, will be addressed in the following chapter. The next section will describe the issues that arose in relation to the elements of the second criterion. In general terms, the main issue of contestation concerned how 'acceptance and recognition' for the purpose of *jus cogens* was to be measured in comparison to how acceptance and recognition might be measured for the purposes of other norms in general international law. In more specific terms, this concerns the question of thresholds, both numerical and quantitative. Section 3 will provide an analysis of the text of Draft Conclusion 6, while Section 4 will provide an analysis of the text of Draft Conclusion 7. Finally, some concluding observations are offered in Section 5.

2. Discussion

As described above, the second criterion, though long and constituted by several distinct elements, constitutes a single composite criterion. At the heart of the criterion is the distinction between *jus dispositivum* and *jus cogens*, which the Commission decided not to explicitly reference in the Draft Conclusions.[1] The criterion is thus meant to distinguish the quality of *jus cogens* norms from other norms of general international law. This distinction is achieved by showing that, in addition to the normal requirements for identifying general rules of international law (the subject of the first criterion), for a peremptory norm of general international law to be shown to exist, an additional criterion must be met, i.e. the composite criterion, which is the subject of this chapter.

This composite criterion raised several issues. The first issue arising in the context of the second criterion is how the lengthy text which makes up the second criterion is to be understood—that lengthy text, it will be recalled is 'accepted and recognised by the international community of States as one from which no derogation is permitted and which can be modified only by a norm having the same character'. This issue was addressed in Chapter 4 and will not be addressed here. The second issue was how the distinction between other norms of general international law and norms having the status of *jus cogens* was to be effectively shown—in other words, whether the identification of *jus*

[1] Dire Tladi *First Report of the Special Rapporteur on Peremptory Norms of General International Law (Jus Cogens)* (A/CN.4/693) proposed Draft Conclusion 2 in which a proposal for such a provision referring to the distinction is made; see Peremptory Norms of General International Law (*Jus Cogens*), Statement of the Chair of the Drafting Committee, Pavel Šturma, 9 August 2016, 4 ('As regards the first paragraph, the Drafting Committee, on the basis of suggestions made in the plenary, decided to reformulate the provision in order to track the language of the second sentence of Article 53 of the Vienna Convention. It was understood that, at this early phase of the work on the topic, it would be difficult to justify adopting a different definition of *jus cogens* than that adopted in the Vienna Convention').

cogens norms required evidence of double acceptance. The last and perhaps the most contentious aspect of this second criterion concerned the phrase 'international community of States as a whole'. For the purposes of the second criterion, this phrase raised two main questions. First, whose acceptance and recognition was relevant for the determination of the peremptory status of a norm? Second, what was the threshold for determining such 'acceptance and recognition'.

Both of these questions—whose acceptance and recognition, and the threshold for such acceptance and recognition—raise the consensualist versus non-consensualist approach discussed in the first chapter. An approach based exclusively on the views of States would tend to suggest a more consensualist approach. Similarly, setting the threshold for acceptance and recognition very high—some States having suggested that the threshold should be virtually all States—would also tend to suggest a more consensualist approach.

While commenting on the work of the Commission, there were some States, notably Israel and the United States, that took the view that to clearly distinguish acceptance and recognition for the purposes of showing the existence of a general norm of international law, on the one hand, and, acceptance and recognition for the purposes of elevating a norm to a *jus cogens* status on the other, required a heightened threshold of acceptance and recognition.[2] Israel, for example, commenting on the first reading text adopted by the Commission, stated that, in its view, the methodology for assessing acceptance and recognition must be 'particularly demanding and rigorous' and that in order to preserve the higher status of *jus cogens*, 'the boundary that divides peremptory norms from other norms must be identified clearly'.[3] More to the point, Israel made the following observation:

> In the view of Israel, the words 'accepted and recognized' require that States must have expressed unequivocal and affirmative support for the status of a particular norm as one of *jus cogens*.[4]

[2] Peremptory Norm of General International Law (*Jus Cogens*): Israel, Comments and Observations received from Governments (A/C.6/74/SR.24), October 2019, para 18; the United States, Comments and Observations received from Governments (A/C.6/74/SR.24), October 2019, para 64.

[3] Israel, Comments and Observations (above note 2), 9. In the same context, Israel stated that '[a]s a general observation, given the significance of *jus cogens* norms, the overall approach to the methodology for identifying them must be at least as rigorous as the methodology proposed by the Commission for identifying rules of customary international law'. Israel went on further to state that because 'of the exceptional character of *jus cogens* norms' there was a 'very high threshold required for their identification'.

[4] Id., 34. See also Israel, Comments and Observations (above note 2), para 18 ('The threshold and process for the identification of *jus cogens* norms under international law must be particularly demanding and rigorous. To preserve the effectiveness and acceptance of a hierarchy of norms international law, the

While not many other States or members of the Commission supported this viewpoint, the point is an important one and goes to the very heart of the second criterion. In responding to the point, the Fifth Report of the Special Rapporteur expressed sympathy with the underlying sentiment of Israel that the criteria should be 'demanding and rigorous'.[5] The Report, however, expressed disagreement with the understanding of 'demanding and rigorous' as implying 'unequivocal and affirmative support'.[6] The approach taken by the Special Rapporteur is that what separates acceptance and recognition for the purposes of identifying rules of general international law from the acceptance and recognition necessary to elevate such norms to the status of *jus cogens* is not the nature or threshold of the acceptance or recognition but rather the quality of the acceptance; or, put differently, it is 'what' is accepted and recognised that is the distinguishing factor. For rules of general international law, it is the quality of the norm in question as a rule of customary international law, while for peremptory norms, it is the acceptance and recognition that the norm in question has peremptory status.[7] The Fifth Report of the Special Rapporteur addressed the matter in the following terms:

> The observations of some States *may suggest* that the threshold for *jus cogens must necessarily* be qualitatively higher than for customary international law. This is a mistake. The standards for the identification of customary international law, on the one hand, and the standard for the identification of *jus cogens*, on the other hand, are different and not comparable. There is a *qualitative* difference between these two processes. For customary international law, what is sought is the widespread opinion of States that a norm constitutes a rule of international law (*jus dispositivum*). For *jus cogens*, the search is for the (collective) opinion of States that a norm is not only a rule of customary international law (or general international law), but is in fact, as a matter of general international law, one that may not be derogated from. The comparison between the quantitative threshold for customary international law and *jus cogens* must therefore be avoided.[8]

boundary that divided peremptory norms from other norms must be identified clearly and monitored vigilantly').

[5] Dire Tladi *Fifth Report of the Special Rapporteur on Peremptory Norms of General International Law (Jus Cogens)* (A/CN.4/747), para 81.
[6] Id.
[7] Fifth Report (above note 5), para 100.
[8] Id., para 91.

The concern raised by Israel is linked to a broader one, namely that it appeared that under the Draft Conclusions, the identification of *jus cogens* would be too easy and not rigorous. This broader concern is also reflected in the concern of several States, including Israel and the United States, over the numerical threshold for acceptance and recognition by the international community of States as a whole. For some States, the numerical threshold implied by the term 'international community of States as a whole' required that virtually all States accept and recognise the peremptory character of the norm in question.[9] The United States, for its part, made the following comment on the text of Draft Conclusion 7 adopted on first reading:

> [The standard of a 'very large majority'] undermines the well-accepted standard for customary international law established by the International Court of Justice in the *North Sea Continental Shelf* cases ['virtually uniform']. Second, it is inconsistent with the draft conclusions on the identification of customary international law.[10]

There are several problems with these arguments for a higher numerical threshold. First, the comparison with customary international law, as already noted above, is inappropriate. Second, the reliance on the *North Sea Continental Shelf* cases is similarly improper. In response to these arguments, the Fifth Report stated as follows:

> [A]s is known, while it is true that the International Court in *North Sea Continental Shelf* cases referred to 'virtually uniform' for the purposes of customary international law, it is also true that the Court has also described the test using different phrases, which could be interpreted in different ways. Moreover, the phrase 'virtually uniform' in [the relevant passage of the decision] refers not to quantity, i.e. how many States, but rather to the quality, i.e., the type of practice. In other words, it [refers not to] how many States participated in the practice, but rather whether the practice of those States that did participate, however many, was uniform. In fact, the quantitative element in the *North Sea Continental Shelf* cases is 'extensive'.[11]

It is unsurprising that the term 'international community of States as a whole' has attracted such widely divergent interpretations. As noted in the Second

9 See, for discussion, id., para 90; See Israel, Comments and Observations (above note 2), 38; See also Russia, Comments and Observations (above note 2), 39.

10 The United States, Comments and Observations (above note 2), 45 (footnotes omitted).

11 Fifth Report (above note 5), para 90.

Report, the term has a rather obscure origin in Article 53.[12] Draft Article 50 of the ILC's Draft Articles on the Law of Treaties provided only that a norm of *jus cogens* is one 'from which no derogation is permitted', without including the element of acceptance and recognition by the international community of States as a whole.[13]

It was the United States that raised the question of acceptance and recognition, by proposing that *jus cogens* norms were those norms 'recognized in common by the national and regional legal systems of the world'.[14] It was in response to this proposal that Finland, Greece, and Spain proposed that *jus cogens* be understood as norms 'recognized by the international community' from which no derogation was permitted.[15] The word 'accepted' was inserted by the Drafting Committee because Article 38(1)(d) of the Statute of the ICJ uses both words.[16] The phrase 'as a whole', which was also not in the proposal of Finland, Greece, and Spain, was inserted by the Drafting Committee 'to indicate that no individual State should have the right of veto' with respect to the recognition of a norm as *jus cogens*.[17] In particular, the phrase was meant to indicate that acceptance and recognition did not have to include all States and that it would be sufficient if 'a very large majority' accepted and recognised the peremptory status of a norm.[18]

3. The Content of Draft Conclusion 6

Draft Conclusion 6

Acceptance and Recognition

1. The criterion of acceptance and recognition referred to in Draft Conclusion 4, subparagraph (b), is distinct from acceptance and recognition as a norm of general international law.

[12] Dire Tladi *Second Report of the Special Rapporteur on Peremptory Norms of General International Law (Jus Cogens)* (A/CN.4/706), para 65 *et seq.*

[13] Draft Article 50, Draft Articles on the Law of Treaties, *Yearbook of the International Law Commission*, 1966, Vol. II.

[14] Summary Records of the Plenary Meetings and of the Meetings of the Committee of the Whole, *Official Records of the United Nations Conference on the Law of Treaties, March–May 1963*, the United States (A/CONF.39/C.1/L.302), para 17.

[15] *Report of the Committee of the Whole on its work at the first session of the Conference*, Official Records of the United Nations Conference on the Law of Treaties (A/CONF.39/14), 1 May 1969, Finland, Greece, and Spain (A/CONF.39/C.1/L.306 and Add.l and 2).

[16] Drafting Committee, Law of Treaties, Statement by Mustafa Kamil Yaseen (A/CN.4/SR.839), 26 January 1966, para 4.

[17] Id., para 7.

[18] Id., para 12.

2. To identify a norm as a peremptory norm of general international law (*jus cogens*), there must be evidence that such a norm is accepted and recognised by the international community of States as a whole as a norm from which no derogation is permitted and which can only be modified by a subsequent norm of general international law having the same character.

According to the Statement of the Chair of the Drafting Committee, the 'basic thrust' of the original proposal of the Special Rapporteur is retained in the final text. However, the text of Draft Conclusion 6 is a significant departure from the text originally proposed in the Second Report of the Special Rapporteur. As originally proposed, Draft Conclusion 6 provided as follows:

1. A norm of general international law is identified as a *jus cogens* norm when it is accepted and recognized as a norm from which no derogation is permitted.
2. The requirement that a norm be accepted and recognized as one from which no derogation is permitted requires an assessment of the opinion of the international community of states as a whole.[19]

In the debate, many members of the Commission felt that the first paragraph of the proposed Draft Conclusion seemed to repeat what was contained in Draft Conclusion 4,[20] while there was some discomfort with the use of the

[19] See Second Report (above note 12), para 91.

[20] Rajput (A/CN.4/SR.3369), 8 ('Of the draft conclusions that related to acceptance and recognition, draft conclusion 6 did not seem to achieve much, other than to reiterate that there had to be recognition and acceptance by the international community as a whole ... Furthermore, given that draft conclusion 8 addressed recognition and acceptance, draft conclusion 6 was perhaps unnecessary and could be deleted'); Park (A/CN.4/SR.3369), 11 ('Draft conclusion 6 seemed to be redundant, because most of its contents were dealt with in draft conclusions 4, 7, 8 and 9. It should therefore be deleted. If there was a particular element in that draft conclusion which deserved emphasis, it could be added to draft conclusion 7, 8 or 9'); Murphy (A/CN.4/SR.3369), 16 ('He had no particular concerns about draft conclusion 6, which addressed the issue of acceptance and recognition. It did, however, include considerable repetition, especially in relation to draft conclusions 3, 4 and 8. Repetition was not necessarily problematic, but it could be confusing if different terms were used in very similar provisions. At a minimum, draft conclusions 6 and 8 could be combined into a single draft conclusion addressing all aspects of acceptance and recognition'); Hmoud (A/CN.4/SR.3370), 6 ('The draft conclusions contained some repetition and would need to be streamlined by the Drafting Committee'); Šturma (A/CN.4/3370), 14 ('He supported the substance of the other draft conclusions but agreed with Mr. Murphy's proposal to merge draft conclusions 6 and 8 into a single draft conclusion'); Lehto (A/CN.4/SR.3371), 7 ('she agreed that draft conclusions 6 and 8 could be merged'); Ruda Santolaria (A/CN.4/SR.3371), 14 ('as had been noted by other members, repetition could be avoided by merging some of the six draft conclusions: they could

word 'opinion' in the second paragraph.[21] On the basis of the debate in plenary, the Special Rapporteur produced a revised proposal for consideration by the Drafting Committee.[22] The idea behind the revised proposal was to take elements from Draft Conclusions 6 and 8 and merge them. The first paragraph would state, in general terms, that acceptance and recognition in the context of *jus cogens* is distinct from acceptance and recognition as general international law;[23] while paragraph 2 would state what had to be accepted and recognised for the purposes of *jus cogens*.

The first reading text adopted by the Commission is based largely on this revised proposal submitted to the Drafting Committee. The final reading, in turn, reproduces the first reading text with minor technical modifications to the first paragraph.[24]

The first paragraph captures the essence of the second criterion, namely that 'acceptance and recognition' as a criterion for *jus cogens* 'is distinct from acceptance and recognition as a norm of general international law'.[25] To further emphasise the distinction, the Commentary to Draft Conclusion 6 refers to the use of the words 'acceptance' and 'recognition' for the purposes of identification of general international law. The Commentary explains that 'acceptance as law (*opinio juris*)' is a constitutive element of customary international

be reduced to three without affecting the substance or diluting the Special Rapporteur's arguments'); Reinisch (A/CN.4/SR.3371), 15 ('draft conclusion 6 was an example of the duplication that might be remedied at the drafting stage. He did not see what it contained that had not already been said in draft conclusions 3 and 4); Peter (A/CN.4/SR.3373), 12 ('He wondered what fundamental difference, if any, there was between draft conclusions 4 and 6').

[21] See e.g. Murase (A/CN.4/SR.3369), 5 ('The Special Rapporteur referred to the "opinion" of the international community in draft conclusion 6 (2) and to the "attitude" of States in draft conclusion 7 (1), but opinions could change and attitudes were always ambiguous'); Rajput (A/CN.4/SR.3369), 8 ('The statement in draft conclusion 6 (2) that the requirement of recognition required "an assessment of the opinion of the international community of States as a whole" was, in his view, problematic and gave rise to a number of questions: What constituted an opinion? How was it to be assessed? Was it related to evidence contained in draft conclusion 9? Or did it require something more or something less?'); Peter (A/CN.4/SR.3373), 11 ('In that connection, the Special Rapporteur should specify who was expected to assess the opinion of the international community of States as a whole, as required in draft conclusion 6').

[22] Drafting Committee, Peremptory Norms of General International Law, Revised Proposal by the Special Rapporteur for the Draft Conclusions 6, 7, 9 ILC(LXIX)/DC/JC/WP.4, 20 July 2017.

[23] Id., para 1.

[24] The first paragraph of the first reading text provided as follows:

> '1. The requirements of "acceptance and recognition" as a criterion for identifying a peremptory norm of general international law (*jus cogens*) is distinct from acceptance and recognition as a norm of general international law.'

[25] While there was some reformulation of the first reading text, this was mainly technical changes for clarity which do not affect the substance at all.

law, which concerns the question of whether States accept a practice as a rule of law.[26] In the same vein, the Commentary explains that recognition for the purposes of identifying general principles of law addresses the question of whether a principle has been recognised as a principle of law within the meaning of Article 38(1)(c) of the Statute of the International Court of Justice.[27] The Commentary then explains that acceptance and recognition 'referred to in Draft Conclusion 6 is qualitatively different' and rather concerns 'the question whether the international community of States as a whole' recognises that norm as having achieved the status of *jus cogens*.[28]

The second paragraph describes how the second criterion is to be shown to have been met. It states that in order to show 'acceptance and recognition', 'there must be evidence' that the norm in question is one 'accepted and recognised by the international community of States as a whole' as having a peremptory character. The emphasis here is that it is not sufficient merely to allege that a norm has peremptory status. Evidence to that effect has to be adduced. The type of evidence required is the subject of Draft Conclusions 8 and 9, and is addressed in Chapter 7. The requirement for evidence does not mean, however, that the assertions by States unsupported by evidence are without any weight. Such assertions, though not conclusive of the existence of *jus cogens*, will constitute evidence of acceptance and recognition by those States, which when taken together with the acceptance and recognition of other States, contribute to the identification of *jus cogens*.[29] In this context, and in response to the comments by Italy and France, the Fifth Report of the Special Rapporteur made the following observation:

> [I]t suffices to say that ... the impression should not be created that 'any assertion made ... between States ... as to the *jus cogens* nature of a given norm would be devoid of legal value, if not accompanied by relevant evidence'. Quite the contrary, any such assertion by a State would be evidence that *those* States (*sic*) accept and/or recognise the norm as *jus cogens*. If evidence can be provided of a similar inclination by a 'large majority of States', that would indicate that the norm has attained peremptory status.[30]

[26] See para 2 of the Commentary to Draft Conclusion 6.
[27] Id.
[28] Id.
[29] See para 5 of Commentary to Draft Conclusion 6.
[30] Fifth Report (above note 5), para 79.

4. The Content of Draft Conclusion 7

Draft Conclusion 7
International Community of States as a Whole

1. It is the acceptance and recognition by the international community of States as a whole that is relevant for the identification of peremptory norms of general international law (*jus cogens*).
2. Acceptance and recognition by a very large and representative majority of States is required for the identification of a norm as a peremptory norm of general international law (*jus cogens*); acceptance and recognition by all States is not required.
3. While the position of other actors may be relevant in providing context and for assessing acceptance and recognition by the international community of States as a whole, these positions cannot, in and of themselves, form part of such acceptance and recognition.

While Draft Conclusion 6 describes the content of acceptance and recognition, Draft Conclusion 7 seeks to explain what is meant by the phrase 'international community of States as a whole'. Draft Conclusion 7 contains three paragraphs. The first and third paragraphs describe the role of various actors relevant to the determination of the 'international community of States as a whole', in the identification of *jus cogens* norms, while the second paragraph describes the threshold for the same.

The first paragraph seeks to emphasise that it is the position of States that is relevant for the determination of *jus cogens* norms and not that of other actors.[31] The Commentary recognises that in recent times there have been calls for greater contributions to law-making by actors other than States, and recalls in this connection that when elaborating the Articles on the Law of Treaties between States and International Organizations or between International Organizations, it had considered using the phrase 'international community as a whole' instead of 'international community of States as a whole'.[32] It is noteworthy that in the debate on the Second Report, not a single member of the Commission opposed the basic proposition that it was the position of States that mattered. Indeed, at least one member thought

[31] See para 3 of the Commentary to Draft Conclusion 7.
[32] Id.

the provision proposed by the Special Rapporteur—which was retained save for the deletion of a sentence that referred to 'attitude of States'—should be strengthened 'to indicate that it was the acceptance and recognition *by States alone* that created *jus cogens* norms, and that attitudes of non-State actors could not provide a basis'.[33] The comments by States similarly supported the idea that it was the acceptance and recognition of States that mattered.[34] The first paragraph of Draft Conclusion 7 was thus not controversial at all.

The Commentary to Draft Conclusion 7 provides support for the proposition that it is the position of States that matters in the form of State practice and decisions of international courts and tribunals.[35]

While paragraph 1 put forward the idea that it is the position of States that matters in the identification of *jus cogens*, paragraph 3 qualifies this somewhat by stating that 'the positions of other actors may be relevant in providing context, and for assessing acceptance and recognition' by States. The view that the positions of other actors may be relevant for providing context was supported both within the Commission and by States. Cyprus, for example, while accepting that 'the main entities whose acceptance and recognition are relevant' for *jus cogens* 'are States' noted that the role of other actors ought not to be disregarded.[36] Yet, at least one

[33] Hassouna (Chair) (A/CN.4/SR.3370), 10 (emphasis added).

[34] See e.g. Peremptory Norm of General International Law (*Jus Cogens*): Cuba, Comments and Observations received from Governments (A/C.6/74/SR.25), October 2019, para 18; Peremptory Norm of General International Law (*Jus Cogens*): Cameroon, Comments and Observations received from Governments (A/C.6/74/SR.27), October 2019, para 57; Argentina, Comments and Observations (above note 2), 7; Brazil, Comments and Observations (above note 2), 93; the Czech Republic, Comments and Observations (above note 2), 6; France, Comments and Observations (above note 2), 38 ('Given the nature of *jus cogens* norms, it seems reasonable, in the view of France, to rule out the possibility of entities other than States (and, to a lesser extent, international organizations), having a role, even a subsidiary one, in the determination of such norms'); Germany, Comments and Observations (above note 2), 38 ('Germany welcomes the clarification in draft conclusion 7 that it is the acceptance and recognition of the international community *of States* as a whole which is relevant'); Japan, Comments and Observations (above note 2), 39; The Netherlands, Comments and Observations (above note 2), 40; Slovenia, Comments and Observations (above note 2), 42; Spain, Comments and Observations (above note 2), 43; United Kingdom, Comments and Observations (above note 2), 43; the United States, Comments and Observations (above note 2), 44.

[35] See para 4 of the Commentary to Draft Conclusion 7; As examples of decisions of international courts and tribunals, the Commentaries refer to *Prosecutor v Katanga Decision on the Application for the Interim Release of Detained Witnesses*, ICC-01/04-01/07-34-05-tENg, 1 October 2013, Trial Chamber II, International Criminal Court, para 30, where the Court states that the peremptory character of non-refoulment 'finds increasing recognition among States' and *Questions relating to the Obligation to Prosecute or Extradite (Belgium v Senegal)*, Judgment, *ICJ Reports* 2012, p. 422, para 99, where the Court referred exclusively to materials reflecting positions of States when identifying the prohibition of torture as *jus cogens*.

[36] Cyprus, Comments and Observations (above note 2), 37; See also Germany, Comments and Observations (above note 2), 38, (which, while also expressing support for the primary role of States,

State—France—seemed to suggest that even the limited role of providing context should be ruled out.[37]

It will not be lost on the reader that paragraph 3 is crafted in rather negative terms. While it positively asserts that the position of other actors is relevant for context and assessment of the acceptance and recognition of States, the accent falls heavily on the qualifier, namely that 'these positions [of other actors] cannot, in and of themselves, form part of such acceptance and recognition'. Indeed, even the relevant part of the Commentary ends on that note.[38]

Two further points can be made about paragraph 3. First, neither the text nor the Commentary explains what is meant by 'providing context' and 'assessing' the acceptance and recognition of States. The best explanation for the phrase 'providing context and for assessing acceptance and recognition', is that such other positions may be used as 'subsidiary means' to support the peremptory status of particular norms. Indeed, the Commentary, in providing justification for this role, uses the words 'subsidiary role'.[39] In fact, for this same reason, there had been a proposal to move paragraph 3 of Draft Conclusion 7 to become part of Draft Conclusion 9 on subsidiary means for the identification of *jus cogens*.[40] It was, however, retained in Draft Conclusion 7 because the paragraph did not concern the materials that are relevant but rather the entities that count.[41]

The more complex issue in Draft Conclusion 7, addressed in paragraph 2, concerns the threshold of support for acceptance and recognition. The Second Report had proposed 'a large majority' as the threshold for the 'international community of States as a whole'.[42] Many members of the Commission thought

stated 'the positions of other States may be relevant only for providing context and assessing' the positions of States); similarly, the Netherlands, Comments and Observations (above note 2), 40, stated that 'the opinions of other actors, such as international organisations, are relevant but not decisive'.

[37] France, Comments and Observations (above note 2), 38 ('it seems reasonable ... to rule out the possibility of entities other than States ... having a role, *even a subsidiary one*, in the determination' of peremptory status).

[38] See para 5 of the Commentary to Draft Conclusion 7 ('Ultimately, however, the positions of entities other States are not, of themselves, sufficient to establish acceptance and recognition required for the elevation of a norm of general international law to peremptory status. This consideration is reflected in paragraph 3 of Draft Conclusion 7').

[39] Id. ('Other actors may provide context and may contribute to the assessment of the acceptance and recognition by the international community of States as a whole. The *subsidiary role* of other actors has been recognised by the Commission in other topics'.)

[40] See e.g. the United Kingdom, Comments and Observations (above note 2), 44; Spain, Comments and Observations (above note 2), 43.

[41] The Fifth Report (above note 5), para 95, while seeing the logic of the suggestion, did not make a proposal to shift para 7 because para 3 could 'fit comfortably in either Draft Conclusion 9 or Draft Conclusion 7'.

[42] See Second Report (above note 12), para 91.

this threshold was too low.[43] The members that questioned the threshold pointed to the fact that the Second Report itself based its reference to the threshold on the statement of the Chair of the Drafting Committee in 1966, which had referred to 'a very large majority'.[44] It was on this basis that the Commission decided, for the first reading text, to refer to 'a very large majority' as the threshold for 'international community of States'.[45]

Yet even this increase in the threshold would be met with criticism by States commenting on the first reading text. Some States believed that even the threshold of 'very large majority' was not sufficiently high, while others believed that the focus on majority placed too much emphasis on numbers.[46]

[43] See e.g. Murase (A/CN.4/SR.3369), 5 ('He personally would favour a more balanced formula requiring the consent of virtually all States in order for a *jus cogens* norm to be identified as such.'); Rajput (A/CN.4/SR.3369), 8 ('To his mind, the word "whole" meant the entire international community, not just a large majority of States. If acceptance and recognition were required from only a "large majority of States", then *jus cogens* norms would be no different than customary international law, evidence of which also required a large majority'); Murphy (A/CN.4/SR.3370), 3 ('Moreover, it was inadequate to assert in draft conclusion 7(3) that "a large majority of States" was sufficient for the identification of a norm as a norm of *jus cogens*, since the threshold should be much higher. It would be more appropriate to refer to "a very large majority", "substantially all States" or "virtually all States" '); Nolte, as Chairperson (A/CN.4/SR.3370), 7 ('he was surprised that the Special Rapporteur considered a "large majority" sufficient to establish the requisite *opinio juris cogentis*. That was all the more surprising because, in paragraph 67 of the report, the Special Rapporteur explained that the reference to the international community of States "as a whole" had been used in article 53 of the Vienna Convention as the equivalent of "a very large majority" of States'); Šturma (A/CN.4/SR.3370), 14 (with regard to Draft Conclusion 7(3), he supported the wording 'a very large majority of States'); Lehto (A/CN.4/SR.3372), 7 ('In paragraph 3, the phrase "a large majority" should be amended to read "a very large majority", in line with the statement by the Chairman of the Drafting Committee at the Vienna Conference referred to in paragraph 67 of the report'); Ruda Santolaria (A/CN.4/SR.3372), 14 ('In draft conclusion 7 (3), "large majority" should be replaced with "overwhelming majority" '); Reinisch (A/CN.4/SR.3372), 16 ('Draft conclusion 7 raised the threshold question: how many States had to accept a norm as *jus cogens* in order for it to qualify as having gained the acceptance of the international community of States as a whole? Paragraph 3 should be clarified by a comparison of the high threshold of acceptance required for a norm to qualify as *jus cogens* with the lower threshold for the emergence of customary norms or general principles of law. It might also be prudent to clarify the fact that the required majority must be something like the "very large majority" described by the Chairman of the Drafting Committee at the Vienna Conference, as cited in paragraph 67 of the report'); Oral (A/CN.4/SR.3373), 10 ('As to draft conclusion 7 (3), which related to the term "international community of States as a whole", she agreed with previous speakers who had said that acceptance and recognition by "a very large majority" of States should be required, in line with paragraph 67 of the report'); Ouazzani-Chahdi (A/CN.4/SR.3373), 13 ('He endorsed the Special Rapporteur's analysis of recognition and acceptance as the second criterion for *jus cogens*, while noting that the bar should perhaps be set higher and another formula should be found to replace the "majority of States" requirement referred to in paragraph 67 of the report and in draft conclusion 7(3)').

[44] Second Report (above note 12), para 67 ('The Chairman of the Drafting Committee explained that the insertion of the words "as a whole" was meant to indicate that it was not necessary for the peremptory nature of the norm in question "to be accepted and recognized by all States" and that it would be sufficient if "a very large majority did so" ').

[45] Special Rapporteur (Tladi) (A/CN.4/SR.3374), 9 ('Observing that many members had expressed concern that the word "very" had been deleted in draft conclusion 7 (3), he said that the phrase "a large majority" had not been intended to signify a less-than-substantial majority. He would therefore be amenable to the proposal to revert to the phrase initially proposed by the Chairman of the Drafting Committee at the Vienna Conference').

[46] See discussion in Section 2 above.

It was in particular because of the criticism that too much emphasis was placed on quantity that the Commission adopted the phrase 'a very large and representative majority'. While there had been suggestions within the Drafting Committee to provide clarification to the meaning of 'representative' in this context, the Committee decided that this was a matter best left for the Commentaries.[47] To this end, the Commentary to Draft Conclusion 7 states that determining whether a very large majority exists is not 'a mechanical exercise in which the number of States [is] counted'.[48] Rather than a qualitative exercise, the assessment of whether the international community of States as a whole accepted and recognised the peremptory status of a norm required a qualitative assessment.[49] According to the Commentary:

> [t]he idea that what is required is a qualitative assessment is captured by the word 'representative' to qualify a 'majority of States'. The acceptance and recognition by the international community of States as a whole requires that the acceptance and recognition be across regions, legal systems, and cultures.[50]

Draft Conclusion 7 thus requires, first, that a very large majority of States accept and recognise the peremptory status of a norm. Second, because a purely quantitative assessment would be inadequate,[51] the Draft Conclusion requires that the very large majority must be representative of different regions, legal systems, and cultures of the world.

The threshold put forward in Draft Conclusion 7 and as explained in the Commentary is open-ended. This open-endedness ought to allow a court, any court, charged with determining the existence of a norm of *jus cogens*, a degree of flexibility and discretion in applying the standard to particular facts. As with open-ended concepts like reasonableness and foreseeability it would be unwise to set in stone a threshold which would prevent a decision-maker taking into account relevant circumstances. Indeed, customary international law, and the question whether there exists a widespread and general practice, is itself open-textured, permitting flexibility.

[47] Peremptory Norms of General International Law (*Jus Cogens*), Statement of the Chair of the Drafting Committee, Ki Gab Park, 17 May 2022, 9.
[48] Paragraph 7 of the Commentary to Draft Conclusion 7.
[49] Id.
[50] Id., para 8.
[51] See, for discussion, Dire Tladi 'The ILC's Draft Conclusion on Peremptory Norms of General International Law: Special Reflections of the Special Rapporteur' (2019) 24 *Austrian Review of International and European Law* 121, 133.

Yet, from the perspective of others, the lack of clarity is dangerous and opens *jus cogens* up to abuse. In a private discussion, one delegate (post adoption of the Draft Conclusions) posed the following question: is the import of Draft Conclusion 7, and its reference to 'very large majority' as the threshold for acceptance and recognition by the international community of States as a whole, that 120 States, which is arguably a very large majority of States, can establish a *jus cogens* norm at the objection of seventy plus States.

In fact, this example illustrates the dangers of focusing too much on the quantity of States. The answer to the question whether the evidence that 120 States accept and recognise the peremptory status of a norm ought to be 'it depends'. In some instances evidence of acceptance and recognition by 120 States will be sufficient and in other instances it will not be sufficient. Writing after the adoption of the first reading text, the Special Rapporteur provided the following illustration of how the qualitative threshold described in Draft Conclusion 7 and its Commentary could operate and how imposing a specific numerical threshold would be damaging:

> An example to explain the problem with a definitive figure might be warranted. Imagine a rule (rule x). Evidence ... can be found in which 180 States have expressed *opinio juris cogentis* (acceptance and recognition). Yet 12 States have vehemently rejected the peremptory status of that same rule. Now imagine another rule (rule y). Evidence ... signifying the *opinio juris cogentis* of only a hundred States can be found. Yet rule y has been communicated in public forums, in debates in diplomatic correspondence without a single State expressing an objection or questioning its peremptory status. All things being equal, the claim to peremptory status of rule y would appear to be stronger than the claim of rule x even though there is qualitatively more evidence of support for rule x than rule y.[52]

5. Concluding Observations

One of the central contributions of these Draft Conclusions is the methodology for identification of *jus cogens*. Of the provisions relevant to identification, the most important are concerned with the second criterion, namely acceptance and recognition, in Draft Conclusions 6 and 7. It is these provisions

[52] Id.

that give *jus cogens* its special character. It is thus unsurprising that these provisions have attracted a significant amount of attention from States.

The most contentious aspect of the second criterion is the threshold necessary for acceptance and recognition. The Commission chose to adopt an open-ended provision to address the threshold. While this choice is accepted by the majority of States, quite a number of States continued to express concern about what is seen as a low threshold.[53] How the Draft Conclusions considered in this chapter are received in practice in the future may well determine the impact of the Draft Conclusions as a whole.

[53] See e.g. Singapore, Sixth Committee of the General Assembly, Seventy-Seventh Session, 25 October 2022 ('my delegation notes with appreciation the Commission's incorporation in Draft Conclusion 7 our comment that, in determining whether there is a "very large majority" of States ... a "large and representative majority of States is required." That said, my delegation continues to take the view that referring to the international community "as a whole" has qualitative as well qualitative elements, and that the term "virtually all States" is required the requisite qualitative meaning').

7
The Second Criterion
Evidence of Acceptance and Recognition

1. Introduction

The second criterion for identification of *jus cogens* is that the norm in question must be accepted and recognised by the international community of States as a whole as a norm from which no derogation is permitted and which can only be modified by a subsequent norm of general international law having the same quality. The main components of this composite criterion, namely 'acceptance and recognition' and 'the international community of States as a whole', are the subject of Draft Conclusions 6 and 7 which were addressed in Chapter 6.

But how are we to determine whether this composite criterion has been met? How are we to determine whether the international community of States as a whole recognises the peremptory character of a norm? Put differently, what evidence is to be used to make the assessment required for the second criterion? This question of evidence is addressed in Draft Conclusions 8 and 9 and is the subject of this chapter. The Draft Conclusions identify two types of evidence: the primary forms of evidence and subsidiary means. The chapter will address them both.

Section 2 provides a general overview of the contestations surrounding 'evidence'. In particular it will address the balance struck by the Commission between materials emanating from the State and those from non-State actors in the identification of *jus cogens*. Needless to say, this balance is relevant for the underlying tension in the Commission's work—the consensualist tradition versus the pull for a non-consensualist approach. Thereafter Section 3 will provide a description of the text of Draft Conclusion 8, while Section 4 will provide a description of the text of Draft Conclusion 9. Finally, Section 5 will offer final observations.

2. Discussion

What evidence is required to show that a norm has peremptory character would invariably depend on the source of acceptance and recognition, i.e.

whose acceptance and recognition was relevant for the purposes of the second criterion. In other words, once the Commission made the choice that it was the acceptance and recognition of the international community *of States* as a whole that was sought (Draft Conclusion 7), and that this meant that it was the position of States that was relevant (Draft Conclusion 7, para 1), it became self-evident that the evidence for acceptance and recognition would have to be found in materials capable of expressing the views or positions of States.[1] Given the overwhelming support for the 'international community of States as a whole' as the relevant element of the second criterion, it is unsurprising that the evidence for acceptance and recognition was generally uncontroversial in the work of the Commission.

The Second Report noted that the International Court of Justice, in *Questions relating to the Obligation to Prosecute or Extradite*, when identifying the prohibition of torture as a norm of *jus cogens*, only referred to State-developed instruments.[2] The Court referred to 'international instruments of universal application', such as the Universal Declaration of Human Rights, the Geneva Conventions of 1949, the International Covenant on Civil and Political Rights, and General Assembly Resolution 3452 (XXX).[3] It also referred to the fact that the prohibition in question was incorporated 'into the domestic law of almost all States'.[4]

Yet, some members questioned whether the oft-quoted extract from the judgment of the International Court of Justice really concerns acceptance and recognition under the second criterion or whether, rather, the Court was referring to evidence of *opinio juris sive necessitatis* (or acceptance of practice as a rule of customary international law)—the first criterion. The exchange in the debate within the Commission, in which Mr Forteau and Mr Jalloh were the main protagonists, is revealing:[5]

> **Mr. Jalloh** said that, in the second sentence of paragraph (2), the reference to 'a wide range of forms' was unclear. It might be helpful to insert after that sentence a quotation from paragraph 99 of the judgment of the International

[1] Dire Tladi *Second Report of the Special Rapporteur on Peremptory Norms of General International Law (Jus Cogens)* (A/CN.4/706), para 79 ('With regard to the nature of the materials that may be used to show acceptance and recognition, it is worth recalling that the phrase "international community of States as a whole" implies that it is the "acceptance and recognition" of States that is at issue. As such, it is materials that are capable of expressing the views of States that are relevant').

[2] *Questions relating to the Obligation to Prosecute or Extradite (Belgium v Senegal)*, Judgment, *ICJ Reports* 2012, p. 422, para 99.

[3] Id.

[4] Id.

[5] Forteau, Jalloh *et al.* (A/CN.4/SR.3596), 7–10.

Court of Justice in the case concerning *Questions relating to the Obligation to Prosecute or Extradite (Belgium v. Senegal)*, which would read: 'That prohibition is grounded in a widespread international practice and on the *opinio juris* of States. It appears in numerous international instruments of universal application (in particular the Universal Declaration of Human Rights of 1948, the 1949 Geneva Conventions for the protection of war victims; the International Covenant on Civil and Political Rights of 1966; General Assembly resolution 3452/30 of 9 December 1975 on the Protection of All Persons from Being Subjected to Torture and Other Cruel, Inhuman or Degrading Treatment or Punishment), and it has been introduced into the domestic law of almost all States; finally, acts of torture are regularly denounced within national and international fora.'

Mr. Forteau said that, in the quotation cited by Mr. Jalloh, the Court had not made clear whether it was establishing that the prohibition of torture was a norm of customary international law or a peremptory norm. In that particular passage, the Court appeared to be establishing the customary character of the prohibition more than its peremptory character. He was therefore not in favour of including the quotation in the commentary. The end of the third sentence of paragraph (2) should be redrafted to read 'as evidence of the prohibition of torture, which the Court characterized as a peremptory norm of general international law (*jus cogens*)'.

The Chair,[6] speaking as a member of the Commission, said that in his view Mr. Forteau's proposal would accurately reflect what the Court had done.

Mr. Jalloh said that paragraph 99 of the Court's judgment stated very clearly, which materials it had relied on in reaching its conclusion. The Universal Declaration of Human Rights and the Geneva Conventions were considered to be customary international law.

The Chair, speaking as a member of the Commission, said that the question was whether the Court had referred to those materials as evidence of the peremptory character of the prohibition of torture.

Mr. Tladi (Special Rapporteur) said that the Commission had debated the same point in 2017. On that occasion, while some members had interpreted paragraph 99 of the judgment in one particular way, the view that had inspired the current text, namely that the Court had used the materials it had

[6] The Chair in this instance was Mr Wood, since the Chair of the Commission was also Special Rapporteur for the topic.

cited to substantiate its claim that the prohibition of torture was a norm of customary international law that had become a *jus cogens* norm, had received overwhelming support. He had chosen not to include the quotation proposed by Mr. Jalloh purely because of its length, but he would be in favour of adding it.

The Chair, speaking as a member of the Commission and supported by Mr. Grossman Guiloff, said that the third sentence of paragraph (2), which included a footnote referring to paragraph 99 of the Court's judgment, should be left unchanged.

Mr. Murphy said that, perhaps the Commission could reconcile the different views expressed by deleting the words 'as evidence of the peremptory character of the prohibition of torture' and replacing them with the phrase 'when stating that, "[i]n [its] opinion, the prohibition of torture is part of customary international law and it has become a peremptory norm (*jus cogens*)" '.

Mr. Jalloh proposed that the entirety of paragraph 99 of the judgment should be quoted in footnote 108.

Mr. Forteau said he was surprised that some members wished to impose a particular interpretation of the Court's judgment at all costs. Paragraph 99 of the judgment referred only to the evidence in support of the two constituent elements of international custom, as shown by the sentence immediately preceding the list of forms of evidence; it said nothing about evidence substantiating the peremptory character of the prohibition of torture and was thus, ambiguous. Mr. Murphy's proposal was therefore a good compromise solution.

Mr. Tladi (Special Rapporteur) suggested that, in order to move forward, the Commission should adopt Mr. Murphy's proposal in part, incorporating the first sentence of paragraph 99 into the text of the commentary but citing the rest of paragraph 99 in the footnote. Considerations of length had been behind his decision not to include the full text suggested by Mr. Jalloh. However, it was not the length of paragraph 99 but rather differences of opinion as to its meaning that had fuelled the current discussion. In the light of the views expressed, and to be faithful to the Court's decision, he had concluded that paragraph 99 should be cited in its entirety to ensure that all members' positions were taken into account.

Mr. Jalloh said that while it was still not clear to him why the entire text could not be incorporated into the commentary itself, in deference to his colleagues, he would accept the compromise proposed by the Special Rapporteur.

Mr. Grossman Guiloff said he agreed that paragraph 99 of the Court's judgment should be cited verbatim in the footnote.

Mr. Saboia said that he supported Mr. Jalloh's proposal, as modified by Mr. Murphy and the Special Rapporteur.

The tension underlying this discussion concerned mainly how resolutions of international organisations ought to be reflected, and will be discussed further below.[7] However, for the purposes of the present discussion, it is sufficient to state only that in 2017, five years before this debate, the Second Report had already noted the ambiguity of the Court's remarks. The Second Report observed that the 'Court is not explicit about whether it is [here] describing *opinio juris cogentis* or *opinio juris*'.[8] The Report notes the possibility that the Court may have conflated the two types of acceptance.[9]

In a sense, however, the debate is a red herring. Whether, in *Questions relating to the Obligation to Prosecute or Extradite*, the Court was referring to *opinio juris sive necessitatis* or *opinio juris cogentis*, is immaterial. What the cited extract illustrates is that, to find the positions of States, what is relevant is State-developed materials.[10] As discussed in the context of Draft Conclusion 6 (see Chapter 6), the difference between the two types of *opinio* is not the form in which they appear (or the evidence), but rather the content, or what they evince.[11] For the former, it is the acceptance of a norm as a rule of law, and for the latter it is the acceptance of a norm (with a quality of law) as one from which no derogation is permitted.

Thus, the approach proposed by the Special Rapporteur, and eventually accepted by the Commission, followed closely (although not exactly), the approach adopted by the Commission for evidence of *opinio juris* in the Draft Conclusions on the Identification of Customary International Law.[12] The suggestion that the evidence relevant for the identification of the peremptory status of a norm is the same as that for customary international law was criticised by only one member:

[7] This background is not reflected in the summary records but was discussed in the Drafting Committee.

[8] Second Report (above note 1), para 81.

[9] Id.

[10] Second Report (above note 1), para 81 ('Alternatively, the Court implies that the materials relevant for assessing "normal" *opinio juris* are the same materials that are relevant for assessing whether the international community of States as a whole has accepted and recognized the peremptory nature of a norm').

[11] Second Report (above note 1), 77.

[12] Draft Conclusions on the Identification of Customary International Law, *Report of the International Law Commission, Seventieth Session* (A/73/10), Draft Conclusion 10.

In Draft Conclusion 9(2),[13] the Special Rapporteur enumerated materials that might provide evidence of *jus cogens*. Those materials were, however, the same as the ones used to identify a normal rule of customary international law. If the Commission wished to prove that such a rule had been elevated to the status of *jus cogens*, it would have to use qualitatively different materials in order to avoid double counting.[14]

The following was offered in response:

One member had suggested that [the approach] was interesting but artificial and amounted to double counting ... The proposed approach could only be seen as double counting if the fact that the two steps were qualitatively different was ignored. In the first step, one was searching for the existence of law, most often customary international law, while in the second, what was at issue was the peremptory character of the rule or norm. It would be double counting only if, in that second stage, it were sufficient to show that a rule was accepted and recognised as having the quality of law.[15]

On this basis, the approach adopted in the Customary International Law Draft Conclusions was followed.

As in the case of identification of customary international law, the Draft Conclusions adopted the approach that other materials, not reflecting the views of States, may also be relevant as subsidiary means. In practice, of course, decisions of international courts and tribunals, in particular the International Court of Justice, and the work of the International Law Commission tend to be regarded as more than 'subsidiary'.[16] This raised the question of whether, in particular, the International Court of Justice should be treated as more than just a subsidiary source.

The Second Report attempted a slightly nuanced approach to the treatment of other materials. With respect to the decisions of international courts and tribunals, the Second Report proposed to qualify their use with 'may also serve' but without referring to them as subsidiary or secondary.[17] This usage

[13] What is currently Draft Conclusion 8 was Draft Conclusion 9 in the proposal in the Second Report.
[14] Murase (A/CN.4/SR.3369), 5.
[15] Tladi (Special Rapporteur) (A/CN.4/SR.3374), 5.
[16] See, for discussion of the frequent reference to decisions of international courts, Second Report (above note 1), para 85. See also para 86, and the accompanying footnotes, for frequent references to the work of the International Law Commission on the peremptory status of norms.
[17] Second Report (above note 1), para 91 (Proposed Draft Conclusion 9(3): 'Judgments and decisions of international courts and tribunals may also serve as evidence of acceptance and recognition for the purposes of identifying a norm as *jus cogens* norm of international law').

of 'may also serve' implies, without explicitly so stating, a secondary status. It was in respect of '[o]ther materials, such as the work of the International Law Commission' that the words 'secondary means' were used.[18] In general, members of the Commission expressed the view that it should be made clear that materials coming from non-State sources ought to be secondary or subsidiary.[19]

3. The Content of Draft Conclusion 8

Draft Conclusion 8
Evidence of Acceptance and Recognition

1. Evidence of acceptance and recognition that a norm of general international law is a peremptory norm (*jus cogens*) may take a wide variety of forms.
2. Forms of evidence include, but are not limited to: public statements made on behalf of States; official publications; governmental legal opinions; diplomatic correspondence; constitutional provisions; legislative and administrative acts; decisions of national courts; treaty provisions; resolutions adopted by an international organisation or at an intergovernmental conference; and other conduct of States.

The text of Draft Conclusion 8 follows closely Draft Conclusion 10 of the ILC's Draft Conclusions on the Identification of Customary International Law. The first paragraph remained unchanged from the first reading and is virtually identical to the first paragraph of Draft Conclusion 10 of the Customary International Law Draft Conclusions. The second paragraph was modified at second reading. Moreover, both the first and the second reading versions of the second paragraph were different from the customary international law version.[20]

[18] Id. (see Proposed Draft Conclusion 9(4)).

[19] Reinisch (A/CN.4/SR.3372), 15 ('The wording of the draft conclusion suggested that the pronouncements of international courts and tribunals were on the same plane as the positions of States themselves').

[20] Draft Conclusions on Customary International Law (above note 12), 140 ('Forms of evidence of acceptance as law (*opinion juris*) include, but are not limited to: public statements made on behalf of States; official publications; government legal opinions, diplomatic correspondence; decisions of

The first paragraph, like its customary international law counterpart, simply provides that the forms of evidence of acceptance and recognition 'may take a variety of forms'. The statement is presented as a statement of fact. The statement in the first paragraph was justified on the basis of the International Court of Justice's oft-cited quote in *Questions relating to the Obligation to Prosecute or Extradite*, where the Court referred to numerous instruments, including resolutions of international organisations.[21] Yet, as the description of the debate above illustrates, not everyone in the Commission believed that the cited text concerned evidence of acceptance and recognition as a criterion for peremptory norms. Rather, these members took the view that the Court was referring to *opinio juris sive necessitatis*.[22] As a compromise, the Commentary adopts an ambiguous approach, citing the chapeau of the judgment in quotation marks, which refers to both customary international law and *jus cogens*,[23] and placing the rest of the text in the footnote.[24] As stated above, the debate is much ado about nothing since the Commission had agreed that the materials relevant for acceptance for the purposes of customary international law are the same as the materials relevant for acceptance and recognition for the purposes of *jus cogens*.[25]

The second paragraph created a more substantive debate. The text adopted on first reading provided as follows:

> Such forms of evidence include, but are not limited to: public statements made on behalf of States; official publications; government legal opinions; diplomatic correspondence; legislative and administrative acts; decisions of national courts; treaty provisions; and resolutions adopted by an international organization or at an intergovernmental conference.[26]

national courts; treaty provisions; and conduct in connection with resolutions adopted by an international organization or at an intergovernmental conference.')

21 *Questions relating to the Obligation to Prosecute or Extradite* (above note 2), para 99.

22 See discussion in Section 2 above.

23 *Questions relating to the Obligation to Prosecute or Extradite* (above note 2), chapeau of para 99 ('In its judgment in *Questions relating to the Obligation to Prosecute or Extradite*, the International Court of Justice relied on a variety of means when stating that, "[i]n [its] opinion the prohibition of torture is part of customary international law and it has become a peremptory norm"').

24 Id. (The footnote states 'Paragraph 99 continued: "that prohibition is grounded in widespread practice and in the *opinio juris* of States . . ."' and continued with the rest of the quote that set out the relevant materials.)

25 See para 2 of the Commentary to Draft Conclusion 8.

26 Dire Tladi *Fifth Report of the Special Rapporteur on Peremptory Norms of General International Law (Jus Cogens)* (A/CN.4/747), 34.

Commenting on the first reading text, several States made particular reference to the resolutions of international organisations. Some of these comments were not substantive and reflected drafting choices. For example, El Salvador suggested that specific mention be made of resolutions adopted by regional organisations.[27] More substantive was the view that Draft Conclusion 8 should not refer to 'resolutions of international organisations' but rather to '*conduct of States in relation* to [or in connection with] resolutions'.[28] Different reasons were put forward for this observation. The first was that decisions or resolutions of international organisations as distinct legal entities did not necessarily reflect the position of States, and that if what was at stake was the position of States, then it was not sufficient to merely refer to resolutions.[29] The second reason provided was that by linking the relevance of resolutions to the conduct of States, Draft Conclusion 8 would be more consistent with the Draft Conclusions on the Identification of Customary International Law.[30]

The view that what matters is not the resolutions themselves but the conduct of States in connection with the resolutions would make the identification of *jus cogens* more dependent on the *practice* of States, rather than on the opinion or position of States. It would place a greater emphasis on what States do and 'action on the ground' rather than the legal view of States. This position would, for example, discount Human Rights Council Resolution 49/28, in which the Human Rights Council accepted and recognised the right of self-determination as a norm of *jus cogens*.[31] On the other hand, referring simply to

[27] Peremptory Norm of General International Law (*Jus Cogens*): El Salvador, Comments and Observations received from Governments (A/CN.4/748), March 2022, 46; Colombia, at 45 (raising questions on whether resolutions of international organisations 'could meet this threshold').

[28] Germany, Comments and Observations (above note 27), 46; Italy, Comments and Observations (above note 27), 49; Russian Federation, Comments and Observations (above note 27), 50; United Kingdom, Comments and Observations (above note 27), 51; the United States, Comments and Observations (above note 27), 51 *et seq*. See also the Comments by France, Commentaires et observations de la République française relatifs aux projets de conclusions de la commission de droit international sur les normes imperatives du droit international général (*jus cogens*), which were not reproduced in A/CN.4/748 but can be found on the website of the Commission https://legal.un.org/ilc/sessions/73/pdfs/french/jc_france.pdf (accessed 22 September 2022), 23.

[29] Italy, Comment and Observations (above note 27), 49 ('In the view of Italy, the above is necessary because oftentimes the resolutions as such are attributable to the international organisation as a distinct legal subject and *per se* cannot constitute evidence of the "acceptance and recognition" by the member States of the relevant international organisations').

[30] Germany, Comments and Observations (above note 27), 46; the United Kingdom, Comments and Observations (above note 27), 51; the United States, Comments and Observations (above note 27), 51 *et seq*.

[31] Human Rights Council Resolution 49/28 of 11 April 2022, preambular para 7 ('Reaffirming the right of the Palestinian people to self-determination in accordance with the provisions of the Charter, relevant United Nations resolutions and declarations, and the provisions of international covenants and instruments relating to the right to self-determination as an international principle and as a right of all peoples in the world, and emphasizing that this *jus cogens* norm of international law is a basic prerequisite for achieving a just, lasting and comprehensive peace in the Middle East').

resolutions, as the first reading text did, would mean that this resolution could be used as evidence. Of course, even under the construction of the first reading text, the resolution would not be conclusive of the peremptory status of the right of self-determination. It would constitute evidence that could be taken into account, together with other factors—for example, how many States supported the resolution, how many voted against it, and how many spoke against that particular paragraph.

Several members of the Commission supported the introduction of 'conduct in connection with'.[32] Other members, however, were opposed to the addition and agreed with the Special Rapporteur that resolutions should not be qualified.[33] More importantly, while many members of the Commission did not express a view in the plenary, there was overwhelming support for retaining the language of the resolution without qualifying it with 'conduct of States' within the deliberations of the Drafting Committee. This does not mean, however, that conduct of States in connection with a resolution, such as an explanation of votes, reservations, and abstentions, is irrelevant. These acts of the State are of course to be taken into account, but not to the exclusion of the resolution itself.[34] To address this, the Drafting Committee decided, in addition to the list, to include a catch-all phrase:

> The Drafting Committee considered various options for how best to capture the concept in the provision. Some proposals included adding the phrase 'and conduct in relation to'. In the end, the Drafting Committee adopted the proposal of the Special Rapporteur to include a more all-encompassing reference to State conduct (and not just in the context of the adoption of resolutions) by means of adding a new phrase at the end 'and other conduct of States'.[35]

Thus, the Drafting Committee added the phrase 'and other conduct of States' at the end of paragraph 2.[36] In fact, the phrase 'include, but are not limited to', makes this insertion unnecessary, but the Commission decided

[32] Park (A/CN.4/SR.3565), 6; Murphy (A/CN.4/SR.3565), 12.

[33] Hassouna (A/CN.4/SR.3565), 13; Grossman (A/CN.4/SR.3356), 5; Argüello Gómez (A/CN.4/SR.3358), 5.

[34] Peremptory Norms of General International Law (*Jus Cogens*), Statement of the Chair of the Drafting Committee, Ki Gab Park, 17 May 2022, 11 ('The view of the Drafting Committee was that it was important to also take into account such conduct of States, including statements made during the process of the adoption of a particular resolution, or votes for and against its adoption').

[35] Id.

[36] Drafting Committee, Peremptory Norms of General International Law, Proposal of Special Rapporteur for Draft Conclusion 8, para 2, ILC (LXXIII)/DC/JC/WP.1, 29 April 2022.

to adopt it regardless. The only other addition to paragraph 2 was 'constitutional provisions'—an insertion made in response to a suggestion by Mr Oauzzani-Chahdi.[37]

While Draft Conclusion 8 of the Draft Conclusions on *Jus Cogens* follows closely Draft Conclusion 10 of the Draft Conclusions on Customary International Law, it does not include the equivalent of paragraph 3 of the latter which provides that 'failure to react over to time . . . may serve as evidence'. Yet this does not mean that inaction is irrelevant for the purposes of identification of peremptory norms. In that context, Israel took the position that '[i]naction or failure to react . . . may not serve as a form of evidence of acceptance and recognition'.[38] To this end, Israel suggested that 'the commentary clearly states that in the case of peremptory norms of general international law (*jus cogens*), inaction may in principle not be said to be evidence of acceptance and recognition'.[39] In response, the Fifth Report stated:

> [T]he Special Rapporteur is not aware of any State practice . . . according to which failure to react *may not serve as evidence of acceptance and recognition* [for the purposes of *jus cogens*]. It is of course the case that silence must not be easily accepted as evidence, but it would be going too far to suggest that it may never serve as evidence of acceptance and recognition.[40]

The role of silence in assessing evidence can perhaps best be illustrated by a comment made by the Special Rapporteur in an academic article in respect of the threshold of the international community. There he stated as follows:

> Imagine a rule (rule x). Evidence from the materials [in Draft Conclusion 8] can be found in which 180 States have expressed *opinio juris cogentis* (acceptance and recognition). Yet 12 States have vehemently rejected the peremptory status of that same rule. Now imagine another rule (rule y). Evidence from materials [in Draft Conclusion 8] signifying the *opinio juris cogentis* of only a hundred States can be found. Yet rule y has been communicated in public

[37] Oauzzani-Chahdi (A/CN.4/SR.3568), 12.
[38] Israel, Comments and Observations (above note 27), 46.
[39] Id.
[40] Fifth Report (above note 26), 105.

forums, in debates in diplomatic correspondence without a single State expressing an objection or question its peremptory status. All things being equal, the claim to peremptory status of rule y would appear to be stronger than that of rule x even though there is qualitatively more evidence of support for rule x than rule y.[41]

Ultimately, no single form of evidence is conclusive of the peremptory status of a norm. What matters is what the various materials when taken together, and taking into account various factors including silence, signify about the position of States concerning the peremptory character of a norm.[42]

4. The Content of Draft Conclusion 9

Draft Conclusion 9
Subsidiary means for the determination of the peremptory character of norms of general international law

1. Decisions of international courts and tribunals, in particular of the International Court of Justice, are a subsidiary means for determining the peremptory character of norms of general international law. Regard may also be had, as appropriate, to decisions of national courts.
2. The works of expert bodies established by States or international organizations and the teachings of the most highly qualified publicists of the various nations may also serve as subsidiary means for determining the peremptory character of a norm of general international law.

The text of the Draft Conclusion is loosely based on Draft Conclusions 13 and 14 of the customary international law study but departs from those provisions in significant ways, as will be illustrated below.

[41] Dire Tladi 'The ILC's Draft Conclusion on Peremptory Norms of General International Law: Special Reflections of the Special Rapporteur' (2019) 24 *Austrian Review of International and European Law* 121, 133.

[42] See para 8 of the Commentary to Draft Conclusion 8 ('it should be recalled that the materials listed in Draft Conclusion 8 provide evidence. As such they are not, individually, conclusive of the peremptory character of a norm. Thus the fact that a resolution . . . a treaty provision, a national court decision, a public statement, or any other conduct by a State indicates a belief that a norm has peremptory status, is not sufficient to establish [that status]. The materials have to be weighed and assessed together, in their context, in order to determine whether they evince acceptance and recognition [as required under the Draft Conclusions]').

Draft Conclusion 9 concerns subsidiary means for the determination of the peremptory status of norms. This is reflected both in the title and in both paragraphs. The role of the materials in Draft Conclusion 9 is subsidiary in the sense that they may be used to support the primary materials referred to in Draft Conclusion 8.[43] The Draft Conclusion contains two paragraphs, structured according to some sort of hierarchical understanding.

The first paragraph refers to courts and tribunals. But the first paragraph itself contains levels of hierarchy. The first sentence refers to '[d]ecisions of international courts and tribunals, and in particular of the International Court of Justice' and states that these '*are* subsidiary means for determining' the *jus cogens* status of norms.[44] As the Commentary notes, this sentence mirrors Article 38(1)(d) of the Statute of the International Court of Justice. On first reading, the first paragraph contained only this sentence. The first hierarchical distinction is in the phrase 'in particular of the International Court of Justice' which establishes an elevated position for the Court.[45]

The Commentary justifies the reference to decisions of international courts and tribunals by pointing to judicial decisions that rely on other decisions of international courts.[46] For example, the Commentary refers to *Prosecutor v Furundžija* which relied, *inter alia*, on a decision of the European Court of Human Rights.[47] With respect to the specific mention of the International Court of Justice, while the Court has been reluctant to invoke *jus cogens*,[48] it has remained very influential in the evolution of doctrines connected to *jus cogens*. Perhaps the single most important driver of the further development of *jus cogens* since the adoption of the Vienna Convention has been, together with the International Law Commission, the concept of *erga omnes* obligations, a concept whose emergence and entrenchment in international law is thanks to

43 See para 1 of the Commentary to Draft Conclusion 9 ('It is important to emphasize that the word "subsidiary" is not meant to diminish the importance of these materials, but is rather aimed at expressing the idea that these materials facilitate the identification of "acceptance and recognition" but do not themselves, constitute evidence of such acceptance and recognition.')

44 Emphasis added.

45 See, however, Argüello Gómez (A/CN.4/SR.3368), 5–6 ('As a last point on draft conclusion 9, he noted that equal value was given to decisions of the International Court of Justice and decisions of other international courts and tribunals, including arbitral tribunals. The words "in particular" were, in his opinion, insufficient to distinguish the Court').

46 See generally para 3 of the Commentary to Draft Conclusion 9. See, in particular, examples cited in footnotes 123, 125, 126, 127, 128, 129, and 130.

47 See *Prosecutor v Anto Furundžija*, Case No. IT-95-17/1-T, Judgment of 10 December 1998, Trial Chamber, International Criminal Tribunal for the Former Yugoslavia, para 144.

48 See, on the reluctance of the Court to identify *jus cogens* norms, Catherine Maia '*Jus Cogens* and the (In)Application of the 1969 Vienna Convention on the Law of Treaties in the Jurisprudence of the International Court of Justice' in Dire Tladi (ed.) *Peremptory Norms of General International Law (Jus Cogens): Disquisitions and Disputations* (Brill, 2021).

the Court.[49] In addition, the Commentary refers to a number of decisions of the International Court of Justice which have often been invoked in support of various arguments concerning *jus cogens*.[50]

The second sentence of the first paragraph, stating that the decisions of national courts may also serve as subsidiary means for the determination of peremptory status, was inserted by the Drafting Committee on second reading. The phrases '[R]egard may also be had' and 'as appropriate' to qualify decisions of national courts are intended to signify hierarchy by placing decisions of domestic courts at a lower level as a subsidiary means for the determination of *jus cogens* status.[51] Curiously, the non-inclusion, on first reading, of decisions of national courts was not raised by a single State in their Comments and Observations. Moreover, only one member during the plenary debate, on first reading, questioned the omission of national courts from the provision.[52] It was the Drafting Committee, of its own volition, that, on second reading, decided to include decisions of national courts. Of course, on the one hand, a cursory read of the Commentaries reveals that there is an abundance of references to decisions of national courts, suggesting that the insertion of the sentence was appropriate. Yet, on the other hand, Draft Conclusion 8 also plays a role, in fact, a more important role as primary evidence for domestic courts, raising the question of why national courts would need to be referred to as a subsidiary means. According to the Chair of the Drafting Committee, the Committee

> considered the possibility, mentioned during the debate in plenary, of referring also to the decisions of national courts. One of the considerations was whether such reference was strictly necessary since such decisions were referred to in draft conclusion 8, paragraph 2. The prevailing view in the Drafting Committee was that a reference to the decisions of national courts in draft conclusion 9 would serve a different purpose: while in draft conclusion 8 the decisions of national courts are one of the forms of evidence of acceptance and recognition of a peremptory norm of general international law (*jus cogens*), in draft conclusion 9, judicial decisions, including the decisions of

[49] See, for discussion, Martha Bradley '*Jus Cogens*' Preferred Sister: Obligations *Erga Omnes* and the International Court of Justice—Fifty Years after the *Barcelona Traction* Case' in Tladi (above note 48).

[50] See para 4 of the Commentary to Draft Conclusion 9.

[51] See para 5 of the Commentary to Draft Conclusion 9 ('The Commission decided to use the phrases "may also" and "as appropriate" to indicate that, although decisions of national courts may serve as subsidiary means for the determination of [*jus cogens* status], they should be resorted to with caution').

[52] Wood, as Chair (A/CN.4/SR.3568), 15 ('In draft conclusion 9, he was not sure that the Commission should omit a reference to decisions of national courts'). See, however, also Murphy (A/CN.4/SR.3367), 3, who had made a similar point in the context of the debate on the Second Report of the Special Rapporteur ('With regard to draft conclusion 9, he queried the lack of reference to decisions of national courts, which were extensively referenced elsewhere in the report').

national courts, are a subsidiary means for determining the peremptory character of norms.[53]

Yet this explanation does not fully address the question. Even if the distinction between decisions of national courts as primary evidence and as subsidiary means were sound—even if theoretically—why would it be necessary to also specify a subsidiary role if they served a primary role? The Commentary responds to this question as follows:

> When relied upon under Draft Conclusion 8, decisions of national courts provide evidence of the acceptance and recognition of *the State in question.* In that context, the relevance of the decision of the court is that it evidences *that State's* position, and not its broader assessment of the recognition and acceptance of a norm in question by the international community of States as a whole as peremptory in nature.[54]

The primary relevance of decisions of national courts is not as a subsidiary means, but rather as primary evidence under Draft Conclusion 8. In the context of Draft Conclusion 8, where decisions of national courts served as primary evidence of acceptance and recognition of a State, the reasoning or assessment of evidence is irrelevant. This is not the case for reliance on judicial decisions as a subsidiary means, where the reasoning and evidence ought to play an important role.

The second paragraph concerns 'the works of experts and teachings of the most highly qualified publicists' as subsidiary means for the determination of peremptory status. The use of the phrase 'may also' is intended to suggest that these forms of evidence should be accorded 'less weight' than decisions of courts.[55] In contrast to the customary international law study, which did not refer to works of expert bodies except in the Commentary, the Commission here refers explicitly to 'works of expert bodies'.[56]

While the Commentary does refer to some authorities in support of the works of experts and teachings,[57] it focuses much more on explaining the role

53 Statement of the Chair of the Drafting Committee (above note 34), 12.
54 See para 6 of the Commentary to Draft Conclusion 9.
55 See para 7 of the Commentary to Draft Conclusion 9.
56 The initial draft proposed by the Special Rapporteur had referred explicitly to the work of the International Law Commission; See Second Report (above note 1), para 91 ('Other materials, such as the work of the International Law Commission, the work of expert bodies and scholarly writings, may provide a secondary means of identifying norms of international law from which no derogation is permitted'); Drafting Committee, Peremptory Norms of General International Law, Revised Proposal of the Special Rapporteur for Draft Conclusion 9 ILC(LXX)/DC/JC.WP.1, 4 May 2018.
57 See para 9 of the Commentary to Draft Conclusion 9.

of the Commission. This was in part a compromise for not having an explicit reference to the Commission in the text because it was generally agreed that the Commission has played a leading role[58] not only in bringing *jus cogens* from the periphery of international law to the mainstream, but in maintaining its place through its inclusion in several outputs, most notably the Articles on State Responsibility.[59]

The works of expert bodies, which may serve as subsidiary means under Draft Conclusion 9 are limited to those expert bodies 'established by States or international organisations'. It is worth noting that this limitation did not exist in the proposal by the Special Rapporteur.[60] This might raise questions about the place of works of expert bodies whose contributions to international law are undeniable, yet which are not created by States or international organisations; such as the *Institut de Droit International* and the International Law Association. According to the Commentary, these works continue to be relevant because they 'qualify as "teaching of the most qualified publicist" '.[61]

The designation of bodies like the *Institut de Droit International* and the International Law Association raises another point of curiosity about Draft Conclusion 9. It is curious that the Commission refers to 'works of expert bodies … *and* teaching of publicists … '. This seems to suggest that the works of expert bodies are a different category altogether from teachings.

Draft Conclusion 9 did attract more fundamental comments about the place of subsidiary forms of evidence in the determination of *jus cogens*. Some States, without objecting to the first paragraph, sought to emphasise that decisions of international courts, including of the International Court of Justice, were merely subsidiary.[62] Some States, however, wanted to emphasise the important

[58] See e.g. Peremptory Norms of General International Law (*Jus Cogens*), Statement of the Chair of the Drafting Committee, Charles Chernor Jalloh, 14 May 2018, 4 ('The Drafting Committee discussed, inter alia, whether the work of the International Law Commission should be explicitly mentioned in the text of the draft conclusion. It was noted that it was worthwhile mentioning the Commission explicitly because of the significant contribution made by the Commission to the emergence and development of peremptory norms of general international law (*jus cogens*) and in light of its mandate and its interaction with States in the process of codification and progressive development. However, the Drafting Committee agreed to delete any explicit reference to its work because this was not in line with its usual practice. It will be explained, in the commentary, that the Commission, as an expert body, has played a significant role in the emergence and development of peremptory norms of general international law (*jus cogens*)').

[59] Articles on the Responsibility of States for Internationally Wrongfully Acts, *Yearbook of the International Law Commission*, 2001, Vol. II, Part II; See especially Articles 26, 40, 41, and 48 and the Commentaries thereto.

[60] Id.

[61] See para 8 of the Commentary to Draft Conclusion 9.

[62] Israel, Comments and Observations (above note 27), 53 ('In this context, Israel would like to recall that the criteria for determining whether a norm is peremptory depend on whether States have accepted and recognised a certain norm as such'); Spain, Comments and Observations (above note 27), 55 ('it is useful to contextualise the relative value of certain decisions of courts and tribunals which sometimes

role of international courts and tribunals, in particular of the International Court of Justice.[63] This division was equally apparent within the Commission, with some members seeking to emphasise the special role of international courts such as the International Court of Justice.[64] Mr Hmoud, for example, took the view that '[d]ecisions of international courts and tribunals could be evidence of the existence of a *jus cogens* rule'.[65] Others, however, sought to emphasise that these decisions of international courts should not be treated as the main source for determining the peremptory character of norms.[66]

Similar issues were raised concerning expert bodies. The views of France were particularly pointed in this regard:

> The second paragraph of Draft Conclusion 9 may raise a number of doubts. It seems risky to classify expert bodies established by States or international organisations as a 'subsidiary source' for the determination of *jus cogens* norms. While there is no doubt that the Commission, given its mandate from the General Assembly, its particularly rigorous working methods, and the recognised quality of its experts, can lay claim to such classification, the same is not necessarily true of all expert bodies. For example, both inside and outside

classify norms as peremptory rather casually'); the United States, Comments and Observations (above note 27), 56.

[63] See e.g. Italy, Comment and Observations (above note 27), 53 ('it is of the view that the commentary should clarify that the Draft Conclusion is without prejudice to the specific, privileged role of the International Court of Justice with regard to the determination of peremptory norms'); Spain, Comments and Observations (above note 27), 55 ('Consequently, Spain agrees, first, that the fundamental importance of the decisions of the International Court of Justice in relation to other international tribunals is highlighted').

[64] Argüello Gómez (A/CN.4/SR.3368), 5–6; Saboia (A/CN.4/SR.3566), 6 ('Some States appeared to have failed to recognize the important role played by international courts and tribunals, particularly the International Court of Justice'); Forteau (A/CN.4/SR.3564), 13 ('It was odd that, in draft conclusion 9, there was no mention of the fact that the International Court of Justice was assigned a special role by the 1969 Vienna Convention in identifying *jus cogens* norms').

[65] Hmoud (A/CN.4/SR.3566), 8; Hmoud (A/CN.4/SR.3566), 10 ('the issue was whether decisions of international courts and tribunals could serve as evidence of the existence of a *jus cogens* norm, not that such decisions were a subsidiary means for determining the peremptory character of norms of general international law' and was thus 'concerned that the use of the term "subsidiary means" in paragraph 1 could undermine the pronouncements of the International Court of Justice on the existence of certain peremptory norms'); Forteau (A/CN.4/SR.3564), 13 ('It was odd that, in draft conclusion 9, there was no mention of the fact that the International Court of Justice was assigned a special role by the 1969 Vienna Convention in identifying *jus cogens* norms').

[66] Park (A/CN.4/SR.3369), 12 ('Paragraph 4 should also reflect the idea that the decisions of international courts and tribunals were subsidiary evidence of acceptance and recognition, along the lines of draft conclusion 13 on the identification of customary international law, which stated that such decisions were subsidiary means of determining rules of customary international law'); Murphy (A/CN.4/SR.3367), 3 ('decisions of international courts and tribunals were not evidence of *jus cogens* in themselves but might serve as a subsidiary means for identifying a norm as one of *jus cogens*'); Reinisch (A/CN.4/SR.3372), 16.

> the United Nations, certain expert bodies, which are not always composed of lawyers, adopt controversial findings, based on legal reasoning that is, to say the least, questionable. The question of the role, even if it is a subsidiary one, that these bodies might have, in the determination of *jus cogens* should be approached with great caution.[67]

Germany had similarly suggested 'a more differentiating approach' that would take into account 'the various existing expert bodies'.[68]

While the subsidiary means have been the subject of some criticism, it is clear that in practice they serve a very important role in the identification of *jus cogens*, and of rules of international law in general.[69] Draft Conclusion 9 attempts to achieve a balance by recognising the role of these means, but by describing them as 'subsidiary'. As with any 'subsidiary means', the value of the evidence will depend on various factors including their acceptance by States, the mandate and expertise of the body, and their reasoning. While this is particularly true of the works of expert bodies and teachings and is stated explicitly in the Commentary to Draft Conclusion itself,[70] there is no reason why it would not be true of decisions of courts and tribunals, including those of the International Court of Justice.

5. Concluding Observations

The second criterion for the identification of *jus cogens* requires that evidence be provided that a norm is accepted and recognised by the international community of States as a whole as a norm from which no derogation is permitted. The type of material that is relevant as evidence is that which reveals the views of States. However, decisions of courts, both national and international, as well as works of expert bodies may also serve, in a subsidiary role, as evidence for the identification of *jus cogens*.

For primary material, what matters is whether the content of the material reveals that the State (or States) in question believe that a particular norm is *jus*

[67] France, Comments and Observations (above note 27), 52; Japan, Comments and Observations (above note 27), 54 ('While the Commission is tasked with the progressive development and codification of international law which includes *jus cogens*, the vast majority of other expert bodies do not possess explicit or implied power to determine *jus cogens* ... Thus the formulation of this paragraph needs to be revised').

[68] Id., 53. See, in even stronger terms, Israel, which stated that it 'objects to' the inclusion of expert bodies. See, however, at 56, Spain, expressing support for the inclusion of expert bodies.

[69] See, for discussion, Section 4.1 in Chapter 1; see also Fifth Report (above note 26), 23.

[70] See paras 7 and 11 of the Commentary to Draft Conclusion 9.

cogens. The reasoning, or whether the position is based on evidence, is less important since that evidence serves to illustrate the position of a particular State (or particular States). It is only if that position is shared by a very large majority (See Chapter 6), that a peremptory norm can be said to exist.

It is common for there to be great reliance placed on subsidiary means in the determination of whether a norm is *jus cogens*. For this, it is necessary to assess, carefully, whether the secondary material in question itself presents sufficient evidence or reasoning in support of the contention that a norm is *jus cogens*. In a sense, the subsidiary means must itself reveal evidence that a very large majority accepts and recognises the peremptory character of the norm in question.

During the debate of the Sixth Committee on the final product of the Commission, Draft Conclusions 8 and 9 were generally well received. One issue, appearing in the interstices of evidence and the threshold for acceptance and recognition by the international community of States as a whole, is the role of silence, to which, it appears, the Commission did not pay sufficient attention.

PART III
CONSEQUENCES

8

Consequences of *Jus Cogens* for Treaties

1. Introduction

The consequence most synonymous with peremptory norms is invalidity of a treaty conflicting with *jus cogens* as provided for in the Vienna Convention. The Commission provides for such invalidity in Draft Conclusion 10. In addition, the Draft Conclusions also describe the consequences of invalidity (Draft Conclusions 11 and 12). The extent of invalidity, and thus the extent of the consequences flowing from invalidity, are dependent on whether those provisions of the treaty that are in conflict with *jus cogens* are severable from the rest of the treaty. The issue of severability—or separability—is addressed in Draft Conclusion 11. Draft Conclusions 10, 11, and 12 concern consequences of treaties, or treaty provisions, conflicting with *jus cogens* and are addressed in this chapter.

The text of the Draft Conclusions also addresses how the *jus cogens* status of a norm may affect reservations (Draft Conclusion 13). While this is different from Draft Conclusions 10, 11, and 12 in that it does not concern invalidity of treaties on account of conflict with a *jus cogens* norm, it does complete the picture of the relationship between *jus cogens* and treaties and is therefore also addressed in this chapter.

The next section will provide a general context of the Draft Conclusions relevant to treaties. Section 3 will address the consequences of treaties conflicting with *jus cogens* (Draft Conclusion 10). Section 4 will address the possibility of severability (Draft Conclusion 11) of treaty provisions conflicting with *jus cogens* norms. Section 5 will address consequences of invalidity of treaties conflicting with *jus cogens* (Draft Conclusion 12). Finally, Section 6 will discuss the effects of *jus cogens* on reservations (Draft Conclusion 13). Concluding remarks are provided at the end of the chapter.

2. Discussion

The primary consequence of *jus cogens* is the invalidity of treaties and it is provided for in Article 53 of the Vienna Convention. It provides that a treaty 'is void if, at the time of its conclusion, it conflicts with a [norm of *jus cogens*]'. At the same time, Article 64 of the Vienna Convention addresses instances of a treaty which, at the time of its conclusion, does not conflict with a norm of *jus cogens*, but subsequently comes into conflict with a norm of *jus cogens* arising after its conclusion (*jus cogens superveniens*). Article 64 provides that if a new norm of *jus cogens* emerges, 'any existing treaty which is in conflict with that norm becomes void and terminates'.

The notion that a treaty is (or becomes) void if it conflicts with a norm of *jus cogens* is the most obvious consequence of peremptoriness. Indeed, once the Commission decided to use the Vienna Convention on the Law of Treaties as its point of departure for the topic, it was to be expected that the consequence of invalidity of treaties would feature prominently. In fact, for many observers, the consequence of invalidity is the primary (and for others even the sole) consequence of peremptoriness.[1] Yet, for others it is doubtful that nullity of treaties is a consequence, in the main, since there is no practice supporting the idea of nullity.[2] Yet, in the course of work on this topic, all members of the Commission, and virtually all States, accepted nullity of a treaty in conflict with *jus cogens* as a consequence of

[1] See, for description of nullity as the 'original consequence', Kyoji Kawasaki 'A Brief Note on the Legal Effects of *Jus Cogens* in International Law' (2006) 34 *Hitotsubashi Journal of Law and Politics* 27. See also, for a general discussion, Maarten den Heijer and Harmen van der Wilt '*Jus Cogens* and the Humanisation and Fragmentation of international Law' (2016) 46 *Netherlands Yearbook of International Law* 3, 7, describing the differences in approaches to the consequences of *jus cogens* ('While the skeptics have denied its very claim to existence, its proponents have enthusiastically claimed *jus cogens* status for a myriad of norms. Moreover, they have sought to extend the functions or effects of *jus cogens* beyond its initial capacity of trumping and invalidating conflicting treaty rules. The presumptive consequences of *jus cogens* have, indeed, been manifold. *Jus cogens* has been mobilized in order to invalidate customary international law and resolutions of the Security Council; it has been invoked in the national context in order to nullify domestic law; and it has been claimed to create obligations, like a duty to prosecute violations of *jus cogens* ("international crimes") or to lift state immunities'). For the view that treaty nullity is the only consequence, see Hugh Thirlway, *The Sources of International Law* (Oxford University Press, 2014), 145 ('The significance of the quality of a norm as *jus cogens*, on the basis of Article 53 of the Vienna Convention, is simply to invalidate any agreement purporting to contradict or evade that norm. There has inevitably been a temptation a temptation for scholars to attach wider effects to the concept').

[2] For doubt on the continued relevance of nullity under Article 53, see Daniel Costelloe *Legal Consequences of Peremptory Norms* (Cambridge, 2017), 55, stating that it is a real question whether the provisions of Article 53 of the Vienna Convention on the Law of Treaties are 'now virtually a dead letter'. See, for general discussion, Catherine Maia '*Jus Cogens* and (In)Application of the 1969 Vienna Convention on the Law of Treaties in the Jurisprudence of the International Court of Justice' in Dire Tladi (ed.) *Peremptory Norms of General International Law (Jus Cogens): Disquisitions and Disputations* (Brill, 2021).

peremptory norms.[3] Only one State, the United States, explicitly questioned this consequence:

> The United States reiterates at the outset that there is little or no State practice with respect to any of these provisions [Draft Conclusions 10–14 and 16]. The United States is therefore of the view that Draft Conclusions 10 to 14 and 16 should be deleted ... If some or all of these draft conclusions remain, the Commission should clearly identify them as proposals for the progressive development of international law.[4]

The Fifth Report of the Special Rapporteur, responding to this position of the United States, stated as follows:

> The Special Rapporteur simply does not understand such proposition. It is not clear to the Special Rapporteur whether the United States, by this recommendation, seeks to suggest that under international law, as it currently stands, a treaty entered by two or more States for the commission of genocide is valid. To this recommendation, the Special Rapporteur can say, very few rules of international law are truly trite: this is one of them.[5]

In the introduction of the Fifth Report, the Special Rapporteur conceded that Draft Conclusion 10 was 'less reliant' on practice 'than others' because the rule contained therein was 'uncontested'.[6] While it is true that there was little practice of a treaty being declared void by a judicial body on account of inconsistency with *jus cogens*, practice is not limited to judicial declarations of invalidity. Assertions or statements by States of invalidity, even potential invalidity, of a treaty or other agreement on account of inconsistency with *jus cogens* are also relevant for the assessment of the rule contained in Draft Conclusion 10.

There are many examples of States casting doubt on the validity of treaties on account of possible conflict with *jus cogens*.[7] The United States itself, the one

[3] See e.g. Colombia, Peremptory Norm of General International Law International Law (*Jus Cogens*): Japan, Comments and Observations received from Governments (A/CN.4/748), 57; id., 59.

[4] The United States, Comments and Observations (above note 3), 59.

[5] *Fifth Report of the Special Rapporteur on Peremptory Norms (Jus Cogens)* (A/CN.4/747), 115.

[6] Special Rapporteur (A/CN.4/SR.3564), 5.

[7] Examples listed in the Fifth Report (above note 5), para 31, include the following: The Netherlands (A/C.6/SR.781), para 2 ('The question of *jus cogens*, dealt with in draft article 37, was not one of classical international law. In an era when the use of force in international relations had been almost unrestricted and when international law had barely begun to recognize human rights, international public order had been the vaguest of concepts. The Agreement concerning the Sudeten German Territory, signed at Munich on 29 September 1938, was one of the few examples of treaties which had come to be regarded as contrary to international public order'); Cyprus (A/C.6/SR.783), para 18, in welcoming

State that expressed doubt about the status of Draft Conclusion 10, has in the past expressed the view that a treaty between the Soviet Union and Afghanistan was void for being in breach of *jus cogens*.[8] Additionally, there is judicial practice to the effect that a treaty inconsistent with *jus cogens* would be invalid.[9] There are also General Assembly resolutions that stand for the proposition that the validity of certain agreements is dependent on their consistency with particular norms of *jus cogens*.[10]

While there was broad agreement on the consequence of invalidity of treaties in conflict with *jus cogens*, the question of whether those provisions of a treaty that conflict with *jus cogens* could be excised (severed or separated) from the rest of the treaty in order to save the rest of the treaty, was slightly more contested. The language of both Articles 53 and 64—'[a] treaty is void' and 'any existing treaty ... becomes void and terminates'—would seem to exclude the possibility of severability. Yet, the particular provision on severability, Article 44, would suggest the possibility of severability in the case of *jus cogens superveniens* (Article 64). Paragraph 5 of Article 44 states that particular cases, including those falling under Article 53, do not permit severability.[11] Article 44 does not mention, however, *jus cogens superveniens* as one of the instances

the Commission's inclusion of Article 37 (predecessor to Article 53), listed a number of international agreements which provided for nullity on account of conflict with a peremptory norm, namely the prohibition on the use of force. For other examples, reflected in the Commentary to Draft Conclusion 10 (para 2), see: *East Timor (Portugal v Australia), Counter-Memorial of the Government Australia of 1 June 1992*, para 223, in which it is stated that the Timor Gap Treaty, if in conflict with the right of self-determination, would be invalid on account of being in breach of a norm of *jus cogens*.

8 Memorandum from Roberts B. Owen, Legal Adviser of the State Department to Warren Christopher, Acting Secretary of State 29 December 1979, in U.S. Digest, chapter 2, section 1, para 4, reproduced in M. L. Nash 'Contemporary Practice of the United States Relating to International Law' (1980) 74 *American Journal of International Law* 418, 419 ('Nor is it clear that the treaty between the USSR and Afghanistan ... is valid. If it actually does lend itself to support of Soviet intervention of the type in question in Afghanistan, it would be void under contemporary principles of international law, since it would conflict with what the Vienna Convention on the Law of Treaties describes as a "peremptory norm of general international law" ... namely that contained in Article 2, paragraph 4 of the Charter' of the United Nations).

9 *Prosecutor v Taylor*, Case No. SCSL-2003-01-I, Decision of 31 May 2004 on Immunity from Jurisdiction, Appeals Chamber, Special Court for Sierra Leone, para 53. See also *Prosecutor v Kallon*, Case No. SCSL-2004-15-AR72(E), Decision of 13 March 2004 on Constitutionality and Lack of Jurisdiction, Appeals Chamber, Special Court for Sierra Leone; *Aloeboetoe and Others v Suriname*, Judgment of 10 September 1993 on Reparation and Costs, InterAmerican Court of Human Rights, Series C, No. 1, para 57.

10 General Assembly resolution 33/28A of 7 December 1978, para 4 ('Declares that the validity of agreements purporting to solve the problem of Palestine requires that they be within the framework of the United Nations Charter ... on the basis of the full attainment and exercise of the inalienable right of self-determination'); General Assembly Res. 34/65 B of 29 November 1979, 36/51 of 24 November 1981 and General Assembly Res. 39/42 of 5 December 1984.

11 Article 44(5) of the Vienna Convention on the Law of Treaties: 'In cases falling under Articles 51, 52 and 53, no separation of the treaty provision is permitted'.

in which severability is precluded. The position that severability is possible for *jus cogens superveniens* but not in the case of treaties conflicting with *jus cogens* at the time of conclusion is also confirmed in the Commentaries to the Draft Articles on the Law of Treaties. In the Commentary to Draft Article 50—which became Article 53—the Commission stated that the 'treaty is wholly void because its actual conclusion conflicts with a peremptory norm'.[12] In contrast the Commentary to Draft Article 61—which became Article 64 of the Vienna Convention—the Commission made the following observation:

> [A]lthough the Commission did not think that the principle of separability is appropriate when a treaty is void *ab initio* under Article 50 by reason of an existing rule of *jus cogens*, it felt that different considerations apply in the case of a treaty which was entirely valid when concluded but is now found with respect to some of its provisions to conflict with a newly established rule of *jus cogens*. If those provisions can properly be regarded as severable from the rest of the treaty, the Commission thought that the rest of the treaty ought to be regarded as still valid.[13]

While this position was generally accepted both within the Commission and by States, there were calls for the Commission to depart from the Vienna framework and to permit severability even for Article 53 cases.[14] For Mr Nolte, while practice was scarce, there was at least one example of States providing for severability even in the case of an agreement being in conflict with *jus cogens* at the time of its conclusion.[15] For Mr Reinisch, the reason that the Commission ought to provide for separability was practical, since 'distinguishing between pre-existing *jus cogens* and *jus cogens superveniens* added yet another layer of evidentiary' complexity to the issues in that 'a State claiming conflict between a treaty provision and *jus cogens*' would be required to identify 'the specific moment in time [that] the *jus cogens* norm had come into existence'.[16] This view was echoed by Austria,[17] Belarus,[18] and South Africa.[19] In response to these

[12] See para 6 of the Commentary to Draft Article 50 of the Draft Articles on the Law of Treaties. *Yearbook of the International Law Commission*, 1966, Vol. II, 248.

[13] Id., para 3 of the Commentary to Article 61.

[14] See Nolte (A/CN.4/SR.3417), 12; Reinisch (A/CN.4/SR.3567), 6.

[15] Nolte (A/CN.4/SR.3417), 12 ('By way of example ... the General Assembly had declared in its resolution 34/65 "that the Camp David accords and other agreements had no validity in so far as they purport to determine the future of the Palestinian people and Palestinian territories occupied by Israel since 1967"').

[16] Reinisch (A/CN.4/SR.3567), 6.

[17] Australia, Comments and Observations (above note 3), 60.

[18] Belarus (A/C.6/74/SR.24), para 83.

[19] South Africa, Comments and Observations (above note 3), 61.

views, the Special Rapporteur seemed to accept the merit of the views, but ultimately decided that it would be best to retain the Vienna framework since the majority of States and members of the Commission accepted it.[20]

Under the Vienna Convention, the consequences of invalidity depend, in part, on whether the inconsistency with *jus cogens* existed at the time of conclusion of the treaty or whether the inconsistency emerged subsequent to the conclusion of the treaty. Article 71 provides that, with respect to an inconsistency existing at the time of conclusion of the treaty, the parties to that treaty are obligated to eliminate 'as far as possible the consequences of any act performed in reliance on any provision [of that treaty] which conflicts with' the *jus cogens* norm.[21] Thus, flowing from the fact that the treaty is void *ab initio*, the consequences are retrospective. For invalidity arising from an inconsistency which emerges subsequent to the conclusion of the treaty, the consequences are prospective, i.e. parties are released 'from any obligation further to perform' and the invalidity does not 'affect any right, obligation or legal situation of the parties created through the execution of the treaty prior to its termination'.[22] While there were some issues concerning how to reflect this framework (see Section 5 below), the framework itself was generally accepted both within the Commission and by States.

The Vienna Convention does not address the effects of *jus cogens* on reservations. On this question the Commission was faced with two possible options. The first option was to follow the approach of the Human Rights Committee which took the view that a reservation that was inconsistent with a norm of *jus cogens* was invalid, with result that the treaty would bind the State making the reservation without the benefit of the reservation.[23] This position finds some support in the literature.[24]

A second approach, one that was suggested by the Special Rapporteur and eventually adopted by the Commission, had been put forward by the

[20] See Fifth Report (above note 5), para 125.

[21] Article 71(1)(a) of the Vienna Convention on the Law of Treaties.

[22] Id., Article 71(2).

[23] See Human Rights Committee, General Comment No. 24 (1994), Issues Relating to Reservations Made Upon Ratification or Accession to the Covenant or the Optional Protocols Thereto, or in Relation to Declarations Under Article 41 of the Covenant, para 8 ('Accordingly, provisions in the Covenant that represent customary international law (and a fortiori when they have the character of peremptory norms) may not be the subject of reservations').

[24] Alain Pellet 'Tenth Report on Reservations to Treaties', *Yearbook of the International Law Commission*, Vol. II, 173; Alexander Orakhelashvili 'The Effect of *Jus Cogens* in the Law of Treaties' in *Peremptory Norms in International Law* (OUP, 2008), 181; Joe Verhoeven 'Invalidity of Treaties: Anything New in/under the Vienna Conventions?' in Enzo Cannizzaro (ed.) *The Law of Treaties Beyond the Vienna Convention* (OUP, 2011), 313.

Commission earlier in the Guide to Practice on Reservations.[25] Unlike the Human Rights Committee, the Guide to Practice does not provide that reservations contrary to peremptory norms are invalid. Rather, the Guide to Practice states simply that such reservations do not 'affect the binding nature of that norm'. The essence of this approach is to emphasise the distinction between the *jus cogens* norm—a norm of general international law—and any treaty provision reflecting such a norm. It proceeds from the understanding that a treaty rule and the general international law norm it reflects, though having the same content, have an independent existence.[26]

While there were some members of the Commission that supported the approach put forward by the Human Rights Committee,[27] the Commission decided to be consistent with its earlier work and not to provide for the invalidity of the reservation itself. According to the Third Report, the effect of this choice is that while a reservation to a treaty provision might 'affect the applicability of the *treaty rule as such*, ... it will have no effect on the norm of *jus cogens* reflected in the treaty rule'.[28] In other words, the *jus cogens* norm, and all its consequences, will continue to apply notwithstanding the reservation. Moreover, according to the Third Report 'it is *difficult* (although not impossible) to conceive of a reservation to a treaty provision embodying a norm of *jus cogens*' which would not be inconsistent with the object and purpose of the treaty and thus invalid in accordance with Article 19 of the Vienna Convention.[29] It is worth pointing out, in this connection, that the Human Rights Committee came to its conclusion that a reservation in conflict with a *jus cogens* norm is invalid, applying the same reasoning.[30] This suggests that the two positions might be closer than they appear at first glance.

[25] See Guideline No. 4.4.3 of the Guide to Practice on Reservations to Treaties, *Yearbook of the International Law Commission, 2011*, Vol. II, Part Two, 35.

[26] See *Case Concerning Military and Paramilitary Activities in and Against Nicaragua (Nicaragua v United State)*, Judgment, Merits, *ICJ Reports* 1986, p. 14, para 94 ('But in addition, even if a treaty norm and a customary norm relevant to the present dispute were to have exactly the same content, this would not be a reason for the Court to take the view that the operation of the treaty process must necessarily deprive the customary norm of its separate applicability').

[27] Saboia (A/CN.4/SR.3415), 4 ('To the extent that such reservations collided with *jus cogens*, they should be considered invalid'); Nguyen (A/CN.4/SR.3415), 7 ('reservation that undermined its non-derogatory and hierarchical character would be invalid'); Ruda Santolaria (A/CN.4/SR.3417), 16 ('In respect of the possibility of formulating reservations to *jus cogens* norms, reference could usefully be made to paragraph 8 of general comment No. 24 of the Human Rights Committee ... which stated that reservations that offended peremptory norms would not be compatible with the object and purpose of the Covenant').

[28] See *Third Report of the Special Rapporteur on Peremptory Norms of General International Law (Jus Cogens)* (A/CN.4/714), para 71.

[29] Id.

[30] See Human Rights Committee, General Comment No. 24 (above note 23), para 8.

3. The Content of Draft Conclusion 10

Conclusion 10

Treaties Conflicting with a Peremptory Norm of General International Law (*Jus Cogens*)

1. A treaty is void if, at the time of its conclusion, it conflicts with a peremptory norm of general international law (*jus cogens*). The provisions of such a treaty have no legal force.
2. Subject to paragraph 2 of Draft Conclusion 11, if a new peremptory norm of general international law (*jus cogens*) emerges, any existing treaty which is in conflict with that norm becomes void and terminates. The parties to such a treaty are released from any obligation further to perform the treaty.

The text of Draft Conclusion 10 follows closely the provisions of the Vienna Convention on the Law of Treaties concerning invalidity of treaties on the basis of conflict with *jus cogens*. The first paragraph concerns treaties conflicting with *jus cogens* at the time of conclusion, while the second paragraph concerns treaties conflicting with a norm of *jus cogens* that emerges subsequent to the conclusion of the treaty. The text generally follows the structure of Draft Conclusion 10 as proposed in the Third Report of the Special Rapporteur, which provided as follows:[31]

> 1. A treaty is void if, at the time of its conclusion, it conflicts with a peremptory norm of general international law (*jus cogens*). Such a treaty does not create any rights or obligations.
> 2. An existing treaty becomes void and terminates if it conflicts with a new peremptory norm of general international law (*jus cogens*) that emerges subsequent to the conclusion of the treaty. Parties to such a treaty are released from any further obligation to perform in terms of the treaty.

The text of the first sentence of paragraph 1 is identical to the text initially proposed in the Third Report and it is taken verbatim from Article 53. While the proposition contained in the second sentence of the Special Rapporteur's proposal was retained, the Commission decided to reformulate it by replicating Article 69 of the Vienna Convention on the Law of the Treaties, which provides

[31] See Third Report (above note 28), 65.

that the provisions of a void treaty 'have no legal force'.[32] The language of the first paragraph is self-explanatory—voidness *ab initio* for any treaty in conflict with *jus cogens* at the time of its conclusion.

The second paragraph, however, underwent several changes. On first reading, while retaining the essence of the proposal in the Third Report, the Commission decided to reformulate the first sentence so that it replicated verbatim the words in Article 64 of the Vienna Convention on the Law of Treaties.[33] The second sentence, which itself replicates part of Article 72(1)(a) of the Vienna Convention, was retained in the form proposed in the Third Report.

The content of the second paragraph is a lot less straightforward than that of the first paragraph. The first point to highlight is that, unlike the position in paragraph 1, the treaty is not void *ab initio* but rather *becomes* void. Thus, before the emergence of the *jus cogens* norm, the treaty is fully valid, with the consequence that the rights and obligations before the emergence of the *jus cogens* are valid and enforceable. It is only from the time of the emergence of the *jus cogens* norm that the rights and obligations cease to exist, hence the word in the second sentence 'further' in relation to the parties being released from the performance of the obligations under the treaty. The precise consequences of this release from further obligation are addressed in Draft Conclusion 12.

In its written comments, the United States had suggested that there is an inconsistency between the second paragraph of Draft Conclusion 10, which states that a treaty becomes void and terminates in the event of conflict with a subsequently emerging *jus cogens* norm, and paragraph 2 of Draft Conclusion 11, which provides for the separability of provisions of a treaty that are in conflict with such a subsequently emerging norm of *jus cogens*.[34] In response to this statement, the Third Report makes the following observation:

> An appreciation and application of the most elementary principles of interpretation would make plain that this statement is simply wrong.

[32] See Peremptory Norms of General International Law (*Jus Cogens*), Statement of the Chair of the Drafting Committee, Mr Charles Chernor Jalloh, of 26 July 2018, 3.

[33] Id.

[34] The United States, Comments and Observations (above note 3), 60 ('this draft conclusion is inconsistent with draft conclusion 11. Draft conclusion 10 paragraph 2 states that if a new *jus cogens* norm emerges, an existing conflicting treaty is void and that the parties are "released" from all obligations under those treaties. Draft Conclusion 11, paragraph 2, on the other, makes clear that [such a treaty] may survive, so long as the offending provision is separable').

> Indeed, in the absence of the application of these elementary principles of interpretation, the chapeau of paragraph 2 of draft conclusion 11 [the treaty 'is void in whole, *unless* ...'] ... the word 'unless' [is] signalling an exception to the general rule set forth in draft conclusion 10.[35]

Notwithstanding this retort, the Commission decided to address the concern of the United States by inserting, at the beginning of the second paragraph the words 'subject to paragraph 2 of Draft Conclusion 11'.[36] Another option, considered but rejected, was to add a third paragraph which would read 'Paragraph 2 of Draft Conclusion 10 is subject to Draft Conclusion 11'.[37]

4. The Content of Draft Conclusion 11

Conclusion 11

Separability of treaty provisions conflicting with a peremptory norm of general international law (*jus cogens*)

1. A treaty which, at the time of its conclusion, conflicts with a peremptory norm of general international law (*jus cogens*) is void in whole, and no separation of the provisions of the treaty is permitted.
2. A treaty which is in conflict with a new peremptory norm of general international law (*jus cogens*) becomes void and terminates in whole, unless: (a) the provisions that are in conflict with a peremptory norm of general international law (*jus cogens*) are separable from the remainder of the treaty with regard to their application; (b) it appears from the treaty or is otherwise established that acceptance of the said provisions was not an essential basis of the consent of the parties to be bound by the

[35] See Fifth Report (above note 5), para 116.

[36] See Peremptory Norms of General International Law (*Jus Cogens*), Statement of the Chair of the Drafting Committee, Mr Ki-Gab Park, of 17 May 2022, 14 ('The main issue confronting the Drafting Committee was the relationship between paragraph 2 of the present Draft Conclusion and paragraph 2 of Draft Conclusion 11, which envisages the possibility of the separability of the provisions of the treaty which are in conflict with the [new *jus cogens* norm]. In order to further clarify the relationship between the two draft conclusions, the Drafting Committee, acting on the recommendation of the Special Rapporteur, added a new opening phrase "[s]ubject to paragraph 2 of Draft Conclusion 11"'). See also Proposal by the Special Rapporteur for Draft Conclusion 10, para 2, ILC(LXXIII)/DC/JC/WP.2, 3 May 2022.

[37] See handwritten comments on Proposal by the Special Rapporteur for Draft Conclusion 10, para 2, ILC(LXXIII)/DC/JC/WP.2, 3 May 2022.

treaty as a whole; and (c) continued performance of the remainder of the treaty would not be unjust.

Draft Conclusion 11 concerns the separability of the provisions of a treaty that are in conflict with a *jus cogens* norm. Whether separability is possible depends on whether the treaty is void *ab initio* on account of a pre-existing *jus cogens* norm, or whether it becomes void and terminates on account of a *jus cogens* norm that emerges subsequent to the conclusion of the treaty. The first paragraph addresses the former while the second addresses the latter situation.

As discussed in Section 2, while there were calls for the Commission to provide for some possibility of separability even in the case of conflict with a pre-existing *jus cogens* norm, the Commission decided to retain the Vienna Convention rule and to not permit separability. The Commission modified the drafting initially proposed in the Third Report,[38] so that it followed more closely language used in the Vienna Convention. The first part of the sentence replicates, again, Article 53. The second part of the sentence is taken from Article 44 of the Vienna Convention, which states that for cases falling under Article 53 'no separation of the provisions of the treaty is permitted'.

The second paragraph addresses separability in cases of *jus cogens superveniens*. The chapeau of paragraph 2 is taken from Article 64 of the Vienna Convention. The rest of the paragraph is based on paragraph 3 of Article 44 of the Vienna Convention. The principle reflected in this paragraph, i.e. the idea that separability is possible under certain circumstances, was generally accepted. Yet, capturing the principle was not without its difficulties. On the first reading, paragraph 2 provided as follows:

> 2. A treaty which becomes void because of the emergence of a new peremptory norm of general international law (*jus cogens*) terminates in whole, unless:
>   (a) the provisions that are in conflict with a peremptory norm of general international law (*jus cogens*) are separable from the remainder of the treaty with regard to their application;

[38] As proposed by the Special Rapporteur, para 1 of Draft Conclusion 11 provided that a 'treaty which, at its conclusion, is in conflict with a peremptory norm of general international law (*jus cogens*) is invalid in whole, and no part of the treaty may be severed or separated'. See Third Report (above note 28), 66.

(b) it appears from the treaty or is otherwise established that acceptance of the said provisions was not an essential basis of the consent of any party to be bound by the treaty as a whole; and
(c) continued performance of the remainder of the treaty would not be unjust.

In the Drafting Committee, Mr Murphy argued that the first reading text did not make any sense since a treaty which 'becomes void' could not be the subject of separability. Voidness, by definition, meant that the treaty was no longer in existence and as such no provisions could be separated from it. Other members of the Drafting Committee preferred to retain the language in the Vienna Convention. It was, in fact, during the *toilletage*, or the final cleaning up of the text, that the Drafting Committee saw the reasoning of Mr Murphy and modified the chapeau to the final text adopted by the Commission.[39]

The import of the chapeau of paragraph 2 is that, as a general rule, the consequence of conflict with a *jus cogens* norm that emerges subsequent to the conclusion of the treaty is voidness, with the result that separability is not permitted. The word 'unless' at the end of the chapeau indicates that, notwithstanding the general rule of voidness and no separability, separability may be permitted in certain limited circumstances as provided for in (a) to (c). However, as noted by Mr Wood, it was important to emphasise that the conditions laid out in (a) to (c) were to be read as cumulative, i.e. all three conditions had to be present for separability.[40] Thus, as a general rule, no separation is permitted. However, where (a) the offending provision is separable, which is to say 'it is possible for the rest of the treaty to be applied without' the offending provision,[41] (b) it appears that the offending provision 'was not an essential basis of' consent, and (c) the continued performance of the treaty without the offending provision would not be unjust, then the offending provision can be severed. In that case, the treaty would not become void, but would continue to apply without the offending provision.

[39] See Drafting Committee, Text of Draft Conclusion 11(2) ILC (LXXIII)/DC/JC/CRP.8, which still contained the first reading version of the *chapeau*.
[40] See Wood (acting as Chair) (A/CN.4/SR.3597), 3.
[41] Paragraph 4 of the Commentary to Draft Conclusion 11.

5. The Content of Draft Conclusion 12

Conclusion 12

Consequences of the invalidity and termination of treaties conflicting with a peremptory norm of general international law (*jus cogens*)

1. Parties to a treaty which is void as a result of being in conflict with a peremptory norm of general international law (*jus cogens*) at the time of the treaty's conclusion have a legal obligation to:
   (a) eliminate as far as possible the consequences of any act performed in reliance on any provision of the treaty which conflicts with a peremptory norm of general international law (*jus cogens*); and
   (b) bring their mutual relations into conformity with the peremptory norm of general international law (*jus cogens*).
2. The termination of a treaty on account of the emergence of a new peremptory norm of general international law (*jus cogens*) does not affect any right, obligation or legal situation of the parties created through the execution of the treaty prior to the termination of the treaty, provided that those rights, obligations or situations may thereafter be maintained only to the extent that their maintenance is not in itself in conflict with the new peremptory norm of general international law (*jus cogens*).

While Draft Conclusion 10 sets forth the consequence of a conflict with a *jus cogens* norm, namely voidness and termination, Draft Conclusion 12 addresses the consequences of that voidness and termination. Like Draft Conclusion 10, Draft Conclusion 12 is divided into two paragraphs, one dealing with consequences of invalidity arising from a treaty's conflict with an existing norm of *jus cogens*, and the other dealing with the consequences of invalidity arising from a treaty's conflict with a *jus cogens* norm emerging subsequent to the conclusion of the treaty.

The text initially proposed by in the Third Report was simpler, leaving out many of the details of Article 71 of the Vienna Convention. Draft Conclusion 12 as proposed in the Third Report provided:

> **Conclusion 12**
>
> **Elimination of consequences of acts performed in reliance of invalid treaty**
>
> 1. Parties to a treaty which is invalid as a result of being in conflict with a peremptory norm of general international law (*jus cogens*) at the time of the

treaty's conclusion have a legal obligation to eliminate the consequences of any act performed in reliance of the treaty.

2. The termination of a treaty on account of the emergence of a new peremptory norm of general international law (*jus cogens*) does not affect any right, obligation or legal situation created through the execution of the treaty prior to the termination of the treaty unless such a right, obligation or legal situation is itself in conflict with a peremptory norm of general international law (*jus cogens*).

While there was general agreement with the content of the proposal, members of the Drafting Committee generally supported following the Vienna Convention more closely.[42]

Under paragraph 1, the consequences of voidness as a result of conflict with a pre-existing norm of *jus cogens* norm are two-fold. The first is to eliminate as far as possible the consequences of any act performed in reliance of the offending provision. The key point is that while the treaty as a whole is void (with the result that there is no duty to perform further under it), the consequences of acts performed in reliance on provisions other than the offending provision of the treaty are not affected. Moreover, the obligation to eliminate consequences of past acts performed in reliance on the offending provision is only to do so 'as far as possible'. In the words of the Commission, this obligation 'is not one of result but of conduct', recognising that 'it may not be possible to eliminate' all consequences.[43] The second consequence, flowing from the first, is that there is a duty on the States to bring their relations into conformity with the *jus cogens* norm. According to the Commission, this duty concerns the parties' future conduct, i.e. that 'moving forward, the parties ... should ensure that their relations are consistent with the' *jus cogens* norm in question.[44]

Paragraph 2 concerns situations of termination of the treaty on account of conflict with a *jus cogens* norm that emerges subsequent to the conclusion of the treaty. The text of paragraph 2 is taken almost verbatim from Article 71(2) of the Vienna Convention, with changes only to the chapeau to account for the particular context of the Draft Conclusions. The first comment to make on the situation of termination on account of *jus cogens*

[42] Statement of the Chair of the Drafting Committee (above note 32), 6.
[43] Paragraph 4 of the Commentary to Draft Conclusion 12.
[44] Id.

superveniens is that the termination is not retrospective, such that, in general, the termination 'does not affect' rights, obligations, or legal situations created through the execution of the treaty. This is the general rule. However, where the right, obligation, or situation created through the performance of the treaty is itself in conflict with the *jus cogens* norm, then this general rule does not apply. In the latter case, the right, obligation, or situation cannot be maintained.[45]

One point to mention is that the rights, obligations, and situations referred to in paragraph 2 of the Draft Conclusion are said to be 'of the parties'. This might seem to suggest that rights, obligations, and situations of third States created through the performance of the treaty prior to its termination may be maintained even if they are consistent with *jus cogens*. One explanation for this appears to be that the Commission sought to be faithful to the text of the Vienna Convention.[46] The explanation provided in the statement of the Chair of the Drafting Committee is that Draft Conclusion 12 deals with treaty law.[47] Whatever the reason for this choice by the Commission, the Commentary makes clear that 'any right, obligation or legal situation of a third State or person, created through the execution of the treaty prior to its invalidation, is not affected'.[48]

6. The Content of Draft Conclusion 13

Conclusion 13

Absence of effect of reservations to treaties on peremptory norms of general international law (*jus cogens*)

1. A reservation to a treaty provision that reflects a peremptory norm of general international law (*jus cogens*) does not affect the binding nature of that norm, which shall continue to apply as such.
2. A reservation cannot exclude or modify the legal effect of a treaty in a manner contrary to a peremptory norm of general international law (*jus cogens*).

---

[45] Id., para 5.
[46] Statement of the Chair of the Drafting Committee (above note 32), 6.
[47] Statement of the Chair of the Drafting Committee (above note 36), 16.
[48] Paragraph 6 of the Commentary to Draft Conclusion 12.

Draft Conclusions 10, 11, and 12 are concerned with invalidity of treaties due to conflict with *jus cogens* norms. Draft Conclusion 13 is different from these since it is not concerned at all with invalidity of treaties. Rather, it concerns the consequences of *jus cogens* for reservations. As discussed in Section 2, the Commission considered adopting the approach adopted by the Human Rights Committee, namely that reservations inconsistent with *jus cogens* are invalid. The Commission decided, instead, not to address the validity of reservations which are regulated in the Vienna Convention, but rather to address the consequences of reservations. It does so by addressing two issues: first, reservations to treaty provisions that constitute *jus cogens*, and second, the effect of a reservation which, on its face, does not affect a *jus cogens* norm, but whose application would impact on a norm of *jus cogens*. The text of Draft Conclusion is the same as that proposed in the Third Report of the Special Rapporteur.

The first paragraph addresses the question of a reservation to a treaty provision that reflects a norm of *jus cogens*. Without addressing the validity of the reservation, it states that such a reservation 'does not affect the binding nature of the *jus cogens* norm which shall continue to apply as such'. As explained in Chapter 5, this rule is based on the independent existence of a treaty law norm reflecting a norm of customary international law.[49] The provision thus means that, even if the reservation is valid and applies in relation to the rule as contained in the treaty, the reservation would have no effect on the *jus cogens* rule as such—the rule as contained in the customary international law forming the basis of the *jus cogens* norm—and the *jus cogens* rule would continue to apply to the reserving State, although not as a treaty rule. The main consequence of this rather fine distinction seems to be that any procedural rule in the treaty, most notably dispute settlement provisions of the treaty, would not apply to the reserving State, since those procedural rules will themselves likely not be *jus cogens*.

The problem of course is Draft Conclusion 5, which states that treaties may also be a basis of *jus cogens*. This might suggest that it could be possible, in those cases where a treaty is *the* basis for a *jus cogens* norm, i.e. where there is no independent customary international law basis for the *jus cogens* norm, for a State to exclude the application of a *jus cogens* norm—a proposition that is inimical to the very idea of *jus cogens*. The answer to this apparent contradiction is to be found in paragraph 8 of the Commentary to Draft Conclusion 5:

[49] *Military and Paramilitary Activities in and against Nicaragua (Nicaragua v United States of America), Jurisdiction and Admissibility*, Judgment, *ICJ Reports* 1984, p. 392, para 73.

> Treaties, in most cases, are not 'general international law' since they do not usually have a general scope of application with 'equal force for all members of the international community.' There is, however, support in scholarly writings that provisions in treaties can form the basis of [*jus cogens*]. While recognising the special character of the Charter of the United Nations, it is noteworthy that in the commentary to Draft Article 50 of the 1966 Draft Articles on the Law of Treaties, the Commission identified 'the law of the Charter ... concerning the prohibition of the use of force' as *jus cogens*. The role of treaties as a basis for [*jus cogens*] may be understood as a consequence of the relationship between treaty rules and customary international law as described by the International Court of Justice in the *North Sea Continental Shelf* cases. In that case, the Court observed that a treaty can codify (or be declaratory of) an existing general rule of international law, or that a treaty rule can help crystallize an emerging general rule of international law, or that a treaty rule can, after the adoption, come to reflect a general rule on the basis of subsequent practice.

The essence of this extract is that a treaty provision can form the basis of a *jus cogens* norm to the extent that the treaty provision itself reflects a rule of customary international law. Seen from this perspective, under paragraph 1 of Draft Conclusion 13, a reservation to a treaty provision reflecting a *jus cogens* norm may be effective in the treaty context, but the *jus cogens* norm itself, based on a rule of customary international law, will continue to apply as a general norm of international law.

7. Concluding Observations

The rules on the impact of *jus cogens* on treaties, contained in Draft Conclusions 10, 11, 12, and 13, were generally not controversial. This was in large part because, here, the Commission erred on the side of consistency with the Vienna Convention. Draft Conclusions 10, 11, and 12 are, in the main, a reproduction of the Vienna Convention. Even where, such as is the case with separability in Draft Conclusion 11, there would have been good cause to depart from the Vienna Convention—there were strong policy reasons and even some support for doing so—the Commission decided to stick religiously to the text of the Vienna Convention. This of course is the safe route, but in opting for the safe route, the Commission may have missed an opportunity to be ambitious and to progressively develop the law.

In the case of reservations, where there is no specific provision in the Vienna Convention, the Commission was faced with the earlier approach of the Human Rights Committee, under which a reservation conflicting with *jus cogens* was invalid, and its own previous work which adopted a narrower approach, under which the reservation would not *necessarily* be invalid but would not affect the binding character or *jus cogens* status of the underlying norm. The Commission again chose the more conservative option, which also happens to be the safer one.

9

Consequences of *Jus Cogens* for Other Sources of Obligations

1. Introduction

The consequences of *jus cogens* for treaties, the subject of the previous chapter, is regulated in the Vienna Convention on the Law of Treaties. But there is no treaty or other international instrument developed by States addressing the consequences of *jus cogens* for other sources of obligations. There are of course some incidental references to consequences of *jus cogens* in the Conclusions of the Study Group on Fragmentation and the Guiding Principles Applicable to Unilateral Declarations.[1]

The Draft Conclusions address the consequences of *jus cogens* for sources of obligations other than treaty law, in Draft Conclusion 14 (customary international law), Draft Conclusion 15 (unilateral acts), and Draft Conclusion 16 (acts and decisions of international organisations). In brief, the Draft Conclusions relevant to these other sources of obligations apply the same framework applicable to treaties to these other sources of obligations. Thus, for each source considered, the Draft Conclusions provide that obligations do not arise in the event of conflict with a *jus cogens* norm. Moreover, as with the framework on the law of treaties, the Draft Conclusions provide that an otherwise validly established obligation will cease to exist if it is in conflict with a new peremptory norm that arises subsequent to the relevant customary international law rule, unilateral act, or decision of an international organisation.

Each of the sources discussed raised their own particular issues. This pertains both to issues that are explicitly addressed and issues that are not. These issues will be addressed in turn in Section 2. Thus, after a general discussion,

[1] See para 41 of the Conclusions of the work of the Study Group on the Fragmentation of International Law: Difficulties arising from the Diversification and Expansion of International Law (A/61/10, para 251), *Yearbook of the International Law Commission, 2006*, Vol. II, Part Two, 183; Guiding Principles Applicable to Unilateral Declarations of States Capable of Creating Legal Obligations, with Commentaries thereto (A/61/10), *Yearbook of the International Law Commission, 2006*, Vol. II, Part Two, 378–9.

Section 2 will discuss particular issues relevant to customary international law, namely persistent objection and the problem of modification. Thereafter, as a particular issue concerning acts of international organisations, binding decisions of the Security Council will be discussed. Sections 3, 4, and 5 will address respectively the textual provisions dealing with the individual sources of obligations.

2. Discussion

2.1 The Basic Approach

The effects of *jus cogens* for treaties are well-documented and, more importantly, are reflected in one of the most important treaties of modern international law—the Vienna Convention on the Law of Treaties. The point of departure of the Draft Conclusions is that the effects of *jus cogens* on other sources of obligations under international law are 'less established'.[2] Yet, it would not make sense for treaty rules—the source of law often described as the most important in international law—to be invalidated on account of conflict with *jus cogens*, while other sources of international law remain unaffected by conflict with *jus cogens*. The application of the rule of invalidity, derived from the law of treaties, is thus a rule of deductive logic. Indeed, the idea that other sources of international law are also subject to *jus cogens*, and are thus invalid when inconsistent with *jus cogens*, flows from the character of *jus cogens* as being hierarchically superior to other norms.[3]

For customary international law, the Third Report of the Special Rapporteur relied primarily on domestic cases as a form of State practice.[4] The Report also

[2] See *Third Report of the Special Rapporteur on Peremptory Norms of General International Law (Jus Cogens)* (A/CN.4/714), para 137.

[3] See para 14 of the Commentary to Draft Conclusion 14 of the Draft Conclusions on Identification and Legal Consequences of Peremptory Norms of General International Law (*jus cogens*), with Commentaries, *Yearbook of the International Law Commission*, 2022, Vol. II, Part Two ('The fact that peremptory norms ... are hierarchically superior to other norms of international law is both a characteristic and a consequence ... It is a consequence in that the identification of a norm as [*jus cogens*] has the effect that it will be superior to other norms not having the same character. Some of the implications of hierarchy are reflected in the consequences of peremptory norms described in Part III of the Draft Conclusions').

[4] (Argentina) *Simón, Julio Héctor y otros s/ privación ilegítima de la libertad*, Case No. 17.768, Judgment of 14 June 2005, Supreme Court of Argentina (original: 'el carácter de ius cogens de modo que se encuentra no sólo por encima de los tratados sino incluso por sobre todas las fuentes del derecho') (translation: 'character of *jus cogens*, meaning that [the prohibition is] above not only treaty law, but above all other sources of international law'); (Kenya) *Kenya Section of the International Commission of Jurists v Attorney-General*, High Court Judgment (on file), stating that *jus cogens* norms 'rendered void

relied on the European Court of Human Rights jurisprudence.[5] Yet, it may be noted that, by and large, the language in the authorities relied upon in the Third Report provides only that the *jus cogens* norm takes priority, is higher than, and prevails over or overrides other sources of law. With the exception of the *Kenya Section of the International Commission of Jurists* case, the cases relied upon do not provide authority for invalidation. The International Court of Justice, in the *Jurisdictional Immunities* case, similarly also referred to Italy's argument that *jus cogens* norms prevail over other rules, without rejecting the proposition.[6] In that case, the Court simply found that there was no conflict between the *jus cogens* norm in question and the customary international law in question (the rule on immunity).

While the balance of authority points only to *jus cogens* norms having priority over norms of customary international law and not necessarily invalidating them, at least not explicitly, the approach that the Commission takes is that the *jus cogens* norms have an invalidating effect over inconsistent norms of customary international law. This is based, it seems, on the desire for congruence with the rule concerning the invalidation of treaty rules.

For unilateral acts, the Third Report relied on the Commission's previous work, i.e. the Guiding Principles Applicable to Unilateral Declarations. Guiding Principle 8 states simply that a 'unilateral declaration which is in conflict with a [norm of *jus cogens*] is void'. In the Commentary to Guiding Principle 8, the Commission stated that the Guiding Principle 'derives from the analogous rule contained in Article 53 of the Vienna Convention'.[7] Also relying on inspiration from Article 53, the Commission's Guide to Practice on Reservations similarly

any other pre-emptory rules which come into conflict with them'; (United States) *Committee of United States Citizens Living in Nicaragua v Reagan*, United States Court of Appeals, 859 F.2d 929 (DC Cir. 1988), p. 940 where the Court observed that *jus cogens* 'enjoy[s] the highest status in international law and prevail over both customary international law and treaties'; (United Kingdom) the Queen's Bench Division of the England and Wales High Court of Justice in *R (Mohamed) v Secretary of State for Foreign and Commonwealth Affairs* [2009] 1 WLR 2579, p. 142 (ii) also referred to the hierarchical superiority of *jus cogens* norms and, consequently, 'that derogation by States through treaties or rules of customary law not possessing the same status [was] not permitted'.

[5] See *Al-Adsani v United Kingdom* [GC], No. 35763/97, European Court of Human Rights, para 30, stating that *jus cogens* norms are those norms that enjoy 'a higher rank in the international hierarchy than treaty law and even "ordinary" customary rules'. See also joint Dissenting Opinion of Judges Rozakis and Caflisch (joined by Judges Wildhaber, Costa, Cabral Barreto, and Vajić) ('By accepting that the rule on prohibition of torture is a rule of *jus cogens*, the majority recognise that it is hierarchically higher than any other rule of international law ... For the basic characteristic of a *jus cogens* rule is that... it overrides any other rule which does not have the same status. In the event of a conflict between a *jus cogens* rule and any other rule of international law, the former prevails').

[6] *Jurisdictional Immunities of the State (Germany v Italy: Greece intervening)*, Judgment, *ICJ Reports* 2012, p. 99, para 92.

[7] See also para 2 of the Commentary to Draft Conclusion 15 of the Draft Conclusions (above note 3) ('Para 1 of Draft Conclusion 15 is inspired by Article 53 of the Vienna Convention').

stated that it is 'certainly true' that 'the rule prohibiting derogation from a rule of *jus cogens* applies not only to treaty relations, but also to all legal acts, including unilateral acts'.[8]

On decisions and acts of international organisations, much of the authority relied upon to substantiate the rule contained in Draft Conclusion 16 concerned the Security Council—which is discussed below in Section 2.4. Yet, as with the rule concerning customary international law and unilateral acts, it is apparent that the rule in Draft Conclusion 16 is inspired by Article 53. The Commentary to the Draft Conclusion explains the rationale for Draft Conclusion 16 in the following terms:

> The rule in Draft Conclusion 16 ... follows from the hierarchical superiority of [*jus cogens* norms]. If rules of international law that are inconsistent with [*jus cogens*] cannot be created through treaties, customary international law and unilateral acts, it follows that such rules cannot be created through resolutions, decisions or other acts of international organisations either.[9]

With the exception of particular issues discussed below (the problem of modification, Section 2.2; the persistent objector rule, Section 2.3; decisions of the Security Council, Section 2.4), the content of the rules in Draft Conclusion 14, Draft Conclusion 15, and Draft Conclusion 16 did not attract much comment, whether by members of the Commission or States.[10] There were, of course, questions of drafting, particularly in relation to customary international law. These will be addressed in Section 3.

While the Commission addressed the legal effects of *jus cogens* on other sources in addition to treaties, there is no consideration of the effects of *jus cogens* on general principles of law within the meaning of Article 38(1)(c) of the Statute of the International Court of Justice. There is, moreover, no explanation whatsoever in the Commentary for this omission. This omission did not go unnoticed. Within the Commission, the issue was raised by several members.[11]

[8] See para 18 of the Commentary to Guideline 3.1.5.3 of the Guide to Practice on Reservations to Treaties, *Yearbook of the International Law Commission, 2011*, Vol. II, Part Two, 224.

[9] Paragraph 4 of the Commentary to Draft Conclusion 16 (above note 3).

[10] See, however, Peremptory Norms of General International Law (*Jus Cogens*): the United States, Comments and Observation received from Governments (A/CN4/748), suggesting that there was insufficient State practice to support any of the Draft Conclusions pertaining to the effects of *jus cogens* on sources of obligations under international law.

[11] Murphy (A/CN.4/SR.3416), 10 ('First, it was curious that the Special Rapporteur had chosen to propose Draft Conclusions relating to customary international law, unilateral acts and acts of international organisations but not general principles of law. The implication was that a general principle

In response, Mr Nolte stated that he agreed with the choice not to address general principles since 'he could not conceive of a situation in which a general principle ... could conflict with a norm of *jus cogens*'.[12] While Mr Nolte is correct that it was inconceivable that a general principle could conflict with *jus cogens*, this consideration was, at least to some degree, applicable also to other sources of obligations. Indeed, in response to the debate, the Special Rapporteur made the following observations:

> Several members had raised the question of why general principles ... had not been covered. Like Mr Nolte, he found it hard to imagine general principles of law that would conflict with norms of *jus cogens*. That said, ... the report made it plain that the same situation pertained to treaties, resolutions of international organisations and customary international law ... He therefore agreed with the majority who had taken the view that general principles should not be excluded.[13]

And yet, even with the concession by the Special Rapporteur, the Draft Conclusions did not address general principles nor is there any indication in the Commentary as to why that source of law was not addressed in the Draft Conclusions.

The issue was considered in the Drafting Committee. The Drafting Committee considered a proposal by the Special Rapporteur which followed the structure of Draft Conclusion 14:[14]

Draft Conclusion 15 *bis*

1. A general principle of law does not come into existence if it conflicts with a peremptory norm of general international law (*jus cogens*). This is without prejudice to the possible modification of a peremptory norm

of law that conflicted with a peremptory norm of general international law might nevertheless be valid'); Rajput (A/CN.4/SR,3418), 4 ('However, such an approach should be taken with caution. The report included a discussion of the relationship between peremptory norms and customary international law, unilateral acts and acts and resolutions of international organisations, including the Security Council, but the relationship between peremptory norms and general principles should also be considered'); Ouazzani-Chahdi (A/CN.4/SR.3418), 11; Galvão Teles (A/CN.4/SR.3419), 4; Grossman Guiloff (A/CN.4/SR.3420), 6; Wood (A/CN.4/SR.3421), 6; Escobar-Hernandez (A/CN.4/SR.3421), 7.

12 Nolte (A/CN.4/SR.3417), 12.

13 Tladi (Special Rapporteur) (A/CN.4/SR.3425), 5.

14 See Drafting Committee, Peremptory Norms of General International Law, Proposal of Special Rapporteur (Draft Conclusion 15 *bis*), ILC(LXXI)/DC/JC/WP.6, 15 May 2019.

of general international law (*jus cogens*) by a subsequent norm of general international law having the same character.

2. A general principle of law not of a peremptory character ceases to exist if and to the extent that it conflicts with a new peremptory norm of general international law (*jus cogens*).

Yet the Drafting Committee decided not to include the provision. The Chair of the Drafting Committee explained the reason for the Drafting Committee's decision not to include a provision as follows:

> [T]he Drafting Committee had a discussion on whether or not to include a provision on general principles of law conflicting with a peremptory norm of general international law (*jus cogens*). It will be recalled that following the debate the Special Rapporteur had expressed a willingness to consider including a provision that would complement the corresponding provisions on treaties, rules of customary international law, unilateral acts of States, and resolutions, decisions or other acts of international organisations. The Drafting Committee decided to recommend that the Commission considers the issue during the second reading, so as to take into account the work that will be undertaken in the topic 'General Principles of Law'.[15]

On second reading, the Commission did not return to the issue. This is mainly because States had not generally raised this issue in their written comments. Indeed, the issue had only been raised by Poland which, in its written comments, recommended the insertion of an additional conclusion addressing the relationship between *jus cogens* and general principles of law in the same way as with other sources of international law.[16] Given that, in the main, the second reading was intended to address issues raised by States, the fact that States did not generally find fault with the absence of a provision on general principles probably contributed to it falling between the cracks. Yet it is hard to deny that general principles ought to have been addressed, at least to avoid the implication raised by Mr Murphy that general principles of law in conflict with *jus cogens* remained valid. It is, however, clear from the comments by members, the response of the Special Rapporteur, and the statement of the Chair of the Drafting Committee that the intention of the Commission

[15] Peremptory Norms of General International Law (*Jus Cogens*), Statement of the Chair of the Drafting Committee, Claudio Grossman Guiloff, 31 May 2019, 4.

[16] Poland, Comments and Observations (above note 10), 59.

was not to suggest that general principles of law in conflict with *jus cogens* remained valid.

2.2 Customary International Law: The Problem of Modification

While the basic idea concerning the invalidity of customary international law rules conflicting with *jus cogens* was not questioned within the Commission, there is one conceptual issue that is not addressed—or at least not addressed in great detail. The issue is, if customary international law is the most common basis of *jus cogens*, it was not clear how peremptory norms could be modified (or new peremptory norms could emerge) if rules of customary international law conflicting with *jus cogens* could not arise.[17] Within the Commission, the issue was raised most sharply by Mr Hmoud. During the debate on second reading, Mr Hmoud made the following comments:

> Among the aspects of the *jus cogens* regime that remained open for debate was the question of how, or under which conditions, a *jus cogens* norm could be modified by the emergence of a subsequent norm of general international law having the same character, including in situations where the subsequent norm nullified the existing one. In his opinion, such a subsequent norm could never emerge, since it would obviously be in conflict with the existing norm.[18]

The view that modification of *jus cogens* was not possible was apparently shared by Mr Nguyen, who stated that 'the authors of the Vienna Convention' had included the possibility of modification 'only as a safety valve in ensuring the non-derogability of norms of general international law or preventing any attempt to change them'.[19] Without expressing a view one way or the other, Mr Forteau also suggested that there was an internal inconsistency in the Draft Conclusions:

> Moreover, Draft Conclusion 14 raised a major problem by implying that *jus cogens* norms were irreversible: if a customary norm contrary to *jus cogens*

[17] See Hmoud (A/CN.4/SR3420), 11.

[18] Hmoud (A/CN.4/SR.3566), 8. See also Hmoud (A/CN.4/SR.3597), 8 ('For the record, his view was that, in practice, it was impossible for a rule of customary international law that acquired a peremptory character to modify a pre-existing *jus cogens* norm').

[19] Nguyen (A/CN.4/SR.3415), 6.

could not exist, then a *jus cogens* norm could never be modified. However, that view ran counter to Article 64 of the 1969 Vienna Convention. Draft Conclusion 14 should therefore be thoroughly revised.[20]

This point was picked up by some States. In its written comments, the Netherlands alluded to the fact that the Commission needed to clarify this point:

> [T]he Kingdom of the Netherlands finds it difficult to imagine how a peremptory norm of international law may be revised by a developing rule of customary international law. This would imply that the required State practice with respect to the developing rule of customary international law would derogate from an already existing norm of *jus cogens*.[21]

The complexity of the question posed by these States, and some members of the Commission, has been acknowledged in the literature. Mehrdad Payandeh observes that neither the Reports of the Special Rapporteur nor the Draft Conclusion focus on modification.[22] He identifies two reasons for this. On the one hand, given the complexity of the more fundamental questions concerning identification, he suggests that the issue of modification might be seen as a second-tier question.[23] Second, he posits that given the fundamental character of *jus cogens* norms, it is difficult to see how they could be modified, making serious consideration of the question of modification seem like a 'pointless academic endeavour'.[24]

Many of the statements pointing to the apparent internal inconsistency in the Draft Conclusions are based on the erroneous assumption that modification always involves an emergent norm in conflict with a norm of *jus cogens*.[25]

[20] Forteau (A/CN.4/SR.3564), 14.

[21] The Netherlands, Comments and Observations (above note 10), 69. See also Slovenia, Comments and Observations (above note 10), 70 stating that additional clarification was required on the process of modification. The statement continued: 'the position of the Republic of Slovenia is that peremptory norm of general international law (*jus cogens*) can only arise from a norm of customary international law. Since the first sentence of draft conclusion 14 stipulates that a rule of customary international law cannot come into existence if it conflicts with [a norm of *jus cogens*], it is unclear how a peremptory norm can be modified by a subsequent norm of general international law.'

[22] Mehrdad Payandeh 'Modification of Peremptory Norms of General International Law' in Dire Tladi (ed.) *Peremptory Norms of General International Law (Jus Cogens): Disquisitions and Disputations* (Brill, 2021), 44.

[23] Id.

[24] Id.

[25] See statement by the Special Rapporteur in Response to the Debate on Cluster One, 27 October 2022 available on UN WebTV https://media.un.org/en/asset/k12/k12iqnldud (accessed 23 December 2022).

After all, the problem does not generally arise in the case where a *jus cogens* norm is expanded, which is also a form of modification.[26] Moreover, even modification in the sense of the emergence of a new conflicting norm is, though extremely difficult, nevertheless possible.[27] According to the Commentary to Draft Conclusion 14, for modification to take place 'the rule of customary international law in question must have the same character as the' *jus cogens* norm.[28] Practically, this means

> that there must be, at the point of the emergence of a peremptory norm of general international law (*jus cogens*), a practice accepted as law (*opinio juris*) and which the international community of States as a whole, at the same time, accept and recognize as having peremptory character.[29]

Seen from this perspective, the possibility of modification does not seem as intractable as might first appear. The process simply requires that the existence of *opinio juris sive necessitatis* coincide with the emergence of the *opinio juris cogentis* (or as often referred to '*opinio cogentis*'). An example to illustrate the point might be warranted. The prohibition on the use of force is a norm of *jus cogens*. There are two exceptions to this prohibition. To show that a new exception has emerged, e.g. the unilateral use of force for humanitarian purposes, would require not only a belief that general international law permits this (*opinio juris sive necessitatis*) but also an acceptance and recognition by the international community of States as a whole of the peremptory status of the permissibility of humanitarian intervention (*opinion juris cogentis*) or, put differently, that the rule of humanitarian intervention has the same *jus cogens* status as the prohibition. In the event that there is a general widespread practice of humanitarian intervention accompanied by *opinio juris sive necessitatis* but without the *opinio cogentis*, then a customary international law does not emerge, because of the conflict with *jus cogens*, and as a result the *jus cogens* norm is not modified. However, if an *opinio cogentis* should subsequently emerge, then the *jus cogens* norm would only then be modified, together with the underlying rule of customary international law.

[26] This point was also acknowledged by the Netherlands, Comments and Observations (above note 10), 69 ('The only situation in which this would be different is when State practice with respect to a developing rule of customary international law would provide the already existing norm of *jus cogens* with a broader scope of application').

[27] See generally Dire Tladi 'Grotian Moments and Peremptory Norms of General International Law: Friendly Facilitators or Fatal Foes?' (2021) 42 *Grotiana* 335.

[28] See para 7 of the Commentary to Draft Conclusion 14 of the Draft Conclusions (above note 3).

[29] Id.

2.3 Customary International Law: The Persistent Objector Rule

The Commission, in 2019, adopted another set of Draft Conclusions: the Draft Conclusions on the Identification of Customary International Law. The Draft Conclusions on Customary International Law provide for the application of the persistent objector doctrine.[30] However, paragraph 3 of Draft Conclusion 15 provided that it was 'without prejudice to any question concerning' *jus cogens*.

The Third Report of the Special Rapporteur stated unequivocally that 'the persistent objector doctrine' does not apply to *jus cogens*.[31] This conclusion was based on the principle that *jus cogens* applied to all subjects of international law.[32] More explicitly, the Inter-American Commission on Human Rights stated that *jus cogens* norms 'bind the international community as a whole, irrespective of protest, recognition or acquiescence'. When introducing the Third Report, the Special Rapporteur described the proposition that the persistent objector doctrine did not apply to *jus cogens* as 'trite'.[33]

This position was generally welcomed by members of the Commission.[34] Only Mr Wood seemed to question the proposition, although even he was rather tentative:

[30] Draft Conclusion 15(1) of the Draft Conclusions on Customary International Law, *Report of the International Law Commission, Seventieth Session* (A/73/10) ('Where a State has objected to a rule of customary international law while that rule was in the process of formation, the rule is not opposable to the State concerned for so long as it maintains its objection').

[31] See para 145 of the Third Report (above note 2).

[32] See, id, paras 143 and 144. Here the Report relied on Swiss Court judgment, *Nada (Youssef) v State Secretary for Economic Affairs and Federal Department of Economic Affairs*, Administrative Appeal, Judgment of 14 November 2007, Federal Supreme Court, Case No. 1A 45/2007, ILDC 461, para 7, stating that *jus cogens* norms 'were binding on all subjects of international law'. The Report also referred to *Belhas v Moshe Ya'Alon*, 515 F.3d 1279, 1291–1292, describing *jus cogens* norms as those that are 'so universally accepted that all States are deemed to be bound by them under international law' and the Advisory Opinion of the Inter-American Court on the *Juridical Conditions and Rights of Undocumented Migrants, Requested by the United Mexican States*, Series A, No. 18, paras 4–5.

[33] Tladi (Special Rapporteur) (A/CN.4/SR.3414), 7.

[34] Members of the Commission that supported the proposition were Saboia (A/CN.4/SR.3415), 5; Nguyen (A/CN.4/SR.3415), 7 ('the universal, hierarchical and non-derogatory character of *jus cogens* left no room for persistent objection'); Zagaynov (A/CN.4/SR.3416), 5 ('he fully agreed with the Special Rapporteur that once a peremptory norm emerged, all States, without exception, were bound by it'); Šturma (A/CN.4/SR.3416), 8; Park (A/CN.4/SR.3416), 15 ('Given the nature of *jus cogens*, it was proper to state that the persistent objector rule was not applicable' to *jus cogens*); Ruda Santolaria (A/CN.4/SR.3417), 17 ('since peremptory norms ... were binding on all subjects, the persistent objector doctrine did not apply'); Lehto (A/CN.4/SR.3417), 18 ('she welcomed the clear statement ... that the persistent objector rule was not applicable to *jus cogens* norms'); Jalloh (A/CN.4/SR.3418), 8; Oauzzani-Chahdi (A/CN.4/SR.3418), 11; Vásquez-Bermúdez (A/CN.4/SR.3418), 13; Galvão Teles (A/CN.4/SR.3419), 4; Hassouna (A/CN.4/SR.3419), 7 ('the non-applicability of the persistent objector doctrine to *jus cogens* was grounded in case law, commentary and logic; the doctrine stood in direct opposition to the universal application of *jus cogens*'); Oral (A.CN.4/SR.3419), 14; Hmoud (A/CN.4/SR.3420), 11; Escobar-Hernández (A/CN.4/SR.3421), 8. See also Valencia-Ospina (Chair) (A/CN.43421), 10, who

> A separate question was whether a State that had established itself as a persistent objector to a rule of customary international law that later achieved *jus cogens* status would be bound by the *jus cogens* norm … The Special Rapporteur had concluded that it would indeed be bound … he was not entirely convinced by the Special Rapporteur's reasoning, although the result was not necessarily wrong.[35]

Similarly, the proposition was generally accepted by States.[36] Only two States explicitly questioned the proposition that the persistent objector doctrine does not apply.[37] On the strength of the Third Report and the views expressed by States and members of the Commission, the Commission decided to retain the proposition that the persistent objector doctrine does not apply to *jus cogens*.

There is, however, one objection to the blanket exclusion of the relevance of the persistent objector doctrine that requires a little more consideration.[38] The point was perhaps best made by Mr Zagaynov:

> Koskenniemi had written that relationship between *jus cogens* and persistent objection was a point where an irresistible force and an immovable object of international legal theory collided. Allowing persistent objection to *jus cogens* norms would undermine the superior nature of those norms … if *jus cogens*

expressed agreement with the conclusion but nonetheless questioned the reasoning; Grossman Guiloff (A/CN.3566), 6.

[35] Wood (A/CN.4/SR.3421), 5.

[36] See e.g. Cyprus, Comments and Observations (above note 10), 67 ('Bearing in mind that peremptory norms are hierarchically superior to ordinary rules of international law, universally applicable and non-derogable, the Republic of Cyprus supports the view that a State cannot be [a] "persistent objector" to a peremptory norm (draft conclusion 14). Accepting the application of the "persistent objector" rule to peremptory norms would contradict and undermine the very essence of the latter concept and negate its constitutive elements'); Greece (A/C.6/74/SR.24), para 37; see also the United States, Comments and Observations (above note 10), 73 ('Finally, with respect to draft conclusion 14, paragraph 3, the United States agrees that the persistent objector rule may not prevent the application of a *jus cogens* norm once that norm has been accepted and recognized consistent with draft conclusions 4 and 6'). See also Brazil, Debate on the *Report of the International Law Commission* (Cluster I), Sixth Committee of the General Assembly, Seventy-Seventh Session available at www.un.org/en/ga/sixth/77/summaries.shtml (accessed 28 December 2022).

[37] Israel, Comments and Observations (above note 10), 68. Although the statement by Israel seemed concerned more with the effect of persistent objection on the formation of *jus cogens*, an issue discussed below, given that it takes the absolute view that persistent objection prevents the formation of *jus cogens*, the effect seems to be the same as the denial of the proposition. See also the United Kingdom, Comments and Observations (above note 10), 72 ('The United Kingdom continues to question whether the status of a persistent objector should be automatically denied if a rule of customary international law were to become a peremptory norm of general international law (*jus cogens*); there is no relevant State practice to support such a contention').

[38] See e.g. Nguyen (A/CN.4/SR.3415), 7, noting that the 'number and representativeness of persistent objectors could prolong the process of formation of a new *jus cogens* norm and influence the international community's acceptance and recognition'.

> could steamroll even otherwise legitimate objections, then it would undermine the idea that persistent objection acted to protect State consent ... the key question was whether, in the event that the international community as a whole accepted and recognised the non-derogability of the norm in question, a persistent objector would be bound by that norm.[39]

The point being made here is that a distinction ought to be made between persistent objection to a norm already established as *jus cogens* and the effects of persistent objection to the norm during its emergence as a *jus cogens*. This view was also expressed by several States commenting on the first reading text.[40] The Fifth Report's response to this position suggests that the objection is based on an unwarranted conflation of persistent objection and the threshold for acceptance and recognition:

> In the view of the Special Rapporteur, persistent objection to the formation of a rule of customary international law cannot prevent the emergence of a *jus cogens* norm. Once the rule of customary international law has been formed, the question that has to be addressed is whether 'the international community as a whole'—as described in the second report of the Special Rapporteur and defined in draft conclusion 7—accepts and recognizes the non-derogability of the norm in question. Needless to say, if there are a sufficient number of objectors, then the *jus cogens* norm does not arise, *not because of the persistent objector rule but because there would not be a large enough majority of States* to qualify as 'recognition of the international community of States as a whole'.[41]

This is the approach ultimately adopted in the Commentary to the Draft Conclusions. To this end, the Commentary states that 'the persistent objector rule does not prevent the emergence of a' *jus cogens* norm 'based on a rule of customary international law to which one or more States have persistently

[39] Zagaynov (A/CN.4/SR.3416), 7.

[40] See e.g. Japan, Comments and Observations (above note 10), 39; The Netherlands, Comments and Observations (above note 10), 69; Russia (above note 10), 70 ('the Commission would do well to revisit paragraph 3 of draft conclusion 14 and consider a formulation that distinguishes between the non-applicability of the persistent objector rule to an existing peremptory norm of general international law (*jus cogens*) and the ability of this rule, provided there is a sufficient number of objections by States, to prevent the emergence or formation of a peremptory norm of general international law (*jus cogens*)'); the United Kingdom, Comments and Observations (above note 10), 72 ('In light of the requirement for acceptance and recognition by the international community of States as a whole, the United Kingdom remains unconvinced that it would even be possible for a norm of *jus cogens* to develop where there is a clear persistent objection or objections from States, especially those States who are specially affected').

[41] Paragraph 142 of the Third Report (above note 2) (emphasis added).

objected'.[42] The Commentary goes on to state that if the *jus cogens* norm does emerge, that is, notwithstanding the persistent objection, there is acceptance and recognition by the international community of States as a whole, then 'the effect of the persistent objection falls away'.[43] Whether there is acceptance and recognition may, however, be affected by the persistent objection.[44] The Commentary notes, in particular, that while the number of persistent objections might not be sufficient to prevent the emergence of a rule of customary international law, it might be large enough to prevent the emergence of a norm of *jus cogens*.[45]

2.4 Decisions of the Security Council

In relation to decisions and other acts of international organisations that are inconsistent with *jus cogens* and thus do not create obligations, the Third Report explicitly referred to resolutions of the UN Security Council in the Draft Conclusion. For this decision, the Report relied on State practice in the form of statements by States and decisions of national courts.[46] The Report

[42] Paragraph 11 of the Commentary to Draft Conclusion 14 of the Draft Conclusions (above note 3).

[43] Id.

[44] Id, para 12.

[45] Id. ('In other words, to the extent that such persistent objection implies that the norm in question is not accepted and recognized by the international community of States as a whole as one from which no derogation is permitted, then a peremptory norm of general international law (*jus cogens*) might not arise.')

[46] For statements by States see Switzerland, 5446th meeting, 30 May 2006 (see S/PV.5446), stating that *jus cogens* norms were norms 'from which neither the Member States nor the United Nations may derogate'; Argentina, and Nigeria, 5474th meeting, 22 June 2006 (see S/PV.5474); Qatar, 5679th meeting, 22 May 2007 (S/PV.5679). See also Qatar, 5779th meeting, 14 November 2007 (S/PV.5779), stating that while, by virtue of Article 103 of the Charter, obligations flowing from Security Council resolutions supersede other obligations, this did not apply to *jus cogens* norms; Finland, speaking on behalf of the Nordic countries (Denmark, Finland, Iceland, Norway, and Sweden) (A/C.6/60/SR.18), para 18; Iran (A/C.6/66/SR.7), para 84, stating that 'the Security Council was subject to and obliged to comply with ... *jus cogens*'. See also the United Kingdom, *R v Secretary of State for Defence (On the Application of Al-Jedda)*, Judgment of 12 December 2007, House of Lords [2008] All ER 28 (Lord Bingham); and the United Kingdom, *R (On the Application of Al-Jedda)*, Judgment of 29 March 2006, Appeal Court, para 71 ('If the Security Council, acting under Chapter VII, considers that the exigencies posed by a threat to peace must override ... the requirements of a human rights convention (seemingly other than *ius cogens*, from which no derogation is possible), the UN Charter has given it the power to do so'); Switzerland, *Nada (Youssef) v State Secretariat for Economic Affairs and Federal Department of Economic Affairs*, Administrative Appeal Judgment of 14 November 2007, Federal Supreme Court, para 7 ('Yet *jus cogens*, the peremptory law binding on all subjects of international law, marks the limit of the obligation to apply Resolutions of the Security Council. For this reason, it must be determined whether, as the petitioner asserts, the Resolutions of the Security Council containing the sanction violate *jus cogens*'). See also *A v State Secretariat for Economic Affairs and Federal Department of Economic Affairs*, Administrative First Instance Judgment, Federal Supreme Court, First Public Law Division, para 7.

also relied on decisions of international courts.[47] The *Kadi* case was particularly noteworthy in this regard because there the European Court recognised the exceptionality of the UN Security Council powers but nonetheless stated that 'there exists one limit to the' powers of the UN Security Council, 'namely that they must observe the fundamental peremptory provisions of *jus cogens*'.[48] Although, as is now well-known, the judgment of the Court of First Instance was overturned, the particular dictum about the impact of *jus cogens* on Security Council decisions was not addressed or overturned and remains thus authority for the proposition.[49] The Third Report also noted that the weight of the literature supported the proposition that the decisions of the Security Council were subject to *jus cogens*.[50]

Finally, the Report refers, as part of an argument of deduction, to the famous Separate Opinion of Judge Lauterpacht in *Application of the Convention on the Prevention and Punishment of the Crime of Genocide*, who, having stated that the priority accorded to decisions of the Security Council 'cannot—as a matter of simple hierarchy of norms—extend to a conflict between a Security Council resolution and *jus cogens*',[51] went on to explain the logic as follows:

[47] *Prosecutor v Duško Tadić*, Case No. IT-94-1-A, Judgment, Appeals Chamber, the International Tribunal for the Former Yugoslavia, 15 July 1999, para 296, stating that that the powers of the Security Council are 'subject to respect for peremptory norms of international law (*jus cogens*)'; Case T-315/01, *Yassin Abdullah Kadi v Council of the European Union and Commission of the European Communities*, Judgment of 21 September 2005, Court of First Instance of the European Communities, para 226, describing *jus cogens* as 'body of higher rules of public international law binding on all subjects of international law, including the bodies of the United Nations, and from which no derogation is possible'.

[48] *Kadi* case (above note 47), para 230. Further, the Court stated that in the event that Security Council resolutions were in conflict with *jus cogens* they 'would bind neither the Member States of the United Nations, nor, in consequence, the Community'.

[49] See Joined Cases C-402/05 P and 415/05 P *Yassin Abdullah Kadi and Al Barakaat International Foundation v Council of the European Union and Commission of the European Communities*, Judgment of 3 September 2008.

[50] See in general Erika de Wet *The Chapter VII Powers of the United Nations Security Council* (Hart, 2004); Anne Peters 'The Security Council, Functions and Powers—Article 25' in Bruno Simma, Daniel-Erasmus Khan, Georg Nolte, and Andreas Paulus (eds) *The Charter of the United Nations: A Commentary (Vol. I)*, 3rd edn (Oxford University Press, 2012), 818 *et seq.*; Thomas Kleinlein '*Jus Cogens* as the "Highest Law"? Peremptory Norms and Legal Hierarchies' (2015) 46 *Netherlands Yearbook of International Law* 173, 186; Dire Tladi and Gillian Taylor 'On the Al Qaida/Taliban Sanctions Regime: Due Process and Sunsetting' (2011) 10 *Chinese Journal of International Law* 771; Hennie Strydom 'Counter-Terrorism Sanctions and Human Rights' in Tiya Maluwa, Max du Plessis, and Dire Tladi (eds) *The Pursuit of a Brave New World in International Law: Essays in Honour of John Dugard* (Brill, 2016), 418. Cf. Daniel Costelloe *Legal Consequences of Peremptory Norms in International Law* (Cambridge, 2017), 128–36. See also para 40 of the Conclusions of the Study Group on Fragmentation of International Law (above note 1), 183.

[51] *Application of the Convention on the Prevention and Punishment of the Crime of Genocide*, Provisional Measures, Order of 13 September 1993, *ICJ Reports* 1993, p. 325 (Separate Opinion of Judge Lauterpacht).

> Indeed, one only has to state the opposite proposition thus—that a Security Council resolution may even require participation in genocide—for its unacceptability to be apparent.[52]

While this proposition is widely accepted in academic circles, it proved difficult to accept within the Commission. It was certainly supported by most members,[53] but there were also several members that did not accept the proposition.[54] It should be said that most of those that questioned the proposition did so mainly because of the practical consideration that it might encourage non-compliance with decisions of the Security Council.[55] Others questioning the proposition simply pointed out that there was no need to single out the Security Council.[56] The view that reference to the Security Council might negatively impact on the Council and that singling out the Council was inappropriate is a view that was held also by some members that generally agreed with the proposition.[57] Finally, it is important to state that only one member, Mr Huang, took the firm position that, under international law, the Security Council was not constrained by *jus cogens* and the Council was bound only by its decision-making rules in Article 27 of the Charter.[58]

[52] Id.

[53] Saboia (A/CN.4/SR.3415), 4; Nguyen (A/CN.4/SR.3415), 7; Sturma (A/CN.4/SR.3416), 8; Nolte (A/CN.4/SR.3417), 12–13; Ruda Santolaria (A/CN.4/SR.3417), 17; Lehto (A/CN.4/SR.3417), 18; Jalloh (A/CN.4/SR.3418), 9; Vásquez-Bermúdez (A/CN.4/SR.3418), 13; Hassouna (A/CN.4/SR.3419), 7; Oral (A/CN.4/SR.3419), 14; Reinisch (A/CN.4/SR.3419), 17; Grossman Guiloff (A/CN.4/SR.3420), 7; Hmoud (A/CN.4/SR.3420), 10; Peter (A/CN.4/SR.3421), 3; Escobar Hernández (A/CN.4/SR.3421), 8; Gómez-Robledo (A/CN.4/SR.3421), 12.

[54] Zagaynov (A/CN.4/SR.3416), 6; Murphy (A/CN.4/SR.3416), 11; Rajput (A/CN.4/SR.3418), 5; Oauzzani-Chahdi (A/CN.4/SR.3418), 11; Huang (A/CN.4/SR.3418), 10; Wood (A/CN.4/SR.3421), 4, 6.

[55] Zagaynov (A/CN.4/SR.3416), 6 ('A signal of that sort from the Commission could have a negative impact on the work of the Security Council to promote international peace and security, which already faced well-known challenges'); Rajput (A/CN.4/SR.3418), 5 ('Although it could in principle be agreed that States would not be bound by a resolution [including of the Security Council] that called for a breach of a peremptory norm ... the expression of doubts about such institutions might in practice have unintended consequences'); Wood (A/CN.4/SR.3421), 4, 6.

[56] See e.g. Murphy (A/CN.4/SR.3416), 11.

[57] See e.g. Nolte (A/CN.4/SR.3417), 12–13 ('he agreed ... that it was useful to cover ... the acts of international organisations that created legal obligations ... however, [the] fact that there had been major debates [on the relationship Security Council and *jus cogens*] did not justify such a narrow focus ... Otherwise, the Commission would risk being misunderstood as taking a generally distrustful position *vis-à-vis* the Security Council'); Lehto (A/CN.4/SR.3417), 18 ('while binding resolutions of the United Nations Security Council were obviously relevant in the context, she agreed with Mr Murphy that other international organisations with competence to take binding decisions should not be excluded'); Grossman Guiloff (A/CN.4/SR.3420), 7 ('However, like other members, he wondered whether the Security Council should be singled out in the Draft Conclusion'); Hmoud (A/CN.4/SR.3420), 10.

[58] See especially Huang (A/CN.4/SR.3597), 11.

The views of States were similarly divergent, with some States supporting the proposition that decisions of the Security Council were subject to *jus cogens*,[59] others opposing it,[60] and others still taking an ambiguous stance.[61]

In the light of the sensitivity of the issue, as well as divergence of views, both within the Commission and among States, the Commission decided on first reading to adopt a compromise with three elements. First, the Draft Conclusion itself would not refer to decisions of the Security Council. Second, references to the Security Council would be included in the Commentaries. Third, the Commentary to the Draft Conclusion would be streamlined, meaning that much of the authority relied on in the Third Report would not be included in the Commentary.[62] In addition, on second reading and in response to the comments from those States that had concerns about the Commentary, the Commentary to Draft Conclusion 16 proposed by the Special Rapporteur added several other elements to the compromise.[63] First,

[59] Austria, Comments and Observations (above note 10), 74 ('It cannot be excluded that Security Council resolutions might in some cases lead to a potential conflict with *jus cogens*. In this context, Austria would like to point out, once again, that the final report of the Austrian initiative (2004 to 2008) on the United Nations Security Council and the rule of law concluded that the Security Council does not operate free of legal constraint, which means that the Council's powers are subject to the Charter of the United Nations and norms of *jus cogens*'); Belgium, Comments and Observations (above note 10), 75 ('Belgium welcomes the Commission's explicit confirmation that resolutions adopted by the Security Council under Chapter VII of the Charter of the United Nations may not violate [*jus cogens* norms]'); Cyprus, Comments and Observations (above note 10), 75 ('In light of the hierarchical superiority of peremptory norms, the Republic of Cyprus shares the view that peremptory norms prevail over resolutions, decisions or other acts of international organizations ... What is also important is that the scope of draft conclusion 16 is broad enough to encompass acts of the Security Council'); Italy, Comments and Observations (above note 10), 76 ('Draft conclusion 16 is consistent with the idea of hierarchical superiority of *jus cogens* norms and, to that extent, Italy supports its insertion'); Slovenia, Comments and Observations (above note 10), 77; South Africa, Comments and Observations (above note 10), 77; Switzerland, Comments and Observations (above note 10), 78–9;

[60] Germany, Comments and Observations (above note 10), 75 ('Germany shares the concerns expressed by States that there is little State practice in support of this conclusion. Furthermore, the draft conclusion in its current wording might imply a risk of abuse by unilaterally disregarding binding Security Council decisions on its basis. This could undermine the authority of the Security Council'); Israel, Comments and Observations (above note 10), 76 ('Accordingly, the commentary's reference to Security Council resolutions in this context cannot be regarded as reflecting existing law and should be omitted'); Russia, Comments and Observations (above note 10), 77; United Kingdom, Comments and Observations (above note 10), 79; the United States, Comments and Observations (above note 10), 79.

[61] Australia, Comments and Observations (above note 10), 74 ('The position of Australia is that States should not be able to unilaterally assert that a Security Council resolution breaches a *jus cogens* norm, and for that unilateral assertion to provide a justification for a State's non-compliance with the resolution'); France, Comments and Observations (above note 10), 75 ('France is concerned that draft conclusion 16 could be interpreted in such a way as to allow a State to unilaterally withdraw from a resolution of the Security Council ... on the ground that, in its view, the resolution is inconsistent with a norm of *jus cogens*'); Spain, Comments and Observations (above note 10), 78;

[62] While much of the discussion leading to this compromise was done in informal consultations and thus not recorded, a comparison of the Commentaries proposed by the Special Rapporteur (A/CN.4/L.929 Add.1 and Add.2) (Annex XX) contains all the authority listed in the Third Report, while the final Commentary does not.

[63] See A/CN.4/L.960 Add.1.

the proposed Commentary specified that it was highly unlikely for a decision of the Security Council to conflict with a *jus cogens* norm.[64] Second, it stated that Draft Conclusion 16 did not provide cover for States to unilaterally decide not to comply with decisions of the Security Council.[65] Finally, the proposed Commentary emphasised that, wherever possible, decisions of the Security Council are to be interpreted in such a way that they are consistent with *jus cogens*.[66]

Yet even with all these compromises, adoption on second reading proved complicated, with one member asserting that failure to accept his position would make it difficult to adopt the Report of the Commission as a whole.[67] The initial exchange on the second reading of the Commentary to Draft Conclusion 16 is reproduced as it reveals the deeply entrenched positions of the protagonists:

> **Mr. Huang,** supported by **Mr. Zagaynov**, said that draft conclusion 16 and the commentary thereto was one of the most controversial sections of the second-reading text. He noted that no big changes had been made to that text. As it was undesirable to touch on Security Council resolutions at all in the text, the best solution would be to delete all references to them. At the Commission's 3595th meeting, he had already made it clear that the Special Rapporteur had taken a step too far on certain major controversial issues, and so it would be impossible to achieve consensus. Paragraph (2) of the commentary to draft conclusion 16 was a case in point. In light of the concerns expressed by some members in plenary meetings and in meetings of the Drafting Committee, he strongly suggested that the sentence concerning Security Council resolutions, and also the references to Security Council resolutions in paragraphs (4) and (5), should be deleted ... The Security Council ... had been given primary responsibility for international peace and security ... It must not therefore be undermined or weakened in any way... The hypothesis of a conflict between a Security Council resolution and a *jus cogens* norm concerned, in

64 Id., para 5 of the Commentary to Draft Conclusion 16 (above note 3) ('Indeed, while the commentary states, unambiguously, that Security Council resolutions are covered by draft conclusion 16, the Commission is conscious that it is highly unlikely that a Security Council resolution would, on its face, be in conflict with a peremptory norm of general international law (*jus cogens*)').

65 Id. ('Draft conclusion 16 should therefore not be read as providing cover for unilateral renunciation of obligations flowing under binding resolutions of the United Nations').

66 Id.

67 See Huang (A/CN.4/SR.3597), 14 ('However, if the Special Rapporteur refused further consultations, it would not be possible to adopt the report' and 'unless paragraph (2) was amended along the lines he had suggested, he would not join the consensus on adopting that or any of the following paragraphs').

substance and essence, a conflict between the Charter and *jus cogens*. Such a hypothesis was entirely a figment of the imagination and implausible in international practice ... It was hard to imagine that the validity of a decision or resolution adopted by the Security Council under Chapter VII of the Charter could be modified. If that happened, what would become of the world?

In paragraph (5) of the commentary to draft conclusion 16, the Special Rapporteur did make it clear that draft conclusion 16 should not be read as providing cover for a unilateral renunciation of obligations under binding resolutions of the United Nations. The wording was, however, rather weak and in practice would not prevent abuses ... The current formulation of the second-reading commentary might well give rise to bewilderment and confusion and was not fit for purpose. It would be highly regrettable if the Special Rapporteur maintained his position and refused to compromise ... He therefore once again urged the deletion of the references to Security Council resolutions from paragraph (2) of the commentary.

Mr. Murphy said that, although he understood many of the points made by Mr. Huang and Mr. Zagaynov and agreed not only that there was a relative lack of State practice that would allow the Commission to develop the commentary in question, but also that there was uncertainty with regard to the interaction of aspects of the Charter with *jus cogens*, the objective of the paragraph was patently to find a balance that would allow the Commission to move forward ...

Mr. Jalloh said that he supported the Special Rapporteur's position: the text was a finely negotiated compromise and should be retained. As for Mr. Murphy's suggestions, he feared that the process of adopting the report would be delayed if the Commission started to debate whether or not to move footnotes.

...

Mr. Huang said that the commentary to draft conclusion 16 was something on which the Commission could hardly reach agreement. Opinion was evenly divided between those in favour of it and those opposed to it. The different views involved some issues of principle. As the Commission was commencing the adoption of its draft report on the work of its seventy-third session, there was no need for any further debate in plenary or for another round of general discussions on a few controversial issues. He therefore proposed two solutions. The first was to delete the whole sentence beginning with the words 'Examples of a resolution' together with footnote 177. It was unnecessary to use Security Council resolutions as an example. The second was to ask the Special Rapporteur to hold private consultations with other members in order to seek a compromise solution to be presented to the Commission the following day

Mr. Tladi (Special Rapporteur) said that he was not amenable to holding consultations on the text of paragraph (2), since the latter was already the result of multiple compromises. The majority of members had wished to have a reference to Security Council resolutions in the text of draft conclusion 16, but instead it had been placed in the commentary. The original commentary discussed at the seventy-first session had been a very lengthy text which had been the result of informal consultations with various Commission members. In fact, it had not included some information which he personally considered to be relevant. The text currently under consideration was a further compromise based on further consultations ... He was not prepared to delete all references to Security Council resolutions or hold consultations on paragraph (2) or the following paragraphs of the commentary.

Mr. Hmoud said that the binding nature of Security Council resolutions was a substantive issue that could not be resolved in the commentary. The majority of Commission members held that the legality of Security Council decisions and resolutions was unquestionable ... He suggested that the statement in paragraph (5) that it was highly unlikely that a Security Council resolution would be in conflict with a peremptory norm of general international law (*jus cogens*) should be moved to paragraph (2).

Mr. Grossman Guiloff said that he supported Mr. Hmoud's proposal and suggested that the statement should be inserted immediately at the end of the sentence beginning 'Examples of a resolution'.

...

Mr. Tladi (Special Rapporteur) said that many States had supported the commentary, although some of them were unhappy that draft conclusion 16 did not itself refer to Security Council resolutions. His modifications to the first-reading text of the commentary had been prompted by a desire to accommodate the States that were unhappy with the commentary.[68]

At the end, the Commission adopted the text of the Commentary with the compromises originally proposed intact:

(a) the Draft Conclusion itself does not refer to acts of the Security Council;
(b) the Commentary would refer to the Security Council;
(c) there would be limited examples of authority justifying the proposition;

[68] A/CN.4/SR.3597, 11–14.

(d) the Commentary would emphasise that it was unlikely for decisions of the Security Council to conflict with *jus cogens*;

(e) the Commentary would also emphasise that it was not to be used as a justification for the unilateral decision not to comply with decisions of the Security Council; and

(f) decisions of the Security Council were to be, as far as was possible, interpreted in such a way as to make them consistent with *jus cogens*.

3. The Content of Draft Conclusion 14

Draft Conclusion 14

Rules of customary international law conflicting with a peremptory norm of general international law (*jus cogens*)

1. A rule of customary international law does not come into existence if it would conflict with an existing peremptory norm of general international law (*jus cogens*). This is without prejudice to the possible modification of a peremptory norm of general international law (*jus cogens*) by a subsequent norm having the same character.
2. A rule of customary international law not of a peremptory character ceases to exist if and to the extent that it conflicts with a new peremptory norm of general international law (*jus cogens*).
3. The persistent objector rule does not apply to peremptory norms of general international law (*jus cogens*).

Draft Conclusion 14 is divided into three paragraphs. The first two paragraphs concern situations where a rule of customary international law conflicts with a norm of *jus cogens*, while the last paragraph addresses the persistent objector doctrine.[69] The first two paragraphs are based on the framework of the Vienna Convention and seek to apply that framework to rules of customary international law. Thus, paragraph 1 concerns conflict with an existing *jus cogens* norm (the Article 53 situation) while paragraph 2 concerns conflict with a *jus cogens* norm emerging after the establishment of a rule of customary international law (the Article 64 situation).

[69] This scheme follows closely the original proposal of the Special Rapporteur in the Third Report (above note 2).

While the Vienna Convention (and Draft Conclusion 10) on treaties speaks of invalidity or voidness of the treaty, Draft Conclusion 14 avoids the use of those terms, which, according to the Commission, are more appropriate for treaties which can exist even if not valid. With respect to the first paragraph, in particular, the view of the Commission was that 'the putative rule of customary international law does not come into existence in the first place'.[70] For that reason the Commission used the phrase 'does not come into existence'. The text of the first paragraph adopted on first reading stated that the rule does not come into existence 'if it conflicts with' a norm of *jus cogens*. Several States commented that there was a contradiction in terms in the text of Draft Conclusion 14, because something that did not exist, i.e. the putative rule, could not be in conflict with something else.[71] It was for this reason that the Commission decided to use the phrase 'if it would conflict' to indicate that there is no conflict if the rule does not exist. Thus, the main thrust of the first paragraph is that a rule of customary international law does not come into existence if it would conflict with an existing norm of *jus cogens*.

The second sentence is a without prejudice clause to ensure that modification is not precluded by the main rule precluding the emergence of customary international law conflicting with *jus cogens*. While modern international law takes for granted that *jus cogens* norms can be modified as implied by the definition in Article 53 and the reference in Article 64 to emergence of a new peremptory norm, as described in Section 2.2, the idea of modification of *jus cogens* norms is not without conceptual difficulties. Nonetheless, the second sentence makes clear that paragraph 1 is not to be read as precluding modification. The conceptual difficulties are addressed in paragraph 7 of the Commentaries to the Draft Conclusion (and expanded upon in Section 2.2 above).

70 See para 2 of the Commentary to Draft Conclusion 14 of the Draft Conclusions (above note 3).

71 See e.g. France, Comments and Observations (above note 10), 68 ('However, the existence of a "conflict" necessarily implies the existence of the conflicting norms. If one of them does not exist, then there can be no conflict'); Italy, Comments and Observations (above note 10), 68 ('paragraph 1 . . . describes an impossible scenario of a conflict between a non-existent rule (of customary international law) and an existent [*sic*] peremptory norm. Either the rule of customary international law has come into existence and may conflict with a peremptory norm . . . or the rule has not come into existence thereby rendering any conflict with a peremptory norm impossible. *Tertium non datur*'); Russia, Comments and Observations (above note 10), 70 ('It is not possible for something that has not yet come into existence to conflict with something else. In that connection, it may be appropriate to consider alternative wording that would affirm that the practice of States that conflicts with an existing *jus cogens* may not give rise to a norm of customary international law'); Spain, Comments and Observations (above note 10), 71 ('The scenario in the first paragraph is one where a conflict is impossible, because if the customary rule does not come into existence, the normative conflict (conflict between norms) would not be possible').

The second paragraph of Draft Conclusion 14 addresses the issue of conflict with a norm of *jus cogens* that emerges subsequent to the establishment of the rule of customary international law. As with the first paragraph, the second paragraph does not speak of the rule of customary international law becoming invalid or void, but rather it states that it 'ceases to exist'. Unlike the first paragraph, the second paragraph provides for the possibility of severability in that it provides that the rule of customary international law ceases to exist 'to the extent that it conflicts' with the subsequently emerging *jus cogens* norm.

The final paragraph is self-explanatory and provides for the non-applicability of the doctrine of persistent objector to *jus cogens*. Thus, unlike rules of customary international law, to which a State can persistently object and thus remain outside the scope of application of the rule, *jus cogens* norms are universally applicable and a State cannot exclude the application of *jus cogens* through persistent objection.

4. The Content of Draft Conclusion 15

Conclusion 15

Obligations created by unilateral acts of states conflicting with a peremptory norm of general international law (*jus cogens*)

1. A unilateral act of a State manifesting the intention to be bound by an obligation under international law that would be in conflict with a peremptory norm of general international law (*jus cogens*) does not create such an obligation.
2. An obligation under international law created by a unilateral act of a State ceases to exist if and to the extent that it conflicts with a new peremptory norm of general international law (*jus cogens*).

Draft Conclusion 15 concerns the relationship between unilateral acts and *jus cogens*. It stems from the understanding that certain unilateral acts by States can create legal obligations for that State. The scope of Draft Conclusion 15 is only those unilateral acts of a State undertaken with the intention to create obligations for the State itself.[72]

It follows the structure and logic of Draft Conclusion 14. Thus, like Draft Conclusion 14, Draft Conclusion 15 is structured on the basis of, on the one

[72] See, for a description of the nature of the act in question, paras 5–7 of the Commentary to Draft Conclusion 15 (above note 3).

hand, conflict with a *jus cogens* norm that exists at the time of the unilateral act and, on the other hand, conflict with a norm of *jus cogens* that emerges after the relevant unilateral act. Thus, the first paragraph of Draft Conclusion 15 concerns conflict with a *jus cogens* norm that exists at the time of the unilateral act. The second paragraph of Draft Conclusion 15 concerns conflict with norms of *jus cogens* that emerge subsequent to the unilateral act. This structure is a departure from that proposed in the Third Report of the Special Rapporteur which only provided one paragraph addressing both scenarios.

Furthermore, like Draft Conclusion 14, Draft Conclusion 15 does not refer to 'invalidity' or 'voidness' because a unilateral act, as an empirical fact, cannot be invalid. The proposal of the Special Rapporteur in his Third Report, however, did refer to invalidity.[73] The Third Report referred to 'invalid' in order to be consistent with the previous work of the Commission, the Guiding Principles Applicable to Unilateral Declarations, which stated that unilateral declarations inconsistent with *jus cogens* are void.[74] Yet, the Commission recognised not only that a unilateral act cannot be valid, but also that what was at issue was not the unilateral act, but rather the obligation that was sought to be created by the unilateral act.

The first paragraph addresses the Article 53 scenario (where the *jus cogens* norm exists at the time of the unilateral act). It focuses on the obligation sought to be created rather than on the unilateral act itself.[75] It captures the idea by referring to a 'unilateral act manifesting an intention to be bound', or, put another way, an intention to accept an obligation. It states that the legal obligations are not created. Thus, if at the time the unilateral act occurs the *jus cogens* norm in question exists, then the obligations that would ordinarily have been created are not created.

The second paragraph addresses the Article 64 scenario (where the *jus cogens* norm emerges only after the unilateral act). In this scenario, there is, at the time of the unilateral act, no impediment to the creation of the obligation and the obligation is therefore created. However, similar to the case of customary international law in Draft Conclusion 14, the second paragraph provides that the obligation ceases to exist. Moreover, as with paragraph 2 of Draft Conclusion 14, the second paragraph of Draft Conclusion 15 provides that the

[73] See Draft Conclusion 16 proposed by the Special Rapporteur in the Third Report (above note 2), para 160 ('A unilateral act that is in conflict with a peremptory norm of general international law (*jus cogens*) is invalid').

[74] See Guiding Principle 8 of the Guiding Principles Applicable to Unilateral Declarations of States Capable of Creating Legal Obligations (above note 1), 378.

[75] See para 2 of the Commentary to Draft Conclusion 15 of the Draft Conclusions (above note 3) ('The focus is therefore on the legal obligations intended to be created by the unilateral act in question').

obligation ceases to exist 'if and to the extent' of its inconsistency with the *jus cogens* norm. In other words, it provides for severability.

Draft Conclusion 15 was generally well accepted by both States and members of the International Law Commission. Much of the discussions in the Drafting Committee pertained to how to reflect the idea of the intention to create an obligation.[76]

5. The Content of Draft Conclusion 16

Draft Conclusion 16

Obligations created by resolutions, decisions or other acts of international organisations conflicting with a peremptory norm of general international law (*jus cogens*)

A resolution, decision or other act of an international organisation that would otherwise have binding effect does not create obligations under international law if and to the extent that they conflict with a peremptory norm of general international law (*jus cogens*).

Draft Conclusion 16 concerns resolutions, decisions, or other acts of international organisations and their relationship with *jus cogens*. The types of acts covered by the Draft Conclusion are those that 'would otherwise have binding effect', i.e. those acts which, but for any inconsistency with *jus cogens*, would be binding under international law.[77]

As with Draft Conclusions 14 and 15, the focus is not on the resolution, decision, or act, but rather on the obligations that may be created by the resolution, decision, or act. While the proposal in the Third Report provided for the invalidity of the resolution or decision,[78] the Commission felt it best to focus on the legal obligations created by the resolution or decision. It provides, in a similar fashion to Draft Conclusions 14 and 15, that the act of the international organisation 'does not create obligations' that it otherwise would have created if those obligations would be in conflict with *jus cogens*. Moreover, as with the

[76] See Drafting Committee, Peremptory Norms of General International Law, untitled document of 1 May 2019 (time stamped 4:45), which is the text produced by the Secretariat drawn from the proposal in the Third Report. It uses the phrase 'capable of creating legal obligations', but also includes a handwritten annotation by the Special Rapporteur suggesting the word 'undertaking' in the place of 'capable of creating'. It is in that handwritten annotation that the phrase 'does not create such obligations' is put forward to replace 'void'.

[77] See para 2 of the Commentary to Draft Conclusion 16 of the Draft Conclusions (above note 3).

[78] See Draft Conclusion 17 proposed by the Special Rapporteur in the Third Report (above note 2), para 160.

second paragraphs of Draft Conclusions 14 and 15, the words 'if and to the extent' are included to indicate that severability is possible and that the obligations that are not in conflict with *jus cogens* will continue to apply.[79]

It is noteworthy that, unlike Draft Conclusions 14 and 15, Draft Conclusion 16 only has one paragraph. There is no equivalent paragraph 2 dealing with *jus cogens superveniens*. This does not mean that *jus cogens* does not affect legal obligations created by acts of international organisations adopted prior to the emergence of a norm of *jus cogens*. Rather, Draft Conclusion 16 should be seen as applying also to cases of *jus cogens superveniens*.

As described in Section 2.4, the main issue of contestation in respect of Draft Conclusion 16 concerned the extent to which it covered decisions of the Security Council. While not including the Security Council in the text of the Draft Conclusion, it bears recalling that the Commission declared, unambiguously, that the Draft Conclusion applies equally to decisions of the Security Council.[80]

6. Concluding Observations

The Draft Conclusions addressed in this chapter represent innovation as they are not sourced from any existing instrument. Yet, at the same time, the basic content of the rules contained in those Draft Conclusions is not controversial. This is not to say that some of the rules do not raise difficult issues. The questions discussed in Section 2.2, e.g. persistent object and modification, of course raise difficult issues of a conceptual and doctrinal nature.

The one issue which could be regarded as controversial in the Draft Conclusions addressed in this chapter was the impact of *jus cogens* on decisions of the Security Council. Yet, by and large, States accepted the final product of the Commission on this question. Indeed, even States that had reservations appeared to be assuaged by the modifications made by the Commission in the Commentary. Questions around modification, however, have remained in the statements of some States post the adoption of the Draft Conclusion.[81]

[79] See para 3 of the Commentary to Draft Conclusion 16 of the Draft Conclusions (above note 3).

[80] See paras 2 and 4 of the Commentary to Draft Conclusion 16 of the Draft Conclusions (above note 3).

[81] Ireland, Sixth Committee of the General Assembly, Seventy-Seventh Session, 25 October 2022; the Czech Republic, Sixth Committee of the General Assembly, Seventy-Seventh Session, 25 October 2022; Hungary, Sixth Committee of the General Assembly, Seventy-Seventh Session, 25 October 2022, noting that the Draft Conclusions 'do not deal with cases of collision between *jus cogens* norms themselves. Therefore, it is unclear how States are supposed to settle cases where collisions between peremptory norms occur.'

10

Consequences of *Jus Cogens* for the Law of State Responsibility

1. Introduction

The previous two chapters concerned the consequences of *jus cogens* for treaties (Chapter 8) and the consequences of *jus cogens* for other sources of obligations under international law (Chapter 9). Beyond the law of obligations, *jus cogens* also has consequences for the law of State responsibility. This chapter addresses those consequences.

The chapter focuses on two specific consequences of *jus cogens* for the law of State responsibility addressed in the Commission's Draft Conclusions, namely the *erga omnes* character of obligations emanating from norms of *jus cogens* (Draft Conclusion 17) and the rule that circumstances precluding wrongfulness may not be relied upon where the act in question involves a breach of *jus cogens* (Draft Conclusion 18). These were perhaps two of the least controversial Draft Conclusions, in large part because they reproduce relevant parts of the Articles on State Responsibility.

Draft Conclusion 19 on the particular consequences of serious breaches of *jus cogens*, which is also based on relevant provisions of the Articles on States Responsibility, is not addressed in this chapter but rather in Chapter 11. This is for two reasons. First, Draft Conclusion 19 raised peculiar problems requiring greater attention and is therefore best addressed separately from Draft Conclusions 17 and 18. Second, while related to State responsibility, particular consequences of serious breaches of *jus cogens* are not strictly speaking about State responsibility in the same way that not every discussion about a breach of international law concerns State responsibility. Of course, the Third Report of the Special Rapporteur did treat particular consequences of *jus cogens* as part of the consequences of State responsibility, as did the Commission,[1]

[1] See *Third Report of the Special Rapporteur on Peremptory Norms of General International Law (Jus Cogens)* (A/CN.4/714), paras 86–111, where particular consequences of serious breaches of *jus cogens*

but this appears to have been more for convenience than as a matter of doctrinal necessity.[2] State responsibility is *a* consequence of breaches of international law (including breaches of *jus cogens*), but it is not the only consequence.[3] Particular consequences of serious breaches seem more to concern consequences related to enforcement of *jus cogens* than State responsibility.

In the next section, a general background discussion of the issues and debates surrounding Draft Conclusions 17 and 18 is provided. Section 3 will provide a discussion of the text of Draft Conclusion 17 while Section 4 will provide a discussion of the text of Draft Conclusion 18.

2. Discussion

2.1 *Jus Cogens* and the Law of State Responsibility

At the very beginning of the project, the question was posed whether the work of the Commission would be limited to the law of treaties or whether it would also cover the law of State responsibility. This issue was a constant theme in the interventions of one member, Mr Murase. In fact, Mr Murase, as the very first speaker in the debate on the First Report of the Special Rapporteur, set the question of the place of law on State responsibility in this topic at the centre of his intervention. Mr Murase said that he

> was puzzled as to why the report limited the scope of the topic to the context of the law of treaties and did not deal with the function of *jus cogens* in the context of the law of State responsibility, which was an equally important aspect of the topic. In 2013, during a meeting of the Working Group on the Long-Term Programme of Work, he had stressed that the Commission could not ignore the concept of *jus cogens* in the context of the law of State responsibility, where it played a distinct role.[4]

are treated under Section C titled Consequences of Peremptory Norms of General international Law (*Jus Cogens*) for the Law of State Responsibility.

[2] See, however, id., para 78.
[3] See also id., para 79 ('The Special Rapporteur pauses here to mention other potential consequences of breaches of *jus cogens* norms which, although related to State responsibility, will not be addressed in the present chapter'). These other consequences are discussed in Chapters 10 and 11.
[4] Murase (A/CN.4/SR.3314), 7.

He continued to state that in his view 'the legal nature, content and function of *jus cogens*' were not the same in the law of treaties and the law of State responsibility.[5] The essence of Mr Murase's position was that the concept of *jus cogens* under the law of State responsibility was distinct from the concept under the law of treaties, thus requiring a distinct definition. While this position was not shared by other members of the Commission, the view that the Commission ought to address the consequences of *jus cogens* for the law of State responsibility was reinforced.[6]

Yet, while the Commission was in general agreement on the need to also cover State responsibility, there was a view expressed in the literature that the law of State responsibility did not entail any particular consequences for *jus cogens*.[7] This view seems to be based on the language of Article 53 of the Vienna Convention on the Law of Treaties, which first sets forth the consequence of *jus cogens* norms in terms of invalidation, and second defines *jus cogens* norms in terms of derogation. On the first point, as the Third Report notes, Article 53 of the Vienna Convention sets forth a consequence, not the consequences.[8] This does not preclude that, under general international law, there may be other consequences flowing from *jus cogens*. On the second point, that *jus cogens* is defined in terms of derogation does not tell us anything, and certainly not everything, about the consequences. The definition only tells us what it is.

2.2 *Erga Omnes* Obligations

That there is a relationship between *jus cogens* norms and *erga omnes* obligations is broadly accepted. Not a single member of the Commission and not a single State questioned the proposition that there was a relationship. If anything, members of the Commission and States explicitly asserted the existence

[5] Id.

[6] See, in response to Mr. Murase's statement, the comments of the Special Rapporteur (A/CN.4/SR.3323), 12 ('He agreed with Mr. Murase that the Commission could not ignore the implications of *jus cogens* in the context of State responsibility; indeed, the Commission could not ignore those implications for any area or subject of international law . . . moreover, the materials referred to in the syllabus and his first report included materials relevant to State responsibility . . . The scope of the topic was certainly broader than just the law of treaties and would also include the law of State responsibility, particularly in relation to consequences').

[7] See e.g. Sévrine Knuchel *Jus Cogens: Identification and Enforcement of Peremptory Norms* (Zurich, Schultess, 2015), 180 ('The peremptory character of *jus cogens* norms has no direct effect on State responsibility; it invalidates conflicting norms, not conflicting behaviour'); see also Daniel Costelloe *Legal Consequences of Peremptory Norms in International Law* (Cambridge, 2017), 185–6 ('the breach, however serious, of [a *jus cogens* norm] does not 'derogate' from such a norm. The breach of an obligation under a peremptory norm entails the legal consequences of the breach of an ordinary obligation').

[8] Third Report (above note 1), para 77.

of a relationship between the two concepts.[9] While the existence of a relationship between the two concepts is generally accepted, what is less settled is the precise nature of this relationship.

The existence of the relationship was generally accepted within the Commission and by States, in part, because it has a strong pedigree, having been established in the jurisprudence of the International Court of Justice and in State practice. The Court, which gave birth to the concept seemingly out of nothing,[10] has been at the forefront of developing the concept and entrenching it in the lexicon of international law. As is now well-known, it was in the *Barcelona Traction* case that the Court drew a distinction between, on the one hand, obligations under international law 'arising vis-à-vis another State', for example in the field of diplomatic protection, and, on the other hand, what the Court referred to as 'obligations of a State towards the international community as a whole'.[11] These latter obligations, the Court said, '[b]y their very nature ... are the concern of all States' and '[i]n view of their importance all States can be held to have a legal interest in their protection; they are obligations *erga omnes*'.[12] This quotation, which was not only not justified by any authority in the judgment, but was also completely gratuitous in the sense that it had no bearing on the Court's decision, has gone on to be repeated in many decisions of the Court.[13]

[9] See e.g. Saboia (A/CN.4/SR.3415), 4 ('analysis, which served as the basis for draft conclusions 19, 20 and 21, was richly documented with international case law, just as was his analysis of the relationship between *jus cogens* norms and *erga omnes* obligations, which led to the conclusion reflected in draft conclusion 18, namely, that peremptory norms of international law (*jus cogens*) established obligations *erga omnes*, the breach of which concerned all States'); Šturma (A/CN.4/SR.3416), 18; Murphy (A/CN.4/SR.3416), 11; Nolte (A/CN.4/SR.3417), 13; Jalloh (A/CN.4/SR.3418), 9; Galvão Teles (A/CN.4/SR.3419), 5; Oral (A/CN.4/SR.3419), 14; Reinisch (A/CN.4/SR.3419), 17; Cisse (A/CN.4/SR.4320), 4; Grossman Guiloff (A/CN.4/SR.3420), 7; Hmoud (A/CN.4/3420), 10. For explicit support from States, see Peremptory Norms of General International Law (*Jus Cogens*): Italy, Comments and Observations received from Governments (A/CN.4/748), 80; Spain, Comments and Observations received from Governments (A/CN.4/748), 81.

[10] Dire Tladi 'The Role of the International Court of Justice in the Development of International Law' in Carlos Esposito and Kate Partlett (eds) *Cambridge Companion of the International Court of Justice* (Cambridge, 2023), 78–9.

[11] *Case Concerning the Barcelona Traction, Light and Power, Limited (Belgium v Spain) (New Application)*, Judgment, *ICJ Reports* 1970, p. 3, para 33.

[12] Id.

[13] See e.g. *Case Concerning East Timor (Portugal v Australia), ICJ Reports* 1995, p. 90, para 29; *Legality of the Threat or Use of Nuclear Weapons*, Advisory Opinion, *ICJ Reports* 1996, p. 226, para 155; *Application of the Convention on the Prevention and Punishment of the Crime of Genocide (Croatia v Serbia)*, Judgment, *ICJ Reports* 2015, p. 3, para 83 *et seq.*; *Legal Consequences of the Separation of the Chagos Archipelago from Mauritius in 1965*, Advisory Opinion, *ICJ Reports* 2019, p. 95, para 180; *Application of the Convention on the Prevention and Punishment of the Crime of Genocide (The Gambia v. Myanmar)*, Provisional Measures, Order, *ICJ Reports* 2020, p. 3, p. 17, para 41; *Application of the Convention on the Prevention and Punishment of the Crime of Genocide (The Gambia v Myanmar)*, Preliminary Objections, Judgment of 22 July 2022, para 107.

While the Court has not explicitly addressed the precise relationship between *jus cogens* and *erga omnes*, national court decisions have often done so. For example, in the case of *Nulyarimma v Thompson*, the Federal Court of Australia accepted the contention of the parties that the prohibition of genocide was a norm of *jus cogens* which gives 'rise to non derogable obligations *erga omnes* that is, enforcement obligations owed by each nation State to the international community as a whole'.[14] The connection between *jus cogens* and *erga omnes* was also drawn in the US District Court for the District of Massachusetts, where the Court described the prohibition against torture as an obligation *erga omnes* that is *jus cogens*.[15] The link between *jus cogens* and *erga omnes* is also generally accepted in the literature.[16]

In the Articles on State Responsibility, the International Law Commission noted that *jus cogens* and *erga omnes* obligations were 'closely related'.[17] The Commission took rather tentative steps to describe the nature of this close relationship:

> [P]eremptory norms of general international law and obligations to the international community as a whole are aspects of a single basic idea. The examples which ICJ has given of obligations towards the international community as a whole all concern obligations which, it is generally accepted, arise under peremptory norms of general international law.[18]

The key point here is that the Commission seems to conceptualise *erga omnes* obligations as '[arising] under peremptory norms of general international law'. In other words, *jus cogens* norms establish *erga omnes* obligations. This means, in effect, that *jus cogens* and *erga omnes* are different but related concepts.[19]

[14] *Nulyarimma and Others v Thompson*, Appeal Decision of 1 September 1999, *ILDC* 2773 (1999, AU), para 81.

[15] *Kane v Winn*, United States District Court for the District of Massachusetts, 31 F Supp 2d 162, 199 (D. Mass. 2004). See also *R and Office of the United Nations High Commissioner for Refugees v Secretary of State for Foreign and Commonwealth Affairs and Secretary of State for Home Affairs*, Appeal Judgment of 12 October 2006 of the High Court, [2006] All ER (D) 138, para 102, referring to '*ius cogens erga omnes*'; and *Jorgić Case, Order of 12 December 2000, 2BvR 1290/99*, Federal Constitutional Court of Germany, para 17, wherein the Court stated that *jus cogens* norms have *erga omnes* effect.

[16] See e.g. generally Martha Bradley '"Jus Cogens" Preferred Sister-Obligations *Erga Omnes* and the International Court of Justice—Fifty Years after the *Barcelona Traction* case' in Dire Tladi (ed.) *Peremptory Norms of General International Law: Disquisitions and Disputations* (Brill, 2021); See also generally Christian Tomuschat 'Reconceptualising the Debate on *Jus Cogens* and Obligations *Erga Omnes*—Concluding Observations' in Christian Tomuschat and Jean-Marc Thouvenin (eds) *The Fundamental Rules of the International Legal Order* (Brill, 2005).

[17] Articles on the Responsibility of States for Internationally Wrongful Acts, *Yearbook of the International Law Commission*, 2001, Vol. II, Part II, para 4 of the Commentary to Part Two, Chapter III.

[18] Id., para 7.

[19] See id. where the Commission notes that while related the two concepts have 'at least a difference in emphasis'.

For Pellet, the difference is that while *jus cogens* refers to 'la qualité du contenu' of the norm, *erga omnes* refers to the addressees of *jus cogens* norms.[20] Along the same lines, Bassiouni sees *jus cogens* as referring to 'the legal status' of a particular norm, while '*obligatio erga omnes* pertains to the legal implications arising out of' that norm's characterisation as a *jus cogens*.[21] Thus, the connection between *jus cogens* and *erga omnes* is that the former creates the latter.

The idea that *jus cogens* norms create *erga omnes* obligations—or put differently that *erga omnes* obligations arise from *jus cogens* norms—itself has a further implication, namely that all *jus cogens* norms have an *erga omnes* quality.[22] However, it is generally accepted that the reverse is not true, i.e. not all *erga omnes* obligations are *jus cogens*. But, beyond *jus cogens* norms, how else are *erga omnes* obligations to be identified? Some members of the Commission have questioned the reference to decisions of the Court referring to *erga omnes* as supporting propositions on *jus cogens*.[23] This view was also echoed by a few States.[24] Yet it seems hard to identify any other norms from which *erga omnes* obligations arise that are not, at the same time, *jus cogens* norms. Of course, we exclude here *erga omnes partes* obligations which are, in this context, a different matter altogether.[25]

Obligations pertaining to common spaces are perhaps the only other example of *erga omnes* obligations under international law not tied to *jus cogens*.[26] The *erga omnes* quality of norms related to common spaces flows from the inherent nature of the obligations imposed by such norms which are, by

[20] Alain Pellet 'Conclusions' in Tomuschat and Thouvenin (above note 16), 418 ('le caractère *cogens* d'une norme concerne la qualité du contenu même de celle-ci; l'expression *erga omnes* attire plutôt l'attention sur des destinataires').

[21] Cherif Bassiouni 'International Crimes: *Jus Cogens* and *Obligatio Erga Omnes*' (1996) 59 *Law and Contemporary Problems* 63, 63.

[22] See Santiago Villalpando *L'émergence de la communauté internationale dans de la responsabilité des États* (Paris, 2005), 107;

[23] See e.g. Wood (A/CN.4/SR.3459), 9 ('Calling something an obligation *erga omnes*, or intransgressible, was not necessarily the same thing as saying that a rule had *jus cogens* character'); Murphy (A/CN.4/SR3460), 9 ('but [the] Court had asserted only that the right to self-determination had an *erga omnes* character. The existence of an obligation *erga omnes* did not necessarily mean that there was an obligation imposed by a norm of *jus cogens*'). In this context, Mr Murphy pointed to obligations relating to common spaces as having *erga omnes* quality without flowing from common spaces.

[24] See e.g. the United States, Comments and Observations (above note 9), 90 and 113; Israel, Comments and Observations (above note 9), 103. This view was, it seems, also supported by Helmut Philipp Aust 'Legal Consequences of Serious Breaches of Peremptory Norms in the Law of State of State Responsibility: Observation in the Light of the Recent Work of the International Law Commission' in Dire Tladi (ed.) *Peremptory Norms of General International Law (Jus Cogens): Disquisitions and Disputations* (Brill, 2021), 244.

[25] First, the *erga omnes* character of those obligations can be explained by adherence to the treaty in question. And second, that *erga omnes* character is itself limited to the parties to the treaties, so it is a qualified *erga omnes* character.

[26] See Murphy (A/CN.4/SR.3460), 9. See also the response of the Special Rapporteur (A/CN.4/SR.3465), 6.

definition, owed to the international community as a whole. At any rate, it seems a fair assumption to state there is a significant overlap between *jus cogens* norms and obligations *erga omnes*.[27]

An important consequence of the *erga omnes* effect of *jus cogens* norms is the idea that any State, including a State not directly harmed by the breach, is entitled to invoke the responsibility of another State for breaching a *jus cogens* norm. This consequence is reflected in Article 48 of the Articles on State Responsibility. This principle was recently affirmed, albeit in the context of *erga omnes partes*, by the Court in *Gambia v Myanmar* where the Court accepted Gambia's right to invoke the responsibility of Myanmar in the commission of genocide against the Rohingya notwithstanding that the genocide was not committed against the Gambia or its people and that the Gambia could not show any other direct interest.[28]

2.3 Non-Applicability of Circumstances Precluding Wrongfulness

Under international law, conduct which would otherwise be wrongful is not wrongful, and the consequences of wrongfulness do not apply, if there exists a ground for precluding wrongfulness.[29] These grounds include, for example, consent, self-defence, necessity, and *force majeure*. This rule of international law, however, does not apply if the conduct in question is in breach of a rule of *jus cogens*. This principle, reflected in Article 26 of the Articles on States Responsibility, attracted the least amount of controversy and discussion throughout the International Law Commission project, both within the Commission and from States.

While the principle has not often been invoked, it has been referred to in a few decisions. An arbitral tribunal of the International Centre for Settlement of Investment Disputes (ICSID) held that Zimbabwe could not rely on necessity, one of the circumstances that would ordinarily preclude wrongfulness,

[27] Articles on State Responsibility (above note 17), para 7 of the Commentary to Part Two, Chapter III. ('The examples which ICJ has given of obligations towards the international community as a whole all concern obligations which, it is generally accepted, arise under peremptory norms of general international law. Likewise the examples of peremptory norms given by the Commission in its commentary to what became article 53 of the 1969 Vienna Convention involve obligations to the international community as a whole.')

[28] *Gambia v Myanmar*, Provisional Measures (paras 41 and 42) and Preliminary Objections (paras 108 and 114) (above note 13).

[29] See para 1 of the Commentary to Part I, Chapter V of the Articles on State Responsibility (above note 17).

because the act complained of amounted to a breach of the prohibition of discrimination.[30] In that case, the Tribunal did not refer to the prohibition of discrimination as *jus cogens*, but it did refer to that prohibition as *erga omnes*.[31] Moreover, removing any doubt that the Tribunal saw the prohibition of discrimination as *jus cogens*, it explicitly invoked the terms of Article 26 of the Articles on State Responsibility.[32] In another ICSID decision, the Tribunal found that it could deny the reliance on necessity as a ground precluding wrongfulness because the act complained of in that case was not a peremptory norm.[33] The proposition contained in Article 26 has also been affirmed by the German Constitutional Court.[34]

Although the principle contained in Draft Conclusion 18 was not opposed by any member of the Commission or any State, some States did suggest that the Commentaries could be improved by addressing particular issues, in particular consistency of the rule with the right of self-defence as an exception to the prohibition on the use of force. In its written comments on the Commission's first reading text, Italy stated that while it accepted the principle, it noted that the Commission

> does not address, not even in its commentary, the thorny issue of the relationship between self-defense, which is a circumstance precluding wrongfulness in accordance with article 21 of the draft articles, and the prohibition on the use of force, which in the past has been considered by the Commission as a peremptory norm of general international law. The problem hinges on the relationship between the *jus ad bellum* primary rules and the secondary rules of State responsibility.[35]

[30] *Bernhard von Pezold and Others v Republic of Zimbabwe*, Case No. ARB/10/15, Award of 28 July 2015, ICSID, para 657.

[31] Id.

[32] Id.

[33] *CMS Gas Transmission Company v the Argentine Republic*, Case No. ARB/01/08, Award of 12 May 2005, ICSID, para 325.

[34] See *Order of 26 October 2004, 2 B v R 1038/01*, Federal Constitutional Court of Germany, para 121.

[35] Italy, Comments and Observations (above note 9), 83. Although not reproduced in the Secretariat's document containing the positions of States, France, in its detailed comments that were not translated, questioned the Commission for not discussing the relationship between the use of force and self-defence. See Commentaires et Observations de la République Française Relatifs aux Projet de Conclusions de la Commission de Droit International sur les Normes Impératives du Droit International General, 35, available at https://legal.un.org/ilc/sessions/73/pdfs/french/jc_france.pdf (accessed 13 January 2023) ('Il peut cependant paraître surprenant que le commentaire sous le projet de conclusion n°18 ne contienne aucun développement concernant l'articulation entre la règle de l'interdiction de l'emploi de la force et l'existence du droit de légitime défense'). A related question was Belgium's suggestion that the Commission consider the relationship between consent and the use of force in the context of intervention by invitation. See Belgium, Comments and Observations (above note 9), 83.

The Third Report of the Commission had already alluded to the issue,[36] but noted that these issues 'concern more the scope of ... the peremptory norm in question, rather than circumstances precluding wrongfulness'.[37] It is noteworthy that even this explanation for why this complex relationship between *jus cogens* norms which permit exceptions and the principle that *jus cogens* norms are not subject to circumstances precluding wrongfulness is not contained in the Commentary. While there is nothing in the summary records to explain this omission, the issue was discussed in the Drafting Committee (for which no summary records exist). In the Drafting Committee, it became apparent that the rules on the use of force and the exceptions thereto are so controversial, and the members of the Commission have such hugely differing views, that it was difficult to imagine that the Commission could agree on something meaningful on the subject, even if only in the Commentary.[38]

3. The Content of Draft Conclusion 17

Draft Conclusion 17

Peremptory norms of general international law (*jus cogens*) as obligations owed to the international community as a whole (obligations *erga omnes*)

1. Peremptory norms of general international law (*jus cogens*) give rise to obligations owed to the international community as a whole (obligations *erga omnes*), in relation to which all States have a legal interest.
2. Any State is entitled to invoke the responsibility of another State for a breach of a peremptory norm of general international law (*jus cogens*), in accordance with the rules on the responsibility of States for internationally wrongful acts.

---

36 Third Report (above note 1), para 81 ('to the extent that the scope of a norm of a *jus cogens* itself incorporates a ground precluding wrongfulness, the existence of such a ground would be relevant in determining whether that *jus cogens* norm has been breached. To take the prohibition on the use of force as an example, while a State could not depend on Article 21 (self-defence) ... the right of self-defence is clearly relevant ... since the use of force in self-defence would not a breach of the *jus cogens* norm. Similarly, in *some cases*, consent by a State to the presence of the military of another State ... may exclude wrongfulness').

37 Id. See also Belgium, Comments and Observations (above note 9), 83.

38 For discussions of this relationship see Mary Ellen O'Connell, Christian Tams, and Dire Tladi *Max Planck Trialogues on the Law of War and Peace (Vol. 1): The Use of Force against Non-State Actors* (Cambridge, 2019), 25–7 and 244–8.

Draft Conclusion 17 contains two paragraphs. The first paragraph describes in general terms the relationship between *jus cogens* and *erga omnes* obligations. The second paragraph describes the main consequence of this relationship, namely the entitlement of a non-injured State to invoke the responsibility of a State that breaches a norm of *jus cogens*. The initial draft proposed in the Third Report did not contain the second element, only the first. It provided:

> **The relationship between peremptory norms of general international law (*jus cogens*) and obligations *erga omnes***
>
> Peremptory norms of general international law (*jus cogens*) establish obligations *erga omnes*, the breach of which concerns all States.

In the Drafting Committee it had been decided to replace the word 'establish' with 'give rise to'. The phrase 'give rise to' is based on the Commentary to the Articles on State Responsibility, which provides that *erga omnes* obligations 'arise under peremptory norms of general international law'.[39] Thus, the *jus cogens* norm is the rule of general international law. This rule is composed of rights and obligations. The obligations are (always) *erga omnes* obligations. The Drafting Committee also decided to replace the phrase 'the breach of which concerns all States' with 'in which all States have an interest'.[40] The first reading text thus provided that *jus cogens* norms 'give rise to' *erga omnes* obligations 'in which all States have a legal interest'.

Spain made the following comments on the first reading text:

> [T]he final phrase of paragraph 1, 'in which all States have a legal interest', could lead to confusion, since States, unless they are injured States, do not have an interest of their own, except that as members of the international community, they have a legal interest in the protection of the collective interest that they reflect and protect. Spain suggests that the final phrase be worded as follows: 'in which all States have a legal interest in ensuring that they are respected'.[41]

[39] Paragraph 7 of the Commentary to Part II, Chapter Three. See for discussion, Peremptory Norms of General International Law (*Jus Cogens*), Statement of the Chair of the Drafting Committee, Claudio Grossman Guiloff, 31 July 2019, 11.

[40] Statement of the Chair of the Drafting Committee (above note 39), 11.

[41] Spain, Comments and Observations (above note 9), 82.

France, in its original written (untranslated comment), made a similar observation:

> La conclusion n°17, paragraphe 1, semble en l'état dépourvue de sens et devrait sans doute faire l'objet d'une reformulation. Elle dispose que « Les normes impératives du droit international général (*jus cogens*) créent des obligations à l'égard de la communauté internationale dans sans [sic] ensemble (obligations *erga omnes*) dans lesquelles tous les États ont un intérêt juridique ». Or l'intérêt juridique des États ne repose pas dans les obligations erga omnes en tant que telles, mais dans le respect de ces obligations. Comme la Cour internationale de Justice a eu l'occasion de le dire au sujet des obligations *erga omnes*, « tous les États peuvent être considérés comme ayant un intérêt juridique à ce que ces droits soient protégés » ou « chaque État partie a un intérêt à ce qu'elles soient respectées ».[42]

In response, the Fifth Report expressed agreement with these sentiments but also a reluctance to make modifications for fear that the modifications might make the text 'heavy'.[43] On second reading, the Draft Committee considered various options to reflect this concern. This discussion reflected the fact that the nature of the legal interests that the non-injured State may have will vary.[44] It is in this sense that the Fifth Report suggested that the modification of the first reading text might make the provision somewhat heavy. The Drafting Committee considered the different formulations in the jurisprudence of the Court. The Court has, for example, described the interest as being in the 'protection',[45] 'observance',[46] 'compliance',[47] 'prevention',[48] and 'accomplishment'.[49] The phrase 'in relation to which' is intended to reflect the idea that the legal interests in Draft Conclusion 17 can refer to any of these ways that an injured State might have an interest in the *erga omnes* obligation.

[42] France, Commentaires et Observations de la République Française (above note 35), 34.

[43] See para 165 of the *Fifth Report of the Special Rapporteur on Peremptory Norms of General International Law (Jus Cogens)* (A/CN.4/747).

[44] See para 5 of the Commentary to Draft Conclusion 17 of the Draft Conclusions on Identification and Legal Consequences of Peremptory Norms of General International Law (*Jus Cogens*), With Commentaries, *Report of the International Law Commission, Seventy-Third Session* (A/77/10).

[45] *Barcelona Traction* (above note 11), para 33; *Questions Relating to the Obligation to Prosecute or Extradite (Belgium v Senegal), ICJ Reports* 2012, p. 422, para 68; *Legal Consequences of the Construction of a Wall in the Occupied Palestinian Territory, ICJ Reports* p. 136, paras 153 and 180.

[46] *Barcelona Traction* (above note 11), para 35.

[47] *Belgium v Senegal* (above note 45), para 68; *Gambia v Myanmar*, Provisional Measures (above note 13), paras 39 and 41.

[48] *Gambia v Myanmar*, Provisional Measures (above note 13), para 41;

[49] *Reservations to the Convention on the Prevention and Punishment of the Crime of Genocide*, Advisory Opinion, *ICJ Reports* p. 15, 23.

The second paragraph follows on from the first paragraph by describing the effects of the legal interest that a non-injured State might have in the *erga omnes* obligation, namely the entitlement to invoke the responsibility of the State in breach of the obligation. The paragraph includes a rather curious appendage, i.e. 'in accordance with the rules on the responsibility of States for internationally wrongful acts'. This caveat is meant to draw attention to the fact that this paragraph, which is based on Article 48 of the Articles on State Responsibility, should be read in the context of the Articles as a whole including their limitation. For example, while a non-injured State could invoke the responsibility of the State in breach of the *jus cogens*, the only forms of relief open to it were cessation and assurances of non-repetition.[50]

4. The Content of Draft Conclusion 18

Conclusion 18

Peremptory norms of general international law (*jus cogens*) and circumstances precluding wrongfulness

No circumstance precluding wrongfulness under the rules on the responsibility of States for internationally wrongful acts may be invoked with regard to any act of a State that is not in conformity with an obligation arising under a peremptory norm of general international law (*jus cogens*).

Draft Conclusion 18 provides for the non-application of circumstances precluding wrongfulness when the act in question concerns a breach of *jus cogens*. Draft Conclusion 18 is based on Article 26 of the Articles on State Responsibility. The original text proposed in the Third Report provided:

> No circumstance may be advanced to preclude the wrongfulness of an act which is not in conformity with an obligation arising under a peremptory norm of general international law (*jus cogens*).[51]

The general idea behind the proposal was retained by the Commission with some minor modifications.[52] For example, 'an act' was replaced with

[50] See para 8 of the Commentary to Draft Conclusion 17 (above note 44).
[51] See Article 19(1) proposed in the Third Report (above note 1), para 160.
[52] See Statement of the Chair of the Drafting Committee, July 2019 (above note 39), 12.

'any act' while 'advanced' was replaced with 'invoked'. These two modifications were made only to follow more closely Article 26 of the Articles on State Responsibility.

The Third Report of the Special Rapporteur had included a second paragraph which provided as follows:

> Paragraph 1 does not apply where a peremptory norm of general international law (*jus cogens*) emerges subsequent to the commission of an act.

This paragraph is not based on anything contained in Articles on State Responsibility. Yet, it seems difficult to argue with the basic premise, which is that in the event that an act occurred prior to the emergence of the norm as a peremptory norm, then the principle contained in the Draft Conclusion would not be applicable or, to put it differently, the circumstances precluding wrongfulness would be applicable. The Commission decided, however, not to include a paragraph on this matter. But this does not mean that the proposition was rejected.

5. Concluding Observations

The Draft Conclusions considered in this chapter were some of the least controversial in the whole set of Draft Conclusions. Yet, as can now be seen through the Gambia's decision to submit a complaint against Myanmar in the International Court of Justice, they are extremely important. In addressing these rules, the Commission decided to stick closely to its previously adopted positions in the Articles on State Responsibility.

There are, of course, particular issues that the Commission avoided, most notably the question of self-defence in the context of Draft Conclusion 18. Yet, as important as this question is, it depends much more on the content of the particular rules on the prohibition on the use of force, rather than on the methodology of *jus cogens*. The decision of the Commission not to address this issue was thus probably prudent.

11

Particular Consequences of *Jus Cogens* Norms

1. Introduction

In addition to the general consequences of *jus cogens* addressed in the previous chapters, there are also particular consequences attached to serious breaches of *jus cogens* as well as specific consequences attached to particular norms of *jus cogens*. Particular consequences of serious breaches are provided for in Draft Conclusion 19, while Draft Conclusion 22 refers to specific consequences of particular norms of *jus cogens*. This chapter addresses both sets of particular consequences.

Draft Conclusion 19 is understandably often associated with State responsibility. First, the particular consequences addressed therein arise after the breach of a peremptory norm, which gives rise to State responsibility. Second, these consequences are provided for in Article 41 of the Articles on State Responsibility. Yet, these particular consequences of *jus cogens* are not about, or at least not just about, the responsibility of States. They are better seen as consequences of *jus cogens* relating to their enforcement and ensuring their respect.

While the particular consequences of *jus cogens* in Draft Conclusion 19 are not purely about State responsibility, there is a strong relationship between these particular consequences and the *erga omnes* character of obligations flowing from *jus cogens* norms. These particular consequences impose duties on third States—States that, in a traditional, bilateralist vision of international law, would be unaffected or unconcerned by the breach. It imposes these duties because the *erga omnes* character of the obligations imposed by the norm means that no State can claim to be unaffected or unconcerned by breaches of *jus cogens*.

While Draft Conclusion 19 is based on the Articles of State Responsibility, unlike the other provisions also based on the Articles of State Responsibility, namely Draft Conclusions 17 and 18 (Chapter 9), Draft Conclusion 19 was the subject of some controversy. While much of the controversy concerned the Commentary to Draft Conclusion 19, there were also some questions about the text of the Draft Conclusion itself and its scope.

Draft Conclusion 22, on the other hand, does not have antecedents in the law of State responsibility. Its antecedents lie rather in international criminal law, although it has wider scope of application than that. It is a without prejudice clause, whose purpose is to capture consequences of particular norms of *jus cogens* that are not addressed in the Draft Conclusions.

Section 2 provides a general discussion of the main issues of contestation under both sets of particular consequences. With respect to particular consequences of serious breaches there were three discrete issues which arose. The first of these is the question whether the consequences addressed in Draft Conclusion 19 should apply only to 'serious' breaches or whether all breaches of *jus cogens* norms should attract these consequences (Section 2.2). Second, whether the consequences referred to in Draft Conclusion 19 are now part of customary international law (Section 2.3). A third issue is how the Russian intervention in Ukraine was to be captured in the Draft Conclusions (Section 2.4). Section 2.5 addresses other consequences that are not addressed in the Draft Conclusions. Section 3 will address the text of Draft Conclusion 19 while Section 4 is dedicated to the text of Draft Conclusion 22.

2. Discussion

2.1 Particular Consequences of *Jus Cogens*

The Articles on State Responsibility provide that, in addition to the normal State responsibility-related consequences of breaches of *jus cogens*, there are particular consequences that attach to serious breaches of *jus cogens*.[1] These consequences are, first, the duty on other States to 'cooperate' to bring to an end the breach.[2] It further specifies the duty not to 'recognise as lawful a situation created' by the breach or to assist in its maintenance.[3] According to the Articles on State Responsibility, however, these consequences are limited to serious breaches.[4]

[1] See Article 41 of the Articles on the Responsibility of States for Internationally Wrongful Acts, *Yearbook of the International Law Commission*, 2001, Vol. II, Part II.

[2] Id., Article 41(1).

[3] Id., Article 41(2).

[4] Id., Article 40.

On the strength of the Articles of State Responsibility, the Third Report proposed that the Commission also adopt provisions on additional consequences of *jus cogens*.[5] The Third Report proposed to depart from the Articles on State Responsibility in two very significant ways, however. First, the Third Report proposed that these consequences, in particular the duty not to recognise or assist, apply not only to serious breaches but to all breaches of *jus cogens*.[6] Second, the Third Report stated that while the Articles on State Responsibility described the duty not to co-operate and to bring to an end serious breaches as progressive development, the duty could now be described as being firmly part of customary international law.[7] However, the status in customary international law of the particular consequences of (serious) breaches of *jus cogens* was disputed. These two departures from the Articles on State Responsibility caused a stir and are discussed below. Since the second reading was adopted in the midst of the Russian war in Ukraine, the Commission also faced an intense debate on how the Commentaries should address the war in Ukraine.

The Third Report also proposed to address what it referred to as the effects of *jus cogens* on individual criminal responsibility under international law and in this respect proposed provisions on the consequences of *jus cogens* for the law on immunity and the principles of jurisdiction. As with particular consequences of serious breaches of *jus cogens*, those proposals concerned consequences arising from the breach of *jus cogens* (and in this way were concerned with responsibility). However, for the most part those proposals addressed principles of individual criminal responsibility, deriving from international criminal law.

2.2 Serious or All Breaches of *Jus Cogens*

The Third Report proposed that the word 'serious', which was central to the framework established by the Articles on State Responsibility, be omitted.[8] First, it should be said that the Third Report's argument for omitting 'seriousness' as a qualifier is limited only to the duties in paragraph 2 of Article 41,

[5] See *Third Report on Peremptory Norms of General International Law (Jus Cogens)* (A/CN.4/714), para 94.
[6] Id., para 101.
[7] Id., para 90.
[8] Incidentally, several States made that observation when commenting on the first reading text of the Articles on State Responsibility. See e.g. the United States, State Responsibility: Comments and Observations received from Government (A/CN.4/515), 69 ('Though the replacement of "international crimes" with the category of "serious breaches" is undoubtedly an important improvement, the United States questions the merit of drawing a distinction between "serious" and other breaches').

i.e. the duty to not recognise or render assistance. Second, the argument is not made in a particularly explicit or detailed way. The Third Report states simply:

> It is noteworthy that the decisions and resolutions described above flow from the character and importance of the rules in question but not from the intensity or the systematic way in which the breach is carried out. While the duty to cooperate to bring to an end situations created by a breach requires positive concerted, perhaps onerous, action, the duty to not to recognize, aid or assist, merely requires State to abstain from conduct. It is thus understandable that the threshold in the case law is not as high as with respect to the duty to co-operate to bring to an end the situation created by a breach.[9]

The Special Rapporteur was more explicit about the departure from the Articles on State Responsibility when introducing the Third Report at the Commission:

> The Commission should note a subtle distinction between draft conclusions 20 and 21. While draft conclusion 20 applied to 'serious' breaches of *jus cogens*, draft conclusion 21 did not contain a similar qualifier, even though it was present in article 41 (2) of the articles on State responsibility. There were two reasons for its exclusion. Firstly, unlike the duty in draft conclusion 20, the duty in draft conclusion 21 only required negative, not positive, conduct. The duty was therefore not onerous, and there was little reason to limit its application only to serious breaches. Secondly, and more importantly, none of the authorities listed in paragraphs 96 to 101 required serious breaches but rather based the duty on the peremptory nature of the rule.[10]

The proposition was supported by a number of members of the Commission,[11] while other members questioned it.[12] There were basically

[9] *Third Report* (above note 5), para 101.
[10] Special Rapporteur (Tladi) (A/CN.4/SR.3414), 9.
[11] Saboia (A/CN.4/SR.3415), 4; Lehto (A/CN.4/SR.3417), 17 ('She could accept the proposal but considered that a departure from the articles on State responsibility should be explained in the commentary'); Jalloh (A/CN.4/SR.3418), 9, who expressed the view that he would expect the deletion of 'serious' also from the duty to co-operate; Hmoud (A/CN.4/SR.3420), 10, although he seemed to suggest that the position would be *lex ferenda*; Reinisch (A/CN.4/SR.3567), 7 ('He concurred with the opinion expressed by a number of States that it might well be misguided to apply the consequences identified in the draft conclusion only in the event of serious breaches of *jus cogens*. On the contrary, any breach of a peremptory norm of international law should entail cooperation to bring it to an end, non-recognition of the situation created by such a breach as lawful, and non-assistance in maintaining that situation'); Ruda Santolaria (A/CN.4/SR.3568), 11.
[12] Murphy (A/CN.4/SR.3416), 12; Nolte (A/CN.4/SR.3417), 13; Rajput (A/CN.4/SR.3418), 5; Galvão Teles (A/CN.4/SR.3419), 4; Huang (A/CN.4/SR.3419), 11; Wood (A/CN.4/SR.3420), 6; Escobar Hernández (A/CN.4/SR.3420), 9.

three arguments advanced by those opposed to the omission of the word 'serious'. The first was the need to remain consistent with the Articles on State Responsibility.[13] The second was that the authorities relied upon in the Third Report for the proposition were the same authorities in the Commentaries to the Articles on State Responsibility. The fact that those authorities did not mention 'serious' was thus insufficient to justify a departure.[14] The third reason was that, while the authorities relied on did not use the word 'serious', the situations they concerned, such as the violations of the right of self-determination of the Palestinian people, were in fact serious.[15]

Recognising the large number of members disagreeing with the proposition that the word 'serious' be dropped, the closing statement by the Special Rapporteur conceded the point but suggested that if the Commission retained the word 'serious', the Commentary (adopted on first reading) would need to make clear that there were opposing views.[16] Most States did not comment on this question.[17] In the end, the Commission decided to retain the word 'serious' but to clarify that this did not mean that there were breaches of *jus cogens* that were not serious, but rather that there were particular consequences that flowed from breaches that met a particular threshold.[18]

2.3 The Status of the Duties in Customary International Law

Perhaps the most serious issue concerned the customary status of the duties to co-operate to bring to an end breaches of *jus cogens* and, to a lesser extent the duties of non-recognition and non-assistance. The starting point

[13] See e.g. Galvão Teles (A/CN.4/SR.3419), 4.
[14] Murphy (A/CN.4/SR.3416), 12.
[15] Huang (A/CN.4/SR.3419), 11.
[16] Tladi (A/CN.4/SR.3425), 12 ('If the Commission insisted on retaining the word "serious", the commentary would need expressly to state that in 2018 the Commission took the view that a State was free to recognize or even assist in breaches of *jus cogens* that were not serious. At the same time, the commentary would have to make it clear that some members, including himself, dissented from that view').
[17] See, for support of retention of the word 'serious', the United Kingdom, Comments and Observations received from Governments (A/CN.4/747), 89. States that were of the view that all breaches of *jus cogens* norms are serious were Poland (A/C.6/74/SR.23), 124 and Egypt (A/C.6/74/SR.26), 4.
[18] Paragraph 17 of the Commentary to Draft Conclusion 19, of the Draft Conclusions on identification and legal consequences of peremptory norms of general international law (*jus cogens*), with Commentaries, *Report of the International Law Commission, Seventy-Third Session* (A/77/10).

for this discussion must be the Articles on State Responsibility of 2001. The Commentary to Article 41 seems to provide a strong indication that the Commission believed the obligations of non-recognition and non-assistance to be grounded in customary international law.[19] Yet, with respect to the duty to co-operate to bring to an end the breach, the Commentary states:

> It may be open to question whether general international law at present prescribes a positive duty of cooperation, and paragraph 1 in that respect may reflect the progressive development of international law. But in fact such co-operation, especially in the framework of international organizations, is carried out already in response to the gravest breaches of international law and it is often the only way of providing an effective remedy.[20]

The Commission did not say that the duty to co-operate was not part of the corpus of customary international law, only that 'it *may* be open to question whether general international law at present prescribes a positive duty' and that the duty '*may* reflect the progressive development of international law'.[21] It is the case that, for paragraph 1 of Article 41, the Commission did not provide any authorities, although there were certainly authorities available, some of which are described below. Yet the position has been put forward that at the time of adoption of the 2001 Articles there was not sufficient authority for the proposition, and that in the intervening period the situation has not changed.[22] This position is made most strongly by Israel, which noted that in 2001 the Commission questioned the customary status of the duty and proceeded to state that the position

> remains true today. The commentary to the current draft conclusions on *jus cogens* does not provide sufficient (if any) evidence of development of State practice regarding the suggestion in article 41, paragraph 1, of the draft articles on the responsibility of States for internationally wrongful acts that

[19] See e.g. para 6 of the Commentary to Article 41, Articles on State Responsibility (above note 1) ('The existence of an obligation of non-recognition in response to serious breaches of obligations arising under peremptory norms already finds support in international practice and in decisions of ICJ'). See also para 12 ('In some respects, the prohibition contained in paragraph 2 may be seen as a logical extension of the duty of non-recognition').

[20] Id., para 3.

[21] Id. (emphasis added).

[22] This position is seemingly advanced in Helmut Philipp Aust 'Legal Consequences of Serious Breaches of Peremptory Norms for the Law of State Responsibility: Observations in the Light of the Most Recent Work of the International Law Commission' in Dire Tladi (ed.) *Peremptory Norms of General International Law (Jus Cogens): Disquisitions and Disputations* (Brill, 2021),

> would indicate a change in this position. Therefore, Israel considers that the particular consequences referred to in draft conclusion 19 do not reflect existing international law.[23]

The United States also expressed similar views.[24] Other States, without questioning the determination that the duties constitute *jus cogens*, called for greater explanation and elaboration in the Commentaries.[25] Most States simply accepted the content of the duties without questioning their status in customary international law, although some did explicitly acknowledge the status in customary international law.[26]

What authority exists that the duties to co-operate to bring an end to breaches of *jus cogens*, and the duties of non-recognition and non-assistance in the maintenance of situations created by the breaches of *jus cogens*, are customary international law? It is perhaps necessary to take each one of the duties in turn.

Taking first the duty to co-operate, the Commentary begins, almost as a chapeau, by citing the general duty to co-operate under international law as the building block for the duty to co-operate.[27] Also referred to in the Commentary is the United Kingdom House of Lords decision in *A, Amnesty International (intervening) and Commonwealth Lawyers Association (intervening) v Secretary of State for the Home Department*, in which the Court referred explicitly to the duty to co-operate to bring to an end breaches of *jus cogens* as existing under international law.[28] It bears mentioning that the House of Lords explicitly referred to the Commission's Articles on State Responsibility for this conclusion. Similarly, the German Federal Constitutional Court referred to the duty of third States to counter serious breaches of *jus cogens*, explicitly invoking the Commission's Articles on State Responsibility.[29] Going further, the Inter-American Court also identified the existence of this duty as part of international law connected with the need to fight impunity.[30]

[23] Israel, Comments and Observations (above note 17), 85.

[24] The United States, Comments and Observations (above note 17), 90.

[25] Australia, Comments and Observations (above note 17), 84; Japan, Comments and Observations (above note 17), 87; The Netherlands (above note 17), 88.

[26] For examples of States explicitly expressing support for the customary status of the duties to co-operate, non-recognition, and non-assistance, see Cyprus, Comments and Observations (above note 17), 85; Austria (A/C.6/74/SR.23), para 73; Cuba (A/C.6/74/SR.25), para 21.

[27] See para 2 of the Commentary to Draft Conclusion 19 (above note 18) ('The obligation to "co-operate ..." builds on the general obligation to cooperate under international law').

[28] *A, Amnesty International Law (Intervening) and Commonwealth Lawyers Association v Secretary of State for the Home Department*, Judgment of the House of Lords [2006] 1 All ER 575, para 34.

[29] *Order of 26 October 2004*, Federal Constitutional Court of Germany, 2 *BvR* 1038/01, para 98.

[30] *Case of La Cantuta v Peru*, Merits, Reparations and Costs, Judgment of the Inter-American Court of Human Rights of 29 November 2006, para 160.

There are also examples in treaty practice of States, collectively, assuming the right to intervene to bring to an end acts which are prohibited as *jus cogens*. These include Article 4(h) of the African Union (AU) Constitutive Act which provides for the right of the AU to intervene in member States in cases of breaches of norms recognised as *jus cogens* such as the prohibition of war crimes and the prohibition of genocide.[31] The Commentary also refers to a large number of resolutions containing examples of the Security Council, General Assembly, and Human Rights Council of the United Nations acting, within the limits of their power, on the duty to co-operate to bring to an end breaches of *jus cogens*, covering situations concerning Southern Rhodesia, South Africa, Portugal, Israeli aggression against several States, the situation in Grenada, the situation in Namibia, use of force by the United States in Panama, breach of the right of self-determination by Portugal, Myanmar, Syria, the right to self-determination of the Palestinian people, and of course the Russian intervention of Ukraine.[32]

Thus, even before accounting for the decisions of the International Court of Justice, both of which are discussed separately below,[33] there is certainly a high degree of evidence to support the duty to co-operate. It also bears mentioning that up until the Commission began working on the topic of peremptory norms of general international law, the customary status of the duty had never openly been questioned before. This is particularly significant since the Court, as we discuss below, had put forward the duty. What the practice shows is that when there has been consensus that particular conduct is in breach of norms accepted as *jus cogens*, the international community has co-operated, including through adoption of resolutions, with a view to end the breaches. Whether the acts in co-operation have been sufficient or effective, or even timely, is a different matter, but on the whole some co-operative action has been taken.

Finally, the duty to co-operate to bring to an end breaches of *jus cogens* has been recognised in the judicial decisions of the International Court of Justice, namely the *Wall* Advisory Opinion and the *Chagos* Advisory Opinion.[34] The point has been made by several members of the Commission,[35] echoed by

[31] See Article 4(h) of the 2000 African Union Constitutive Act.

[32] The Commentary refers to more than twenty resolutions. For the full references, see footnotes 250–2 of the *Report of the International Law Commission, Seventy-Third Session* (A/77/10).

[33] The practice relating to Russia is discussed in Section 2.

[34] *Legal Consequences of the Construction of the Wall in the Occupied Palestinian Territories*, Advisory Opinion, *ICJ Reports* 2006, p. 136, para 155, noting that there is a duty to co-operate to bring to an end breaches of the rights of self-determination and obligations under international humanitarian law, and *Legal Consequences of the Separation of the Chagos Archipelago from Mauritius in 1965*, Advisory Opinion, *ICJ Reports* 2019, p. 95, para 180.

[35] See e.g. Rajput (A/CN.4/SR.3418), 6 ('In paragraph 97 of his report, the Special Rapporteur referred to the advisory opinion of the Court in *Legal Consequences of the Construction of a Wall in the*

several States,[36] that in those decisions the Court never refers to *jus cogens*.[37] But this argument makes little sense and, at best, amounts to obfuscation. For one thing, as has already been noted, the norms to which the Court attached the duty to co-operate in these decisions are widely regarded as *jus cogens*.[38] Indeed, as the Commentary notes, the UK House of Lords assumed, as do many other observers, that the International Court of Justice in these decisions meant to

Occupied Palestinian Territory but once again the Court appeared to have been more concerned with the relationship between *erga omnes* obligations and *jus cogens*, because the norm in question was an *erga omnes* obligation which itself imposed a duty on States to cooperate').

[36] Israel, Comments and Observations (above note 17), 85 ('As for the two advisory opinions that are cited in paragraph (2) of the commentary in support of draft conclusion 19, it should be recalled that in both opinions the Court did not explicitly identify a norm of *jus cogens*, but rather referred to the *erga omnes* character of the rules in question'); Japan, Comments and Observations (above note 17), 87 ('In this regard, first, it is doubtful whether some cases cited in the commentary support draft conclusion 19. For example, in the advisory opinion on the *Legal Consequences of the Separation of the Chagos Archipelago from Mauritius in 1965*, the International Court of Justice stated that all Member States are under an obligation to cooperate with the United Nations in order to complete decolonization, without referring to *jus cogens*. Similarly, according to the Advisory Opinion of *Legal Consequences of the Construction of a Wall in the Occupied Palestinian Territory* [above note 34] "all States are under an obligation not to recognize the illegal situation resulting from the construction of the wall", but there was no explicit reference to *jus cogens*'); the United States, Comments and Observations (above note 17), 90 ('The commentary to draft conclusion 19, paragraph 1, relies heavily on the International Court of Justice advisory opinions on the *Legal Consequences of the Construction of a Wall in the Occupied Palestinian Territory* and the *Legal Consequences of the Separation of the Chagos Archipelago from Mauritius in 1965*. Each of these opinions referred to third-State obligations arising in relation to breach of an obligation *erga omnes*, but neither referred to such obligations in relation to a *jus cogens* norm. The Commission cannot rely on these cases to support an assertion that there now exist new obligations on non-breach').

[37] Other States have referred to this argument, not in support, but only to press the Commission to respond to the argument. See e.g. Italy, Comments and Observations (above note 17), 86 ('Italy sees the need for the Commission to clarify its reference to the advisory opinions of the International Court of Justice on the *Legal Consequences of the Construction of a Wall in the Occupied Palestinian Territory* and the *Legal Consequences of the Separation of the Chagos Archipelago from Mauritius in 1965*. In fact, both advisory opinions grounded the identification of legal consequences for third parties on the *erga omnes* nature of the obligations breached, rather than on the peremptory nature of the corresponding norm and/or the serious violation of those obligations/norms.... The Commission may be of the view that, given the factual and legal circumstances, the reluctance of the Court to employ the normative category of *jus cogens* and the strict interconnection between *erga omnes* obligations and *jus cogens* norms, the International Court of Justice, in those two advisory opinions, had indeed identified a serious violation of a peremptory norm (without explicitly stating that). And yet, if that is the case, the point should be clarified in the commentary').

[38] The Commission had already, in para 7 of the Commentary to Part Two, Chapter III of the Articles on State Responsibility (above note 1), noted that 'the examples which ICJ has given of obligations towards the international community as a whole all concern obligations which, it is generally accepted, arise under peremptory norms of general international law'. See also response of the then President of the Court of Justice, Yusuf, to a question from the Special Rapporteur on why the Court had not referred to *jus cogens* in the *Chagos* Advisory Opinion, (A/CN.4/SR.3478), stating that 'the Court had deemed it unnecessary to address the matter of whether the right to self-determination was a peremptory norm of international law in its advisory opinion on the *Legal Consequences of the Separation of the Chagos Archipelago from Mauritius in 1965*, because that had not been the point at issue', and that, in his view, '[t]he General Assembly's question had been whether the decolonization process of Mauritius had been lawfully completed'. See, however, Julia Sebutinde 'Is the Right to Self-Determination *Jus Cogens*: Reflection on the Chagos Advisory Opinion' in Tladi (above note 22).

refer to *jus cogens*.[39] Moreover, since it is universally accepted that all *jus cogens* norms give rise to *erga omnes* obligations—this proposition by the Commission was not challenged by any member of the Commission or any State (see Chapter 10)—it must follow that any duty under customary international law that attaches to *erga omnes* obligations must also attach to *jus cogens* norms.

On the basis of the above, it is difficult to conclude that the duty not to co-operate is not part of customary international law.

This section will turn now to the duties of non-recognition and non-assistance. Given that the duties to not recognise and assist in the maintenance of situations were already regarded by the Commission in 2001 as customary international law and were subject to less challenge in the current work of the Commission, their substantiation will be less comprehensive.

This duty not to recognise situations created by the breach of *jus cogens* has been affirmed in some domestic case law.[40] As with the duty to co-operate, the duty of non-recognition has also been affirmed in the decisions of international courts.[41] There is also practice in the form of resolutions of the General Assembly and the Security Council affirming the duty on States not to recognise situations created by breaches of norms widely recognised as being *jus cogens*. Examples cited in the Commentary relate to the Turkish Republic of Northern Cyprus, occupation of Kuwait, Chagos, the situation in Palestine, Russian aggression in Ukraine, and the South African policy of Apartheid.[42] The duty of non-assistance, which was described by the Commission in the Articles on State Responsibility as an expression of the duty of non-recognition, has also been affirmed in decisions of the International Court of Justice and resolutions of organs of the United Nations.[43]

[39] See *A v Secretary of State for the Home Department* (above note 28), 34.

[40] Id., 34; *Kuwait Airways Corporation v Iraqi Airways Company and Others*, Judgment of the House of Lords [2002] UKHL 19, [2002] 2 AC 883, para 29.

[41] See *Wall* Advisory Opinion (above note 34), para 159, where the Court, in the context of norms widely recognised as constituting *jus cogens*, stated that all States were 'under an obligation not to recognize the illegal situation resulting from' that breach. See also *The Prosecutor v Bosco Ntaganda*, Case No. ICC-01/04-02/06-1707, *Second Decision on the Defence's Challenge of the Jurisdiction of the Court on Counts 6 and 9*, Trial Chamber IV of the International Criminal Court, para 54, which described the duty of non-recognition as a general principle of law.

[42] See references in footnotes 264–5 of the *Report of the International Law Commission, Seventy-Third Session* (above note 32).

[43] See e.g. *Wall* Advisory Opinion (above note 34), para 159; General Assembly res. 3411 D (XXX), para 3; General Assembly res. ES-11/1, para 10 ('Deplores the involvement of Belarus in this unlawful use of force against Ukraine, and calls upon it to abide by its international obligations'); General Assembly res. 2022 (XX), para 5 ('Condemns any support or assistance rendered by any State to the minority régime in Southern Rhodesia') and para 6 ('Calls upon all States to refrain from rendering any assistance whatsoever to the minority régime in Southern Rhodesia'); General Assembly res. 36/27, para 3 ('Reiterates its call to all States to cease forthwith any provision to Israel of arms and related material of all types which enable it to commit acts of aggression against other States').

Thus, notwithstanding doubts that have been expressed about the customary international law status of the duties to co-operate to bring to an end serious breaches of peremptory norms, of non-recognition of situations created by such breaches, and non-assistance in the maintenance of such situations, these duties are sufficiently supported in practice and jurisprudence.

2.4 Reflecting on the Russian Invasion of Ukraine

The adoption of the Draft Conclusions took place just a few months after the start of the Russian intervention in Ukraine. Russia's intervention has been deemed by UN organs to constitute a violation of the prohibition on the use of force as well as other breaches of norms that qualify as *jus cogens*—war crimes and self-determination to mention but a few. Moreover, given the grand scale and widespread impact of the offensive, potential breaches also probably met the threshold of 'serious' (Section 2.2 above). More importantly, in the face of the Security Council's inability to act on account of the Russian veto, several organs of the United Nations adopted decisions pursuant to the duty to co-operate as well as the duties of non-assistance and non-recognition.[44] Measures were also adopted unilaterally and in the context of regional organisations in response to the Russian intervention. The question facing the Commission was how to reflect these in the Commentaries.

The Fifth Report was submitted prior to the outbreak of war and could thus not capture these various acts or suggest ways to address them. While the Fifth Report itself did not address the question of how to capture the responses to the Russian intervention, the oral introduction of the Fifth Report stated only that the commentaries would need to be 'strengthened significantly'.[45]

The view that the Commentaries would need to be strengthened to account for the Russian intervention was shared by a very large number of members of the Commission.[46] There were, however, some members that cautioned that the Commentaries should not be used as a vehicle to politically address the situation in Ukraine. Without specifically referring to the Russian invasion of Ukraine, Mr Argüello Gómez made the following statement:

[44] These are referred to in the Commentary to Draft Conclusion 19 (above note 18).
[45] Special Rapporteur (Tladi) (A/CN.4/SR.3564), 10.
[46] Murase (A/CN.4/3565), 3; Lehto (A/CN.4/SR.3567), 8; Oral (A/CN.4/SR.3567), 9; Escobar-Hernandez (A/CN.4/SR.3569), 4.

> [I]n September 2002, the Government of the United States of America had announced a national security strategy that authorized recourse to preventive wars. That had been the prelude to the 2003 invasion of Iraq, which had allegedly resulted in violations of several of the peremptory norms of international law ... At the Commission's fifty-fifth session, in 2003, an attempt had been made to speak out on the issue, in response to which Michael J. Matheson, a citizen of the United States serving on the Commission at the time, had written, in the American Journal of International Law, that 'the Commission wisely avoided the temptation of taking actions that might be interpreted as commenting on current political events—specifically the conflict in Iraq'. One hopes that the Commission will continue to approach its work in this careful and orderly way, avoiding any step that might politicize its deliberations to the detriment of its long-term credibility.[47]

Subsequent to the adoption of the text of the Draft Conclusions, the Special Rapporteur presented a draft set of Commentaries.[48] The draft Commentaries contained a detailed description of the measures adopted by States in response to the Russian intervention.[49] This resulted in a lengthy debate with most members calling for the streamlining of the text.[50] Based on the debate, the Special Rapporteur redrafted the Commentary, essentially moving the measures adopted by States to the footnotes. Madam Oral, however, expressed disagreement with the compromise in particularly strong terms:

> [W]hile she was grateful to the Special Rapporteur for having taken the time to draft an alternative text, she regrettably could not support the proposed new paragraph, not least because of the reasons for which the new text had had to be proposed. At the Commission's 3599th meeting, she had made clear that she would not agree to the deletion of paragraphs (3) and (4); the replacement of those paragraphs with the proposed new text would amount to their deletion *de facto*. The reference to the resolutions that concerned the Russian Federation and Ukraine had been buried deep in one of the lengthy new footnotes.[51]

[47] Argüello Gómez (A/CN.4/SR.3468), 5.
[48] See marked-up version of *Draft Report of the International Law Commission, Seventy-Third Session*, Chapter IV, Peremptory Norms of General International Law (*Jus Cogens*), (A/CN.4/L.960.Add.1), reproduced as an Annex.
[49] See id., paras 3, 4, and 11.
[50] (A/CN.4/SR.4599), 5–12.
[51] Oral (A/CN.4/SR.3600), 7.

2.5 Other Consequences of Breaches of *Jus Cogens*—Serious or Not

The duty to co-operate as well as the duties of non-recognition and non-assistance do not constitute the entire universe of particular consequences of *jus cogens*. While the status of the duty to co-operate and the duties of non-recognition and non-assistance in relation to serious breaches of *jus cogens* was questioned in some quarters, in other quarters the question was posed whether there were consequences beyond these duties under international law. For example, it has been suggested that the Draft Conclusions would be incomplete if counter-measures were not addressed.[52]

There were also suggestions that, in the event of serious breaches of *jus cogens*, there should be restrictions on the use of the veto.[53] Other possible 'aggravated circumstances' include increased amounts in the calculations of damages.[54]

Responding to these suggestions after the debate on second reading text in the Sixth Committee, the Special Rapporteur made the following observations:

> I turn now to Draft Conclusion 19. On Draft Conclusion 19, the debate this year has revealed two conflicting criticisms. Three States have suggested that the Commission went too far to suggest that the contents of DC 19 reflected customary international law. On the other hand, three other States suggested that DC 19, by simply restating Arts 40 and 41 of the Arts on SR did not go far enough and could have provided further aggravated consequences for serious breaches of *jus cogens*.

[52] The Netherlands, Comments and Observations (above note 17), 87–8 ('the Netherlands notes that twenty years have passed since the Commission concluded in its work in 2001 on the draft articles on the responsibility of States for internationally wrongful acts, and that, at that time, State practice was not yet sufficiently developed in regard of the question whether States that are not affected by a particular breach of international law are entitled to take countermeasures. According to the Kingdom of the Netherlands, subsequent developments warrant that the Commission resume its research on this point'). France, Commentaires et observations de la république française relatifs aux projets de conclusions de la commission de droit international sur les normes impératives du droit international général, 35, https://legal.un.org/ilc/sessions/73/pdfs/french/jc_france.pdf (accessed 18 January 2023), 37 ('En effet, le paragraphe 3 du commentaire sous le projet de conclusion paraît aller au-delà du compromis plus équilibré trouvé à l'article 54 de ces articles. La Commission n'y avait pas exclu expressément les contre-mesures collectives, en se limitant, dans ses commentaires, à souligner que « l'incertitude plane en ce qui concerne les contre-mesures prises dans l'intérêt général ou collectif »'.

[53] Japan, Comments and Observations (above note 17), 87. See also Saboia (A/CN.4/SR.3566), 7. See in this respect Jennifer Trahan *Existing Legal Limits to Security Council Veto Power in the Face of Atrocity Crimes* (Cambridge, 2020).

[54] See generally Rosalind Elphick (with John Dugard) '*Jus Cogens* and Compensation' in Tladi (above note 22).

The first criticism was already addressed in the Fifth Report and so I wish to make some observations about the second. The Commission could have come up with all sorts of extra consequences, including aggravated responsibility. We could have decided that the application of the veto in matters of *jus cogens* was invalid or States automatically lost their seats in international organizations in the event of serious breaches.

But the question would have to be asked: on the basis of what practice? On the basis of what jurisprudence? Now it is the case that both this year, and in 1974 we have seen examples of States being suspended from organs of international organisations, but these were, rather than automatic consequences, examples of the implementation of the duty to cooperate to bring to an end serious breaches. In other words, these actions by States, acting collectively, are intended to put pressure on the State in serious breach of its duties arising from a breach of a *jus cogens* norm and are reflected as such in the commentary.[55]

There are three main messages here. First, the Commission is caught between those wanting the Commission to go further, i.e. that the Commission is overly conservative, and those that believe that the Commission is too progressive and has gone too far. Second, even if desirable, the Commission cannot put forward provisions that are not based on some practice. Finally, the statement is suggesting that there is a large measure of discretion on how States implement the duty to co-operate and the duties of non-recognition and non-assistance, which provide possibilities for some of these aggravated consequences. Together, these messages call for a balance between ambition and faithfulness to practice and positive law.

Some States called for the Commission to address other consequences of *jus cogens*, such as the impact of *jus cogens* on immunity.[56] This was addressed in the Special Rapporteur's Third Report which included a proposal that read as follows:

Draft Conclusion 22

Duty to exercise domestic jurisdiction over crimes prohibited by peremptory norms of general international law

[55] Statement of the Special Rapporteur in Response to the Debate on the Sixth Committee, 27 October 2022 (on file). A video recording of the statement is available at https://media.un.org/en/asset/k12/k12iqnldud (accessed 18 January 2023).

[56] See e.g. Japan, Comments and Observations (above note 17), 98; Italy, Comments and Observations (above note 17), 104. See, however, Austria, Comments and Observations (above note 17), 74.

1. States have a duty to exercise jurisdiction over offences prohibited by peremptory norms of international law (*jus cogens*), where the offences are committed by the nationals of that State or on the territory under its jurisdiction.
2. Paragraph 1 does not preclude the establishment of jurisdiction on any other ground as permitted under its national law.

Draft Conclusion 23

Irrelevance of official position and non-applicability of immunity *ratione materiae*

1. The fact that an offence prohibited by a peremptory norm of general international law (*jus cogens*) was committed by a person holding an official position shall not constitute a ground excluding criminal responsibility
2. Immunity *ratione materiae* shall not apply to any offence prohibited by a peremptory norm of general international law (*jus cogens*).

For the proposition that immunity *ratione materiae* does not apply, the Third Report relied on the interpretation of a number of domestic cases.[57] The Report also criticises the reliance on arguments in favour of retaining immunity for *jus cogens*-related crimes based on civil proceedings-related cases.[58] Amongst other points, the Third Report states that civil proceedings-related cases themselves often make the distinction between immunity from foreign criminal jurisdiction and immunity of a State from civil proceedings.[59]

[57] See para 125 of the Third Report (above note 5). Some of the cases referred to in the Report include: *Attorney-General of the Government of Israel v Eichmann*, Judgment of the Supreme Court, English translation available in (1968) 36 International Law Reports 277; *Re Bouterse (Desire)*, Judgment on Appeal, Netherlands Supreme Court, Decision No. LJN: AB1471, Case No. HR 00749/01 CW 2323, NJ 2002, 559, ILDC 80 (NL 2001), 18 September 2001; *Guatemala Genocide, Menchú Tumm and Others v Two Guatemalan Government Officials and Six Members of the Guatemalan Military*, Judgment of the Constitutional Court of 26 September 2005; *Scilingo Manzorro (Alolfo Francisco) v Spain*, Judgment of the Supreme Court of Spain of 1 October 2007; *R v Bartle and the Commissioner of Police for the Police and Others, Ex Parte Pinochet*, Judgment of the House of Lords of 24 March 1999, reproduced in International Legal Materials, Vol. 38 (1999), p. 581, opinion of Lord Brown-Wilkinson (para 56), opinion of Lord Hope (para 196), opinion of Lord Millet (para 330 *et seq.*), and opinion of Lord Phillips (para 366). See, for discussion, Dire Tladi 'The International Law Commission's Recent Work on Immunity: Charting the Course for a Brave New World in International Law' (2019) 32 *Leiden Journal of International Law* 169; A.P.V. Rogers 'War Crimes Trials under the Royal Warrant: British Practice 1945–1949' (1990) 39 *International and Comparative Law Quarterly* 780.

[58] See Third Report (above note 5), especially para 130.

[59] Id. The Third Report refers to, for example, *Jurisdictional Immunities of the State (Germany v Italy: Greece intervening)*, Judgment, *ICJ Reports* 2012, p. 99, paras 87 and 91 ('The Court concludes that, under customary international law as it presently stands, a State is not deprived of immunity by

It is important to outline a few points of context. First, with respect to immunity, the exceptions to immunity are limited to immunity *ratione materiae* and criminal proceedings. As a practical matter, this means that under the proposal, the *jus cogens* norm would have no effect on immunity of the State itself, immunity of heads of States and heads of government, and immunity of any official in civil proceedings. The second point of context is that the Draft Conclusion was proposed in 2018, a year after the Commission had adopted Draft Article 7 providing exceptions to immunity *ratione materiae* of State officials from foreign criminal jurisdiction in respect of certain *jus cogens*-related crimes.[60] It is also an important point of context that Draft Article 7 was adopted by vote, a rare occurrence in the International Law Commission.

Against this background, the Special Rapporteur's proposal was not well-received. Of course, members of the Commission that opposed the notion of exceptions to immunities and had voted against Article 7 of the Draft Articles of Immunity expressed strong objection to the Special Rapporteur's proposal.[61] What was a surprise, however, was that even members that had supported the exceptions in Draft Conclusion 7 expressed doubt about the proposal in the Third Report.[62] Only a few members supported the

reason of the fact that it is accused of serious violations of international human rights law or the international law of armed conflict. In reaching that conclusion, the Court must emphasize that it is addressing only the immunity of the State itself from the jurisdiction of the courts of other States; the question of whether, and if so to what extent, immunity might apply in criminal proceedings against an official of the State is not in issue in the present case'); *Al-Adsani v the United Kingdom*, Grand Chamber, No. 35763/97, European Court of Human Rights, ECHR 2001-XI, 20 ('A number of decisions from foreign national courts have reflected a willingness to deny official-act immunity in the criminal context for alleged *jus cogens* violations' while noting that 'the *jus cogens* exception appears to be less settled in the civil context').

[60] Draft Article 7 of the Articles on the Immunity of State Officials from Foreign Criminal Jurisdiction, *Report of the International Law Commission, Sixty-Ninth Session* (A/72/10).

[61] Sagaynov (A/CN.4/SR.3416), 6 ('It was his view that the issues raised in those draft conclusions, having to do with the criminal responsibility of individuals, lay outside the scope of the topic at hand. It was also impossible to comprehend why the focus was on those aspects in particular'); Murphy (A/CN.4/SR.3416), 12–13. Although omitted from the summary records, Mr Murphy described the proposal as Draft Article 7 'on steroids'; Nolte (A/CN.4/SR.3417), 13; Rajput (A/CN.4/SR.3418), 6; Huang (A/CN.4/SR.3419), 11; Wood (A/CN.4/SR.3421), 6.

[62] Ruda Santaloria (A/CN.4/SR.3417), 17 ('he agreed with the draft conclusions in general but, in respect of immunity *ratione materiae* under draft conclusion 23, he was concerned that any overlap with immunity of State officials from foreign criminal jurisdiction should be avoided'); Lehto (A/CN,4/Sr.3417), 19; Jalloh (A/CN.4/SR.3418), 10 ('That said, in view of the sensitive nature of the issue, he wondered whether it might not be wiser to revisit the matter at a later date in order to assuage the concerns of those members who had strongly opposed the adoption of draft article 7 on the immunity of State officials from foreign criminal jurisdiction'); Vásquez-Bermúdez (A/CN.4/SR.3418), 13 ('While not disagreeing with draft conclusions 22 and 23, he cautioned against duplicating the Commission's work on immunity of State officials from foreign criminal jurisdiction, particularly in terms of exceptions to such jurisdiction *ratione materiae*. To that end, the Drafting Committee should postpone discussion of paragraph 2 of draft conclusion 23 at least until draft article 7 of the Commission's draft articles on immunity of State officials from foreign criminal jurisdiction had been approved on second

proposal.[63] It seems members of the Commission feared that addressing immunity in the Draft Conclusions would make it difficult to find consensus on the topic of immunity.

Having listened to the debate, the Special Rapporteur agreed to withdraw the proposal and replace it by a without prejudice clause:

> On that basis, he proposed that the two draft conclusions should be transmitted to the Drafting Committee on the understanding that they should be redrafted as 'without prejudice' clauses. He proposed that the two draft conclusions should be accompanied by a text to the effect that: 'The present draft conclusions are without prejudice to the consequences of specific/individual/particular peremptory norms of general international law (*jus cogens*).' That text did not include the word 'immunity', but it would of course be mentioned in the commentary that immunity was one of those consequences, and he undertook to draft the commentary in a non-prejudicial manner. His proposal was, he believed, an optimal one from a substantive perspective and from the perspective of the internal harmony of the Commission.[64]

3. The Content of Draft Conclusion 19

Draft Conclusion 19

Particular consequences of serious breaches of peremptory norms of general international law (*jus cogens*)

1. States shall cooperate to bring to an end through lawful means any serious breach by a State of an obligation arising under a peremptory norm of general international law (*jus cogens*).
2. No State shall recognize as lawful a situation created by a serious breach by a State of an obligation arising under a peremptory norm of general

reading'); Galvão Teles (A/CN.4/SR,3419), 5 ('She agreed with the proposed text of paragraph 2 and favoured its referral to the Drafting Committee; however, given its close link to the topic "Immunity of State officials from foreign criminal jurisdiction", she concurred with Mr. Jalloh and Mr. Vázquez-Bermúdez that its consideration by the Drafting Committee should be suspended until the first reading of the draft articles on immunity had been completed'); Hassouna (A/CN.4/SR.3419), 8; Oral (A/CN.4/SR.3419), 15 (A/CN.4/SR.3419), 15; Grossman Guiloff (A/CN.4/SR.3420), 7; Hmoud (A/CN.4/SR.3420), 11; Escobar Hernandez (A/CN.4/SR.3421), 9–10;

[63] Saboia (A/CN.4/SR.3415), 4–5; Šturma (A/CN.4/SR.3416), 8; Cisse (A/CN.4/SR.3420), 4; Peter (A/CN.4/SR.3421), 3.

[64] Special Rapporteur (Tladi) (A/CN.4/SR.3422), 16.

international law (*jus cogens*), nor render aid or assistance in maintaining that situation.

3. A breach of an obligation arising under a peremptory norm of general international law (*jus cogens*) is serious if it involves a gross or systematic failure by the responsible State to fulfil that obligation.
4. This draft conclusion is without prejudice to the other consequences that any breach by a State of an obligation arising under a peremptory norm of general international law (*jus cogens*) may entail under international law.

Draft Conclusion 19 contains four paragraphs. The first three paragraphs are based on Article 41 of the Articles on State Responsibility. In the Third Report, the duties were presented in two separate Draft Conclusions.[65] Motivated in part by the objective of remaining faithful to the Articles on State Responsibility, the Commission decided to place all three duties under one Draft Conclusion.

The first paragraph contains the duty to co-operate to bring to an end breaches of *jus cogens*. There are two caveats to this duty. The first is that, under the Draft Conclusion, the duty applies only to 'serious' breaches of *jus cogens*. What is meant by 'serious' breaches is discussed further below. The second caveat is that the duty to co-operate has to be given effect 'through lawful means'. This means that, under Draft Conclusion 19, measures which would otherwise be unlawful may not be taken as an application of the duty contained in Draft Conclusion 19. Put differently, Draft Conclusion 19 cannot itself be a justification precluding the wrongfulness of a measure. This raises a number of questions about the utility of the duty.

It raises, for example, the question whether co-ordinated unilateral measures, including decisions to act in non-compliance with existing treaties with the State in serious breach of *jus cogens* norms, would be valid under the Draft Conclusions. It is in this context that the International Court of Justice in the *Wall* Advisory Opinion, while stating that States, individually, should take measures with a view to ensuring the end of the serious breach, qualified the permissible measures as ones 'respecting the [UN Charter] and international law'.[66] Thus, in the event that a measure which, on the face of it, appears unlawful is adopted as part of implementing the duty to co-operate, the lawfulness

[65] See Draft Conclusion 20 (duty to cooperate) and Draft Conclusion 21 (Duty of non-recognition and non-assistance), in the Third Report (above note 5), para 160.

[66] *Wall* Advisory Opinion (above note 34), para 159.

of the measure would have to be found on some other grounds, for example the grounds in Section 3 of Part V of the Law of Treaties.

The current situation, and the provision of arms by Western States to Ukraine, can be advanced as an example. This measure of co-operation is no doubt an example of the implementation of the duty to co-operate in Draft Conclusion 19. Yet, the lawfulness of the provision of arms cannot be justified by Draft Conclusion 19. The lawfulness of the provision of arms *could* be justified by other rules of international law such as the right of States to intervene militarily when invited by the territorial State or, alternatively, the right of collective self-defence.[67]

The requirement for co-operative measures to be lawful can significantly constrain actions necessary to end serious breaches of *jus cogens*. It is, in part, for this reason that according to the Commentary, the emphasis on the duty to co-operate falls on collective measures.[68]

The second paragraph contains two duties. The first duty is the duty not to recognise as lawful situations created by serious breaches of *jus cogens*, while the second is the duty not to assist in the maintenance of such situations. There are a few general points that can be made about these two duties. First, these duties concern not the breach itself, but situations created by the breach. The typical example here is the acquisition of territory by the use of force. Nonetheless, while the Commentary states that Draft Conclusion 19 does not cover assistance in the commission of the breach as such,[69] this point should not be overstated for at least two reasons. First, if assistance or aid in the maintenance of a situation is prohibited, it can be logically argued that assistance in the breach itself is unlawful. Second, there is a general duty not to assist or aid in the perpetration of a breach of international law and *jus cogens* norms are norms of international law.

The second general point to be made is that these two duties are related and, in fact, the Commentary has described the duty of non-assistance as a 'logical consequence of the obligation of non-recognition'.[70] Third, these two duties are different from the duty to co-operate in that, while the latter is to be

[67] See generally, for discussion of these, Dire Tladi 'The Extraterritorial Use of Force against Non-State Actors' (2021) 418 *Collected Courses of the Hague Academy of International Law* 237.

[68] See para 7 of the Commentary to Draft Conclusion 19 (above note 18) ('Although international law does not prohibit unilateral measures to bring to an end a serious breach of a peremptory norm of general international law (*jus cogens*) if such unilateral measures are consistent with international law, the emphasis in para 1 of draft conclusion 19 is on collective measures. This is the essence of "cooperation" ').

[69] Id., para 16.

[70] Id.

implemented through positive action, the duties in paragraph 2 require States refraining from action.

All three duties—the duty to co-operate, the duty of non-recognition, and the duty of non-assistance—apply to serious breaches. What is meant by serious breaches is explained in the third paragraph of the Draft Conclusion. Taken from Article 40, a breach of *jus cogens* is said to be serious if it is 'gross or systematic'. This threshold means, for example, that a single act of torture would not give rise to the particular consequences mentioned in Draft Conclusion 19.

As described in Section 2.2 above, the limitation of the particular consequences to 'serious' breaches provoked some disagreement, with some members arguing that these particular consequences of *jus cogens* should apply to all breaches of *jus cogens*. The Commission responded to the issue in two ways. First, the Commission emphasised that the reference to serious did not mean that other breaches of *jus cogens* were not serious, but rather to indicate the sense that there were additional (particular) consequences that flowed from breaches that were gross and systematic.[71]

Second, the debate in the Drafting Committee on the question led to the modification of the without prejudice clause contained in paragraph 4 of Draft Conclusion 19. Paragraph 4 provides that Draft Conclusion 19 is without prejudice to other consequences that any breach of *jus cogens* might entail under international law. At first reading, paragraph 4 provided that Draft Conclusion 19 was without prejudice to other consequences that serious breaches of *jus cogens* might entail. This would include, for example, the duties of cessation, payment of compensation, including whether a higher amount of compensation is applicable in the event of a serious breach of *jus cogens*. At second reading, the Commission decided to delete the word 'serious' from the without prejudice clause to make clear that these other consequences could also be applicable to breaches of *jus cogens* that did not meet the threshold in paragraph 3.

There is, however, a second possible implication of the reformulated without prejudice clause in paragraph 4. Given its genesis in the debate on whether the consequences in Draft Conclusion 19 should apply only to 'serious' breaches or to all breaches,[72] the without prejudice clause might be seen as leaving open the possibility that the particular consequences described in Draft Conclusion 19 may also apply to other breaches of *jus cogens* that do not meet

[71] Id., para 17.

[72] See Peremptory Norms of General International Law (*Jus Cogens*), Statement by Chair of the Drafting Committee, Ki Gab Park, 17 May 2022, 22.

the paragraph 3 threshold. The word 'other' may suggest a contrary meaning. Moreover, the Commentary itself does not mention this potential implication. Nonetheless, this possibility was certainly on the minds of several members of the Commission when paragraph 4 was adopted.

Finally, this without prejudice clause does not address the possible consequences of breaches of particular norms of *jus cogens*. A separate without prejudice clause, in Draft Conclusion 22, which addresses consequences that arise from the breach of particular norms of *jus cogens*, is the subject of the next section.

4. The Content of Draft Conclusion 22

Draft Conclusion 22
Without prejudice to consequences that specific peremptory norms of general international law (*jus cogens*) may otherwise entail
The present draft conclusions are without prejudice to consequences that specific peremptory norms of general international law (*jus cogens*) may otherwise entail under international law.

Draft Conclusion 22 states that the Draft Conclusions are without prejudice to consequences that specific *jus cogens* norms may have under international law. The Commentary explains that the reason for the without prejudice clause lies in the nature of the Draft Conclusions which are concerned with methodology. To identify consequences flowing from particular *jus cogens* would require a substantive study of those norms of *jus cogens* which, according to the Draft Conclusion, falls outside the methodological scope of the Draft Conclusions.[73]

The without prejudice clause is thus intended to emphasise that the Draft Conclusions' silence on consequences flowing from particular norms of *jus cogens* should not be understood as suggesting that particular norms do not produce peculiar consequences. Examples identified in the Commentary are the same examples that were contained in the Third Report, namely 'the

[73] See para 2 of the Commentary to Draft Conclusion 22 (above note 18) ('As described in paragraph (3) of the commentary to draft conclusion 1, the present draft conclusions are not intended to address the content of individual peremptory norms of general international law (*jus cogens*). In addition to the methodology and process for identifying … *jus cogens*, the draft conclusions also address, in general, the legal consequences flowing from … *jus cogens* … The contents of individual peremptory norms of general international law (*jus cogens*) may themselves have legal consequences that are distinct from the general legal consequences identified in the present draft conclusions').

possible consequences for immunity and the jurisdiction of national courts'.[74] According to the Commentary, these 'consequences are not general consequences of' *jus cogens* but flow from 'specific peremptory norms' and are therefore 'not addressed in the ... Draft Conclusions'.[75]

The original text proposed by the Special Rapporteur provided that the Draft Conclusions were 'without prejudice to the consequences of specific/individual/particular peremptory norms'.[76] The Commission modified the text by adding 'may otherwise entail' to leave open the possibility that there were particular *jus cogens* norms which did not produce their own consequences.

5. Concluding Observations

The conclusion of treaties conflicting with *jus cogens* is not a common phenomenon. Nor is the emergence of customary international law rules that are inconsistent with *jus cogens*. The consequences of *jus cogens* addressed in Draft Conclusions 10, 11, 12, 13, 14, 15, and 16 are thus unlikely to be resorted to. What is more common, however, is the breach of *jus cogens* (or at least allegations of such breaches). The Russian intervention in Ukraine, allegations of genocide against Myanmar, allegations of genocide and crimes against humanity in the Darfur region of Sudan, allegations of serious breaches of humanitarian law against Israel in Palestine, the occupation of Palestine, the recent presence of the United Kingdom in the Chagos, and the occupation of Western Sahara by Morocco are all examples of situations that have been alleged to constitute breaches of *jus cogens*. The consequences addressed in this chapter are thus far more likely to arise than the rules addressed in the previous chapters dealing with consequences.

Because these particular consequences are likely to be raised more frequently, States are understandably more concerned about the framing of these provisions. While other States wanted the Commission to be more expansive,[77] other States would have preferred the Commission to be cautious.[78] To this

[74] Id., para 3.

[75] Id.

[76] See Drafting Committee, Peremptory Norms of General International Law, Revised Proposal of the Special Rapporteur for Draft Conclusions 22 and 23, ILC(LXXI)DC/JC/WP.1, 16 April 2019.

[77] See e.g. Italy, Sixth Committee of the General Assembly, Seventy-Seventh Session, 25 October 2022, expressing disappointment that the Commission chose not to address 'the thorny issue of the legal consequences of some peremptory norms such as those prohibiting genocide, war crimes and crimes against humanity'.

[78] An example in this regard is Brazil, Sixth Committee of the General Assembly, Seventy-Seventh Session, 25 October 2022 emphasising that, in its view, 'cooperation to put to an end this violation must

end, the Commission's text sought a balance. First, it reinforced the consequences that have generally been accepted. Second, it did not exclude the possibility of consequences that are currently being debated. In the third place, it did not include potentially controversial consequences such as limits on the powers of the Security Council and unilateral counter-measures.

As a final matter, while there remain a handful of States that, post final adoption, still question whether the contents of Draft Conclusion 19 reflect customary international law,[79] these States are in the minority with many more States simply accepting that the Draft Conclusion reflects customary international law.[80]

be carried out in multilateral institutions and should be focused on the peaceful—not coercive' measures and, in this context, it rejected 'unilateral sanctions adopted under the pretext of reacting' to serious breaches of *jus cogens*.

[79] See the United Kingdom, Sixth Committee of the General Assembly, Seventy-Seventh Session, 26 October 2022 ('As we have previously stated, those provisions do not, in their entirety, reflect existing customary international law. Further, the United Kingdom questions whether the State conduct cited in the commentaries to this draft conclusion evidences a legal duty to cooperate'); the United States, Sixth Committee of the General Assembly, Seventy-Seventh Session, 25 October 2022 ('Fourth, the provisions of Draft Conclusion 19 on consequences of *jus cogens* breaches on non-breaching states do not reflect customary international law. It is therefore inappropriate to suggest in this document, which will not be negotiated as a treaty, that such provisions are mandatory through use of the word "shall"').

[80] See e.g. making an explicit statement to that effect, Slovenia, Sixth Committee of the General Assembly, Seventy-Seventh Session, 25 October 2022; Cyprus, Sixth Committee of the General Assembly, Seventy-Seventh Session, 27 October 2022.

PART IV
MISCELLANEOUS

12
Jus Cogens and Interpretation of International Law

1. Introduction

Many of the Draft Conclusions in the previous Part concern consequences of *jus cogens* in the event of a breach of a *jus cogens* norm, either in the sense of conduct inconsistent with a norm of *jus cogens* (Chapter 11), or the establishment (or attempt to establish) of obligations inconsistent with *jus cogens* (Chapters 8 and 9). In contrast, Draft Conclusion 20, the subject of this chapter, seeks to prevent inconsistency with *jus cogens*. In particular, it seeks to prevent conflict between other rules of international law and *jus cogens* by requiring the interpretation of other rules of international law consistent with *jus cogens*, if possible.

Moreover, unlike Draft Conclusions 10 to 19, Draft Conclusion 20 is not based on any particular provision of either the Vienna Convention or the Articles on State Responsibility. It is, of course, inspired by a general rule of interpretation and the principle of systemic integration. Although not based on any provision of an existing instrument, Draft Conclusion 20 has proved to be relatively uncontroversial both within the Commission and with States.

Section 2 will discuss briefly issues that arose in the consideration of Draft Conclusion 20, while Section 3 will describe the text of Draft Conclusion 20.

2. Discussion

The main consequence of *jus cogens* is that rules inconsistent with it are invalid. Thus, treaties freely entered into, and otherwise validly concluded, can be rendered void on account of conflict with *jus cogens*. Decisions of the Security Council that impose obligations inconsistent with *jus cogens* can be rendered without legal effect. This invalidating effect of *jus cogens* contradicts one of the most central pillars of international law, that of *pacta sunt servanda*. It is, in part, this quality that has caused some to be sceptical about *jus cogens* on the basis that it has the potential to undermine the stability of international relations. Its far-reaching impacts have been described as 'draconian'.[1]

The Third Report identified this problem in the context of treaty invalidity on account of conflict with *jus cogens*.[2] It sought to lessen this 'draconian' consequence of invalidity.[3] It found the solution in the application of the rules of treaty interpretation. Whether a treaty provision conflicts with a norm of *jus cogens* leading to the invalidity of the rule can only be determined by establishing the meaning of the rule, which in turn depends on the interpretation of the treaty.

The main rule of treaty interpretation under customary international law, reflected in Article 31 of the Vienna Convention, requires that treaties be interpreted in good faith, with the ordinary meaning to be given to its terms, in their context and in light of the treaty's object and purpose. To find the ordinary meaning of the text, in their context and in light of the object and purpose of the treaty, the Vienna Convention calls for the application of particular elements, including 'any relevant rules of international law applicable in the relations between the parties'.[4] The purpose of this principle—systemic integration—is described in the Commission's Study Group on Fragmentation as follows:

> All treaty provisions receive their force and validity from general law and set up rights and obligations that exist alongside rights and obligations established by other treaty provisions and rules of customary international law. None of these rights and obligations has any intrinsic priority over the others. The question of their relationship can only be approached through a process of reasoning that makes them appear as parts of some coherent and meaningful whole.[5]

It should go without saying that norms of *jus cogens* form part of the 'coherent and meaningful whole' which are to be taken into account in the interpretation

[1] Daniel Costelloe *Legal Consequences of Peremptory Norms in International Law* (Cambridge, 2017), 69.

[2] *Third Report of the Special Rapporteur on Peremptory Norms of General International Law (Jus Cogens)* (A/CN.4/714), para 55 *et seq.*

[3] See generally, on the problem and its solution, Sâ Benjamin Traoré 'Peremptory Norms and Interpretation' in Dire Tladi (ed.) *Peremptory Norms of General International Law (*Jus Cogens*): Disquisitions and Disputations* (Brill, 2021).

[4] Article 31(3)(c) of the 1969 Vienna Convention on the Law of Treaties.

[5] *Yearbook of the International Law Commission* 2006, Vol. II, Part 1 (Addendum 2) Fragmentation Report, para 414.

of treaties. Moreover, it would be expected that, given their hierarchical superiority, *jus cogens* norms would have priority in the factors and means to be taken into account in the interpretation of treaties.[6] On the strength of this reasoning, the Third Report made the following observation:

> [T]hese two legal elements would require that the application of the rules of interpretation in articles 31 and 32 should, as far as possible, seek to achieve a meaning that is consistent with *jus cogens* and thus avoid the 'draconian' effect of invalidity.[7]

The Third Report did caution that this conclusion did not mean that an interpretation of consistency should be achieved at all costs and that the ordinary meaning of the terms of the treaty cannot be jettisoned in favour of the search for consistency with *jus cogens*.[8]

While generally uncontroversial, some members raised concerns about the idea that a consequence of *jus cogens* is that treaty interpretation should go as far as possible to seek to achieve a meaning that is consistent with *jus cogens*. Mr Saboia, for example, stated that the conclusion 'was a helpful mode of interpretation but one that, if stretched, could lead to unforeseen results'.[9] In his view, a statement by the Commission that treaty interpretation should be undertaken with a view to preventing conflict 'could be seen as undermining the peremptory nature of *jus cogens*'.[10] Mr Rajput similarly expressed concern about the proposal and did so in particularly strong terms:

> [A]lthough he agreed with the overall objective of avoiding conflicts between peremptory norms and interpretations of treaties, he was uncomfortable with [the proposal] as it risked giving the impression that, even when there was no inconsistency between the interpretation of a treaty and peremptory norms, and the treaty operated independently of the scope of peremptory norms, it was nevertheless preferable that the treaty should be interpreted in a manner consistent with such a norm.... [In his view] it was important to preclude any

[6] Sâ Benjamin Traoré *L'interprétation des résolutions du Conseil de Sécurité des Nations Unies: contribution à la théorie de l'interpretation dans la société internationale* (Helbing, 2020), 369.

[7] Third Report (above note 2), para 58.

[8] Id. ('this does not mean that the other elements of interpretation in the 1969 Vienna Convention can be ignored in order to achieve a meaning consistent with *jus cogens*. The latter would not be "interpretation" but rather modification, an exercise that should be left to the parties').

[9] Saboia (A/CN.4/SR.3415), 4; he went on to state that while 'he did not disagree with the Special Rapporteur's conclusion, he was reluctant to have the Commission issue it as a recommendation'.

[10] Id.

> interpretation of the draft conclusions that could upset the negotiated outcome of a treaty in force.[11]

In the same light, Mr Park suggested that the approach put forward in the Third Report 'could lead to a misuse of interpretation as a means of saving a treaty from invalidation'.[12] In his view, relying on interpretation to 'save' a treaty from invalidation might go against the basic principle of good faith underlying treaty interpretation.[13] Mr Park, however, did offer that it would be possible to craft a provision on interpretation, but that the Commission would need to be careful about how to do so:

> It would be important to study the zero-sum game between the annulment and the interpretation of a treaty in order to distinguish between them. Without further guidance, almost no treaties would ever be annulled on account of a conflict with a rule of *jus cogens*. While he supported the [proposal], that issue needed to be clarified in order for the draft conclusion to effectively serve its purpose.[14]

Mr Park's concern seemed to flow from the use of the qualifier 'as far as possible'.[15] This same concern was raised by Ms Lehto, stating that the Commentary would need to explain what this concept means.[16] At their heart, these concerns seem to point to the possibility of undermining the rules of interpretation in the pursuit of some greater good.[17]

Of course, the interpretation of any instrument must respect the limits of interpretation. Merkouris, relying on Hart, describes this as the set of correct possible interpretations:

> Hart's oft-quoted passage that every legal rule has a 'core of settled meaning' but also a 'penumbra of uncertainty' is predicated on an understanding that there exist sets of correct and incorrect interpretations. A core of settled meaning and a penumbra of uncertainty require the existence of a frame of reference outside of these two ... This would be the surrounding space where

[11] Rajput (A/CN.4/SR.3418), 3.
[12] Park (A/CN.4/SR.3416), 14.
[13] Id.
[14] Id.
[15] Id.
[16] Lehto (A/CN.4/SR.3417), 18.
[17] Hassouna (A/CN.4/SR.3419), 6 ('commentary should emphasize that such interpretation should not override the interpretative rules enshrined in the 1969 Vienna Convention or customary international law').

the rule's scope and interpretation cannot penetrate. This surrounding space would include amongst others, interpretations that clearly go beyond the limits of the legal rule's scope.[18]

Notwithstanding these concerns, in general, the Commission supported the thrust of the proposal which,[19] though not reflected in any instrument, had a good basis in international practice. The Third Report refers, as an example of practice, to the statements by Cyprus and the United Kingdom in the Security Council, in respect of the Treaty of Guarantee between Cyprus, Greece, Turkey, and the United Kingdom.[20] The statement of Cyprus, in particular, stated explicitly that the treaty would be void if it were interpreted in such a way as to conflict with *jus cogens*, suggesting *a contrario sensu*, that an alternative interpretation would save the treaty from the consequence of invalidity.[21]

The Report also referred to the decision of the European Court of Justice concerning the Fisheries Partnership Agreement between the European Community and the Kingdom of Morocco of 2006, and the European Council decision giving effect to it.[22] While the Council decision was annulled by the General Court of the European Court of Justice on account of being inconsistent with the *jus cogens* norm of self-determination,[23] the Grand Chamber adopted a more nuanced approach, effectively saving the European Council decision (and therefore the Partnership Agreement) from invalidity by restrictively interpreting the agreement in a way that rendered it consistent with the right of self-determination.[24] In particular, the Court determined that the

[18] See generally Panos Merkouris 'Interpretation of Customary International Law: Methods and Limits: You'll Never Walk Alone' in Panos Merkouris, Jörg Kammerhofer, and Noora Arajärvi (eds) *The Theory, Practice and Interpretation of Customary International Law* (Cambridge, 2022).

[19] See e.g. Hmoud (A/CN.4/SR.3420), 9 ('In any case, the rules of interpretation contained in articles 31 and 32 of the Vienna Convention should be applied [and the proposal] was appropriate in that it did not attempt to redefine the Vienna interpretation rules. The superior nature of *jus cogens* norms necessarily meant that rules of *jus cogens* would play a primary role in the interpretation of a given treaty, as already demonstrated in a number of cases').

[20] See Third Report (above note 2), paras 59–61.

[21] Cyprus (S/PV.1098), 27 February 1964, paras 93–102. See, however, the statement of the United Kingdom which seems to interpret the *jus cogens* norm in question, the prohibition on the use of force, in such a way as to render it consistent with the treaty.

[22] See Third Report (above note 2), paras 61–3.

[23] Case T-512/12, *Front Populaire pour la Libération de la Aaguia-el-Hamra et du Rio de Oro (Front Polisario) v Council of the European Union*, Judgment of the General Court (Eighth Chamber), European Court of Justice, 10 December 2015, para 247 (the action of the Front Polisario 'must be upheld and the contested decision must be annulled in so far as it approves the application of the agreement'). Paragraph 2 of the order itself (id., para 251) reads as follows: 'Declares that the Council Decision ... on the conclusion of [the Fisheries Partnership Agreement] ... is annulled in so far as it approves the application of that agreement to Western Sahara.'

[24] Case C-104/16 P, *Council of the European Union v Front Populaire pour la Libération de la Saguia-el-Hamra et du Rio de Oro (Front Polisario)*, Judgment of the Grand Chamber, European Court of Justice, 21 December 2016 [2017] OJ C53/19 (20 February 2017), paras 101–14.

term 'territory of Morocco' in the Partnership Agreement must be interpreted as excluding the territory of Western Sahara.[25]

The most explicit invocation of the principle of using interpretation to achieve consistency with *jus cogens* was in the *Oil Platforms* case.[26] Iran was particularly explicit in its invocation of the rule, stating that the far-reaching provision in Article 53 of the Vienna Convention 'must ... generate a stringent principle of interpretation, so that any provision of a treaty is to be interpreted, if at all possible, so as not to conflict' with *jus cogens*.[27] The Court, without referring to *jus cogens*, itself endorsed the notion that the treaty provision in question was to be interpreted taking into account the prohibition on the use of force.[28]

The Third Report applied the rule to treaties and to decisions of international organisations but not to customary international law. To this end, some members suggested that the rule should be one of general application. Mr Nolte was the first member to question the restricted scope of application of the proposal in the Third Report:

> While supporting the thrust of [the proposal in the Third Report], he did not see why the rule of interpretation contained therein should not also apply to rules of customary international law and other sources of obligations that were addressed in other proposed draft conclusions, especially draft conclusions 15 to 17. Moreover, if there were a general rule of interpretation, it would not be necessary to repeat the rule in draft conclusion 17 (2), specifically for resolutions of international organizations.[29]

[25] Id. See, for discussion, Makane Moïse Mbengue and Apollin Koagne Zouapet 'Ending the Splendid Isolation—*Jus Cogens* and International Economic Law' in Tladi (above note 3), 252, noting that the Grand Chamber 'opted for a conciliatory interpretation that would preserve the treaty while reaffirming the peremptory nature of the right of self-determination'.

[26] *Case Concerning Oil Platforms (Islamic Republic of Iran v United States of America)*, Judgment, *ICJ Reports* 2003, p. 161, paras 64–6.

[27] *Oil Platforms (Islamic Republic of Iran v United States of America), Reply and Defence to Counter-Claim Submitted by the Islamic Republic of Iran, Vol. I,* 10 March 1999, pp. 164–5.

[28] *Oil Platforms* (above note 26), 40–1. See especially Separate Opinion of Judge Simma ('The Court, in paragraph 41 of the Judgment, thus accepts, and rightly so, the principle according to which the provisions of any treaty have to be interpreted and applied in the light of the treaty law applicable between the parties as well as of the rules of general international law ... If these general rules of international law are of a peremptory nature, as they undeniably are in our case, then the principle of interpretation just mentioned turns into a legally insurmountable limit to permissible treaty interpretation').

[29] Nolte (A/CN.4/SR.3417), 11.

This position was reiterated by other members of the Commission, notably Mr Jalloh[30] and Mr Vásquez-Bermúdez.[31] In light of this, the Commission decided to adopt the provision and apply it broadly to sources of obligations under international law, including customary international law. It may well be asked whether customary international law rules are open to being interpreted.[32] For our purposes, it is sufficient only to state that the content of rules of customary international law, including their scope of application and the obligations they impose, have to be determined and it is that search for content and scope that is referred to here.[33]

The notion that rules of international law have to be interpreted in such a way as to be consistent with *jus cogens* was accepted by States. In fact, there was not a single State that included comments on the relevant text in their written observations.[34]

3. The Content of Draft Conclusion 20

Draft Conclusion 20

Interpretation and application consistent with peremptory norms of general international law (*jus cogens*)

Where it appears that there may be a conflict between a peremptory norm of general international law (*jus cogens*) and another rule of international law, the latter is, as far as possible, to be interpreted and applied so as to be consistent with the former.

Draft Conclusion 20 provides that rules of international law are to be interpreted in such a way as to render them consistent with *jus cogens*. As initially proposed in the Third Report, the provision covered the interpretation of

30 Jalloh (A/CN.4/SR.3418), 8 ('He agreed with Mr. Nolte that, in principle, there was no reason why the rule of interpretation set forth in draft conclusion 10(3) could not be broadened to apply to other rules of customary international law and, perhaps, even other sources of obligations addressed in other draft conclusions. Perhaps that paragraph would be more appropriately located in a different draft conclusion dealing specifically with that issue').

31 Vásquez-Bermúdez (A/CN.4/SR.3418), 12, also agreeing with Mr Nolte. See also implicitly Huang (A/CN.4/SR.3419), 9.

32 See Traoré (above note 3), 158 *et seq*. See also generally Merkouris (above note 18), who identifies several arguments that have been put forward for the non-interpretability of customary international law and proceeds to debunk them.

33 Traoré (above note 3), 159.

34 See Peremptory Norms of General International Law (*Jus Cogens*): Comments and Observations received from Governments (A/CN.4/748).

treaties and resolutions of international organisations. In respect of treaties, it provided:

> To avoid conflict with a peremptory norm of general international law, a provision in a treaty should, as far as possible, be interpreted in a way that renders it consistent with a peremptory norm of general international law (*jus cogens*).[35]

In respect of international organisations, the Third Report proposed the following text:

> To the extent possible, resolutions of international organizations, including those of the Security Council of the United Nations, must be interpreted in a manner consistent with peremptory norms of general international law (*jus cogens*).[36]

On the strength of the proposal made by Mr Nolte in the plenary,[37] the Special Rapporteur proposed a general provision (Draft Conclusion 17bis) which would provide as follows:

> A rule of international law should, as far as possible, be interpreted in a way that renders it consistent with peremptory norms of general international law (*jus cogens*).[38]

Within the Drafting Committee, several issues were raised with this formulation. First, it was felt that the rule was too automatic. In the view of most members of the Drafting Committee, the rule should only be activated when there was a possibility of conflict and not as an automatic part of the interpretation process. Second, the word 'should' was identified as suggesting that the provision was hortatory when in fact it was mandatory. Third, there was some consternation at the use of the word 'rendered' which it was said suggested that the interpreter would be creating an interpretation rather than finding meaning in the text. Finally, the point was made that the search for consistency

[35] Draft Conclusion 10(3) proposed in the Third Report (above note 2), para 160.

[36] Id., Draft Conclusion 17(2).

[37] See Special Rapporteur (Tladi) (A/CN.4/SR.3424), 5 ('He agreed with the view expressed by many members that paragraph 3 should also apply to the other sources of international law. His preference would be a single draft conclusion applicable to all the sources').

[38] Drafting Committee, Peremptory Norms of General International Law, Proposals of Special Rapporteur ILC(LXXI)/DC/JC/WP.6, 15 May 2019.

with the *jus cogens* was relevant not only for the interpretation of rules of international law but also in their application.

As finally adopted, the Draft Conclusion is intended to capture all these concerns. Thus, the phrase 'where it appears' is intended to make clear that the rule is not applicable in all cases of interpretation (and application) but only in those instances where there was a potential for conflict.[39] The concern expressed by several members in the plenary, that the rule ought not to be applied to 'misuse of interpretation as a means of saving a treaty from invalidation',[40] is captured in the phrase 'as far as possible'. These words are supposed to make clear that 'the bounds of interpretation may not be exceeded' to achieve the purpose of the provision and that the rule of international law in question 'may not be given a meaning or content that does not flow from the normal application' of the interpretative processes in order to save the treaty.[41] Finally, the Commentary explains that the text uses the words 'interpreted and applied' and not only 'interpreted' to cover also cases where the rule in question was, on its face, consistent with *jus cogens*, but where the said rule could be applied in a way that would be contrary to *jus cogens*.[42]

4. Concluding Observations

Draft Conclusion 20 on the interpretation of rules of international law to avoid inconsistency is an example of a rule designed for treaties but applied to other sources of international law. Given the far-reaching consequences of nullity, the rule is a necessity for the Draft Conclusions. It is an example of a rule which, though not found in any authoritative text, is generally well-accepted. It was thus unsurprising that the States did not criticise Draft Conclusion 20.

[39] See para 2 of the Commentary to Draft Conclusion 20.
[40] See e.g. Park (A/CN.4/SR.3416), 14.
[41] Paragraph 2 of the Commentary to Draft Conclusion 20.
[42] Paragraph 3 of the Commentary to Draft Conclusion 20.

13
Recommended Dispute Settlement Procedure

1. Introduction

Draft Conclusion 21, the subject of Chapter 13, provides a recommended procedure for addressing disputes relating to the invalidation of a rule of international law on account of conflict with *jus cogens*. Draft Conclusion 21 is, thus, an essential part of the set of Draft Conclusions and is intended to prevent, or more accurately, reduce the potential of auto-interpretation inherent in the system of international law.[1]

Draft Conclusion 21 has two things in common with Draft Conclusion 20. First, like Draft Conclusion 20, Draft Conclusion 21 is not based on any one provision of an international instrument. Thus, while many provisions of the Draft Conclusions are based on the Vienna Convention or the Articles on State Responsibility, there is no particular provision of a previous instrument on which this Draft Conclusion is based. Second, Draft Conclusion 21 and Draft Conclusion 20 are both, in different ways, designed to avoid conflict or reduce some far-reaching consequences of *jus cogens*. Draft Conclusion 20, by requiring rules of international law to be interpreted consistently with *jus cogens*, reduces potential conflict and invalidation. Draft Conclusion 21, on the other hand, seeks to avoid the unilateral determination of conflict with *jus cogens*.

Unlike Draft Conclusion 20, however, Draft Conclusion 21 was not met with general approval from States. It was the subject of criticism from a large number of States. Much of the criticism centred around the status of the provision and the extent to which it reflected existing law. Moreover, the Commission itself recognised that the contents of Draft Conclusion 21 did not reflect existing international law.

[1] *Third Report of the Special Rapporteur on Peremptory Norms of General International Law (Jus Cogens)* (A/CN.4/714).

Section 2 will describe the issues surrounding the adoption of Draft Conclusion 21. Thereafter, Section 3 will describe the structure and text of Draft Conclusion 21.

2. Discussion

As alluded to in Chapter 11, the consequences of *jus cogens* are, or can be, very far-reaching. This is particularly true of the consequence of invalidation. This consequence is exacerbated by the horizontal nature of international law which does not provide for compulsory jurisdiction. This promotes auto-interpretation, where each actor reserves the right to determine the content of law and the consistency of conduct with international law. The implications of auto-interpretation with *jus cogens*, and its far-reaching consequences, are that, potentially, any State can decide that any treaty, decision of the Security Council, or rule of customary international law is invalid or inapplicable. It is this power to decide, unilaterally, that a rule will not be applied that is of concern to some.

The problem of auto-interpretation as an obstacle for the acceptance of *jus cogens* was already discussed in the First Report:

> French concerns with the Commission's draft article 50, which were shared by some other delegations, centred on the criteria for identifying these rules to avoid abuse of *jus cogens* through unilateral invocation. The concerns of the United States are equally instructive in this regard. The United States 'accepted the principle of *jus cogens* and its inclusion in the convention'. In its view, however, 'a State could not seek release from a treaty by suddenly adopting a unilateral idea of *jus cogens* in its international rules'.[2]

The Third Report, however, described the issue as one that is not peculiar to *jus cogens*, but that applies in international law generally:

> While it is correct, as has been pointed out that 'it would be difficult to claim authoritatively that a treaty is void' on the basis of 'unilateral statements' under article 53, this is not a result of a consequence flowing from *jus cogens*. Rather, it is a general problem of international law that arises from

[2] *First Report of the Special Rapporteur of Jus Cogens* (A/CN.4/SR.693), para 36.

> auto-interpretation resulting from a decentralized legal system without a compulsory system of adjudication. The problem applies equally to invalidity on account of fraud or coercion.[3]

Nonetheless, while the problem of auto-interpretation is endemic to international law, it is particularly problematic in the context of *jus cogens*, in part because *jus cogens* norms are not based on the consent of States. When faced with this problem in the Vienna Conference, States decided to elaborate a comprehensive dispute settlement provision. Article 65, a general provision, provides that in the event that a State wishes to invalidate or terminate a treaty it 'must notify the other parties of its claim'.[4] In the event that 'no party has raised any objection' the termination or invalidity can be given effect.[5] In the event that there is an objection Article 65 provides for the recourse to amicable dispute settlement mechanisms as provided for in Article 33 of the UN Charter.

Yet, what happens when the amicable mechanisms do not produce a solution? Article 66 provides for third party settlement of disputes. In situations not involving *jus cogens*, Article 66 provides for a non-binding conciliation mechanism.[6] With respect to disputes concerning *jus cogens*, Article 66(a) provides:

> [A]ny one of the parties to a dispute concerning the application or the interpretation of article 53 or 64 may, by a written application, submit it to the International Court of Justice for a decision unless the parties by common consent agree to submit the dispute to arbitration.

Thus, for disputes involving *jus cogens* the Convention creates a framework for compulsory judicial settlement. The question for the Commission was whether the solution provided for in Article 66 could also help to address the potential for auto-interpretation outside of the Vienna Convention context. The Third Report notes, as a point of departure, that 'treaties are only binding on ... parties to the relevant treaties'.[7] Thus, the Article 66 solution could not be reproduced in the Draft Conclusions since it only applied to States Parties

[3] Third Report (above note 1), 48.
[4] Article 65(1) of the 1969 Vienna Convention on the Law of Treaties.
[5] Id., Article 65(2) ('If, after the expiry of a period which, except in cases of special urgency, shall not be less than three months after the receipt of the notification, no party has raised any objection, the party making the notification may carry out in the manner provided in article 67 the measure which it has proposed').
[6] See id., Article 66(b) read with the Annex.
[7] Third Report (above note 1), para 51.

while the Draft Conclusions ought to apply to all States, including non-Party States. Article 66, however, could be relied on if it reflected a rule of customary international law. Yet, the Third Report stated that there is 'no evidence of practice or *opinio juris* to support the conclusion that article 66 (a)' reflects customary international law.[8] That might suggest that Article 66 could not be used in the Draft Conclusions. At the same time, the Third Report noted that without this process (or some process), the risk of 'the far-reaching possibility of unilateral claims of invalidity' that led to Article 66 remains.[9]

Thus, while Article 66 is not general international law, applicable beyond the Vienna Convention, the Third Report proposed that a procedure be included in the Draft Conclusions:

> [T]he Special Rapporteur proposes that the Commission recommends, as a practice, that, even in cases where the Vienna Convention does not apply because one or both of the States are not party to the Vienna Convention, the procedure in article 66 (a) should be applicable.[10]

The Third Report did, however, stipulate two caveats. The first caveat is that it should be made clear the procedure is not binding under international law.[11] The second caveat is that the jurisdictional rules under international law, such as Article 36 of the Statute of the International Court of Justice, could not be affected by the Draft Conclusion.[12] The main purpose of the proposal appears, therefore, to be to pressure States into agreeing to judicial settlement under the normal rules applicable to dispute settlement:

> [A] State that withholds its consent for judicial settlement runs the risk of a State unilaterally declaring a treaty invalid on account of conflict with *jus cogens* or conversely, its declaration of invalidity of a treaty on account of conflict of *jus cogens* not being recognized. These practical considerations, coupled with a draft conclusion by the Commission, may encourage both the party seeking to invalidate a treaty, and the party seeking to maintain the treaty, to submit to international adjudication.[13]

[8] Id.
[9] Id.
[10] Id., para 52.
[11] Id. (the Draft Conclusion should 'spell[s] out clearly that the provision is only recommended practice and does not reflect the state of international law').
[12] Id.
[13] Id.

With these caveats in mind, the Third Report proposed Draft Conclusion 14 titled 'Recommended Procedure Regarding the Settlement of Disputes Involving Conflict between a Treaty' and a *jus cogens* norm:

1. Subject to the jurisdictional rules of the International Court of Justice, any dispute concerning whether a treaty conflicts with a peremptory norm of general international law (*jus cogens*) should be submitted to the International Court of Justice for a decision, unless the parties to the dispute agree to submit the dispute to arbitration.
2. Notwithstanding paragraph 1, the fact that a dispute involves a peremptory norm of general international law (*jus cogens*) is not sufficient to establish the jurisdiction of the Court without the necessary consent to jurisdiction in accordance with international law.

The proposal for a recommended procedure received a mixed reaction within the Commission.[14] Some members supported the idea of referring disputes concerning *jus cogens* to a binding dispute settlement process.[15] Other members, while supporting in broad terms the proposal, sought to have amicable solutions highlighted in the text.[16] There were, however, members that expressed serious concerns.

In this regard, three types of general objections can be identified. The first type of objection was that the proposal seeks to impose the procedures in Article 66 of the Vienna Convention on States that were not party to the Vienna Convention and States that were party to the Vienna Convention but that had made a declaration not accepting Article 66. Examples of this view can be seen

[14] There were even members that, uncharacteristic of the Commission, showed a great deal of equivocation. See e.g. Part (A/CN.4/SR.3416), 14.

[15] See e.g. Saboia (A/CN.4/SR.3415), 3 ('he endorsed the Special Rapporteur's suggestion in paragraph 54 that it should be stated in a draft conclusion that any dispute concerning whether a treaty conflicted with a peremptory norm of international law (*jus cogens*)'); Šturma (A/CN.4/SR.3416), 7 ('Draft conclusion 14 at first sight seemed more like a provision for an intended treaty; however, its careful wording as a recommendation on procedure, together with the analysis in the report, had convinced him that it was appropriate'); Nolte (A/CN.4/SR.3417), 10 ('The procedural rules set out in articles 42 and 65 of the 1969 Vienna Convention on the Law of Treaties were of great importance for ensuring the stability of treaty relations and for preventing incorrect or abusive invocations of jus cogens. It was therefore crucial that those articles should be taken as the point of departure when considering the relationship between the rules regarding the consequences of jus cogens and the procedure by which the existence of a jus cogens norm was determined. Such rules needed to be reaffirmed'); Lehto (A/CN.4/SR.3417), 18; Vásquez Bermúdez (A/CN.4/SR.3418), 12; Oral (A/CN.4/SR.3419), 14; Grossman Guiloff (A/CN.4/SR.3420), 5; Wood (A/CN.4/SR.3420), 4.

[16] See e.g. Nguyen (A/CN.4/SR.3415), 8 ('Under that chapeau, other amicable procedures should be suggested as options before the matter could be referred to the International Court of Justice'); Escobar Hernández (A/CN.4/SR.3421), 8. The position concerning amicable solutions was also put forward by members that opposed the recommended procedure, e.g. Huang (A/CN.4/SR.3419), 10.

in the statement by Mr Zagaynov, who noted that as crafted the 'recommendation appeared to apply even to States that were not party to the Convention' and also noted that 'many States Parties [that] had formulated reservations and objections to Article 66'.[17] The second type of objection, which seemed to pull in the opposite direction, was that the provision would have the impact of undermining the Vienna Convention by making it seem like a non-binding procedure when it was in fact binding for those States that are party to it. An example of this view can be seen in the statement by Mr Murphy in which it was observed that describing the procedure as 'a "recommended procedure"' was 'problematic' because the procedure was 'actually legally binding on States parties to the Vienna Convention'.[18] The third objection was that, regardless of the merits of the content of the proposal, dispute settlement procedures were inappropriate for an instrument that was not drafted as a treaty. Mr Rajput is an example of a member that held this view.[19]

Most of the views, whether for or against the proposal, proceeded from the assumption that Article 66 did not reflect customary international law. It was mainly Mr Nolte who seemed to proceed from a different assumption, namely that, at the very least, the principles underlying Article 66, in particular the duty to seek good faith solutions to international disputes, was part of customary international law.[20]

Another question that arose from the debate was the extent to which the right to refer a matter in dispute to the International Court of Justice should be restricted to States Parties to the treaty in question.[21] While the proposed provision itself was silent, the Third Report seemed to suggest that the right ought to be open to States that were not party to the treaty.[22] Some members, however, took the view that the right to submit a dispute to binding dispute resolution, if provided for, should be limited to States that were party to the relevant treaty.[23]

[17] Zagaynov (A/CN.4/SR.3416), 4.
[18] Murphy (A/CN.4/SR.3416), 9.
[19] Rajput (A/CN.4/SR.3418), 4; Huang (A/CN.4/SR.3419), 10.
[20] Nolte (A/CN.4/SR.3414), 11 ('Rather, article 65 expressed certain generally recognized rules that should be recognized in the draft conclusions. After all, in paragraph 109 of its judgment in the case concerning the *Gabčíkovo-Nagymaros Project (Hungary/Slovakia)*, the International Court of Justice had noted the following regarding articles 65 to 67: "if not codifying customary international law, [they] at least generally reflect customary international law and contain certain procedural principles which are based on the obligation to act in good faith."'). See, however, support from Lehto (A/CN.4/SR.3417), 18, who 'welcomed' Mr Nolte's comment. See also Grossman Guiloff (A/CN.4/SR.3420), 5.
[21] Nolte (A/CN.4/SR.3417), 10.
[22] See Third Report (above note 1), paras 53–4, where, having established that Article 66 is meant to operate to parties to the treaty, it was stated that 'the nature of jus cogens requiring absolute invalidity and non-recognition should permit any State to invoke *jus cogens* to invalidate a treaty where such a treaty is in conflict with a norm of *jus cogens*'.
[23] See e.g. Zagaynov (A/CN.4/SR.3416), 4.

The proposal in the Third Report was based on Article 66 of the Vienna Convention and as such was applicable only to treaties. Yet, as noted by Mr Nolte, the issue did not apply 'only to treaties but also to other sources of law and of obligations' and, therefore, a similar recommended procedure should be crafted for other sources of obligations.[24]

These views largely matched those of States. Thus, several States supported the procedures to resolve disputes, albeit with suggestions for improvements.[25] Many States expressed strong objections and did so for many of the reasons expressed in the debates of the Commission.[26]

The Fifth Report, commenting on the views from States, stated that it came 'as no surprise' that the procedure had 'attracted as much comment' or that the comments largely reflected those expressed within the Commission.[27] Nonetheless, the Fifth Report stressed that it was important to retain the provision while making necessary amendments to address the comments of States:

> This draft conclusion is not, as the Commission tries to make clear in its commentary, reflective of international law. Moreover, it seeks to balance

[24] Nolte (A/CN.4/SR.3417), 11; Oral (A/CN.4/SR.3419), 14.

[25] Peremptory Norms of General International Law (*Jus Cogens*): Colombia, Comments and Observations received from Governments (A/CN.4/748), 91; the Czech Republic, Comments and Observations received from Governments (A/CN.4/748), 92; El Salvador, Comments and Observations received from Governments (A/CN.4/748), 98; Slovenia, Comments and Observations received from Governments (A/CN.4/748), 95; Spain, Comments and Observations received from Governments (A/CN.4/748), 96; the United Kingdom, Comments and Observations received from Governments (A/CN.4/748), 96.

[26] France, Comments and Observations (above note 25), 92 ('The very presence of a "procedural" draft conclusion in the text transmitted by the Commission raises questions about the status of the text. Such a draft conclusion would undoubtedly have a place in a draft treaty instrument . . . However, in the view of France, the 23 draft conclusions and their annex should not be adopted in the form of an international treaty'); Germany, Comments and Observations (above note 25), 93 ('First, the Commission itself found that detailed dispute resolution provisions did not operate as a matter of customary international law, but were embedded in treaties and bound treaty parties only. Second, the commentary rightly points out that not every aspect of the detailed procedure set forth in the draft conclusion constitutes customary international law'); Israel, Comments and Observations (above note 25), 93 ('does not reflect existing international law, and the procedure offered in it is novel'); Italy, Comments and Observations (above note 25), 93 ('unnecessary for the purpose of the current project and potentially problematic, especially in its relation to the Vienna Convention on the Law of Treaties. Therefore, Italy suggests its deletion'); Japan, Comments and Observations (above note 25), 94; Poland, Comments and Observations (above note 25), 94; Russian, Comments and Observations (above note 25), 94 (noting that the procedure does 'not reflect *lex lata* and do not contribute to the formation of *lex ferenda*'); Singapore, Comments and Observations (above note 25), 95; Spain, Comments and Observations (above note 25), 96, the United States, Comments and Observations (above note 25), 97 ('The dispute resolution provisions in the Convention are not customary international law applying to *jus cogens* disputes, as the commentary to the draft conclusions itself recognizes').

[27] *Fifth Report of the Special Rapporteur on Peremptory Norms of General International Law (Jus Cogens)* (A/CN.4/747), para 208.

> two factors that are particularly difficult to balance, i.e., the need to ensure the effectiveness of the consequences for breaches of peremptory norms, while also discouraging the unilateral invocation of the rules contained in the draft conclusion. The Special Rapporteur recognizes that the comments and concerns by States cannot be fully addressed because of the vexed nature of those questions. Nonetheless, the Special Rapporteur believes that to simply not have this draft conclusion would be dangerous. For these reasons, it is important to address, as much as possible, the comments made, both in the text of the draft conclusion and the commentary thereto.[28]

It was on the basis of this view that the Commission decided to retain the provision, notwithstanding the discomfort it caused to many States and indeed many members of the Commission.

3. The Content of Draft Conclusion 21

Draft Conclusion 21
Recommended procedure

1. A State which invokes a peremptory norm of general international law (*jus cogens*) as a ground for the invalidity or termination of a rule of international law should do so by notifying other States concerned of its claim. The notification should be in writing and should indicate the measure proposed to be taken with respect to the rule of international law in question.
2. If none of the other States raises an objection within a period which, except in cases of special urgency, will not be less than three months, the invoking State may carry out the measure which it has proposed.
3. If, however, any State concerned raises an objection, the States concerned should seek a solution through the means indicated in Article 33 of the Charter of the United Nations. If no solution is reached within a period of twelve months, and the objecting State offers to submit the matter to the International Court of Justice or to some other procedure entailing binding decisions, the invoking State should not carry out the measure which it has proposed until the dispute is resolved.

[28] Id.

4. This draft conclusion is without prejudice to the procedures set forth in the Vienna Convention on the Law of Treaties, to the relevant rules concerning the jurisdiction of the International Court of Justice, or to other applicable dispute settlement provisions agreed by the States concerned.

Draft Conclusion 21 is a provision that has gone through significant modifications throughout the project. As discussed in Section 2, the original proposal in the Third Report contained only two paragraphs. The first paragraph provided that in the event there was a dispute concerning a conflict between a treaty provision and a norm of *jus cogens*, the parties to the dispute should refer the dispute to the International Court of Justice. The second paragraph recalled the jurisprudence of the Court, that the mere fact that a dispute involved a norm of *jus cogens* was insufficient to establish the jurisdiction of the Court.[29]

The debate in the Commission revealed several concerns. First, any dispute settlement provision would have to include the provisions concerning notification and amicable dispute settlement as provided in Article 65 of the Vienna Convention. Second, the provision would need to make clear that it does not create any legally binding obligations nor does it seek to impose the provisions of the Vienna Convention on non-consenting States. Third, at the same time, the provision would need to ensure that the rights and obligations of States Parties to the Vienna Convention, or any other instrument providing for a binding settlement of dispute mechanism, were not undermined by the provision. Finally, the suggestion that the provision ought to apply to other sources of obligations was also one that had to be considered.

Against this background, the Drafting Committee considered how best to improve the proposal in the Third Report. At the outset of the consideration of the text in the Drafting Committee, Mr Nolte proposed two alternative approaches, Alternative A and Alternative B.[30] Alternative A would retain the proposal in the Third Report but insert a first paragraph, the objective of which would be to include a requirement for notification and an attempt at amicable dispute settlement solutions based on Article 65 of the Vienna Convention.[31]

[29] *Armed Activities on the Territory of the Congo (New Application: 2002) (Democratic Republic of the Congo v Rwanda)*, Jurisdiction and Admissibility, Judgment, *ICJ Reports* 2006, p. 6.

[30] See Drafting Committee, Peremptory Norms of General International Law (*Jus Cogens*), Proposal by Georg Nolte, ILC(LXX)/DC/JC/WP.3, 10 July 2018.

[31] Id., Alternative A, para 1 ('A State Party which invokes the invalidity of a treaty as resulting from a conflict with a peremptory norms of general international law (*jus cogens*) shall notify the other Parties of its claim. If another Party raises an objection, the State Parties concerned shall negotiate in good faith with a view to agreeing on a solution or an appropriate procedure to resolve the dispute. The invoking Party may give effect to its claim in relation to any objecting Party after the invalidity of the treaty has been determined as agreed by them').

Alternative B proposes a general, one-paragraph Draft Conclusion, which would cover both treaties and other obligations under international law.[32]

This proposal did not address all the concerns. In response, the Special Rapporteur proposed an untitled paper that was produced containing four paragraphs.[33] It is this informal paper that eventually formed the basis of Draft Conclusion 21. The first paragraph provided for the notification in the event of a belief that a rule of international law conflicted with *jus cogens*. If there were no objections received within a determined time, the State may give effect to its claim. The second paragraph provided for the recourse to amicable dispute settlement processes if there was an objection to the notification. The third paragraph applied in the event that there was no amicable solution. It sought to prevent the invoking State from giving effect to its claim if there was no agreement unless it had offered to submit the matter to the International Court of Justice.[34] Finally, a without prejudice clause designed to protect jurisdictional rules under the Vienna Convention and the Statute of the International Court of Justice was inserted as the final element of the package.[35]

The version of Draft Conclusion 21 adopted by the Commission on first reading was contained in Part III of the Draft Conclusions and provided as follows:

Conclusion 21

Procedural requirements

1. A State which invokes a peremptory norm of general international law (*jus cogens*) as a ground for the invalidity or termination of a rule of international law is to notify other States concerned of its claim. The notification is to be in writing and is to indicate the measure proposed to be taken with respect to the rule of international law in question.

[32] Id., Alternative B ('A State which invokes the invalidity of an obligation as resulting from a conflict with a peremptory norm of general (*jus cogens*) shall notify other States concerned of its claims. If another State raises an objection, the States concerned shall negotiate in good faith with a view to agreeing on a solution or an appropriate procedure to resolve the dispute. The invoking State may give effect to its claim in relation to any objecting State after the invalidity of the obligation has been determined as agreed by them').

[33] See unofficial informal paper, with the heading 'Replace DC 14 with:', 12 July 2018, 3:00pm.

[34] This particular provision, which is the real innovation of the provision, was inspired by a suggestion by Mr Wood.

[35] This paper was replaced by another informal paper, with the same heading 'Replace DC 14 with:', 12 July 2018, 5:00pm.

2. If none of the other States concerned raises an objection within a period which, except in cases of special urgency, shall not be less than three months, the invoking State may carry out the measure which it has proposed.
3. If any State concerned raises an objection, then the States concerned are to seek a solution through the means indicated in Article 33 of the Charter of the United Nations.
4. If no solution is reached within a period of twelve months, and the objecting State or States concerned offer to submit the matter to the International Court of Justice, the invoking State may not carry out the measure which it has proposed until the dispute is resolved.
5. This draft conclusion is without prejudice to the procedural requirements set forth in the Vienna Convention on the Law of Treaties, the relevant rules concerning the jurisdiction of the International Court of Justice, or other applicable dispute settlement provisions agreed by the States concerned.

It is this version of Draft Conclusion 21 that drew criticism from States that the procedure was not based on international law. The Fifth Report proposed to address the concerns by making amendments that would emphasise that the procedure 'is not binding, nor does it imply the establishment of jurisdiction' and also that it does not 'affect' the jurisdictional rules applicable to international tribunals.[36] It was these elements that formed the basis of the final text adopted on second reading.

The first two paragraphs of Draft Conclusion 21 are based on Article 65 of the Vienna Convention. The first paragraph provides that a State which invokes *jus cogens* as a ground for invalidation of a treaty has to notify other States, while the second paragraph provides that if there are no objections, the invoking State may carry out the measure which it has proposed.

Several elements are meant to indicate that the Draft Conclusion is non-binding. First, Draft Conclusion 21 is now placed in Part IV, to indicate that it is not part of the 'legal' consequences, the subject of Part III. Second, and most importantly, unlike Article 65 of the Vienna Convention, Draft Conclusion

[36] See para 209 of the Fifth Report (above note 27). See also Chapter IV of the Fifth Report titled 'Marked up Text of Draft Conclusions adopted on First Reading' for the particular textual changes proposed. See also proposal made in the Drafting Committee, Peremptory Norms of General International Law (*Jus Cogens*), Proposal of the Special Rapporteur for Draft Conclusion 22, ILC(LXXIII)/DC/JC/WP.5, 5 May 2022.

21 uses the hortatory language 'should', while the Vienna Convention uses the binding words 'shall' and 'must'.

The third paragraph is the central provision of the procedure and concerns cases where the disputing parties are not able to reach an agreement. The first sentence of the third paragraph provides that in such cases the disputing parties should resort to amicable means for dispute settlement in Article 33 of the UN Charter, in particular negotiation, enquiry, mediation, and conciliation. The second sentence addresses those cases in which the amicable solutions for dispute settlement listed in Article 33 do not yield an agreement. It provides that the State invoking conflict with *jus cogens* 'should not carry out the measure which it has proposed until the dispute is resolved' if the objecting State has offered to submit the matter to the International Court of Justice.

Initially, two different interpretations had been put forward and intensely debated during the adoption of the Commentary to Draft Conclusion 21 on first reading. Under the first possible interpretation, in the event that no agreement is reached and there is, for whatever reason, no adjudication by the International Court of Justice, then the invoking State may not carry out the measure it had proposed.[37] This means, in effect, that the effect of any objection is to prevent the effectiveness of *jus cogens*. Under an alternative interpretation, if no agreement is reached, the invoking State may carry out the proposed measures if the objecting State does not offer to submit the

[37] Wood (A/CN.4/.SR.3502), 10 ('noting that the first sentence stated that the import of paragraph 4 was that if after the expiration of the twelve-month period no offer to submit the matter to the International Criminal Court was made, the invoking State "may carry out the measure that it has proposed"), said that it was important to state that it did not follow from the fact that the invoking State had not brought the matter to the Court that it was free lawfully to carry out the measure. A new sentence could be inserted after the first sentence to read: "This is of course without prejudice to the question whether taking the measures is justified under international law since the dispute concerning the effect of any possible peremptory norm will not have been resolved"'); Zagaynov (A/CN.4/SR.3502), 11 ('said that he too had concerns with regard to the first sentence. His understanding of paragraph 4 of the draft conclusion was that if the objecting State did not offer to submit the matter to the International Court of Justice, the situation remained as it was. In other words, the dispute situation continued. He was unsure whether it was right for the Commission to say that the invoking State "may carry out" the measures proposed but that those measures might be unlawful. Moreover, the interpretation of paragraph 4 proposed in paragraph (9) was not compatible with the idea that the provision did not establish the compulsory jurisdiction of the International Court of Justice, since it seemed to suggest that the objecting State had a choice between bringing the matter before the Court or accepting that the invoking State could do what it proposed to do'); Murphy (A/CN.4/SR.3502), 11 ('generally speaking, he agreed with Mr. Zagaynov. It would help to see a redrafted version of the paragraph in writing. Even with the proposals put forward by Sir Michael Wood and Mr. Tladi, the clause in the first sentence that stated that the invoking State "may carry out" the measure remained problematic. If that was simply a factual claim, it was correct. It seemed to him, however, that it was a claim about propriety. To make such a claim and then try to soften it created a disconnect that was problematic. His own view was that paragraph 4 of the draft conclusion stopped short of saying what paragraph (9) was saying. One solution would be to delete the first sentence of paragraph (9)').

matter to the International Court of Justice.[38] In other words, in the event that there is no agreement, the invoking State is entitled to carry out the proposed measure if the objecting State has not offered to submit the matter to the International Court of Justice. It is this latter interpretation that the Commentary adopts. In particular, the Commentary states that it is adopted 'in the spirit of avoiding unilateralism' and, 'without obliging submission to the International Court of Justice' and seeks 'to encourage submission of the dispute to the International Court of Justice'.[39] More definitely, the Commentary states as follows:

> If, after the expiration of the twelve-month period, no offer to submit the matter to the International Court of Justice is made by the other States concerned, the invoking State is no longer precluded by the procedural provisions of draft conclusion 21 from taking the proposed measures.[40]

The practical effect of paragraph 3, under the interpretation accepted in the Commentary, is that if objecting States offer to submit the matter to the International Court of Justice, the invoking State may not carry out its measures until the dispute is resolved by the International Court of Justice. If, on the other hand, the objecting States do not offer to submit the matter to the International Court of Justice, the invoking State may carry out the measures it proposed. The paragraph thus places pressure on any objecting State, if it believes that there is no conflict with a norm of *jus cogens*, to submit the matter to

[38] See Special Rapporteur (Tladi) (A/CN.4/SR.3502), 10 ('said that he would be willing to agree to add the sentence proposed by Sir Michael Wood if it was amended to read: "This is of course without prejudice to the lawfulness of such measures." The question of lawfulness would be left open. A further sentence could then be added at the end of the paragraph to read: "If the invoking State rejects the offer to submit the matter to the International Court of Justice, it may not carry out the proposed measures and will continue to be bound by the rule or obligations." The whole point of the draft conclusion was to avoid unilateralism. Both of the proposed new sentences contributed to that aim'). Nolte (A/.CN.4/SR.3502), 11 ('said that he agreed with the Special Rapporteur's proposal for an additional sentence at the end of the paragraph. However, the second part of the proposed sentence, which read "and will continue to be bound by the rule or obligations", should be deleted. The question of whether or not the State was bound was not a matter that the Commission addressed') and ('that the Commission should not, in the commentary, backtrack on the adopted draft conclusion. It could be explained that the draft conclusion did not equate to an obligation to submit the matter to the International Court of Justice. The Special Rapporteur's proposals explained the issue well. Perhaps the adoption of the paragraph should be suspended to allow for further refinement'); Jalloh (A/CN.4/SR.3502), 11 ('said that he agreed with Mr. Nolte. While he understood the concerns raised by Mr. Murphy and Mr. Zagaynov, it was important to remember that the paragraphs of the draft conclusion applied in sequence. If one considered paragraph 4 in isolation, it could be misconstrued as giving rise to compulsory jurisdiction. However, such a conclusion could not be reached if the paragraph was read in conjunction with the preceding paragraphs').

[39] Paragraph 9 of the Commentary to Draft Conclusion 21.

[40] Id., para 10.

the International Court of Justice if it wants to preclude the invoking State from acting on its belief that there is a conflict with *jus cogens*.

Paragraph 4 of the Draft Conclusion is a self-explanatory without prejudice clause which serves to make clear that the Draft Conclusion does not undermine any rules establishing the jurisdiction of international courts, whether under the Vienna Convention, the Statute of the International Court of Justice, or any other instrument, i.e. those other instruments continue to be binding. At the same time, it emphasises that the Draft Conclusions do not serve as a basis for the jurisdiction of the International Court of Justice.

A final word on the status of Draft Conclusion 21. The textual changes described above, i.e. placement in Part IV, insertion of 'should' to replace 'shall' and 'must', and the change of the title to 'Recommended Procedure', already make plain that the procedure is not binding under customary international law. The Commentary, however, buttresses this point further. Having noted that, in the *Gabčíkovo-Nagymaros Project* case, the Court stated that Articles 65 to 67 of the Vienna Convention 'if not codifying customary international law at least generally reflect ... customary international law', proceeded to state that the Court did not mean by this 'that there was a customary international law rule concerning the establishment of jurisdiction of the Court' in respect of conflicts between *jus cogens* norms and other obligations.[41]

4. Concluding Observations

Draft Conclusion 21 is the most innovative provision in the whole of set of Draft Conclusions. While its basic framework is based on the Vienna Convention, it departs from the Vienna framework in significant ways. Moreover, the Vienna Convention is only binding on States Parties. While other provisions of the Convention relied upon in the Draft Conclusions are generally regarded as well-established in customary international law, Draft Conclusion 21 is not.

Leading up to the adoption of the Draft Conclusions, Draft Conclusion 21 received criticisms from many different quarters. One might have expected the Commission to delete the Draft Conclusion given the extensiveness of the criticism. However, not only did the Commission not delete Draft Conclusion 21, that Draft Conclusion is one of those provisions that received a considerable amount of support from members of the Commission—and more significantly members of the Commission that are generally on opposing sides of the aisle.

[41] Id., para 4.

There is a reason for this. The fear of auto-interpretation led the Commission to the view that the Draft Conclusion could not be adopted without some kind of failsafe mechanism, even if not foolproof, against auto-interpretation. Still the Commission made some changes, both to the text and to the Commentaries, in an attempt to address the concerns by States.

While most States maintained their concerns,[42] there was certainly a degree of appreciation for the attempts by the Commission to address those concerns.[43] Whether this would lead to an acceptance, over time, of the procedure, remains to be seen.

[42] The Czech Republic, Sixth Committee of the General Assembly, Seventy-Seventh Session, 25 October 2022.

[43] Singapore, Sixth Committee of the General Assembly, Seventy-Seventh Session, 25 October 2022; Romania, Sixth Committee of the General Assembly, Seventy-Seventh Session, 25 October 2022.

14

Non-Exhaustive List of *Jus Cogens* Norms

1. Introduction

Draft Conclusion 23 provides for a non-exhaustive list of *jus cogens* norms previously identified by the Commission in an Annex. It is the only Draft Conclusion in the whole set that dedicates itself to primary rules of international law.

The list in the Annex is made up of *jus cogens* norms reflected in the commentaries of various works of the International Law Commission, most notably the Articles on State Responsibility.[1] The examples in the Annex include the prohibition of genocide, the right of self-determination, and the prohibition of torture. The question of the list proved to be perhaps the most controversial and contested issue in the whole set of Draft Conclusions. This is somewhat counter-intuitive because the list is really a peripheral part of the project in that it does not address the core aspects of the project, namely the identification and legal consequences of *jus cogens*. The Commission itself, as will be seen in Section 2, had to grapple with the issue of whether to have the list at all. Entangled into the assessment was a series of interrelated and overlapping questions. These questions included whether to undertake a *de novo* assessment to determine the *jus cogens* status of candidate norms; once the *jus cogens* status of particular norms is determined, which norms to include and which norms to exclude; how to ensure that the *jus cogens* status of norms that did qualify but were not included was not undermined; how to ensure that the list did not have a freezing effect preventing new *jus cogens* from emerging; and how to account for norms whose recognition and acceptance was not assured but whose *jus cogens* status was desirable.

The next section will offer a broad discussion of these issues. Section 3 will describe the text, focusing on the nuances of Draft Conclusion 23 and the

[1] Articles on the Responsibility of States for Internationally Wrongful Acts, *Yearbook of the International Law Commission*, 2001, Vol. II, Part II.

formulation of the norms in the list. Finally, concluding observations are provided in Section 4.

2. Discussion

2.1 General

The syllabus on which the inclusion of the topic on the programme of the International Law Commission was based identified what it termed 'an illustrative list' of norms as one of the main elements of the project.[2] The other elements were the nature of *jus cogens*, identification of *jus cogens*, and consequences and effects of *jus cogens*. According to the syllabus, the list 'would be based on an assessment of the judgment of the International Court of Justice and other courts and tribunals'.[3] Importantly, the syllabus, no doubt because of some of the issues raised in the Working Group on the Long-Term Programme of Work, addresses some of the issues that have plagued the question of the list from the beginning. It states that there 'may well be fears that a list, even with the most careful drafting, could lead to the conclusion that it is exclusive (*sic*)'.[4] Yet, the syllabus points out that while this is a possibility the point 'should not be overstated' and that the Commission would need to take extra care to avoid any such misunderstanding.[5]

Also, in the context of the Long-Term Programme of Work, Mr Forteau made a telling prediction.[6] The overall point he sought to make was that there was little that the Commission could contribute to the development of the project. As an illustration, he pointed to the illustrative list and suggested that it could either be achieved in five minutes or else it would take fifty years. By this Mr Forteau meant that the Commission could attempt to prepare its own list, applying whatever methodology it had arrived at under the second element of the work programme—the identification of *jus cogens*. This, in his view would take fifty years, which then makes the project unfeasible. Alternatively, the Commission could simply take the norms listed in the Articles on State Responsibility, an endeavour that he said, tongue-in-cheek,

[2] Annex, *Report of the International Law Commission, Sixty-Sixth Session* (A/69/10), para 13.
[3] Id., 16.
[4] Id.
[5] Id.
[6] The deliberations of the Long-Term Programme of Work are confidential. However, permission has been given by Mr Forteau to attribute this particular point to him.

would take five minutes. This, in his view, would make the value of the endeavour questionable.

Thus, it was clear from the beginning that the question of the list would raise the question of which norms to include. Unsurprisingly, the very First Report of the Special Rapporteur sought the views of members of the Commission notwithstanding that the subject of that First Report did not deal with the question of the list.[7] Moreover, the question of the list was raised also in the Second, Third, and Fourth Reports, although it was only an issue for the last report.[8] This suggests that there was consternation on the part of the Special Rapporteur on the question of the list. This consternation was most explicitly expressed in the First Report, which, having declared support for the list, made the following observations:

> Nonetheless, there may be different reasons to reconsider the illustrative list. The topic, as proposed in the syllabus, is inherently about process and methodology rather than the content of specific rules and norms. In other words, like the Commission's consideration of the topic of customary international law, it is not concerned with the substantive rules; rather, the present topic is concerned with the process of the identification of the rules of *jus cogens* and its consequences. An illustrative list might have the effect of blurring the fundamentally process-oriented nature of the topic by shifting the focus of discussion towards the legal status of particular norms, as opposed to the identification of the broader requirements and effects of *jus cogens*.[9]

Given the difficulties identified in the statement, the Fourth Report proposed that the Commission 'refer, in a single Draft Conclusion, to norms recognized by the Commission and to qualify the draft conclusion appropriately'.[10] According to the Fourth Report, this was 'a creative way of elaborating an illustrative list . . . while respecting the understanding that the Commission should be discussing process and method, as opposed to the content of the peremptory norms'.[11] The basic proposition was thus not to elaborate a list as such, but rather a statement of norms that the Commission had previously identified

[7] *First Report of the Special Rapporteur on Jus Cogens* (A/CN.4/693), para 16.
[8] *Second Report of the Special Rapporteur on Jus Cogens* (A/CN.4/706), paras 8 and 9; *Third Report of the Special Rapporteur on Peremptory Norms of General International Law (Jus Cogens)* (A/CN.4/714), para 162; generally *Fourth Report of the Special Rapporteur on Peremptory Norms of General International Law* (A/CN.4/747).
[9] First Report (above note 7), para 16.
[10] Fourth Report (above note 8), para 55.
[11] Id., para 53.

as *jus cogens*. In a sense, the proposal was to adopt Mr Forteau's 'five minutes' approach.

2.2 Divergence of Views

Yet, even with the Fourth Report's adoption of the five-minute approach, the question of the list engendered great division among both members of the Commission and States.[12]

To begin with the division within the Commission, some members thought it was important to include an illustrative list. These members felt that the value of the project would be significantly reduced if the Commission did not produce a list.[13] In this context, Mr Park noted that a list of norms would help States 'to identify *jus cogens* norms and to gain a better understanding of the criteria' for the identification of norms of *jus cogens*.[14] Mr Saboia, for his part, pointed out that a list would reveal a lot about the nature of *jus cogens*.[15] It had also been noted by, for example, Mr Forteau, that there was simply an expectation that the Commission, having placed them on the agenda, would, at the very least, confirm the list that it had put forward in its previous work.[16]

Still other members expressed serious doubt about the prospects of drawing up a list. The questions arose as to which norms would be included

[12] For a broad description of these see Fourth Report (above note 8), paras 50–2.

[13] Caflisch (A/CN.4/SR.3314), 9–10 ('the work undertaken by the Commission would be of much less relevance and value if an attempt was not made to at least draw up such a list. Despite the uncertainties, it would be regrettable if the Commission, instead of drawing up just an "illustrative" and "provisional" list, limited itself to citing "examples" on the pretext that "the topic ... is inherently about process and methodology rather than the content of specific rules and norms"'); Kittichaisaree (A/CN.4/SR.3415), 5; Candiotti (A/CN4/SR.3317), 13 ('In principle he supported the proposal to provide a list of norms that currently qualified as *jus cogens*. It was hard to see how [the methodological issues could be addressed] *in abstracto* without identifying [the norms]'); Jalloh (A/CN.4/SR.3372), 12; Cisse (A/CN.4/SR.3373), 5; Galvão Teles (A/CN.4/SR.3373), 8–9; Oral (A/CN.4/SR.3373), 10; Peter (A/CN.4/SR.3373), 12.

[14] Park (A/CN.4/SR.3316), 13; Hmoud (A/CN.4/SR.3322), 12; Hassouna (A/CN.4/SR.3370), 10.

[15] Saboia (A/CN4/SR.3316), 16. See also Vásquez Bermúdez (A/CN.4/SR.3322), 5. See especially Šturma (A/CN.4/SR.3322), 11 ('first, it seemed difficult to identify true peremptory norms if the Commission gave no examples of *jus cogens* norms. Second, the general characteristics of, or criteria for, *jus cogens* should be supported by at least some examples of such norms'); Reinisch (A/CN.4/SR.3372), 15.

[16] See Forteau (A/CN.4/SR.3317), 13 ('He was in favour of establishing an illustrative list ... Fourthly he could not fully understand why concerns were being expressed over the proposal for a list. In 1966 and 2001, the Commission's decision to draw up similar lists had hardly been contested. It would be at the very least surprising for the Commission to refrain from repeating the exercise after having opted to include the topic of *jus cogens* in its agenda'). See, in a similar vein, Vásquez Bermúdez (A/CN.4/SR.3322), 5 ('given that it had already drawn up lists of examples of *jus cogens* in the context of other work, the Commission should *a fortiori* compile one as part of the study of *jus cogens*').

and which excluded.[17] In particular, the real possibility that such a list would result in freezing development and preventing the emergence of new *jus cogens* norms was raised.[18] A related point was that to properly put together a list applying the methodology of the Commission would be near impossible.[19]

These views were largely replicated in the written comments received from States on the Draft Conclusions adopted on first reading, with several States expressing support for the list,[20] while other States expressed concern and doubt over the inclusion of the list.[21] Other States supported the list but preferred that the Commission justify its choices—an approach that would be akin to Forteau's fifty-year approach.[22]

The main criticism against the Commission's approach is that the Commission had not, in producing the list, been faithful to its own methodology.[23] The five-minute approach—i.e. simply reproducing the Commission's

[17] See e.g. Wood (A/CN.4/SR.3414), 12 ('Which examples would be included in the list ... What would be the status of such a list and why should norms be included simply because they had been included in the commentaries by way of examples?'); Nolte (A/CN.4/SR.3315), 9 ('concerned that it would lead fruitless debate about why certain norms were included over others'); Murphy (A/CN.4/SR.3316), 10; Jacobsson (A/CN.4/SR.3322), 15 ('Experience showed that, as well as being time consuming, the establishment of a list, even an indicative or open-ended one, entailed making a final choice about which elements should or should not be included'); Lehto (A/CN.4/SR.3372), 7.

[18] Jacobsson (A/CN.4/SR.3322), 15 ('It would thus be difficult to add new norms').

[19] Rajput (A/CN.4/SR.3369), 8 ('Indeed, each item on the tentative list would have to be discussed at great length, pass the tests that the Commission would devise as part of the outcome of its work on the topic and require a separate report, which would make such a task unmanageable').

[20] Peremptory Norms of General International Law (*Jus Cogens*): Austria, Comments and Observations received from Governments (A/CN.4/748), 100; Belgium, Comments and Observations received from Governments (A/CN.4/748), 100; Slovenia, Comments and Observations received from Governments (A/CN.4/748), 108; South Africa, Comments and Observations received from Governments (A/CN.4/748), 109; Spain, Comments and Observations received from Governments (A/CN.4/748), 109; Switzerland, Comments and Observations received from Governments (A/CN.4/748), 110; Romania (A/C.6/74/SR.23), para 79; Belarus (A/C.6/74/SR.24), para 85; Brazil (A/C.6/74/SR.24), 92; Micronesia (A/C.6/74/SR.24), para 99; Mexico (A/C.6/SR.25), para 11.

[21] Australia, Comments and Observations (above note 20), 99; Czech Republic, Comments and Observations (above note 20), 101; Denmark (on behalf of the Nordic Countries), Comments and Observations (above note 20), 101; France, Comments and Observations (above note 20), 101; Germany, Comments and Observations (above note 20), 101; Israel, Comments and Observations (above note 20), 102; Italy, Comments and Observations (above note 20), 104; The Netherlands, Comments and Observations (above note 20); Russian Federations, Comments and Observations (above note 20), 106–7; Singapore, Comments and Observations (above note 20), 108; United Kingdom, Comments and Observations (above note 20), 112–13; United States, Comments and Observations (above note 20), 113; China (A/C.6/74/SR.23), para 55; Nicaragua (A/C.6/74/SR.23), para 71; Ireland (A/C.6/74/SR.24), para 41; Thailand (A/C.6/74/SR.24), para 108; Republic of Korea (A/C.6/74/SR.26), para 59; Turkey (A/C.6/74/SR.26), 73.

[22] See e.g. Japan, Comments and Observations (above note 20), 105–6; Portugal, Comments and Observations (above note 20), 106; Slovakia (A/C.6/74/SR.23), para 86.

[23] See Wood (A/CN.4/SR.3459), 7 ('It would be especially harmful if the way in which the Commission set about formulating the draft conclusion were to set a poor example in terms of methodology and rigour. There was a risk that readers might look at the evidence referred to in the commentary to any draft conclusion and take it as reflecting a sufficient standard for the identification of a peremptory norm').

previous list—is an attempt to respond to that. There is a related but broader question about the list, namely, whether the norms that were included in the Commission's list were worthy of inclusion and whether other norms ought to have been included. This question of over- and under-inclusiveness is discussed in Section 2.3.

2.3 Which Norms to Include and Which to Exclude

The norms referred to in the Commission's Annex are the prohibition of aggression, the prohibition of genocide, the prohibition of crimes against humanity, basic rules of international humanitarian law, the prohibition of racial discrimination and apartheid, the prohibition of slavery, the prohibition of torture, and the right of self-determination.[24] This list correlates with the list proposed in the Fourth Report.[25]

The first criticism that has been raised is that the list is too narrow and does not include other norms that are also *jus cogens*. This criticism itself has two categories.[26] In the first category, it had been noted that traditional norms regarded as fundamental in international law such as sovereignty, equality of States, and *pacta sunt servanda* had not been included. Proponents of this were Mr Murase,[27] Mr Nguyen,[28] Mr Aurescu,[29] Mr Argüello Gómez,[30] and Mr Zagaynov.[31] There were also several States that made this observation.[32]

[24] See Annex to the Draft Conclusions on Peremptory Norms of General International Law (*Jus Cogens*).

[25] See para 137 of the Fourth Report (above note 8).

[26] See Special Rapporteur (Tladi) (A/CN.4/SR.3465), 10 ('With regard to the absence from the list of some important norms of international law, some members had expressed the view that the Commission seemed to be stuck in the 1960s, noting that the list did not address concerns of modern international law such as the rights of lesbian, gay, bisexual, transgender and intersex persons or the protection of the environment. Others, on the contrary, had noted that traditional norms such as sovereignty, non-intervention and *pacta sunt servanda* were not included').

[27] Murase (A/CN.4/SR.3459), 12 ('It was perhaps naivety on his part, but his initial reaction had been to question why respect for State sovereignty was not at the top of the list of *jus cogens* norms, since sovereignty, or sovereign equality, was the most fundamental norm in international law. Was not respect for international law or *pacta sunt servanda* supposed to be the basic norm, or *Grundnorm*, of international law and therefore a *jus cogens* norm?').

[28] Nguyen (A/CN.4/SR.3460), 18, referring to the Declaration of Principles of Friendly Relations, which contains these types of norms.

[29] Aurescu (A/CN.4/SR.3462), 4.

[30] Argüello Gómez (A/CN.4/SR.3462), 12.

[31] Zagaynov (A/CN.4/SR.3463), 10.

[32] See e.g. Switzerland, Comments and Observations (above note 20), 112; Nicaragua (A/C.6/74/SR.23), para 71; Russian Federations, Comments and Observations (above note 20), 107; Croatia (A/C.6/74/SR.25), para 56.

A second category of members pointed out more contemporary candidates for *jus cogens* status, such as in the field of the environment and gender rights.[33] It was in this context that Mr Jalloh said he was struck that we appeared to be stuck in the 1960s.[34] Members that supported this view referred to rules on, for example, environmental protection, human trafficking, and gender discrimination.[35] There were, likewise, States that also noted that these more contemporary humanitarian concerns ought to have been captured.[36]

On the first category, i.e. that more traditional norms related to sovereignty ought to have been included, it is of course possible to simply respond to the criticism by noting that the list is non-exhaustive. But there is also a more substantive possible response. While these norms are certainly regarded as fundamental to the international law system, and thus of a higher status than other norms, their categorisation as *jus cogens* is less generally accepted. Of course, in its Commentary to the 1966 Articles on the Law of Treaties, those principles make an appearance,[37] but even there, the Commission does not seem to recognise those norms as *jus cogens* but rather points out that some members in the course of the debate had done so.[38]

[33] See e.g. Mary Hansel '"Magic" or Smoke and Mirrors? The Gendered Illusions of *Jus Cogens*' in Dire Tladi (ed.) *Peremptory Norms of General International Law (Jus Cogens): Disquisitions and Disputations* (Brill, 2021) and in the same volume Nilufer Oral 'Environmental Protection as a Peremptory Norm of General International Law: Is it Time?'.

[34] Mr Jalloh's statement can be found in (A/CN.4/SR.3461), however, that particular statement has been edited out of the summary records and instead contained the following sentiment (at 9): 'Members should consider, for example, the implications of using a list dating back to the immediate post-decolonization period, to a bipolar world characterized by the Cold War and the fear of nuclear annihilation. The International Bill of Human Rights had just been completed and its implications had not yet been fully absorbed. It was the age before computers, the Internet and social media. The world today was significantly different from that world. The list proposed by the Special Rapporteur reflected the most widely recognized examples of peremptory norms at that time and the preoccupations of that period.'

[35] Murase (A/CN.4/SR.3459), 12 ('He noted that, while torture and the basic rules of international humanitarian law were new additions to the fourth report, which also made reference to the catastrophic destruction of the environment as a possible candidate for inclusion in the illustrative list of *jus cogens* norms, no mention was made of massive pollution of the atmosphere and of the sea'); Oral (A/CN.4/SR.3460), 7 ('Unlike genocide, however, "gecocide" was not a *jus cogens* norm. While protection of the environment and natural resources might not have been recognized as a peremptory norm in the past, it was a potential candidate for inclusion on a future list of *jus cogens* norms. The manner in which the Commission elaborated an illustrative list should not hinder the potential inclusion of such norms'); Argüello Gómez (A/CN.4/SR.3462), 11 ('It was hard to understand how, at the current stage of human development, norms such as the prohibitions of enforced disappearance, human trafficking, discrimination and terrorism, the right to life and environmental rights, all of which were mentioned in paragraph 123 of the report, could be excluded').

[36] See e.g. Portugal, Comments and Observations (above note 20), 106; Romania (A/C.6/74/SR.23), para 79; Federated States of Micronesia (A/C.6/74/SR.24), para 24.

[37] See Commentary to Article 50 of the 1966 Articles on the Law of Treaties, *Yearbook of the International Law Commission*, 1966, Vol. II, para 3.

[38] Id. ('*Other members* expressed the view that, if examples were given, it would be undesirable to appear to limit the scope of the article to cases involving acts which constitute crimes under international law; treaties violating human rights, the equality of States or the principle of self-determination were mentioned as other possible examples') (emphasis added).

The prevailing view seems to be that endorsed by Viñuales.[39] Under this view, norms found in the Friendly Relations Declaration certainly occupy a higher status than other norms and to this extent reflect a stratification of international law. Yet this stratification 'is based on a number of essentially State-centric rationales' (with the exception of self-determination which has, in addition to its State-centric character, a humanitarian rationale).[40] The rationale for the stratification of *jus cogens*, however, is different in that it is to be found in humanitarian concerns, with the main exceptions being the prohibition on the use of force,[41] while the rationale for self-determination appears to straddle both categories of higher norm. While Viñuales suggests that this may be the reason why norms relating to the environment struggle to get recognition as *jus cogens*,[42] I would suggest that those norms would easily meet the humanitarian rationale test. Of course, this 'stratification rationale' is not a criterion for peremptory status under the Draft Conclusions (Draft Conclusion 4 in Chapter 3), but it may be implicit in the general nature of *jus cogens* (Draft Conclusion 2) and this may in part explain why that Draft Conclusion was so contentious.[43]

With respect to the second category of norms, i.e. those related to contemporary issues of human co-existence, there is certainly a strong argument to be made for many of those norms. Indeed the Fourth Report identified certain rules of international law which normatively were deserving of *jus cogens* status, namely the prohibition of enforced disappearance, the prohibition of arbitrary deprivation of life, the principle of *non-refoulement*, the prohibition of non-discrimination (broadly), and some norms aimed at protecting the environment.[44] Moreover, the Fourth Report suggested that there was also some evidence of acceptance and recognition of the first three of these norms, while such evidence was as yet lacking for the last two.[45]

Thus, at least with the second category of norms that were identified, it remains a possibility that, first, even if not included in the non-exhaustive list, they do meet the criteria for peremptory status. That, after all, is the nature of a non-exhaustive list. Second, there remains the possibility that, assuming

[39] Jorge E. Viñuales 'The Friendly Relations Declaration and Peremptory Norms' in Tladi (above note 33).
[40] Id., 686.
[41] Id.
[42] Id.
[43] See, for discussion, Chapter 2.
[44] See Fourth Report (above note 8), paras 125–36.
[45] Id.

they do not as yet have sufficient evidence of acceptance and recognition of their peremptory status, they could in the future acquire that recognition and acceptance.

In addition to the criticism of under-inclusiveness, i.e. that there were norms of *jus cogens* that ought to have been included in the list, there is also a criticism of over-inclusiveness, i.e. the idea that there are norms on the list that ought not to have been included. The norm in the list that has attracted the most attention in this regard is self-determination. Within the Commission, the peremptory status of the norm has been questioned by Mr Wood, Mr Murphy, and Mr Ouazzani Chahdi.[46] Amongst States, the peremptory status of self-determination has been called into question by Israel, Morocco, the United Kingdom, and the United States.[47]

It bears mentioning that, for the most part, the arguments against the *jus cogens* status of self-determination have focused on the Fourth Report's reliance on sources that refer to self-determination as establishing *erga omnes* obligations and the fact that the International Court of Justice did not describe self-determination as *jus cogens* in the *Chagos* Advisory Opinion.[48] The first of these concerns was addressed in Chapter 10 in the context of the relationship between *erga omnes* and *jus cogens*. There it was pointed out that while there are obligations *erga omnes* that do not arise out of *jus cogens*, these generally seem to be obligations arising from rules relating to open spaces, such as the deep seabed. It is thus hard to imagine on what basis, other the *jus cogens* character, the duty to respect the right of self-determination could have acquired its *erga omnes* character.

On the second concern, while it is certainly true that the Court did not determine that self-determination was *jus cogens* in the *Chagos* Advisory Opinion, it is equally true that the Court does not deny the *jus cogens* character of self-determination which it could have done had it believed self-determination was not *jus cogens*. This is because so many States invoked the *jus cogens* character of self-determination. Furthermore, it might also be noted that, in fact, while several judges explicitly declared self-determination as *jus cogens*,[49]

[46] Wood (A/CN.4/SR.3459), 10; Murphy (A/CN.4/SR.3460), 9; Ouazzani Chahdi (A/CN.4/SR.3463), 12.

[47] See e.g. Israel, Comments and Observations (above note 20), 104; the United States, Comments and Observations (above note 20), 113.

[48] *Legal Consequences of the Separation of the Chagos Archipelago from Mauritius in 1965*, Advisory Opinion, *ICJ Reports* 2019, p. 95.

[49] See *Chagos* Advisory Opinion (above note 48), Separate Opinion of Judge Cançado Trindade, Joint Declaration of Judge Cançado Trindade and Judge Robinson, Separate Opinion of Judge Sebutinde, and Separate Opinion of Judge Robinson.

not a single judge made the opposite determination. Indeed, according to the then President of the Court, the Court did not make a statement about the *jus cogens* status of self-determination, not because it did not believe that self-determination was not a *jus cogens* norm, but because that determination was not necessary for the legal question put before it.[50]

Moreover, the consequences that ordinarily flow from the *erga omnes* character of a norm concern the entitlement to invoke responsibility.[51] Yet the Court went further to find that the consequences of self-determination in the context of the Chagos Archipelago include the duty to co-operate to bring to an end the breach.[52] This duty, it will be recalled, is a *particular consequence* of serious breaches of *jus cogens*.[53] This would seem to affirm that self-determination is not only *erga omnes* but also *jus cogens*, since the particular consequences of serious breaches of *jus cogens* attach also to its breach.

Finally, in the summation of the debate on the Fourth Report, and specifically responding to comments about the *Chagos* Advisory Opinion, the Special Rapporteur said the following:

> A third point relates to the fact that several States, in the proceedings before the International Court of Justice relating to the request for an advisory opinion on the Chagos Archipelago identified self-determination as a peremptory norm of general international law. These states are Belize, Cyprus, the Netherlands, Brazil, South Africa, Mauritius, Kenya, Nicaragua, Serbia and representing 54 States, the African Union. Now, one member of our Commission drew a negative conclusion from this, suggesting that the fact that these arguments were made but not taken up by the International Court of Justice is an indication that the right of self-determination is not a peremptory norm of general international law. It is interesting that this is the same member that decried the reliance on the International Court of Justice more than State practice. But in this case State practice in the form of public statements before the International Court of Justice is not only irrelevant, but negates the content of that state practice if not taken up by the International

50 See, in this regard, the response of President of the Court of Justice, Yusuf, to a question from the Special Rapporteur on why the Court had not referred to *jus cogens* in the *Chagos* Advisory Opinion (A/CN.4/SR.3478): 'the Court had deemed it unnecessary to address the matter of whether the right to self-determination was a peremptory norm of international law in its advisory opinion on the *Legal Consequences of the Separation of the Chagos Archipelago from Mauritius in 1965*, because that had not been the point at issue'. He stated further that, in his view, '[t]he General Assembly's question had been whether the decolonization process of Mauritius had been lawfully completed'.

51 See Draft Conclusion 17.

52 *Chagos* Advisory Opinion (above note 48), para 180.

53 See Draft Conclusion 19 discussed in Chapter 10.

> Court of Justice. So in other cases State practice is more important than the ICJ except where that State practice points to a conclusion not favoured by this member.[54]

In connection with the views of States, it is worth noting that before the elaboration of Draft Conclusion 23, there is little evidence of any State, even as late as 2018, objecting to the peremptory status of the right of self-determination, notwithstanding its frequent inclusion in lists of norms. Indeed, when the Commission included a list in the 2001 Articles on State Responsibility, and included the right to self-determination, States did not question that list,[55] nor did they question the inclusion of the right to self-determination on that list—not even those States that have now begun to question the *jus cogens* status of the norm.[56]

3. The Content of Draft Conclusion 23

Draft Conclusion 23
Non-exhaustive list
Without prejudice to the existence or subsequent emergence of other peremptory norms of general international law (*jus cogens*), a non-exhaustive list of norms that the International Law Commission has previously referred to as having that status is to be found in the annex to the present draft conclusions.
Annex
(a) The prohibition of aggression;
(b) the prohibition of genocide;
(c) the prohibition of crimes against humanity;
(d) the basic rules of international humanitarian law;
(e) the prohibition of racial discrimination and apartheid;
(f) the prohibition of slavery;

[54] Verbatim statement on file with the author. In the summary records, Special Rapporteur (Tladi) (A/CN.4/SR.3465), 7, makes the same point but omits the reference to the numbers of States.
[55] See, for a recent description of the right to self-determination as *jus cogens*, Case T-160/19, *LTTE v Council*, Judgment of the European Union General Court, para 289.
[56] See the following summary records where the Report of the International Law Commission was considered in 2001: A/C.6/56/SR.11; A/C.6/56/SR.12; A/C.6/56/SR.13; A/C.6/56/SR.14 (here the delegate of India, without questioning the status of self-determination as a *jus cogens* norm, circumscribed it as excluding secession); A/C.6/56/SR.15; A/C.6/56/SR.16; A/C.6/56/SR.17; A/C.6/56/SR.18; A/C.6/56/SR.19; A/C.6/56/SR.20; A/C.6/56/SR.21; A/C.6/56/SR.22; A/C.6/56/SR.23; A/C.6/56/SR.24.

(g) the prohibition of torture;
(h) the right of self-determination.

Draft Conclusion 23 and its accompanying Annex provide a list of *jus cogens* norms. The basic approach of the Draft Conclusion and the Annex is to provide norms that the Commission had previously identified as having the status of *jus cogens* without undertaking any *de novo* assessment of the peremptory status of the norms. To capture this approach, the Fourth Report proposed the following text for Draft Conclusion 23:

> Without prejudice to the existence of other peremptory norms of general international law (*jus cogens*), the most widely recognized examples of peremptory norms of general international law (*jus cogens*) are:
> (a) the prohibition of aggression or aggressive force;
> (b) the prohibition of genocide;
> (c) the prohibition of slavery;
> (d) the prohibition of apartheid and racial discrimination;
> (e) the prohibition of crimes against humanity;
> (f) the prohibition of torture;
> (g) the right to self-determination; and
> (h) the basic rules of international humanitarian law.

The current structure, where the list of norms is contained in the Annex, was proposed in the plenary debate by Madam Galvão Teles. She proposed that the Draft Conclusion would provide as follows:

> A non-exhaustive list of norms that have been generally accepted as having attained the status of peremptory norms of general international law (*jus cogens*) is contained in the annex to the present draft conclusions.[57]

The Annex itself would contain a chapeau in the following terms:

> Without prejudice to the existence or emergence of other peremptory norms, the following norms have been generally accepted as having attained the status of peremptory norms of general international law (*jus cogens*).[58]

[57] Galvão Teles (A/CN.4/SR.3460), 4.
[58] Id.

In plenary, and on the basis of the proposal by Madam Galvão Teles, the Special Rapporteur presented a new textual proposal.[59] This proposal, which formed the basis of discussions in the Drafting Committee,[60] differed from Madam Galvão Teles' proposal in that the latter described the norms in the list as 'the most widely recognised' as being *jus cogens*, whereas the proposal submitted to the Drafting Committee described the norms as those 'that the Commission has previously referred to as having attained' *jus cogens* status. Yet, like the proposal of Madam Galvão Teles, the proposal in the Drafting Committee retained structure that necessitated an introductory paragraph in the Annex. Within the Drafting Committee, that structure was deemed too complex and the Special Rapporteur put forward a simplified text in an informal paper.[61] Under this simplified text, a chapeau would not be necessary, and the text of the Draft Conclusion would read:

> Without prejudice to the existence or future emergence of other peremptory norms of general international law (*jus cogens*), the Commission has previously referred to the norms contained in the Annex as having attained the status of peremptory norms of general international law (*jus cogens*).[62]

It was this text, with some minor modifications of an editorial and cosmetic nature, that was eventually adopted by the Commission.

Draft Conclusion 23 is a fine balance that seeks to account for two conflicting concerns. On the one hand, that it would be impractical to seek to elaborate a list of *jus cogens* norms applying the methodology developed in the Draft Conclusion—Forteau's fifty-year dilemma. On the other hand, that a list of norms serving as examples was seen by many as a useful exercise. For this reason, the Commentary emphasised that 'in putting together this list, it did not apply the methodology' it had established in the Draft Conclusions.[63] Rather, the Commission explained, the 'list is intended to illustrate … the types of norms that have routinely been identified as having peremptory character' and that it itself had not, in this project, made 'an assessment of those norms'.[64]

[59] See Special Rapporteur (Tladi) (A/CN.4/SR.3465), 10.
[60] Drafting Committee, Peremptory Norms of General International Law (*Jus Cogens*), Proposal of Special Rapporteur, ILC(LXXI)/DC/JC/WP.7, 16 May 2019.
[61] Informal, untitled paper, 21 May 2019, 5:15pm.
[62] Id.
[63] Paragraph 3 of the Commentary to Draft Conclusion 23.
[64] Id.

This is the first disclaimer and it is reflected in the text of the Draft Conclusions by the phrase 'the International Law Commission has previously referred to as having that status'. In keeping with this disclaimer, the Commentaries only refer to the previous references of the Commission to support the norms—this is to emphasise that no independent assessment of the individual norms has been undertaken.

A major concern with the list in the discussion is that the list has excluded (or may have excluded) other norms—the issue of under-inclusion. This concern is addressed in the text by the phrase 'Without prejudice to the existence or subsequent emergence of other' norms. This message is reinforced by the description of the list as 'non-exhaustive'.

The without prejudice nature of the list is described by the Commission as operating on two mutually reinforcing levels. The most obvious level is that it is without prejudice generally to norms that currently exist or that will emerge in the future.[65] Thus, while the right against arbitrary deprivation of life is not mentioned, this does not mean that the Commission is rejecting its current *jus cogens* status. Similarly, the fact that the prohibition of discrimination broadly speaking is not referred to in the list does not mean that the Commission is excluding the possibility that it may now be, or in the future become, *jus cogens*. The second level at which the without prejudice clause operates is that 'the Commission has also referred previously to other norms' when addressing *jus cogens* and while there may be differences of opinion as to whether the Commission, by those references, was making a definitive claim about their peremptory status, their non-inclusion in the list should 'not be seen as excluding [their] peremptory character'.[66] These norms are referred to in the Commentary and include the prohibition of piracy, sovereign equality of States, and rules relating to the preservation of the environment.[67]

While the Commentary links the without prejudice clause to these two levels, there is a third level at which the without prejudice clause operates, namely the formulation of the individual norms and their content. The Commission decided to rely on the formulation that was previously used by the Commission.[68] For some of the norms, the Commission had used different

[65] Id., para 4.
[66] Id.
[67] Id., para 15.
[68] See id., para 5 of the Commentary.

formulations. For example, the Commission has variously referred to 'the prohibition of aggression', 'the law of the Charter concerning the prohibition of the use of force', and 'the prohibition of aggressive use of force'.[69] Similarly, the Commission has referred to both the 'right to self-determination' and 'the right of self-determination'.[70] In the main, the Commission relied on the formulations in the Articles on State Responsibility, with the exception of 'crimes against humanity' for which the formulation relied on was taken from the preamble of the Draft Articles on the Prevention and Punishment of Crimes against Humanity.[71]

These formulations are without prejudice to the scope of the individual rules. Thus, while aggression is much narrower than the use of force, the list should be seen as without prejudice to the *jus cogens* status of the broader prohibition of the use of force, whose status is beyond doubt.[72] By the same token, the reference to the basic principles of international humanitarian law as *jus cogens* should be seen as being without prejudice to the *jus cogens* scope of principles of international humanitarian law.

4. Concluding Observations

Draft Conclusion 23 and the Annex accompanying it attracted perhaps the most attention from States, both negative and positive, in the debate following the Commission's completion of the work. In general, those States that had opposed the list continued to oppose it,[73] and those that supported it continued to

[69] Id., para 7.
[70] Id., para 14.
[71] Id., para 9. In the Articles on States Responsibility, the prohibition of crimes against humanity is combined with the prohibition of torture. See para 5 of the Commentary to Article 26 of the Articles on State Responsibility (above note 1).
[72] Olivier Corten and Vaios Koutroulis 'The *Jus Cogens* Status of the Prohibition on the Use of Force: What is Its Scope and Why Does it Matter?' in Tladi (above note 33). See also Dire Tladi *The Extraterritorial Use of Force against Non-State Actors* (Brill, 2022).
[73] The Czech Republic, Sixth Committee of the General Assembly, Seventy-Seventh Session, 25 October 2022; Nordic States, Sixth Committee of the General Assembly, Seventy-Seventh Session, 25 October 2022; Germany, Sixth Committee of the General Assembly, Seventy-Seventh Session, 25 October 2022; Australia, Sixth Committee of the General Assembly, Seventy-Seventh Session, 25 October 2022; The United States, Sixth Committee of the General Assembly, Seventy-Seventh Session, 25 October 2022; The United Kingdom, Sixth Committee of the General Assembly, Seventy-Seventh Session, 26 October 2022; Morocco, Sixth Committee of the General Assembly, Seventy-Seventh Session, 26 October 2022; Cameroon, Sixth Committee of the General Assembly, Seventy-Seventh Session, 26 October 2022; Israel, Sixth Committee of the General Assembly, Seventy-Seventh Session, 25 October 2022.

support it.[74] Others, however, such as Italy, have taken a more measured stance in which they have expressed understanding for the Commission's approach without being in favour of it.[75] Moreover, there remained those States, such as Austria, which, while generally supportive, would have preferred to see particular norms being included.[76]

Yet, Draft Conclusion 23 is not the central part of the Draft Conclusions. In truth, the Draft Conclusion is not even *a* central element of the Draft Conclusions. This much is clear from the Commentaries to the Draft Conclusions—both the Commentary to Draft Conclusion 1 and the Commentary to Draft Conclusion 23. The Commentary to Draft Conclusion 1, for example, recalls that the Draft Conclusions are concerned with methodology and do not seek to identify the content of individual norms of *jus cogens*.[77] The Commentary to Draft Conclusion 23, for its part, having recalled the methodological nature of the project states that the elaboration of a list of *jus cogens* norms 'falls beyond the scope of the exercise of elaborating Draft Conclusions on identification and legal consequences of' *jus cogens*.[78] The list appears to have been appended merely for the sake of completeness and not for any substantive purpose. Indeed, with all caveats, it is clear that the list is not of much normative value, save to highlight the norms that the Commission had already identified as *jus cogens*—norms which, up to the adoption of the Draft Conclusions, were hidden in the commentaries of various outputs of the Commission.

[74] Pakistan, Sixth Committee of the General Assembly, Seventy-Seventh Session, 25 October 2022; Estonia, Sixth Committee of the General Assembly, Seventy-Seventh Session, 26 October 2022; Slovenia, Sixth Committee of the General Assembly, Seventy-Seventh Session, 25 October 2022; Brazil, Sixth Committee of the General Assembly, Seventy-Seventh Session, 25 October 2022; Switzerland, Sixth Committee of the General Assembly, Seventy-Seventh Session, 25 October 2022; Sierra Leone, Sixth Committee of the General Assembly, Seventy-Seventh Session, 26 October 2022; Jordan, Sixth Committee of the General Assembly, Seventy-Seventh Session, 25 October 2022.

[75] See Italy, Sixth Committee of the General Assembly, Seventy-Seventh Session, 25 October 2022 ('we partly appreciate the reasons behind the decision to elaborate a non-exhaustive list'). See also Ireland, Sixth Committee of the General Assembly, Seventy-Seventh Session, 25 October 2022 ('We note also the adoption of the Annex to the Conclusions which sets out a non-exhaustive list of peremptory norms ... As my delegation was one of those that expressed some reservations about such a list ... and in particular the risk of it being misunderstood as comprehensive, we welcome the clarification provided by Conclusion 23. Accordingly we regard the list in the Annex as purely illustrative even if, in Ireland's view, each of the norms listed is indeed a peremptory norm of general international law').

[76] See Austria, Sixth Committee of the General Assembly, Seventy-Seventh Session, 25 October 2022 ('By drawing up a list of peremptory norms, even if such list is only indicative, the Commission made an important step towards clarifying basic notions of international law. However, Austria would have preferred that the non-exhaustive list refer to the prohibition on the use of force as a peremptory norm rather than to the prohibition of aggression').

[77] See paras 3 and 4 of the Commentary to Draft Conclusion 1.

[78] Para 2 of the Commentary to Draft Conclusion 23.

While the list is not central to the project, it is important, in assessing the criticisms of the list of norms, including individual norms on the list, to recall that the list is one with a pedigree and which has been repeated several times without much objection, at least until recently. Sudden criticism from a small number of States, no matter how vociferous, is unlikely to be sufficient to undo the list.

15

Prospects and Concluding Thoughts

1. Introduction

When, in August 2022, the Commission adopted the Draft Conclusions on the Identification and Legal Consequences of Peremptory Norms (*Jus Cogens*), it marked the end of the elaboration of the Draft Conclusions by the Commission. What happens to the Draft Conclusions now will depend on their reception in the community of international law, which is broader than just States, but includes courts, scholars, and other actors.

2. Post-Adoption Reception

The Commission's Draft Conclusions have already been the subject of intense debate in the Sixth Committee of the General Assembly during its Seventy-Seventh Session. In general, the output of the work of the Commission was well received by States in the General Assembly debate.[1] Unsurprisingly, there was a minority of States that adopted an overall negative attitude to the Draft Conclusions.[2] There were other States, whose statements were, on balance, neutral.[3]

Of course, even States that generally supported the product did not agree with every provision. To take the statement of the Nordic States as an example,

[1] There were forty-one States that were, on balance, in support of the Draft Conclusions. They are, in the chronological order of their statements: Norway (on behalf of Denmark, Finland, Iceland, and Sweden), Jordan, Greece, Islamic Republic of Iran, Italy, El Salvador, Hungary, Austria, India, Mexico, Egypt, Belarus, Brazil, Slovenia, Slovakia, Estonia, Pakistan, Romania, Czech Republic, Colombia, Cuba, Portugal, Ireland, Sierra Leone, Peru, Switzerland, Vietnam, Chile, Thailand, the Netherlands, the Republic of Korea, Spain, Cyprus, Croatia, Lebanon, New Zealand, State of Palestine.

[2] There were ten States whose statements were, on balance, negatively disposed to the Draft Conclusions. These are, in the chronological order of the statements: China, the United States, the United Kingdom, the Russian Federation, Armenia, Israel, Morocco, Japan, France, and Turkey.

[3] There were nine States whose statements were, on balance, neutral. These are, in the chronological order of the statements: Singapore, Australia, Canada, the Philippines, Germany, Poland, Cameroon, Bulgaria, and the Holy See.

it 'commend[ed]' and 'applaud[ed]' the Commission for its work on *jus cogens*.[4] At the same time, the Nordic States identified a number of provisions in the Draft Conclusions that were of concern to them. For example, the Nordic States believed that the precise role of non-State actors in the identification of *jus cogens* should be made clearer.[5] They also expressed caution about the Annex with the non-exhaustive list.[6] This pattern is visible with other States that generally supported the Draft Conclusions. South Africa, for example, while expressing support for the Draft Conclusions,[7] also took issue with the fact that the text of Draft Conclusion 5 provides the possibility for treaty provisions to form the basis of *jus cogens*.[8] Similarly, Greece welcomed the adoption of the Draft Conclusions on second reading, but nonetheless expressed the view that the characteristics in Draft Conclusion 2 (general nature), should play a greater role in the criteria for the identification of *jus cogens*.[9] Similarly, the Islamic Republic of Iran, while praising the work of the Commission,[10]

[4] See Statement of Norway (on behalf Denmark, Finland, Iceland, Sweden, and Norway), *Report of the International Law Commission*, Sixth Committee of the General Assembly, Seventy-Seventh Session, 25 October 2022, 3 ('We commend the contribution of the International Law Commission in providing this guidance to practitioners who may be called upon to determine the existence of peremptory norms of general international law and their legal effects, and applaud the Commission for submitting its work on the draft conclusions regarding this very important topic to the General Assembly'). In addition to this general support, the Nordic States also expressed their appreciation for particular provisions, such as Draft Conclusion 2, Draft Conclusion 7, and Draft Conclusion 19 amongst others.

[5] Id., 4 ('We feel that the need for clarity is particularly pressing with regard to the definition of the term "other actors" in draft conclusion 7, paragraph 3. However, in the commentary [paragraph 3] it is rightly stated—and it should be stressed—that it is the position of States that is relevant; and not that of other actors. The same applies to draft conclusion 9, paragraph 2, and the reference to the works of expert bodies, etc., as subsidiary means for the determination of the peremptory character of norms of general international law. The Nordic countries continue to hold the view that the question of the role of these organs should be approached with caution').

[6] Id. ('The Nordic countries also sustain our reservations on the non-exhaustive list of *jus cogens* norms mentioned in draft conclusion 23 and annexed to the draft conclusions. Although we note that the list is without prejudice to the existence or subsequent emergence of other peremptory norms, we find it important to emphasize that this list shall not be interpreted as preventing the emergence of State practice and opinio juris in support of other norms.')

[7] See South Africa, Sixth Committee of the General Assembly, Seventy-Seventh Session, 25 October 2022, expressing support for the text as a whole as well as particular provisions, e.g. Draft Conclusion 2, Draft Conclusion 7, Draft Conclusion 16, Draft Conclusion 17, and Draft Conclusion 18.

[8] Id., 2. ('South Africa notes that paragraph 2 of Draft Conclusion 5 was retained in its previous form, in which treaty provisions are identified as basis for peremptory norms. Nonetheless, we remain unconvinced by the ambiguity of the Commission's treatment of treaty provisions as basis for *jus cogens*. We note the suggestion at various places in the commentary to suggest that treaty provisions can only form basis of *jus cogens* to the extent that such provisions reflect customary international law. Yet, we believe that this ought to be made clear in the text of the Draft Conclusions.')

[9] See Greece, Sixth Committee of the General Assembly, Seventy-Seventh Session, 25 October 2022, 2. ('We also note with appreciation that conclusion 2 [*sic*] provides, inter alia, that *jus cogens* norms reflect and protect fundamental values of the international community. We are however of the view that this cardinal characteristic of *jus cogens* norms provides also a criterion for their identification given that, for a norm to qualify as peremptory, it should be accepted and recognized by the international community of States as reflecting and protecting such values.')

[10] See the Islamic Republic of Iran, Sixth Committee of the General Assembly, Seventy-Seventh Session, 25 October 2022, 1, stating that it 'commend[s]' the Commission on its work on *jus cogens* and

did identify aspects of the Draft Conclusions that it did not (fully) support.[11] Jordan also adopted an overall positive view of the Draft Conclusions. In its statement, Jordan welcomed the fact that the Commission 'maintained a cautious approach to the topic' and that the Draft Conclusions 'mostly reflected existing practice of States'.[12] Yet, even with all this praise, Jordan was not convinced by the Commission's treatment of the bases of *jus cogens*, believing that only customary international law could form the basis of *jus cogens*. Nor was Jordan convinced of the decision by the Commission to include a recommended procedure. Ireland also said that it 'generally welcomes' the adoption of the Draft Conclusions, but still had 'questions in respect of a small number of [the] Conclusions'.[13] The main issues of concern for Ireland were the distinction between 'international community' in Draft Conclusion 2 and 'international community of States as a whole' in Draft Conclusion 3. The statement of Slovakia, which concurred, 'in general, with the outcome of the Commission's work', raised concerns about the inclusion of resolutions amongst the materials that can serve as evidence of acceptance and recognition.[14] A final example is the statement of Italy which, having described the Draft Conclusions as 'an important milestone in the contribution of the [Commission] to the clarification and development of international law', went on to express the failure of the Commission to 'address the thorny issue of the legal consequences of some peremptory norms such as those prohibiting genocide, war crimes and crimes against humanity'.[15]

In the same way that those States that generally supported the Draft Conclusions had some concerns, even those States that were not positively disposed to the Draft Conclusions adopted on second reading expressed positive views about some aspects. An example in this respect is the United States, which, while adopting an overall negative view of the Draft Conclusions,[16]

adding, at 3, that it 'supports the general approach taken by the Commission to identify peremptory norms of general international law'.

[11] Id., 3. ('With respect to the notion of "fundamental values" referred to in draft conclusion 3 on "General nature of peremptory norms of general international law", while it is agreed that the peremptory norms of general international law reflect and protect fundamental values of the international community, this concept has not been addressed by the 1969 Vienna Convention on the Law of Treaties (VCLT) and it appears that a new criterion has been appended to 1969 Vienna Convention for acceptance and recognition of *jus cogens*. Hence, this phrase should have been either omitted from the main text or clarified more vividly in the commentaries.').

[12] Jordan, Sixth Committee of the General Assembly, Seventy-Seventh Session, 25 October 2022.

[13] Id.

[14] Slovakia, Sixth Committee of the General Assembly, Seventy-Seventh Session, 25 October 2022.

[15] Italy, Sixth Committee of the General Assembly, Seventy-Seventh Session, 25 October 2022.

[16] See the United States, Sixth Committee of the General Assembly, Seventy-Seventh Session, 2. ('The United States nonetheless continues to disagree with several of the draft conclusions. We refer the Sixth

expressed positive comments in respect of some of the adaptations to the Draft Conclusions on the basis of the written comments by States.[17] Particular modifications on which the United States expressed positive views were Draft Conclusion 2 on the general nature of *jus cogens*, Draft Conclusion 16 and the relationship between *jus cogens* and decisions of the Security Council, and Draft Conclusion 21 on the recommended dispute resolution procedure. Japan similarly expressed appreciation for the Commission's modifications, while still maintaining 'substantial concerns'.[18]

What is more important, however, is that even the few States that took an overall negative view of the Commission's work on *jus cogens* generally supported (or did not oppose) the central elements of the Commission's work, namely the basic rule concerning the identification of *jus cogens* and the general rules on consequences. Indeed, only one State, namely Armenia, opposed the basic methodology to identification of *jus cogens*. In its intervention, Armenia stated that it has 'ongoing concerns about the positivist' approach of the Commission and that, in its view, 'the moral law is the foundation for their historical recognition, not State practice'.[19] Not even the biggest critics of the Draft Conclusions throughout the project—the United States and Israel—have shared this rather damning view of the project. On the criteria for the identification of *jus cogens* norms, for example, the United States stated that it 'favours ... the retention of draft conclusion 4 which, unlike draft conclusion 3 (*sic*), is reflective of Article 53 of the Vienna Convention on the Law of Treaties'.[20] Similarly, it seems apparent from its intervention in the Sixth Committee that, while Israel does not believe that the Commission accurately captured the threshold of evidence for the second criterion in Draft Conclusion 4, it accepts the basic framework for the criteria established in the Draft Conclusion.[21]

Committee to our written comments and past statements in this Committee. Rather than reiterate those comments here, I will highlight our remaining concerns with five of the draft conclusions.')

[17] Id. ('We recognize that the Commission has addressed some of those concerns, including with respect to the adjusted placement of what is now draft conclusion 2 and with significant edits to draft conclusion 21 on recommended procedures. We also note the additional explanations included in the commentary to draft conclusion 16 that make clear that states cannot unilaterally invoke *jus cogens* to avoid binding Security Council resolutions, and that "it is highly unlikely that a Security Council resolution would, on its face, be in conflict with a" norm of *jus cogens*.')

[18] Japan, Sixth Committee of the General Assembly, Seventy-Seventh Session, 25 October 2022.

[19] Armenia, Sixth Committee of the General Assembly, Seventy-Seventh Session, 1 and 3.

[20] See United States, Comments and Observations received from Governments on the Draft Conclusions on the Identification of Peremptory Norms (*Jus Cogens*) (A/CN.4/748), 27.

[21] See Israel, Sixth Committee of the General Assembly, Seventy-Seventh Session, especially at 5. See also Morocco, Sixth Committee of the General Assembly, Seventy-Seventh Session.

There were in fact, for those States that had a decidedly negative view of the Draft Conclusions, three main areas of concern. The first area of concern was the inclusion of the characteristics in Draft Conclusion 2. Second, several States questioned the specific reference, albeit in the Commentary, to decisions of the Security Council as decisions that do not create obligations under international law if they conflict with *jus cogens*. Finally, the inclusion of a non-exhaustive list has caused a degree of consternation for several States. Of course, there were other issues,[22] but it is these three issues that caused many States to adopt the particularly negative stance towards to the project.

The General Assembly was unable to adopt a resolution to 'commend the Draft Conclusions … to the attention of States and to all who may be called upon to' apply *jus cogens* as recommended by the Commission.[23] Instead the General Assembly decided to defer consideration of the topic to the following session.[24] It was only in 2023 that the General Assembly adopted a resolution taking note of the Draft Conclusions.

3. Prospects

The prospects for the Draft Conclusions will ultimately depend on how they are received. From the above, notwithstanding the failure of the General Assembly to adopt a resolution at the first attempt, the Draft Conclusions were generally well received by States. It is still too early to tell how useful the Draft Conclusions will be in practice. Judging by the extent of their invocation in scholarly writings shortly after their adoption on final reading, it seems safe to assume that they will inform discourse and discussion in academic circles.[25]

[22] The other issues that caused consternation were Draft Conclusion 7 (the threshold, with some States believing it should be virtually all States); Draft Conclusion 19 (with some States taking issue with the claim in the Commentary that the duties contained therein are customary international law); and Draft Conclusion 21 (with some States believing that it was inappropriate to have a dispute settlement provision in a set of Draft Conclusions).

[23] *Report of the International Law Commission, Seventy-Third Session* (A/77/10), para 41.

[24] General Assembly Resolution on the Report of the International Law Commission on the Work of its Seventy-Third Session (GA Res/77/103), para 3 ('*Decides* that the consideration of chapter IV of the report of the International Law Commission on the work of its seventy-third session, dealing with the topic "Identification and legal consequences of peremptory norms of general international law (*jus cogens*)", shall be continued at the seventy-eighth session of the General Assembly, during the consideration of the report of the Commission on the work of its seventy-fourth session').

[25] See e.g. Łukasz Kułaga 'Prohibition of Massive and Serious Pollution of Marine Environment as a Jus Cogens: Identification, Legal Bases and Consequences in View of the Recent Work of the International Law Commission' (2022) 144 *Marine Policy*; Dinah Shelton *Jus Cogens* (Oxford University Press, 2022), especially chapter 4; Ana Zdravkovic ' Finding the Core of International Law—Jus Cogens in the Work of International Law Commission' (2019) 5 *South Eastern Europe and European Union—Legal Issues* 141; Francesco Maiello 'The Intervention in the Light of the Provisions of Serious Breaches

Within a few weeks of being adopted, these Draft Conclusions had already been referred to in the report of a UN Special Rapporteur.[26]

At the same time, it seems safe to say that *jus cogens* will continue to be invoked in practice, whether before courts or any other forum in which international law is invoked. Thus, the situation depicted by Abi Saab and Brownlie's words, to the effect that *jus cogens* is a car stuck in the garage, is well and truly behind us.[27] What the Draft Conclusions offer is a common language with which to engage when *jus cogens* is invoked. The use of the Draft Conclusions offers the possibility for us to assess their existence, their breach, and their main consequences from a common prism. Without this common language, *jus cogens*, though no longer stuck in the garage, will remain in the eye of the beholder, with determinations of peremptoriness ultimately being dependent on policy preferences, and the consequences varying, depending only on the decision-maker.

of *Jus Cogens*' (2022) 8 *Italian Law Journal* 447; Patricia V. Sellers '*Jus Cogens*: Redux' (2022) 116 *AJIL Unbound* 281; Kateryna Vazhna 'The Obligation Not to Recognise as Lawful the Situation which has Arisen as a Result of Violations of Peremptory Norms of General International Law (*Jus Cogens*) in the Current International Law' [2021] *Ukrainian Journal of International Law* 59.

[26] *Report of the Special Rapporteur on the Situation of Human Rights in the Palestinian Territories Occupied since 1967* (Francesca Albanese) (A/77/356), 9.

[27] See Georges Abi-Saab 'The Third World and the Future of the International Legal Order' (1973) 29 *Revue egyptienne de droit international* 27, 53; Ian Brownlie 'Comment' in Antonio Cassese and Joseph Weiler (eds) *Change and Stability in International Law-Making* (Walter de Gruyter, 1988), 110.

APPENDIX

ILC(LXVIII)/DC/JC/WP.1
ENGLISH AND FRENCH ONLY

20 July 2016

INTERNATIONAL LAW COMMISSION
Sixty-eighth session
Geneva, 2 May to 10 June and 4 July to 12 August 2016

Drafting Committee

Jus Cogens

Proposal of the Special Rapporteur regarding draft conclusion 3, paragraph 1

Draft conclusion 3

…

1. A peremptory norm of general international law (*jus cogens*) is a norm accepted and recognized by the international community [of States] as a whole as a norm from which no derogation is permitted and which can be modified only by a subsequent norm of general international law having the same character.

delete (?)

…

ILC(LXXIII)/DC/JC/WP.3
4 May 2022
English, French and Spanish only

INTERNATIONAL LAW COMMISSION
Seventy-third session
Geneva, 18 April–3 June and 4 July–5 August 2022

Drafting Committee

Peremptory norms of general international law (*jus cogens*)

Proposal by the Special Rapporteur for Draft Conclusion 17, paragraph 1

1. Peremptory norms of general international law (*jus cogens*) give rise to obligations owed to the international community as a whole (obligations *erga omnes*), in relation to which all States have a legal interest.

Someone should point out para 3

27 April 2022

Proposal by Mr. Wood for draft conclusion 3

Peremptory norms of general international law (jus cogens) reflect and protect fundamental values of the international community. They are universally applicable and are superior to other rules of international law.

13 July 2017
4:30pm

Draft conclusion 4

Criteria for *jus cogens*

To identify a peremptory norm of general international law *(jus cogens)*, it is necessary to establish that the norm in question meets the following criteria:

(a) it is a norm of general international law; and
(b) it is accepted and recognised by the international community of States as a whole as a norm from which no derogation is permitted and which can be modified only by a subsequent norm of general international law having the same character.

Projet de conclusion 4

Critères du *jus cogens*

Pour identifier une norme péremptoire du droit international *(jus cogens)*, il est nécessaire de démontrer que la norme en question satisfait les critères suivants:

a) être une norme du droit international général; et
b) être acceptée et reconnue par la communauté internationale des États dans son ensemble en/ tant que norme dont aucune dérogation n'est permise et qui ne peut être modifiée que par une nouvelle norme du droit international général ayant le même caractère.

—

ILC(LXIX)/DC/JC/WP.1
ENGLISH AND FRENCH ONLY

13 July 2017

INTERNATIONAL LAW COMMISSION
Sixty-ninth session
Geneva, 1 May – 2 June and 3 July – 4 August 2017

Drafting Committee

Peremptory norms of general international law *(jus cogens)*

Revised proposal for draft conclusion 4, by the Special Rapporteur

Draft conclusion 4

Criteria for *jus cogens*

To identify a norm as one of *jus cogens*, it is necessary to show that the norm in question meets two criteria:

(a) It must be a norm of general international law; and
(b) It must be accepted and recognised by the international community of States as a whole as:
  (i) a norm from which no derogation is permitted;
  (ii) a norm that can be modified only by a subsequent norm of general international law having the same character.

ILC(LXIX)/DC/JC/WP.3
ENGLISH AND FRENCH ONLY

20 July 2017

INTERNATIONAL LAW COMMISSION
Sixty-ninth session
Geneva, 1 May – 2 June and 3 July – 4 August 2017

Drafting Committee

Peremptory norms of general international law *(jus cogens)*

Revised proposal by the Special Rapporteur for draft conclusion 5

Draft Conclusion 5

General International Law

1. [adopted]
2. Treaty provisions and general principles of law may also serve as bases for peremptory norms of general international law (*jus cogens*).

—

ILC(LXIX)/DC/JC/WP.2
ENGLISH AND FRENCH ONLY

17 July 2017

INTERNATIONAL LAW COMMISSION
Sixty-ninth session
Geneva, 1 May – 2 June and 3 July – 4 August 2017

Drafting Committee

Peremptory norms of general international law *(jus cogens)*
Proposal for draft conclusion 5, by the Special Rapporteur

Draft Conclusion 5

Sources of General International Law

1. ~~A norm of general international law is one which has a general scope of application.~~

2. Customary international law is the most common **source** ~~for the formation~~ of peremptory norms of general international law (*jus cogens*). ~~norms of general international law.~~

3. General principles of law can **also serve as a source of peremptory norms** of **general international law *(jus cogens)*** ~~and treaty law can reflect or give rise to a norm of general international law capable of becoming a jus cogens norm.~~

4. Provisions in multilateral treaties may reflect **and give rise to peremptory norms of general international law (*jus cogens*).**

ILC(LXIX)/DC/JC/WP.2
ENGLISH AND FRENCH
ONLY

17 July 2017

INTERNATIONAL LAW COMMISSION
Sixty-ninth session
Geneva, 1 May – 2 June and 3 July – 4 August 2017

Drafting Committee

Peremptory norms of general international law *(jus cogens)*
Proposal for draft conclusion 5, by the Special Rapporteur

Draft Conclusion 5

Sources of General International Law

1. ~~A norm of general international law is one which has a general scope of application.~~

2. Customary international law is the most common **source** ~~for the formation~~ of peremptory norms of general international law *(jus cogens)*. ~~norms of general international law.~~

3. General principles of law can **also serve as a source of peremptory norms of general international law *(jus cogens)*** ~~and treaty law can reflect or give rise to a norm of general international law capable of becoming a jus cogens norm.~~

4. Provisions in multilateral treaties may reflect **and give rise to peremptory norms of general international law *(jus cogens)*.**

ILC(LXIX)/DC/JC/WP.4
ENGLISH AND FRENCH ONLY

20 July 2017

INTERNATIONAL LAW COMMISSION
Sixty-ninth session
Geneva, 1 May – 2 June and 3 July – 4 August 2017

Drafting Committee

Peremptory norms of general international law *(jus cogens)*

Revised proposal by the Special Rapporteur for draft conclusions 6, 7 and 9

Draft Conclusion 6

Acceptance and Recognition

1. The requirement of "acceptance and recognition" as a criterion for peremptory norms of general international law (*jus cogens*) is distinct from acceptance and recognition as law.

2. To identify a norm as a peremptory norm of general international law (*jus cogens*), it is necessary to present evidence that such a norm is accepted and recognized as one from which no derogation is permitted.

3. Evidence that a norm of general international law protects and reflects fundamental values of the international community, is hierarchically superior to other norms of general international law and is universally applicable can contribute to the criterion of acceptance and recognition.

Chair:
Please ask them
to be brief!

ILC(LXIX)/DC/JC/WP.3
ENGLISH AND FRENCH ONLY

20 July 2017

INTERNATIONAL LAW COMMISSION
Sixty-ninth session
Geneva, 1 May – 2 June and 3 July – 4 August 2017

Drafting Committee

Peremptory norms of general international law *(jus cogens)*

Revised proposal by the Special Rapporteur for draft conclusion 5

Draft Conclusion 5
General International Law

1. [adopted]

2. Treaty provisions and general principles of law may also serve as bases for peremptory norms of general international law (*jus cogens*).

—

Draft Conclusion 7

International Community of States as a Whole

1. It is the acceptance and recognition of the international community of States as a whole that is relevant in the identification of peremptory norms of general international law (*jus cogens*).

2. Acceptance and recognition by a very large majority of States is sufficient for the identification of a norm as a peremptory norm of general international law (*jus cogens*). Acceptance and recognition by all states is not required.

3. While the attitudes of other actors may be relevant in providing context and assessing the acceptance and recognition of the international community of States as a whole, these cannot, in and of themselves, constitute acceptance and recognition by the international community of States as a whole.

Draft Conclusion 9

....

ILC(LXXIII)/DC/JC/WP.1
29 April 2022
English, French and Spanish only

INTERNATIONAL LAW COMMISSION
Seventy-third session
Geneva, 18 April–3 June and 4 July–5 August 2022

Drafting Committee

Peremptory norms of general international law (*jus cogens*)

Proposal by the Special Rapporteur for Draft Conclusion 8, paragraph 2

2. Forms of evidence of acceptance and recognition include, but are not limited to: public statements made on behalf of States; official publications; government legal opinions; diplomatic correspondence; constitutions, legislative and administrative acts; decisions of national courts; treaty provisions; and resolutions adopted by an international organization or at an intergovernmental conference; and other conduct of States.

ILC(LXXIII)/DC/JC/WP.1
29 April 2022
English, French and Spanish only

INTERNATIONAL LAW COMMISSION
Seventy-third session
Geneva, 18 April–3 June and 4 July–5 August 2022

Drafting Committee

Peremptory norms of general international law (*jus cogens*)

Proposal by the Special Rapporteur for Draft Conclusion 8, paragraph 2

2. Forms of evidence of acceptance and recognition include, but are not limited to: public statements made on behalf of States; ~~official publications~~; government legal opinions; diplomatic correspondence; constitutions, legislative and administrative acts; decisions of national courts; treaty provisions; ~~and~~ resolutions adopted by an international organization or at an intergovernmental conference; and other conduct of States.

Draft conclusion 9.

2 May 2018

4:20 pm

<u>Draft conclusion 9, paragraph 1, as provisionally adopted</u>

1. **Evidence of acceptance and recognition that a norm of general international law is a peremptory norm (*jus cogens*) may take a wide range of forms.**

1. **Les preuves de l'acceptation et de la reconnaissance qu'une norme du droit international general est une norme impérative (*jus cogens*) peut revêtir une large variété de formes.**

ILC(LXX)/DC/JC/WP.1
ENGLISH AND FRENCH ONLY

4 May 2018

INTERNATIONAL LAW COMMISSION
Seventieth session
New York, 30 April – 1 June, and Geneva, 2 July – 10 August 2018

Drafting Committee

Peremptory norms of general international law *(Jus cogens)*

Revised proposal by the Special Rapporteur for draft conclusion 9 [9 (3), (4)]

Draft Conclusion 9

Judicial decisions and Teachings

1. Judicial decisions of international courts and tribunals, in particular of the International Court of Justice, are a subsidiary means for determining **the** peremptory character of norms of general international law (*jus cogens*).
2. The work of the International Law Commission, the pronouncement of expert bodies and the teachings of the most highly qualified publicists of various nations may also serve as a subsidiary means for determining the peremptory character of norms of general international law (*jus cogens*).

ILC(LXX)DC/JC/WP.1
4 mai 2018

ANGLAIS ET FRANÇAIS SEULEMENT

Commission du droit international
Soixante-dixième session
New York, 30 avril – 1er juin, et Genève, 2 juillet – 10 août 2018

Comité de rédaction

Normes impératives du droit international général (*jus cogens*)

Projet de conclusion 9 [9(3), (4)] révisé par le Rapporteur spécial

Décisions judiciaires et doctrine

1. Les décisions judiciaires des cours et tribunaux internationaux, notamment de la Cour internationale de justice, constituent un moyen auxiliaire de détermination du caractère impératif des normes du droit international général (*jus cogens*).
2. Les travaux de la Commission du droit international, les déclarations des organes d'experts et la doctrine des publicistes les plus qualifiés des différentes nations peuvent aussi constituer un moyen auxiliaire de détermination des normes du droit international général (*jus cogens*).

ILC(LXX)DC/JC/CRD.2
17 avril 2018

ANGLAIS ET FRANÇAIS SEULEMENT

Commission du droit international
Soixante-dixième session
New York, 30 avril – 1er juin, et Genève, 2 juillet – 10 août 2018

Comité de rédaction

Normes impératives du droit international général (*jus cogens*)

Projet de conclusion 9, tel que proposé par le Rapporteur spécial dans son second rapport

Projet de conclusion 9

Preuves de l'acceptation et de la reconnaissance

1. Les preuves de l'acceptation et de la reconnaissance d'une norme du droit international général en tant que norme de *jus cogens* peuvent prendre des formes et être reflétées dans des documents divers.
2. Les documents ci-après peuvent fournir la preuve de l'acceptation et de la reconnaissance du fait qu'une norme du droit international général a été élevée au rang de jus cogens : traités, résolutions adoptées par des organisations internationales, déclarations publiques faites au nom des États, publications officielles, avis juridiques gouvernementaux, correspondance diplomatique et décisions des juridictions nationales.
3. Les jugements et décisions des cours et tribunaux internationaux peuvent également servir de preuve de l'acceptation et la reconnaissance pour l'identification d'une norme en tant que norme de *jus cogens* du droit international.
4. D'autres documents, comme ceux issus des travaux de la Commission du droit international, des travaux d'oranges d'experts et de la doctrine, peuvent constituer un moyen secondaire d'identification des normes du droit international auxquelles aucune dérogation n'est permise. Ces documents peuvent également être utiles pour évaluer le poids des documents principaux.

---

10 July 2018, 3:30 pm

Texts and titles provisionally adopted by the Drafting Committee thusfar

Draft conclusion 10 [10 (1), (2)]

Invalidity and termination of treaties in conflict with a peremptory norm of general international law (*jus cogens*)

1. A treaty is void if, at the time of its conclusion, it conflicts with a peremptory norm of general international law (*jus cogens*). The provisions of such a treaty have no legal force.
2. If a new peremptory norm of general international law (*jus cogens*) emerges, any existing treaty which is in conflict with that norm becomes void and terminates. The parties to such a treaty are released from any obligation further to perform the treaty.

Draft conclusion 11

. . .

1. A treaty which, at the time of its conclusion, conflicts with a peremptory norm of general international law (*jus cogens*) is void in whole, and no separation of the provisions of the treaty is permitted.

. . .

ILC(LXXIII)/DC/JC/WP.2
3 May 2022
English, French and Spanish only

INTERNATIONAL LAW COMMISSION
Seventy-third session
Geneva, 18 April–3 June and 4 July–5 August 2022

Drafting Committee

Peremptory norms of general international law (*jus cogens*)

Proposal by the Special Rapporteur for Draft Conclusion 10, paragraph 2

2. Subject to paragraph 2 of Draft Conclusion 11, if a new peremptory norm of general international law (*jus cogens*) emerges, any existing treaty which is in conflict with that norm becomes void and terminates. The parties to such a treaty are released from any obligation further to perform the treaty.

3. Para 2 of DC 11 is subject to

5:35 pm

Draft conclusion 11

2. A treaty which becomes void because of the emergence of a new peremptory norm of general international law (*jus cogens*) terminates in whole, unless:
   (a) the provisions that are in conflict with a peremptory norm of general international law (*jus cogens*) are separable from the remainder of the treaty with regard to their application;
   (b) it appears from the treaty or is otherwise established that acceptance of those provisions that are in conflict with a peremptory norm of general international law (*jus cogens*) was not an essential basis of the consent to the treaty; and
   (c) continued performance of the remainder of the treaty would not be unjust.

ILC(LXX)/DC/JC/WP.5
ENGLISH AND FRENCH ONLY

11 July 2018

INTERNATIONAL LAW COMMISSION
Seventieth session
New York, 30 April –1 June, and Geneva, 2 July –10 August 2018

Drafting Committee

Peremptory norms of general international law (*jus cogens*)

Revised proposal by the Special Rapporteur for draft conclusion 12, paragraph 1

1. Parties to a treaty which is void as a result of being in conflict with a peremptory norm of general international law (*jus cogens*) at the time of the treaty's conclusion have a legal obligation to:
   (a) eliminate as far as possible the consequences of any act performed in reliance on any provision of the treaty which conflicts with a peremptory norm of general international law (*jus cogens*); and
   (b) bring their mutual relations into conformity with the peremptory norm of general international law (*jus cogens*).

11 July 2018, 1:00 pm

Texts and titles provisionally adopted by the Drafting Committee thusfar

Draft conclusion 12

Consequences of the invalidity and termination of a treaty which conflicts with a peremptory norm of general international law *(jus cogens)*

1. Parties to a treaty which is void as a result of being in conflict with a peremptory norm of general international law (*jus cogens*) at the time of the treaty's conclusion have a legal obligation to:
   (a) eliminate as far as possible the consequences of any act performed in reliance on any provision of the treaty which conflicts with a peremptory norm of general international law (*jus cogens*); and
   (b) bring their mutual relations into conformity with the peremptory norm of general international law (*jus cogens*).
2. The termination of a treaty on account of the emergence of a new peremptory norm of general international law (*jus cogens*) does not affect any right, obligation or legal situation created through the execution of the treaty prior to the termination of the treaty, provided that those rights, obligations or situations may thereafter be maintained only to the extent that their maintenance is not in itself in conflict with the new peremptory norm of general international law (*jus cogens*).

11 July 2018, 1:00 pm

Texts and titles provisionally adopted by the Drafting Committee thusfar

Draft conclusion 12

Consequences of the invalidity and termination of a treaty which conflicts with a peremptory norm of general international law *(Jus cogens)*

1. Parties to a treaty which is void as a result of being in conflict with a peremptory norm of general international law (*jus cogens*) at the time of the treaty's conclusion have a legal obligation to:
   (a) eliminate as far as possible the consequences of any act performed in reliance on any provision of the treaty which conflicts with a peremptory norm of general international law (*jus cogens*); and
   (b) bring their mutual relations into conformity with the peremptory norm of general international law (*jus cogens*).
2. The termination of a treaty on account of the emergence of a new peremptory norm of general international law (*jus cogens*) does not affect any right, obligation or legal situation created through the execution of the treaty prior to the termination of the treaty, provided that those rights, obligations or situations may thereafter be maintained only to the extent that their maintenance is not in itself in conflict with the new peremptory norm of general international law (*jus cogens*).

Texts and titles provisionally adopted by the Drafting Committee thusfar

Draft conclusion 12

Consequences of the invalidity and termination of a treaty which conflicts with a peremptory norm of general international law *(Jus cogens)*

1. Parties to a treaty which is void as a result of being in conflict with a peremptory norm of general international law (*jus cogens*) at the time of the treaty's conclusion have a legal obligation to:
   (a) eliminate as far as possible the consequences of any act performed in reliance on any provision of the treaty which conflicts with a peremptory norm of general international law (*jus cogens*); and
   (b) bring their mutual relations into conformity with the peremptory norm of general international law (*jus cogens*).
2. The termination of a treaty on account of the emergence of a new peremptory norm of general international law (*jus cogens*) does not affect any right, obligation or legal situation created through the execution of the treaty prior to the termination of the treaty, provided that those rights, obligations or situations may thereafter be maintained only to the extent that their maintenance is not in itself in conflict with the new peremptory norm of general international law (*jus cogens*).

ILC(LXXI)DC/JC/WP.2
1 mai 2019

ANGLAIS ET FRANÇAIS SEULEMENT

Commission du droit international
Soixante et onzième session
Genève, 29 avril – 7 juin et 8 juillet – 9 août 2019

Comité de rédaction

Normes impératives du droit international général (*jus cogens*)

Projet de conclusion 15 (1) révisé par le Rapporteur spécial

1. Une règle de droit international coutumier ne peut se former si elle est en conflit avec une norme impérative du droit international général (*jus cogens*). Ceci est sans préjudice de la possible modification d'une norme impérative du droit international général (*jus cogens*) par une nouvelle norme ayant le même caractère.

30 April 2019
4:40 pm

Draft conclusion 15

1. A rule of customary international law does not come into existence if it conflicts with a peremptory norm of general international law (*jus cogens*), unless the underlying rule itself attains the status of a peremptory norm of general international law (*jus cogens*).

ILC(LXXI)/DC/JC/WP.2
ENGLISH AND FRENCH ONLY

1 May 2019

INTERNATIONAL LAW COMMISSION
Seventy-first session
Geneva, 29 April – 7 June and 8 July – 9 August 2019

Drafting Committee

Peremptory norms of general international law *(jus cogens)*

Revised proposal by the Special Rapporteur for draft conclusion 15, paragraph 1

1. A rule of customary international law does not come into existence if it conflicts with a peremptory norm of general international law (*jus cogens*). This is without prejudice to the possible modification of a peremptory norm of general international law *(jus cogens)* by a subsequent norm having the same character.

1 May 2019

4:45 pm

Draft conclusion 16

1. A unilateral act capable of creating legal obligations that conflict with a peremptory norm of general international law *(jus cogens)* is void.

2. A unilateral act that has created legal obligations that conflict with a new peremptory norm of general international law *(jus cogens)* becomes void.

ILC(LXXI)/DC/JC/WP.4
ENGLISH AND FRENCH ONLY

2 May 2019

INTERNATIONAL LAW COMMISSION
Seventy-first session
Geneva, 29 April – 7 June and 8 July – 9 August 2019

Drafting Committee

Peremptory norms of general international law (*jus cogens*)

Revised proposal by the Special Rapporteur for draft conclusion 16 (2)

1. [...]
2. Obligations under international law produced by a unilateral act cease to exist if and to the extent that they conflict with a new peremptory norm of general international law (*jus cogens*).

ILC(LXXI)/DC/JC/WP.4
ENGLISH AND FRENCH ONLY

2 May 2019

INTERNATIONAL LAW COMMISSION
Seventy-first session
Geneva, 29 April – 7 June and 8 July – 9 August 2019

Drafting Committee

Peremptory norms of general international law *(jus cogens)*

Revised proposal by the Special Rapporteur for draft conclusion 16 (2)

1. [...]

2. Obligations under international law produced by a unilateral act cease to exist if and to the extent that they conflict with a new peremptory norm of general international law (*jus cogens*).

ILC(LXXI)/DC/JC/WP.3
ENGLISH AND FRENCH ONLY

2 May 2019

INTERNATIONAL LAW COMMISSION
Seventy-first session
Geneva, 29 April – 7 June and 8 July – 9 August 2019

Drafting Committee

Peremptory norms of general international law *(jus cogens)*

Revised proposal by the Special Rapporteur for draft conclusion 16 (1)

1. A unilateral act manifesting the will to undertake obligations under international law that are in conflict with a peremptory norm of general international law (*jus cogens*) does not produce such obligations.

ILC(LXXI)/DC/JC/WP.4
ENGLISH AND FRENCH ONLY

2 May 2019

INTERNATIONAL LAW COMMISSION
Seventy-first session
Geneva, 29 April – 7 June and 8 July – 9 August 2019

Drafting Committee

Peremptory norms of general international law (*jus cogens*)

Revised proposal by the Special Rapporteur for draft conclusion 16 (2)

1. [. . .]
2. Obligations under international law produced by a unilateral act cease to exist if and to the extent that they conflict with a new peremptory norm of general international law (*jus cogens*).

2 May 2019

16:50

Draft conclusion 16

1. A resolution, decision or other act of an international organization that would otherwise be binding does not create obligations under international law if and to the extent that it conflicts with a peremptory norm of general international law *(jus cogens)*.

ILC(LXXIII)/DC/JC/WP.3
4 May 2022
English, French and Spanish only

INTERNATIONAL LAW COMMISSION
Seventy-third session
Geneva, 18 April–3 June and 4 July–5 August 2022

Drafting Committee

Peremptory norms of general international law (*jus cogens*)

Proposal by the Special Rapporteur for Draft Conclusion 17, paragraph 1

1. Peremptory norms of general international law (*jus cogens*) give rise to obligations owed to the international community as a whole (obligations *erga omnes*), in relation to which all States have a legal interest.

ILC(LXXI)DC/JC/WP.6
15 mai 2019

ANGLAIS ET FRANÇAIS SEULEMENT

Commission du droit international
Soixante et onzième session
Genève, 29 avril – 7 juin et 8 juillet – 9 août 2019

Comité de rédaction

Normes impératives du droit international général (*jus cogens*)

Projet de conclusion 15 *bis* proposé par le Rapporteur spécial

Conséquences des normes impératives du droit international général (*Jus cogens*) sur les principes généraux du droit

1. Un principe général du droit ne peut exister s'il est en conflit avec une norme impérative du droit international général (*jus cogens*). Ceci est sans préjudice de la possible modification d'une norme impérative du droit international général (*jus cogens*) par une nouvelle norme du droit international général ayant le même caractère.
2. Un principe général de droit n'ayant pas un caractère impératif cesse d'exister si et dans la mesure où survient une nouvelle norme impérative du droit international général (*jus cogens*) en conflit avec elle.

Projet de conclusion 17 *bis* proposé par le Rapporteur spécial

Interprétation conforme aux normes impératives de droit international général *(jus cogens)*

Une règle de droit international devrait, dans la mesure du possible, être interprétée de manière à la rendre compatible avec les normes impératives du droit international général (*jus cogens*).

ILC(LXXI)/DC/JC/WP.6
ENGLISH AND FRENCH ONLY

15 May 2019

INTERNATIONAL LAW COMMISSION
Seventy-first session
Geneva, 29 April – 7 June and 8 July – 9 August 2019

Drafting Committee

Peremptory norms of general international law (*jus cogens*)

Proposals of the Special Rapporteur

Draft conclusion 15 *bis*

Consequences of peremptory norms of general international law (*jus cogens*) for general principles of law

1. A general principle of law does not come into existence if it conflicts with a peremptory norm of general international law (*jus cogens*). This is without prejudice to the possible modification of a peremptory norm of general international law (*jus cogens*) by a subsequent norm of general international law having the same character.
2 A general principle of law not of a peremptory character ceases to exist if and to the extent that it conflicts with a new peremptory norm of general international law (*jus cogens*).

Draft conclusion 17 *bis*

Interpretation consistent with peremptory norms of general international law (*jus cogens*)

A rule of international law should, as far as possible, be interpreted in a way that renders it consistent with peremptory norms of general international law (*jus cogens*).

Draft conclusions on peremptory norms of general international law (*jus cogens*)

List of issues for the toilettage

- In DC 14, para. 1, the words "**a conflict with**" might need to be inserted after the word "invokes".
- Harmonize the use of "effects" v. "consequences" in the text and titles of the draft conclusions. The scope of the draft conclusions covers the "**legal effects**" of peremptory norms of general international law (*jus cogens*).
  - In this regard see also the reference to "under international law" in DCs 16, 17 and 21.
- Consider adding a draft conclusion 15*bis* on general principles.
- Consider when to refer to States only and when to include other actors such as international organizations
  - For example: In DC 16, Nolte suggest adding "by a State" or "of a State"
- DC 17 should read: "A resolution, decision or other act of an international organization that would otherwise be binding does not create obligations under international law if and to the extent that **they** conflict~~s~~ with a peremptory norm of general international law (*jus cogens*)".
- The titles of DC 15, 16 and 17 should be harmonized with the title of DC10 ("[Non-existence] of a rule of customary international law in conflict with a peremptory norm of general international law (*jus cogens*)")
  - Note: finding a title that follows the structure of DC 10 for unilateral acts and acts of IOs will be more difficult because it is not the act itself that does not exist/ceases to exist but rather the obligation created by that act
- In the text and title of 17, "or" should be replaced by "and" so that it would read: "Resolutions, decisions, **and** other acts of international organizations"
  - This is consistent with the definition of "rules of the organization" in article 2(b) of the articles on the responsibility of international organization
  - It might also be better to use "international organization" in the singular (also in line with the articles on the responsibility of international organizations"
- In DCs 15, 16 and 17 "to the extent that" should be place within commas, i.e. "... if, and to the extent that, ..."
- In DC 18, it may be necessary to add a comma before "in accordance with the rules on State responsibility for internationally wrongful acts"

2 May 2019

16:50

Draft conclusion 17

1. A resolution, decision or other act of an international organization that would otherwise be binding does not create obligations under international law if and to the extent that it conflicts with a peremptory norm of general international law (*jus cogens*).

ILC(LXXI)/DC/JC/WP.5
ENGLISH AND FRENCH ONLY

6 May 2019

INTERNATIONAL LAW COMMISSION
Seventy-first session
Geneva, 29 April – 7 June and 8 July – 9 August 2019

Drafting Committee

Peremptory norms of general international law (*jus cogens*)

Revised proposal by the Special Rapporteur for draft conclusion 18

Peremptory norms of general international law (*jus cogens*) give rise to obligations *erga omnes*, in which all States have an interest.

Proposal by the Special Rapporteur for draft conclusion 18 *bis*

Any state is entitled to invoke the responsibility of another State for a breach of a peremptory norm of general international law (*jus cogens*).

ILC(LXXI)/DC/JC/WP.8
ENGLISH AND FRENCH ONLY

20 May 2019

INTERNATIONAL LAW COMMISSION
Seventy-first session
Geneva, 29 April – 7 June and 8 July – 9 August 2019

Drafting Committee

Peremptory norms of general international law *(jus cogens)*

Proposal of the Special Rapporteur

Draft conclusion 17 *bis*

Interpretation consistent with peremptory norms of general international law *(jus cogens)*

Where there is an apparent conflict between a peremptory norm of general international law *(jus cogens)* and another rule of international law, the latter is, as far as possible, to be interpreted and applied so as to avoid such conflict.

Some members → Saboia

may be applied

20 May 2019

4:45 pm

Draft conclusion 17 *bis*

Interpretation and application consistent with peremptory norms of general international law *(jus cogens)*

Where it appears that there may be a conflict between a peremptory norm of general international law *(jus cogens)* and another rule of international law, the latter is, as far as possible, to be interpreted [and applied] so as to be consistent with the former.

Wood: "and applied" → can go ✓ dele

Oral/Ch: ~~and~~ "applied" → ✓ ~~delete~~ keep

– Murphy: "~~and~~ delete ✓ dele

Nolte: no indep application ⊗ keep

~~Saboia:~~

~~Saboia: Jalloh~~

Jalloh: Nolte → ⊗ / → keep

~~Cissé~~ Huang: ⊗ ✓ dele

Saboia: keep ⊗

Cissé: keep [ask in PG]

Park: delete

Argüello Gómez: → "may be applied"

Vasquez Bermudez: [applied] → keep

Aurescu: keep

ESH: keep [former ⇒ PN] → Jalloh

ILC(LXX)/DC/JC/WP.3
ENGLISH ONLY

10 July 2018

INTERNATIONAL LAW COMMISSION
Seventieth session
New York, 30 April – 1 June, and Geneva, 2 July – 10 August 2018

Drafting Committee

Peremptory norms of general international law (*jus cogens*)

Proposal by Georg Nolte

Alternative A: Draft conclusion 14, new paragraph 1 (if adopted, current paragraphs 1 and 2 would become paragraphs 2 and 3)

1. A State party which invokes the invalidity of a treaty as resulting from a conflict with a peremptory rule of general international law (*jus cogens*) shall notify the other parties of its claim. If another party raises an objection, the States parties concerned shall negotiate in good faith with a view to agreeing on a solution or an appropriate procedure to resolve the dispute. The invoking party may give effect to its claim in relation to any objecting party after the invalidity of the treaty has been determined as agreed by them.

Alternative B: General draft conclusion on procedure

A State which invokes the invalidity of an obligation as resulting from a conflict with a peremptory rule of general international law (*jus cogens*) shall notify other States concerned of its claim. If another State raises an objection, the States concerned shall negotiate in good faith with a view to agreeing on a solution or an appropriate procedure to resolve the dispute. The invoking State may give effect to its claim in relation to any objecting State after the invalidity of the obligation has been determined as agreed by them.

12 July 2018

3:00 pm

Replace DC 14 with:

1. A State which invokes a peremptory norm of general international law (*jus cogens*) as a ground for the invalidity or termination of a rule of international law must notify other States concerned of its claim. If none of the other States concerned raises an objection within a period which, except in cases of special urgency, shall not be less than three months, the invoking State may give effect to its claim.
2. If any State concerned raises an objection, then the States concerned shall seek a solution through the means indicated in Article 33 of the Charter of the United Nations.
3. If no solution is reached within a period of twelve months, and the objecting State or States concerned offer to submit the matter to the International Court of Justice, the invoking State may not give effect to its claim until the dispute is resolved.
4. This draft conclusion is without prejudice to the procedural obligations set forth in the Vienna Convention on the Law of Treaties and the relevant rules concerning the jurisdiction of the International Court of Justice.

Rev.1

12 July 2018

5:00 pm

Replace DC 14 with:

1. A State which invokes a peremptory norm of general international law (*jus cogens*) as a ground for the invalidity or termination of a treaty or other rule of international law or binding decisions of an international organisation must notify other States and international organisations concerned of its claim. The notification shall be in writing and shall indicate the measure proposed to be taken with respect to the rule of international law in question.

1 *bis*. If none of the other States concerned raises an objection within a period which, except in cases of special urgency, shall not be less than three months, the invoking State may give effect to its claim.

2. If any State concerned raises an objection, then the States concerned shall seek a solution through the means indicated in Article 33 of the Charter of the United Nations.

3. If no solution is reached within a period of twelve months, and the objecting State or States concerned offer to submit the matter to the International Court of Justice, the invoking State may not give effect to its claim until the dispute is resolved.

4. This draft conclusion is without prejudice to the procedural obligations set forth in the Vienna Convention on the Law of Treaties and the relevant rules concerning the jurisdiction of the International Court of Justice.

12 juillet 2018

15:00

Remplacez DC 14 par:

1. Un État qui invoque une norme impérative du droit international général (*jus cogens*) comme cause de nullité ou d'extinction d'une règle de droit international doit notifier sa prétention aux États concernés. Si aucun de ces Etats concernés ne soulève une objection dans un délai qui, sauf en cas d'urgence spéciale, ne peut être inférieur à trois mois, l'Etat invoquant la nullité ou l'extinction peut donner suite à sa prétention.

2. Si un Etat concerné soulève une objection, les Etats concernés doivent rechercher une solution par les moyens indiqués à l'article 33 de la Charte des Nations Unies.

3. Si aucune solution n'est trouvée dans un délai de douze mois et que l'État ou les États concernés soulevant une objection proposent de soumettre l'affaire à la Cour internationale de justice, l'État invoquant la nullité ou l'extinction ne peut donner suite à sa prétention qu'après la résolution du différend.

4. Ce projet de conclusion est sans préjudice aux obligations procédurales énoncées dans la Convention de Vienne sur le droit des traités et aux règles pertinentes concernant la compétence de la Cour internationale de Justice.

I want to make a proposal at some [illegible]

mean

12 July 2018

3:00 pm

Replace DC 14 with:

1. A State which invokes a peremptory norm of general international law (*jus cogens*) as a ground for the invalidity or termination of a rule of international law must notify other States concerned of its claim. If none of the other States concerned raises an objection within a period which, except in cases of special urgency, shall not be less than three months, the invoking State may give effect to its claim.
2. If any State concerned raises an objection, then the States concerned shall seek a solution through the means indicated in Article 33 of the Charter of the United Nations.
3. If no solution is reached within a period of twelve months, and the objecting State or States concerned offer to submit the matter to the International Court of Justice, the invoking State may not give effect to its claim until the dispute is resolved.
4. This draft conclusion is without prejudice to the procedural obligations set forth in the Vienna Convention on the Law of Treaties and the relevant rules concerning the jurisdiction of the International Court of Justice.

ILC(LXXIII)/DC/JC/WP.5
5 May 2022
English, French and Spanish only

INTERNATIONAL LAW COMMISSION
Seventy-third session
Geneva, 18 April–3 June and 4 July–5 August 2022

Drafting Committee

Peremptory norms of general international law (*jus cogens*)

Proposal by the Special Rapporteur for Draft Conclusion 22

Recommended procedure

1. A State which invokes a peremptory norm of general international law (*jus cogens*) as a ground for the invalidity or termination of a rule of international law should do so by notifying other States concerned of its claim. The notification should be in writing and should indicate the measure proposed to be taken with respect to the rule of international law in question.

2. If none of the other States raises an objection within a period which, except in cases of special urgency, will not be less than three months, the invoking State may carry out the measure which it has proposed.

3. If any State concerned raises an objection, then the States concerned should seek a solution through the means indicated in Article 33 of the Charter of the United Nations. If no solution is reached within a period of twelve months, and the objecting State offers to submit the matter to the International Court of Justice or to some other procedure entailing binding decisions, the invoking State should not carry out the measure which it has proposed until the dispute is resolved.

4. This draft conclusion is without prejudice to the procedures set forth in the Vienna Convention on the Law of Treaties, or to the relevant rules concerning the jurisdiction ~~and procedure~~ of the International Court of Justice or other applicable dispute settlement provisions agreed by the States concerned.

ILC(LXXI)DC/JC/WP.1
6 mai 2019

ANGLAIS ET FRANÇAIS SEULEMENT

Commission du droit international
Soixante et onzième session
Genève, 29 avril – 7 juin et 8 juillet – 9 août 2019

Comité de rédaction

Normes impératives du droit international général (*jus cogens*)

Projets de conclusion 22 et 23 révisés par le Rapporteur spécial

Les présents projets de conclusion sont sans préjudice aux conséquences de normes impératives [spécifiques] [individuelles] [particulières] du droit international général (*jus cogens*).

ILC(LXXI)DC/JC/WP.I
6 mai 2019

ANGLAIS ET FRANÇAIS SEULEMENT

Commission du droit international
Soixante et onzième session
Genève, 29 avril – 7 juin et 8 juillet – 9 août 2019

Comité de rédaction

Normes impératives du droit international général (*jus cogens*)

Projets de conclusion 22 et 23 révisés par le Rapporteur spécial

Les présents projets de conclusion sont sans préjudice aux conséquences de normes impératives [spécifiques] [individuelles] [particulières] du droit international général (*jus cogens*).

ILC(LXXI)DC/JC/WP.I
6 mai 2019

ANGLAIS ET FRANÇAIS SEULEMENT

Commission du droit international
Soixante et onzième session
Genève, 29 avril – 7 juin et 8 juillet – 9 août 2019

Comité de rédaction

Normes impératives du droit international général (*jus cogens*)

Projets de conclusion 22 et 23 révisés par le Rapporteur spécial

Les présents projets de conclusion sont sans préjudice aux conséquences de normes impératives [spécifiques] [individuelles] [particulières] du droit international général (*jus cogens*).

ILC(LXXI)/DC/JC/WP.1
ENGLISH ONLY

16 April 2019

INTERNATIONAL LAW COMMISSION
Seventy-first session
Geneva, 29 April – 7 June and 8 July – 9 August 2019

Drafting Committee

Peremptory norms of general international law (*jus cogens*)

Revised proposal by the Special Rapporteur for draft conclusions 22 and 23

The present draft conclusions are without prejudice to the consequences of [specific] [individual] [particular] peremptory norms of general international law (*jus cogens*).

ILC(LXXIII)/DC/JC/WP.4
5 May 2022
English, French and Spanish only

INTERNATIONAL LAW COMMISSION
Seventy-third session
Geneva, 18 April–3 June and 4 July–5 August 2022

Drafting Committee

Peremptory norms of general international law (*jus cogens*)

Proposal by the Special Rapporteur for Draft Conclusion 21, paragraph 2

[2. These draft conclusions do not address consequences arising from other breaches of peremptory norms (*jus cogens*).]

21 May 2019

5:15 pm

Draft conclusion 24

Non-exhaustive list of peremptory norms of general international law *(jus cogens)*

Without prejudice to the existence or future emergence of other peremptory norms of general international law (*jus cogens*), the Commission has previously referred to the norms contained in the annex as having attained the status of peremptory norms of general international law (*jus cogens*).

Annex

(a) the prohibition of aggression;

(b) the prohibition of genocide;

(c) the prohibition of crimes against humanity;

(d) the prohibition of war crimes;

(e) the prohibition of apartheid;

(f) the prohibition of slavery;

(g) the prohibition of torture;

(h) the right of self-determination.

ILC(LXXI)DC/JC/WP.7
16 mai 2019

ANGLAIS ET FRANÇAIS SEULEMENT

Commission du droit international
Soixante et onzième session
Genève, 29 avril – 7 juin et 8 juillet – 9 août 2019

Comité de rédaction

Normes impératives du droit international général (*jus cogens*)

Proposition du Rapporteur spécial

Projet de conclusion 24

Liste non exhaustive de normes impératives du droit international général (*jus cogens*)

L'annexe aux présents projets de conclusion contient une liste non exhaustive de normes que la Commission a précédemment qualifiées d'atteignant le statut de normes impératives du droit international général (*jus cogens*).

Annexe

Sans préjudice de l'existence ou de l'émergence future d'autres normes impératives du droit international général (*jus cogens*), les normes suivantes ont été précédemment considérées comme ayant atteint le statut de normes impératives du droit international général (*jus cogens*):

a) L'interdiction de l'agression;
b) L'interdiction du génocide;
c) L'interdiction des crimes contre l'humanité;
d) L'interdiction des crimes de guerre;
e) L'interdiction de l'apartheid;
f) L'interdiction de l'esclavage;
g) L'interdiction de la torture;
h) Le droit à l'autodétermination.

ILC(LXXI)DC/JC/CRD.3
15 mai 2019

ANGLAIS ET FRANÇAIS SEULEMENT

Commission du droit international
Soixante et onzième session
Genève, 29 avril – 7 juin et 8 juillet – 9 août 2019

Comité de rédaction

Normes impératives du droit international général (*jus cogens*)

Projet de conclusion 24, tel que proposé par le Rapporteur spécial dans son quatrième rapport

Projet de conclusion 24

Liste non exhaustive de normes impératives du droit international général *(jus cogens)*

Sans préjudice de l'existence d'autres normes impératives du droit international général (*jus cogens*), les exemples les plus largement reconnus de normes impératives du droit international général (*jus cogens*) sont les suivants:

a) L'interdiction de l'agression ou de l'emploi agressif de la force;
b) L'interdiction du génocide;
c) L'interdiction de l'esclavage;
d) L'interdiction de l'apartheid et de la discrimination raciale;
e) L'interdiction des crimes contre l'humanité;
f) L'interdiction de la torture;
g) Le droit à l'autodétermination;
h) Les règles fondamentales du droit international humanitaire.

—

ILC(LXXI)/DC/JC/CRD.3
ENGLISH AND FRENCH ONLY

15 May 2019

INTERNATIONAL LAW COMMISSION
Seventy-first session
Geneva, 29 April–7 June and 8 July–9 August 2019

Drafting Committee

Peremptory norms of general international law (*jus cogens*)

Draft Conclusions 24, as proposed by the Special Rapporteur in his fourth report

Draft conclusion 24

Non-exhaustive list of peremptory norms of general international law (*jus cogens*)

Without prejudice to the existence of other peremptory norms of general international law (*jus cogens*), the most widely recognized examples of peremptory norms of general international law (*jus cogens*) are:

(a) the prohibition of aggression or aggressive force;
(b) the prohibition of genocide;
(c) the prohibition of slavery;
(d) the prohibition of apartheid and racial discrimination;
(e) the prohibition of crimes against humanity;
(f) the prohibition of torture;
(g) the right to self-determination; and
(h) the basic rules of international humanitarian law.

ILC(LXXI)/DC/JC/WP.7
ENGLISH AND FRENCH ONLY

16 May 2019

INTERNATIONAL LAW COMMISSION
Seventy-first session
Geneva, 29 April–7 June und 8 July–9 August 2019

Drafting Committee

Peremptory arms of general international law (*jus cogens*)

Proposal of the Special Rapporteur

Draft conclusion 24

Non-exhaustive list of peremptory norms of general international law *(jus cogens)*

A non-exhaustive list of norms that the Commission has previously referred to as having attained the status of peremptory norms of general international law (*jus cogens*) is contained in the annex to the present draft conclusions.

Annex

Without prejudice to the existence or future emergence of other peremptory norms of general international law (*jus cogens*), the following norms have previously been referred to as having attained the status of peremptory norms of general international law (*jus cogens*)

(a) the prohibition of aggression;
(b) the prohibition of genocide;
(c) the prohibition of crimes against humanity;
(d) the prohibition of war crimes;
(e) the prohibition of apartheid;
(f) the prohibition of slavery;
(g) the prohibition of torture;
(h) the right of self-determination.

Select Bibliography

Textbooks and Chapters in Textbooks

Aust, Helmut Philipp 'Legal Consequences of Serious Breaches of Peremptory Norms in the Law of State of State Responsibility: Observation in the Light of the Recent Work of the International Law Commission' in Dire Tladi (ed) *Peremptory Norms of General International Law (Jus Cogens): Disquisitions and Disputations* (Brill, 2021).

Bianchi, Andrea 'The Fight for Inclusion: Non-State Actors and International Law' in Ulric Fastenrath, Rudolf Geiger, Daniel-Erasmus Khan, Andreas Paulus, Sabine von Schorlemer, and Christoph Vedder (eds) *From Bilateralism to Community Interest: Essays in Honour of Judge Bruno Simma* (Oxford University Press, 2011).

Bradley, Martha 'Jus Cogens' Preferred Sister: Obligations Erga Omnes and the International Court of Justice—Fifty Years after the Barcelona Traction Case' in Dire Tladi (ed) *Peremptory Norms of General International Law (Jus Cogens): Disquisitions and Disputations* (2021, Brill).

Brownlie, Ian 'Comment' in Antonio Cassese and Joseph Weiler (eds) *Change and Stability in International Law-Making* (Walter de Gruyter, 1988).

Corten, Olivier and Vaios Koutroulis 'The Jus Cogens Status of the Prohibition on the Use of Force: What is Its Scope and Why Does it Matter?' in Dire Tladi (ed) *Peremptory Norms of General International Law (Jus Cogens): Disquisitions and Disputations* (Brill, 2021).

Costelloe, Daniel *Legal Consequences of Peremptory Norms in International Law* (Cambridge, 2017).

de Wet, Erika *The Chapter VII Powers of the United Nations Security Council* (Hart, 2004).

Elphick, Rosalind (with John Dugard) 'Jus Cogens and Compensation' in Dire Tladi (ed) *Peremptory Norms of General International Law: Disquisitions and Disputations* (Brill, 2021).

Hannikainen, Lauri *Peremptory Norms (Jus Cogens) in International Law: Historical Development, Criteria, Present Status* (Helsinki, Finnish Lawyers' Publishing Company, 1988).

Hansel, Mary '"Magic" or Smoke and Mirrors? The Gendered Illusion of Jus Cogens' in Dire Tladi (ed) *Peremptory Norms of General International Law (Jus Cogens): Disquisitions and Disputations* (Brill, 2020).

Knuchel, Sévrine *Jus Cogens: Identification and Enforcement of Peremptory Norms* (Schultess, 2015).

Kolb, Robert *Peremptory International Law Jus Cogens: A General Inventory* (Hart, 2015).

Kolb, Robert 'Peremptory Norms as a Legal Technical Rather than Substantive Super Norms' in Dire Tladi (eds) *Peremptory Norms of General International Law (Jus Cogens): Disquisitions and Disputations* (Brill, 2021).

Koskenniemi, Martti *From Apology to Utopia: The Structure of Legal Argument (Reissue with new Epilogue)* (Cambridge University Press, 2006).

Linderfalk, Ulf *The Creation of Jus Cogens—Making Sense of Article 53 of the Vienna Convention* (Zeitschrift für ausländisches öffentliches Recht und Völkerrecht, 2011).

Linderfalk, Ulf *Understanding Jus Cogens in International Law and International Legal Discourse* (Edward Elgar, 2020).

Maia, Catherine 'Jus Cogens and (In)Application of the 1969 Vienna Convention on the Law of Treaties in the Jurisprudence of the International Court of Justice' in Dire Tladi (ed) *Peremptory Norms of General International Law: Disquisitions and Disputations* (Brill, 2021).

Mbengue, Makane Moïse and Apollin Koagne Zouapet 'Ending the Splendid Isolation: Jus Cogens and International Economic Law' in Dire Tladi (ed) *Peremptory Norms of General International Law: Disquisitions and Disputations* (Brill, 2021).

Merkouris, Panos 'Interpretation of Customary International Law: Methods and Limits: You'll Never Walk Alone' in Panos Merkouris, Jörg Kammerhofer, and Noora Arajärvi (eds) *The Theory, Practice and Interpretation of Customary International Law* (Cambridge, 2022).

O'Connell, Mary Ellen, Christian Tams, and Dire Tladi *Max Planck Trialogues on the Law of War and Peace (Vol 1): The Use of Force against Non-State Actors* (Cambridge, 2019).

Orakelashvili, Alexander *Peremptory Norms in International Law* (Oxford University Press, 2008).

Oral, Nilufer 'Environmental Protection as a Peremptory Norm of General International Law: Is it Time?' in Dire Tladi (ed) *Peremptory Norms of General International Law (Jus Cogens): Disquisitions and Disputations* (Brill, 2021).

Pellet, Alain 'Conclusions' in Christian Tomuschat and Jean Thouvenin (eds) *The Fundamental Rules of the International Legal Order: Jus Cogens and Obligations Erga Omnes* (Martinus Nijhoff, 2005).

Peters, Anne 'The Security Council, Functions and Powers—Article 25' in Bruno Simma, Daniel-Erasmus Khan, Georg Nolte, and Andreas Paulus (eds) *The Charter of the United Nations: A Commentary (Vol. I)*, 3rd edn (Oxford, 2012).

Pinto, Monica 'The Authority and the Membership of the Commission in the Future' in *United Nations Seventy Years of the International Law Commission: Drawing a Balance for the Future* (Brill/Nijhoff, 2021).

Santalolaria, Juan José Ruda 'The Treatment of Peremptory Norms of General International Law (Jus Cogens) in the Inter-American Human Rights System' in Dire Tladi (ed) *Peremptory Norms of General International Law: Disquisitions and Disputations* (Brill, 2021).

Shelton, Dinah *Jus Cogens: Elements of International Law* (Oxford University Press, 2020).

Strydom, Hennie 'Counter-Terrorism Sanctions and Human Rights' in Tiya Maluwa, Max du Plessis, and Dire Tladi (eds) *The Pursuit of a Brave New World in International Law: Essays in Honour of John Dugard* (Brill, 2016).

Šturma, Pavel 'Is There Any Regional Jus Cogens in Europe? The Case of the European Court of Human Rights' in Dire Tladi (ed) *Peremptory Norms of General International Law: Disquisitions and Disputations* (Brill, 2021).

Teles, Patrícia Galvão 'Peremptory Norms of General International Law and the Fundamental Values of the International Community' in Dire Tladi (eds) *Peremptory Norms of General International Law (Jus Cogens): Disquisitions and Disputations* (Brill, 2021).

Thirlway, Hugh *The Sources of International Law* (Oxford University Press, 2014).

Tladi, Dire (ed) *Peremptory Norms of General International Law: Disquisitions and Disputations* (Brill, 2021).

Tladi, Dire *The Extraterritorial Use of Force against Non-State Actors* (Brill, 2022).

Tladi, Dire 'The Role of the International Court of Justice in the Development of International Court' in Kate Parlett and Carlos Esposito (eds) *The Cambridge Companion to the International Court of Justice* (Cambridge, 2023).

Tomuschat, Christian 'Reconceptualising the Debate on Jus Cogens and Obligations Erga Omnes—Concluding Observations' in Christian Tomuschat and Jean-Marc Thouvenin (eds) *The Fundamental Rules of the International Legal Order* (Brill, 2005).

Trahan, Jennifer *Existing Legal Limits to the Security Council Veto Power in the Face of Atrocity Crimes* (Cambridge, 2020).
Traoré, Sâ Benjamin *L'interprétation des résolutions du Conseil de sSécurité des Nations Unies: Contribution à la théorie de l'interprétation dans la société internationale* (Helbing, 2020).
Traoré, Sâ Benjamin 'Peremptory Norms and Interpretation' in Dire Tladi (ed) *Peremptory Norms of General International Law (Jus Cogens): Disquisitions and Disputations* (Brill, 2021).
Trávníčková, Zuzana 'The International Law Commission and the International Law Codification Market' in *United Nations Seventy Years of the International Law Commission: Drawing a Balance for the Future* (Brill/Nijhoff, 2021).
Villalpando, Santiago *L'émergence de la communauté internationale dans de la responsabilité des États* (Paris, 2005).
Viñuales, Jorge E 'The Friendly Relations Declaration and Peremptory Norms' in Dire Tladi (ed) *Peremptory Norms of General International Law (Jus Cogens): Disquisitions and Disputations* (Brill, 2021).

Journal Articles

Abi-Saab, Georges 'The Third World and the Future of the International Legal Order' (1973) 29 *Revue egyptienne de droit international* 27.
Alexidze, Levan 'Legal Nature of Jus Cogens in Contemporary International Law' (1981) 172 *Collected Courses of the Hague Academy of International Law* 219.
Bassiouni, Cherif 'International Crimes: Jus Cogens and Obligatio Erga Omnes' (1996) 59 *Law and Contemporary Problems* 63.
Bianchi, Andrea 'Human Rights and the Magic of Jus Cogens' (2008) 19 *European Journal of International Law* 491.
D'Amato, Anthony 'It's a Bird, It's a Plane, It's Jus Cogens' (1990) 6 *Connecticut Journal of International Law* 1.
de Wet, Erika 'The Emergence of International and Regional Value Systems as a Manifestation of the Emerging International Constitutional Order' (2006) 19 *Leiden Journal of International Law* 611.
den Heijer, Maarten and Harmen van der Wilt 'Jus Cogens and the Humanisation and Fragmentation of International Law' (2016) 46 *Netherlands Yearbook of International Law* 3.
Dupuy, Pierre-Marie 'The Danger of Fragmentation or Unification of the International Legal System and the International Court of Justice' (1999) 31 *New York University Journal of International Law and Policy* 791.
Essawy, Rana 'The Responsibility Not to Veto Revisited under the Theory of "Consequential Jus Cogens"' (2020) 12 *Global Responsibility to Protect* 299.
Gaja, Giorgio 'Jus Cogens Beyond the Vienna Convention' (1981-III) 172 *Collected Courses of the Hague Academy of International Law* 271.
Janis, Mark W 'The Nature of Jus Cogens' (1988) 3 *Connecticut Journal of International Law* 359.
Kawasaki, Kyoji 'A Brief Note on the Legal Effects of Jus Cogens in International Law' (2006) 34 *Hitotsubashi Journal of Law and Politics* 27.
Kleinlein, Thomas 'Jus Cogens as the "Highest Law"? Peremptory Norms and Legal Hierarchies' (2015) 46 *Netherlands Yearbook of International Law* 173.
Kułaga, Łukasz 'Prohibition of Massive and Serious Pollution of Marine Environment as a Jus Cogens: Identification, Legal Bases and Consequences in View of the Recent Work of the International Law Commission' (2022) 144 *Marine Policy* 1.

Linderfalks, Ulf 'Understanding the Jus Cogens Debate: The Pervasive Influence of Legal Positivism and Legal Idealism' (2015) 46 *Netherlands Yearbook of International Law* 51.

Maiello, Francesco 'The Intervention in the Light of the Provisions of Serious Breaches of Jus Cogens' (2022) 8 *Italian Law Journal* 447.

Moulin, Thibault 'Un nouveau "cheval de Troie"? Regard sur la codification des normes impératives du droit international général (jus cogens)' (2020) 58 *Canadian Yearbook of International Law* 225.

Nash, Marian L 'Contemporary Practice of the United States relating to International Law' (1980) 74 *American Journal of International Law* 418.

Orakhelashvili, Alexander 'Audience and Authority—the Merit of the Doctrine of Jus Cogens' (2015) 46 *Netherlands Yearbook of International Law* 115.

Park, Leo 'The International Court and Rule-Making: Finding Effectiveness' (2018) 39 *University of Pennsylvania Journal of International Law* 1965.

Pellet, Alain 'Comments in Response to Christine Chinkin and in Defense of Jus Cogens as the Best Bastion against the Excesses of Fragmentation' (2006) 17 *Finnish Yearbook of International Law* 83.

Rosene, Shabtai 'International Court of Justice' *Max Planck Encyclopedia of Public International Law* (online 2006).

Sellers, Patricia 'Jus Cogens: Redux' (2022) 116 *AJIL Unbound* 281.

Simma, Bruno 'From Bilateralism to Community Interests in International Law' (1994) 217 *Recueil des Cours de l'Academie de Droit International de la Haye* 217.

Tladi, Dire 'Codification, Progressive Development, New Law, Doctrine, and the Work of the International Law Commission on Peremptory Norms of General International Law (Jus Cogens): Personal Reflections of the Special Rapporteur' (2019) 13 *FIU Law Review* 1137.

Tladi, Dire 'The ILC's Draft Conclusions on Peremptory Norms of General International Law: Personal Reflections of the Special Rapporteur' (2019) 24 *Austrian Review of International and European Law* 121.

Tladi, Dire 'The International Law Commission's Draft Conclusions on Peremptory Norms of General International Law (Jus Cogens): Making Wine from Water or More Water than Wine?' (2020) 89 *Nordic Journal of International Law* 244.

Tladi, Dire 'Grotian Moments and Peremptory Norms of General International Law: Friendly Facilitators or Fatal Foes?' (2021) 42 *Grotiana* 335.

Tladi, Dire 'The Extraterritorial Use of Force against Non-State Actors' (2021) 418 *Collected Courses of the Hague Academy of International Law* 237.

Tladi, Dire and Gillian Taylor, 'On the Al Qaida/Taliban Sanctions Regime: Due Process and Sunsetting' (2011) 10 *Chinese Journal of International Law* 771.

Vazhna, Kateryna 'The Obligation Not to Recognise as Lawful the Situation which has Arisen as a Result of Violations of Peremptory Norms of General International Law (Jus Cogens) in the Current International Law' (2021) 2 *Ukrainian Journal of International Law* 59.

Weatherall, Thomas 'Jus Cogens and Sovereign Immunity: Reconciling Divergence in Contemporary Jurisprudence' (2015) 46 *Georgetown Journal of International Law* 1151.

Zdravkovic, Ana 'Finding the Core of International Law—Jus Cogens in the Work of International Law Commission' (2019) 5 *South Eastern Europe and European Union—Legal Issues* 141.

Index

For the benefit of digital users, indexed terms that span two pages (e.g., 52–53) may, on occasion, appear on only one of those pages.